Politics
in Russia

The Longman Series in Comparative Politics

Almond/Powell/Strøm/Dalton — *Comparative Politics Today: A World View*, Eighth Edition

Almond/Powell/Strøm/Dalton — *Comparative Politics: A Theoretical Framework*, Fourth Edition

Country Studies

Aborisade/Mundt — *Politics in Nigeria*, Second Edition

Bill/Springborg — *Politics in the Middle East*, Fifth Edition

Remington — *Politics in Russia*, Third Edition

Regional Studies

Almond/Dalton/Powell — *European Politics Today*, Second Edition

Politics in Russia

THIRD EDITION

Thomas F. Remington
Emory University

New York   San Francisco   Boston
London   Toronto   Sydney   Tokyo   Singapore   Madrid
Mexico City   Munich   Paris   Cape Town   Hong Kong   Montreal

Vice President/Publisher: Priscilla McGeehon
Executive Editor: Eric Stano
Senior Marketing Manager: Megan Galvin-Fak
Supplements Editor: Kristi Olson
Production Manager: Eric Jorgensen
Project Coordination, Text Design, and Electronic Page Makeup: Pre-Press Company, Inc.
Cover Design Manager: John Callahan
Cover Designer: Keithley and Associates
Cover Image: Courtesy of Map Resources, Inc.
Manufacturing Manager: Dennis J. Para
Printer and Binder: Courier Corporation—Stoughton
Cover Printer: The Lehigh Press, Inc.

Library of Congress Cataloging-in-Publication Data

Remington, Thomas F., 1948–
    Politics in Russia / Thomas F. Remington.— 3rd ed.
        p. cm.— (The Longman series in comparative politics. Country studies)
    Includes bibliographical references and index.
    ISBN 0-321-15974-8 (alk.paper)
        1.Russia (Federation)— Politics and government—1991-2. Constitutional
    history— Russia (Federation) 3. Soviet Union— Politics and government. I. Title.
    II. Country studies (Longman (Firm)).

    JN6695 .R46 2003
    320.947—dc21   2003047034

Please visit us at http://www.ablongman.com

ISBN 0-321-15974-8

1 2 3 4 5 6 7 8 9 10—CRS—06 05 04 03

PEARSON
Longman

Contents

Preface

The third edition of *Politics in Russia* has been substantially revised to take account of the many developments that have occurred in Russian political life since the second edition was published. It assesses President Putin's efforts to reshape political and economic policy as well as his strategy in international affairs, and takes account of the modest improvements in the country's economic performance since 1999. The book takes the view that the post-Soviet Russian political system has stabilized after a protracted period of difficult regime change, that the present regime incorporates both democratic and authoritarian elements, and that President Putin has made the strengthening of state power his central priority. Russian statehood has been under deep stress many times in Russian history, but the attempt to reconcile a strong state with the principles of democracy, the market economy, and the rule of law is new.

The main focus of the book is on Russia's political institutions and processes since the end of the Soviet regime. At the same time, we need to recognize how strongly the Soviet legacy has shaped post-Soviet developments. The Soviet system had an enormous impact on international relations for most of the twentieth century, as a revolutionary challenge to the world order, as a model and sponsor for many other communist movements and regimes, as a rival to the United States in the global power competition, and as the hegemonic power in Eastern Europe. It also transformed political and economic institutions in Russia. Therefore the book discusses the way the dynamics of the Soviet regime have influenced the evolution of the present system. A chapter of the book covers the Soviet system, in particular the period of Gorbachev's reforms which ended in the disintegration of the Soviet state, while another chapter traces the establishment of Russia's present day political arrangements out of the turmoil of the late 1980s and early 1990s.

Russia's political life remains subject to rapid change. This edition of *Politics in Russia* covers events roughly through the beginning of 2003. It proceeds from the premise that the immediate postcommunist transition period is over and that a new system has come into being. I have tried to identify some of the forces influencing the development of this system, particularly those stemming from the transformation of its economy from a centrally planned state-socialist system to one with private property and market relations. The severe economic depression that Russia only began to escape at the end of the 1990s has provoked fierce disputes in Russia and around the world about how reform might have been conducted differently. This edition discusses some of these issues and invites readers to work through the evidence and arguments themselves, in order to come to their own conclusions about why things have turned out as they have, and what, if anything, could have been done differently by policy makers.

The evolution of the post–Cold War international order remains subject to uncertainty in many ways; whether the structure of power is "unipolar" or "multipolar" is still unclear, and the power of international institutions such as the United Nations is in doubt again after a brief period in the late 1980s and early 1990s when multilateral cooperation in a variety of international crises was evident. Russia's place in the international system is also affected by the success of its efforts to rebuild its economy and state capacity, and by the skill of its international diplomacy. These themes are central to the final chapter, which looks broadly at the relationship between Russia's political evolution and its international role.

ACKNOWLEDGMENTS

In preparing this edition, I have benefited from the advice of a number of readers. Among them I would like to thank Martha Merritt and Nikolai Petrov in particular for their valuable and constructive comments. I would also like to thank Scott Erb of the University of Maine at Farmington and Kurt W. Jefferson of Westminster College for their comments on the second edition, which were extremely useful in preparing this third.

As before, I am deeply indebted to friends and colleagues in Russia for generously sharing with me their knowledge and understanding of developments in their country. I would also like to express my appreciation to colleagues in this country whose studies of Russian politics have advanced our knowledge of present-day Russia and enriched the field of political science.

I would like to acknowledge with deep gratitude the guidance and encouragement of the late Gabriel Almond, who helped to create the modern field of comparative politics. His influence continues to be felt in this book and the comparative politics series of which it is a part.

Like the first and second editions, the third edition of this book is dedicated to my son, Alexander Frederick Remington.

THOMAS F. REMINGTON

Regions of the Russian Federation, 1993

69 Kaliningrad Oblast

Northern region

1 Karelia Republic
  Komi Republic
2 Nenets AOkr
  Other Arkhangel'sk Oblast
3 Nenets AOkr
  Arkhangel'sk Oblast
4 Vologda Oblast
  Murmansk Oblast

Northwestern region

5 Leningrad
  St. Petersburg city
  Leningrad Oblast
6 Novgorod Oblast
7 Pskov Oblast

Central region

8 Bryansk Oblast
9 Vladimir Oblast
10 Ivanovo Oblast
11 Kaluga Oblast
12 Kostroma Oblast
13 Moscow
  Moscow city
  Moscow Oblast
14 Orel Oblast
15 Ryazan' Oblast
16 Smolensk Oblast
17 Tver' Oblast
18 Tula Oblast
19 Yaroslavl' Oblast

Volgo-Vyatsk region

20 Mariy El Republic
21 Mordova Republic
22 Chuvash Republic
23 Kirov Oblast
24 Nizhnii Novgorod Oblast

Central Black Earth region

25 Belgorod Oblast
26 Voronezh Oblast
27 Kursk Oblast
28 Lipetsk Oblast
29 Tambov Oblast

Volga region

30 Kalmykia Republic
31 Tatarstan Republic
32 Astrakhan' Oblast
33 Volgograd Oblast
34 Penza Oblast
35 Samara Oblast
36 Saratov Oblast
37 Ul'yanovsk Oblast

Volga region

38 Adygei Republic
39 Dagestan Republic
40 Kabardino-Balkar Republic
41 Karachay-Cherkess Republic
42 North Osetian Republic
43 Chechen and Ingush Republics
44 Krasnodar Krai
45 Stavropol' Krai
46 Rostov Oblast

Urals region

47 Bashkortostan Republic
48 Udmurt Republic
49 Kurgan Oblast
50 Orenburg Oblast
51 Perm' Oblast
52 Komi-Permyat AOkr
  Other Perm' Oblast
53 Sverdlovsk Oblast
54 Chelyabinsk Oblast

West Siberian region

55 Altai Republic
  Altai Krai
56 Kemerovo Oblast
57 Novosibirsk Oblast
58 Omsk Oblast
  Tomsk Oblast
59 Tiumen' Oblast
  Khanty-Mansiisk AOkr
60 Yamalo-Nenetsk AOkr
  Other Tiumen' Oblast

East Siberian region

61 Buryatia Republic
62 Tuva Republic
63 Khakassia Republic
  Krasnoyarsk Krai
  Taymyr AOkr
  Evenki AOkr
  Other Krasnoyarsk Krai
64 Ust'-Ordyn Buryat AOkr
  Other Irkutsk Oblast
  Chita Oblast
65 Agin AOkr
  Other Chita Oblast

Far Eastern region

  Sakha Republic
  Primorsk Krai
  Khabarovsk Krai
66 Jewish AO
  Other Khabarovsk
  Amur Oblast
67 Kamchatka Oblast
68 Koryak AOkr
  Other Kamchatka Oblast
  Magadan Oblast
  Chukotka AOkr
  Other Magadan Oblast
  Sakhalin Oblast

AO—Autonomous Oblast
AOkr—Autonomous Okrug

Note: There are 89 territorial units of the Russian Federation. The 69 numbered regions in this listing correspond to the numbered units on the following map. The remaining 20 regions are indicated by name.

The 89 Territorial Units of the Russian Federation

Source: Center for International Research, U.S. Bureau of the Census

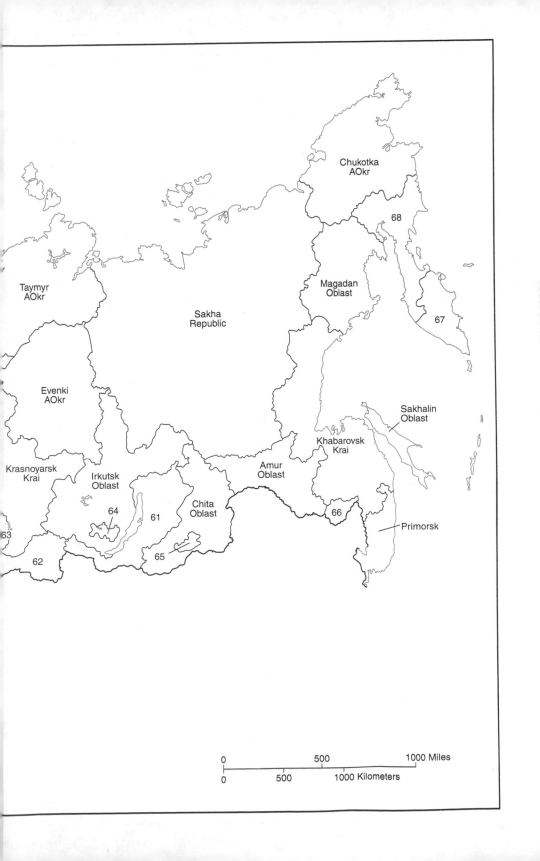

Chukotka
AOkr

68

Taymyr
AOkr

Magadan
Oblast

Sakha
Republic

67

Evenki
AOkr

Sakhalin
Oblast

Krasnoyarsk
Krai

Khabarovsk
Krai

Amur
Oblast

Irkutsk
Oblast

64

61

Chita
Oblast

66

63

Primorsk

62

65

| 0 | 500 | 1000 Miles |
| 0 | 500 | 1000 Kilometers |

Location of the Regions of Western Russia

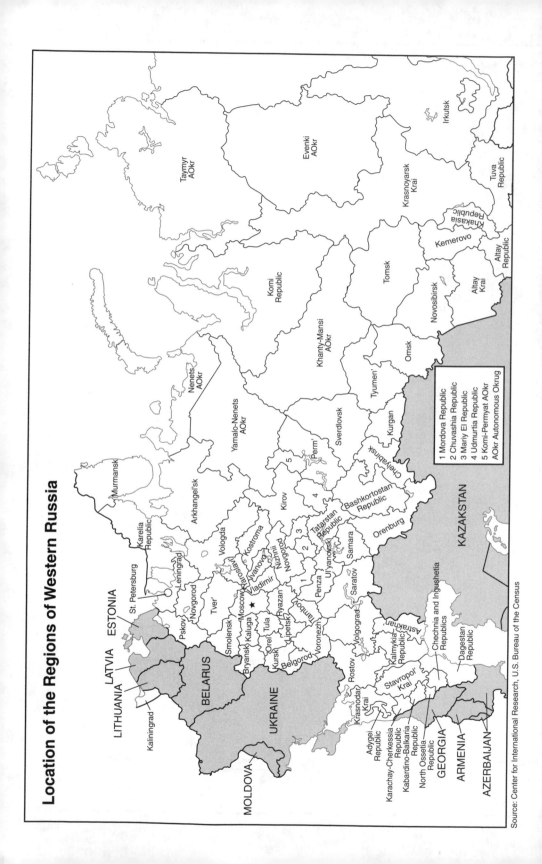

1 Mordova Republic
2 Chuvashia Republic
3 Mariy El Republic
4 Udmurtia Republic
5 Komi-Permyat AOkr
AOkr Autonomous Okrug

Source: Center for International Research, U.S. Bureau of the Census

Russia's Federal Districts

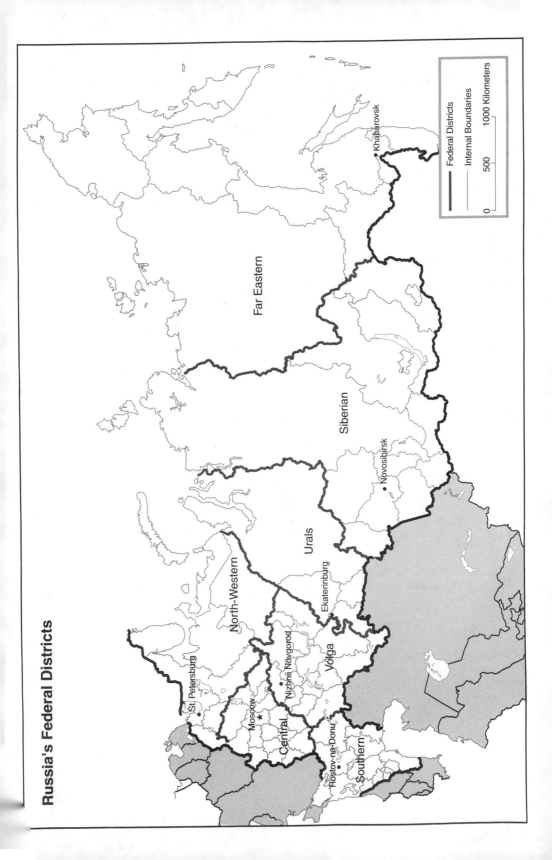

Far Eastern

Siberian

Novosibirsk

Urals

Ekaterinburg

North-Western

St. Petersburg

Nizhnii Novgorod

Moscow

Volga

Central

Rostov-na-Donu

Southern

Khabarovsk

Federal Districts
Internal Boundaries

0   500   1000 Kilometers

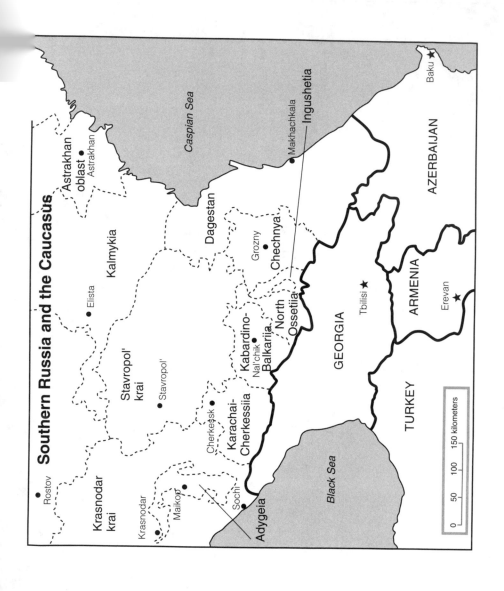

Southern Russia and the Caucasus

Rostov

Krasnodar krai

Krasnodar

Maikop

Sochi

Adygeia

Cherkessk

Karachai-Cherkessiia

Stavropol'

Stavropol' krai

Nal'chik

Kabardino-Balkariia

North Ossetiia

Elista

Kalmykia

Grozny

Chechnya

Astrakhan

Astrakhan oblast

Dagestan

Makhachkala

Ingushetia

Caspian Sea

Black Sea

Tbilisi ★

GEORGIA

TURKEY

ARMENIA

Erevan ★

AZERBAIJAN

Baku ★

0   50   100   150 kilometers

1 Rebuilding the Russian State

The year 2000 opened with a dramatic change of leadership in Russia. On December 31, 1999, President Boris Yeltsin appeared on Russian national television to announce that he was resigning as president of Russia. Although Yeltsin's term was not due to expire until June 2000, he had decided to leave office early. Under the constitution, the prime minister is next in line to the president in the event that the president leaves office, so Yeltsin's preterm resignation made Vladimir Putin acting president. Parliamentary elections had just been held, and had shown that Putin was strong and popular. Yeltsin was leaving in such a way as to give Putin all the advantages of incumbency in launching his own bid for the presidency, which according to the constitution had to be held within three months of the president's leaving office. Putin's very first decree as acting president was to grant Yeltsin and his family lifetime immunity from all criminal prosecution. The manner in which the succession occurred was not illegal, but it hinted strongly of a deal: the presidency for Putin in return for security for Yeltsin.

With the change in presidents came a marked shift in the tenor of politics in Russia. The tumultuous confrontations that had rocked the country during the previous decade came to an end. Putin called for stability and order, based on firm adherence to the rule of law. In both his rhetoric and his actions, he made it clear that there were to be no more revolutionary transformations, no more showdowns between the supporters and enemies of reform. Observers wondered who Putin really was: Was this career KGB official, colorless and lacking in experience with open electoral politics, truly committed to democracy, the market, and the rule of law? (See Close Up 1.1: Who Is Vladimir Putin?)

Boris Yeltsin, on the other hand, had been a vivid, dominating presence on the Russian political scene since the late 1980s.[1] He was Russia's president for nearly a decade. He was first elected Russian president in June 1991, at a time of intense struggle between forces of change and the forces defending the old, communist order. By the end of 1991 those battles climaxed with the end of communist rule and the disintegration of the Soviet Union. Yeltsin's Russia was now a separate country and the Soviet Union as a sovereign legal entity in the

Close Up 1.1   Who Is Vladimir Putin?

Vladimir Vladimirovich Putin was born on October 7, 1952, in Leningrad (called St. Petersburg since 1991), and grew up in an ordinary communal apartment. From early on, he took an interest in martial arts and became expert at judo. Inspired by heroic tales of the secret world of espionage, at the age of sixteen he paid a visit to the local headquarters of the KGB (Committee on State Security), hoping to become an agent. There he was told, however, that he needed to go to university, and to specialize in a field such as law. In 1970 he entered the law faculty at Leningrad State University and specialized in civil law. Upon graduation in 1975, Putin went to work for the KGB and was assigned to work first in counterintelligence and then in its foreign intelligence division. Proficient in German, he was sent to East Germany in 1985. In 1990, after the Berlin Wall fell, Putin went back to Leningrad, working at the university there but still employed by the KGB. When a former professor of his, Anatolii Sobchak, became mayor of Leningrad in 1991, he went to work for Sobchak. In the mayor's office he handled external relations, dealing extensively with foreign companies interested in investing in the city, and rose to become deputy mayor.

In 1996, Putin moved to Moscow to take a position in Yeltsin's presidential administration. His career ascended rapidly. In July 1998, Yeltsin named Putin head of the FSB (Federal Security Service, the successor to the KGB), and in March 1999, Yeltsin named him secretary of the Security Council as well. In August 1999, President Yeltsin appointed him prime minister. Thanks in part to his decisive handling of the federal military operation in Chechnia, following a wave of bombings of apartment houses in several cities in Russia, which were attributed to Chechen terrorists, Putin's popularity ratings quickly rose. On December 31, 1999, Yeltsin resigned, making Putin acting president. Putin went on to run for the presidency and, on March 26, 2000, won with an outright majority of the votes in the first round.

Because Putin's career as a public politician had been quite short, he was something of an enigma to both Russian and foreign observers when he took office as president. Yet as time passed, his own political instincts became somewhat clearer. They suggested that he was a pragmatist and modernizer who strongly desired to move Russia forward, restoring its economic vigor and status as a great power in the world. He was not inclined to look back at the old regime with nostalgia, yet he consciously aimed to construct his own political strategy on a foundation of continuity with the past rather than a radical rupture with it. Skilled at projecting an affable, relaxed demeanor, he is also self-possessed and disciplined. More than one observer has called attention to the significance of his mastery of judo, a martial art in which one uses one's opponent's own strength and momentum to defeat him.

world had disappeared. Yeltsin was reelected in 1996 under a new constitution adopted in 1993 and, despite growing infirmity, held on to power until his resignation in 1999. For better or for worse, Yeltsin was the principal architect of Russia's transition from communism.

In his resignation speech, Yeltsin struck an unexpectedly contrite tone:[2]

> Today, on this incredibly important day for me, I want to say more personal words than I usually do. I want to ask you for forgiveness, because many of our hopes have not come true, because what we thought would be easy turned out to be painfully difficult. I ask [you] to forgive me for not fulfilling some hopes of those people who believed that we would be able to jump from the gray, stagnating, totalitarian past into a bright, rich and civilized future in one go.
>
> I myself believed in this. But it could not be done in one fell swoop. In some respects I was too naive. Some of the problems were too complex. We struggled on through mistakes and failures. At this complex time many people experienced upheavals in their lives. But I want you to know that I never said this would be easy. Today it is important for me to tell you the following. I also experienced the pain which each of you experienced. I experienced it in my heart, with sleepless nights, agonizing over what needed to be done to ensure that people lived more easily and better, if only a little. I did not have any objective more important than that.

Yeltsin's words of regret about how the transition had turned out were a belated acknowledgment of the disappointment and bitterness felt by many Russians about the effect of the changes on their lives. For most people, the passage from the Soviet, communist regime to a system with the superficial trappings of democracy and the market had worsened living standards and increased insecurity. It had created a society with gaping inequality and widespread poverty, suffering from pervasive corruption and criminality, and waging a brutal military campaign against a secessionist region on its southern borders. What had brought Russia to this pass? Were there any signs of progress toward a healthier society and political system?

In this book we will look for answers to these questions as we analyze the changes Russia has undergone during its transition following the collapse of the communist regime and the Soviet state. We will inquire into the reasons that the change in regime has been so painful and difficult. We will study the evolution of Russia's political institutions. We will also discuss the shift away from a socialist economy characterized by central planning and state ownership of property to an economy with elements of market capitalism, and we will describe Russia's efforts to create a new national identity.

Russia's history as a postcommunist state is brief: It dates only to the dissolution of the Soviet Union as a formal legal entity in 1991. But Russia has existed as a state for over a thousand years, and for most of the twentieth century, Russia was the core of the larger communist state called the Union of Soviet Socialist Republics (USSR, or Soviet Union). Russia today shares many continuities of political culture and social structure with its Soviet and earlier past. At the same time, we should recognize how deeply Russia's political institutions have changed since the Soviet regime ended.

Today, Russia—formally called the Russian Federation (*Rossiiskaia Federatsiia*)—is a sovereign state formally adhering to democratic principles such as open and competitive elections, multiparty competition, and a free press. In some respects its political institutions are comparable to those of Western democracies. Examples are the presidency, the Constitutional Court, the Federal Assembly, and federalism. In this book we will discuss these and other institutions and processes of Russia's present-day political system. But to understand how they work in practice, we will also need to refer to the predecessor regimes of the Soviet and pre-Soviet eras. For example, Russia's presidency strongly resembles the office of General Secretary of the Communist Party of the Soviet Union and the institution of the tsar in both form and function.[3] And enormous behind-the-scenes power is wielded by a small number of barons of industry and by a number of regional bosses. Real power in Russia diverges from the formal scheme of political institutions laid out by the constitution. But this is true to some extent of all political systems, and Russia today differs from its predecessor regime in that the degree of divergence between *actual* power and *formal* power is lower now than in the Soviet era.

It is helpful to think of the changes that have taken place in Russia over the past decade as occurring in four broad domains: *state structure, political regime, economic system,* and *national identity.*

First, the Soviet Union as a sovereign state broke apart into its fifteen constituent parts, the union republics, of which Russia was the largest.

Second, communist political rule collapsed and gave way to a quasi-democratic system. The old regime was known as communist because the Communist Party of the Soviet Union held a monopoly on the exercise of political power.

Third, the state socialist economy, where the state owned all productive property and the country's political leadership decided what the economy was to produce, gave way to a partially market-oriented system with elements of private property.

Finally, Russians had to redefine the national identity of their state. The Soviet Union had been a multinational union made up of fifteen nominally equal national republics; in its place, they needed to find a new conception of the Russian nation that fit the post-Soviet Russian state.

Because these changes have occurred simultaneously, they have been much more wrenching than regime transitions in other societies that have witnessed the fall of an authoritarian regime and establishment of democratic institutions. They have created enormous uncertainty for Russia's citizens. Citizens' lack of confidence in the future tends to undermine the forms of social behavior and relations that would reinforce stable democratic institutions. Many people yearn for the security and order of the old Soviet regime. In the political system, elements of a pluralistic, competitive democracy are intermingled with authoritarian patterns of political action. People fear the breakdown of order and statehood, but are reluctant to give up their hopes for political and economic rights.

By *democracy* we mean a political system in which the citizens invest leaders with political power through free and fair elections and in turn hold leaders accountable for their use of political power. Democracy requires not just that all adult citizens have the right to participate in competitive, fair elections, but also that other political rights, such as freedom of association, conscience, and media, are honored as well so that society can participate meaningfully in political life. By *authoritarianism* I mean a political system in which these rights are limited to a part of the citizenry or to a restricted set of political issues, and those who make decisions about policy are not held accountable to the citizenry in any meaningful way.[4] The Soviet regime, which was established in 1917, represented a distinctive form of authoritarian rule known as *communism.* The communist system of rule spread widely throughout Europe and Asia in the second half of the twentieth century, but now has collapsed or fundamentally changed nearly everywhere. Under communism, the state owned all productive property and political power was monopolized by the Communist Party.

Communist regimes were often called *totalitarian* because, like the Nazi regime under Hitler in Germany in 1933–1945, they aspired to give the rulers of the state total control over society. These regimes concentrated far more power in the party and government leaders than is found in other types of authoritarian regimes because the rulers controlled both economic and political processes.

Most also used far-reaching violence to enforce their rule and eliminate enemies, sometimes destroying whole categories of their populations.[5] The vast scope of political and social control, and the destructiveness of the Soviet regime help explain why the transition from communist rule in Russia to a democratic system has been so difficult.[6]

Russia's transformation over the past decade gives us a unique opportunity to analyze the factors shaping regime change. How do long-term, slow-acting social changes combine with short-term conjunctures of circumstance to produce new patterns of political life? As we shall see, the Soviet regime pursued a program of social modernization that had cumulative effects over the decades of Soviet rule, creating pressures for adaptation that the regime could not accommodate. Changes such as urbanization, mass education, and industrialization resulted in a more demanding and articulate society in the Soviet Union. When the reformist Gorbachev[7] leadership in the late 1980s opened up greater freedom of speech and association, Soviet citizens responded with explosive energy to voice demands and to organize for collective action. Politics became freer, more open, and more contested. Leaders such as Gorbachev and Yeltsin strove to create new political institutions that would enable them to realize their designs for policy and power. Not surprisingly, though, in view of the huge uncertainty and rapid change surrounding them in the late 1980s and early 1990s, they often miscalculated the consequences of their actions. For instance, it is clear now that the central party leadership in the late 1980s seriously underestimated the strength of ethnic-national attachments in the union republics, so that when they granted greater political liberty to Soviet citizens, much of the new ferment that followed swelled into nationalist movements demanding independence for the union republics.

Another critical issue in understanding regime change is the relationship between economic and political liberalization. The monopoly on productive property—that is, wealth such as factories, banks, and land that produces wealth—held by the state meant that the state's rulers could dispose of the country's resources as they saw fit with no effective check on their power. Marx and Lenin had taught that the institution of private property is inimical to communism because it is associated with a class of independent property owners who will defend their rights against a government that tries to confiscate their wealth. The reformers fighting for freedom and democracy in Russia therefore regarded the demand to institute private property rights, the rule of law, and a market economy as being inseparable from the demand for democratic rights in the political sphere. Communists fought intensely to prevent the restoration of private property and a market economy. They argued—quite accurately—that privatizing state assets would lead to the concentration of huge wealth and power in the hands of a small number of owners. They downplayed the point that privatization would also deprive them of their lock on political power.

The communist regime's monopoly on power and property also meant that there were few autonomous social groups that could lend support to newly rising political movements. One of the most distinctive features of communist systems is their effort to transform all social associations into instruments furthering the reach of the state into people's lives. Trade unions, youth leagues, hobby groups, professional associations, communications media, religious bodies, educational institutions, and the arts were all forced to become instruments of mass mobilization on behalf of the regime. Among the impediments to the establishment of a fully democratic regime in Russia, the weakness of civil society—the sphere of organized social associations that link people by their common interests outside family and friends—has proven to be one of the most powerful.[8] This weakness has continued to hold back Russia's postcommunist political development.

The study of Russia's transformation is not only of academic interest. It is also a case study from which policy makers throughout the world have drawn lessons for their own development strategies. For some observers, Russia's poor performance in the 1990s stands as a devastating indictment of the strategies pursued by the International Monetary Fund (IMF) and Western governments in their aid and advice to transitional economies; instead of preaching open markets and fiscal austerity, critics argue, the world should have been promoting efforts to increase the state's ability to steer the economy.[9] Russia and China are often contrasted as alternative models of reform. Those who consider China to be a successful example of economic reform argue that under Gorbachev, the Soviet leadership democratized the political system before opening up the economy, resulting in the deepening of nationalism, corruption, civil war, and administrative decomposition that ultimately brought about the collapse of the state—all without improving the economy. Moreover, they claim, under Yeltsin the post-Gorbachev Russian leadership abandoned its controls over the economy before new market-oriented institutions were in place. The result was a catastrophic decline in production, the loss of much of the country's economic capacity, the flourishing of barter, corruption, and underground economic activity, and the takeover of most of Russia's most profitable resources by a few unscrupulous tycoons. In contrast, say the critics, China has preserved its communist political controls and privatized industry only gradually, but encouraged entrepreneurship, foreign investment, and profit making in agriculture, with the result that it has enjoyed a long period of extremely high economic growth without experiencing a loss of political order.[10]

However, it is not clear that the model of reform that Russia attempted to pursue was intrinsically flawed—perhaps the model simply was not carried out fully or properly. For example, other newly postcommunist states carried out similar programs of radical economic reform with far better results. The reasons for Russia's problems may lie in the particular path it took to postcommunism. Moreover, we should be careful of assuming that Russian leaders had the same options that Chinese leaders had. We will take this subject up in more detail in Chapter 7.

Another reason for studying the transition in Russia is the country's importance in the international system. As the heir of the Soviet Union, Russia inherited an enormous military arsenal and vital geopolitical location. Russia's military might has declined considerably since the 1980s, but, with around 6,000 nuclear weapons still in its active inventory, it remains one of the two world nuclear superpowers.[11] Of far greater concern for international security than its active nuclear stockpiles, however, is the legacy of its history as a producer of nuclear, chemical, and biological weapons. Many of its factories and laboratories still have the capability of supplying nuclear fuel and other raw materials that could be used to produce weapons of mass destruction. Loose control over nuclear, biological, and chemical materials in the former Soviet Union, in fact, is considered to be the weakest link in international efforts to prevent the proliferation of weapons of mass destruction. The Soviet Union built up a large pool of scientific and technical expertise in the production of biological, chemical, and nuclear weapons, and there is widespread concern about their willingness to sell their services to radical states or terrorist groups.

The stockpiles of weapons of mass destruction and their associated labs, factories, raw materials, and technical expertise that exist in the United States and Russia are the legacy of decades of competition between the two superpowers during the Cold War. From the late 1940s until the late 1980s, the United States and other Western democracies fought with the Soviet Union for influence over Europe, Asia, the Middle East, and other regions of the world. The United States committed itself by treaty obligations to defending the security of Europe and other regions, with the threat of nuclear war backing up its commitment. The Soviet Union, in turn, countered by building up its arsenal of nuclear, biological, and chemical weapons to levels that would allow it to deter any military threat to its national interests.[12] In the end, of course, the huge military power at the disposal of the regime proved incapable of preventing its collapse. Indeed, the system's insatiable appetite for military spending was one reason its economy lagged far behind the West in most other areas.

The origins of the strategic conflict between the superpowers lie in the revolutionary aims of the communist movement in the first half of the century, when Russia sponsored an international communist movement aimed at overthrowing international capitalism and *bourgeois* (liberal democratic) governments around the world. From the time that the communists took power in Russia in 1917, their regime adopted a posture of fundamental hostility to the West. For most of the period of communist rule (1917–1991), Soviet rulers alternated between an aggressive, expansionist policy toward the Western world and an accommodative and pragmatic one. They pursued "peaceful coexistence" but competed for influence by supporting radical socialist movements and fought the spread of the basic democratic and capitalist values of the West. Observers long noted that in its external relations, the Soviet Union proceeded along two tracks simultaneously.[13] On one track, the regime sought stable economic and diplomatic relations with the powerful countries of the capitalist world. On the other, it constructed a network of political and military alliances with socialist and revolutionary regimes and groups with the goal of increasing its global influence at the expense of that of the West. In turn, the United States constructed a network of alliances and treaty relationships around the world to try to contain the expansion of Soviet influence, provided economic assistance to developing countries, and exerted its power to prevent communism from spreading. The antagonism between the democratic and market-oriented states of the West and the socialist bloc led by the Soviet Union created a bipolar structure of power in world politics that lasted from shortly after World War II until the momentous reforms of Mikhail Gorbachev.[14]

The strategic rivalry between the two superpowers, the United States and the Soviet Union, shaped both political and military relations. Both countries devoted enormous efforts to preparing for possible war. Each side came to accept that a general nuclear war between them would be so devastating to each side, no matter which began it, that it could never be fought; but each accepted that the terrible threat of such a war served to deter the other from taking excessive or provocative risks. Both, moreover, continually upgraded their nuclear arsenals during this period, emphasizing qualities such as destructive power, accuracy, invulnerability, and mobility. The Soviet Union and the United States each built about 10,000 long-range nuclear weapons capable of striking each other's military, industrial, political, and communications centers. They also accumulated tens of thousands more shorter-range nuclear weapons that were part of the military forces stationed in Europe and Asia.[15] Most of these weapons have been dismantled as a result of arms reduction agreements signed between the two sides, but, as of the year 2000, Russia still possessed about 20,000 nuclear weapons deployed or in storage, and the United States about 9,000.[16] Although the two countries no longer regarded each other as their principal adversaries, each still posed a major potential threat to the other. Moreover, the relative security of command and control over Russia's nuclear forces remained a major concern, as did the substantial breakdown in Russia's early-warning capability; as a result, Russia's nuclear missiles are permanently kept on a high state of alert.[17]

Russia and the United States have agreed on the desirability of deep reductions in their nuclear arsenals. In Helsinki in 1997, Presidents Yeltsin and Clinton committed themselves to the goal of reducing the number of long-range warheads that each side possessed to the level of 2,000 to 2,500 warheads by the end of 2007. The two sides have also discussed making still deeper reductions. In May 2002, Presidents Bush and Putin signed a treaty in Moscow committing each side to removing around two-thirds of their remaining nuclear weapons from deployment over the next ten years, leaving between 1,700 and 2,200 warheads for each country.[18]

During the Cold War, the United States and the Soviet Union embodied the opposite poles of a great ideological contest between capitalist democracy and Marxist-Leninist socialism. Soviet doctrine claimed that the socialist system was intrinsically superior to capitalism both because it did away with the exploitation of labor by capitalists, and because it concentrated control over productive resources in the hands of leaders who could build up the country's productive potential. The doctrine held that unlike capitalism, socialism had a clear goal and would one day bring society to the "communist" stage of development, where all property and power would be held in common and all people would be equal. In earlier periods, many Soviet citizens as well as sympathetic foreign observers believed that the Soviet system did indeed offer an alternative model of economic development and social justice to that represented by capitalism. Over time, however, the socialist model showed that it was unable to generate self-sustaining economic growth, technological progress, or political liberty. The Soviet populace lost faith that the bright future of communism would ever arrive. When the communist system collapsed, it collapsed quickly, indicating how little popular support communist rule in fact possessed. In place of the Soviet Union the fifteen national republics making up the Soviet Union became sovereign new states. But it has proven far easier to dismantle the former structures of communist rule than to replace them with new structures. For many people in the former Soviet Union, the hopes that the construction of a democratic and prosperous new order would be relatively smooth have been frustrated, and replaced with bitterness or anger at the authorities. The transition period has left many living in the former Soviet Union materially worse off, at least for the present. Many individuals who thought of themselves as "Soviet" people now feel that they have lost their national identity.

A democratic, open political system in Russia would mean, therefore, that Russia and the West would be able to cooperate in countering the global proliferation of weapons of mass destruction and terrorism rather than engaging in an arms race or political competition. An economically healthy and democratic Russia would be a stabilizing factor in the multiple regions on which Russia borders: Eastern Europe, the Middle East, and Northeast and Northwest Asia. On the other hand, the renewal of authoritarianism in Russia would very likely herald a return to a climate of international tension, a new division of Europe, and a new arms race between East and West.

FOUR DOMAINS OF CHANGE

Let us review the changes that have occurred in the last several years in four basic areas: state structure, political regime, economic system, and national identity.

State Structure: From Soviet Union to Russian Federation

As of January 1, 1992, the Union of Soviet Socialist Republics (USSR, also often called Soviet Union) ceased to exist. The Soviet Union's red flag with its hammer and sickle no longer flew over Moscow's Kremlin, which had been the symbolic center of Soviet power since 1918. In its place was Russia's white-blue-red tricolor flag. Soviet communism had come to an end, and a newly sovereign Russia took control of that portion of the USSR's territory—comprising some three quarters of the physical area and half the population—that had formed the Russian Soviet Federative Socialist Republic (RSFSR). Today the RSFSR has been renamed the *Russian Federation* or simply Russia.

The relationship between the Soviet Union and postcommunist Russia can be confusing, both for outside observers and for the people who suddenly found themselves citizens of a new state. Many people thought of Russia and the Soviet Union as interchangeable names for the same country. This was an understandable mental shortcut given Russia's dominance of the union politically and culturally. Formally, however, Russia was only one of fifteen nominally equal federal republics making up the union. Each republic had an ethnic-national identity but the union itself had no ethnic or national affiliation—only an ideological one.

The union collapsed when the governments of Russia and other member republics refused to accept the authority of the central government any longer. Mikhail Gorbachev, the reform-minded leader of the Soviet Union, struggled to find some new framework to preserve the unity of the union, but he was outmaneuvered by Boris Yeltsin, head of the Russian Republic, and frustrated by the powerful aspirations for self-rule on the part of peoples in many of the republics. On June 12, 1990, the Russian Congress of People's Deputies—the newly elected legislative assembly of the RSFSR—approved a sweeping endorsement of Russian sovereignty within the USSR, according to which Russia would only observe those USSR laws that it consented to acknowledge. A year later, on June 12, 1991, Boris Yeltsin was elected president of Russia in the first direct popular presidential elections that Russia had ever had. Probably few Russians foresaw that the union itself would eventually collapse as an outgrowth of these developments. Other events were equally momentous. The Communist Party ceased to rule the country. The familiar contours of the state-owned, state-planned economy were giving way to contradictory tendencies: Production in the state enterprises fell, while energetic if frequently corrupt private entrepreneurship spread. Inequality and poverty increased sharply. Everyone agreed that the old Soviet system was breaking down, while a new system had not fully formed.

The final breakup came in 1991. In August 1991, a group of leaders of the main bureaucratic structures of the union government (army, KGB, state economic ministries, and so on) arrested Gorbachev and made a desperate attempt to restore the old Soviet order. Their coup attempt failed, however, on the third day when key elements of the army and security police refused to follow their orders. Thereafter, through the fall of 1991, the breakdown of Soviet state authority accelerated. One by one the union republics issued declarations of independence. The power structures of the union soon were unable to exercise authority. The Finance Ministry could not collect taxes, and the military could not conscript soldiers. Trade ties were breaking down across regions and republics. As revenues fell, the Central Bank pumped more and more money into circulation that was not backed up by real values. The economy was sinking into chaos. Union bureaucracies operating on Russian territory were taken over by the Russian government, and those in other republics were similarly nationalized by those republics.

In October 1991, Yeltsin announced that Russia would proceed with radical market-oriented reform designed to move the economy from communism to the market irreversibly. On December 1, 1991, a referendum was held in the Ukrainian republic on national independence. When the proposal to declare Ukrainian independence passed with 90 percent of the vote, politicians throughout the Soviet Union recognized that the breakup of the union was inevitable, and they looked for ways to preserve at least some of the formal ties among the republics. The leaders of the three Slavic core states—Russia, Ukraine, and Belorussia—met near Minsk, capital of Belorussia, on December 8, and on their own authority declared the USSR dissolved. In its place they agreed to form a new entity, a framework for coordinating their economic and strategic relations, called the *Commonwealth of Independent States* (CIS). Thirteen days later the CIS was expanded to include all the former republics except for Georgia and the three Baltic states of Lithuania, Latvia, and Estonia. In 1993, Georgia also joined.

Although it is not a functioning government, the CIS is more than a purely symbolic organization. It has gained some coordinating powers in the realms of trade, finance, lawmaking, and security. The great obstacle to the growth of integration and hence of coordinating power for the CIS is the enormous difference between Russia's power and size and the power and size of the other members: Russia's population is almost three times larger than that of the next most populous member, Ukraine. Russia is unwilling to turn over sovereign power to any organization not under its immediate control, and the other member states of the CIS are to turn over much power to Russia. This issue illustrates the point that the Soviet Union functioned as a sovereign state only by weakening Russia's own status as a political actor, and investing power instead in the Communist Party–dominated structures of the union. For this reason, it is probably the case that Russia had no chance of becoming a democratic state unless in fact it jettisoned the union. But without Russia, of course, there could be no union.

Although movement toward making the CIS an effective coordinating structure for managing relations among the former republics of the Soviet Union has been quite limited, the leaders of Russia and its smaller Western neighbor, Belarus (formerly known as Belorussia), have made sporadic attempts to form a union. Belarus, with a population of 10 million, is led by its dictatorial president, Alexander Lukashenka, who has pinned his hopes for a political future on a union of Belarus and Russia. This would elevate his own political stature to that of a coequal with Russia's president and tie his country's failing economy to Russia. Six times between 1996 and 1999, Presidents Yeltsin and Lukashenka held showy ceremonies at which they signed agreements promising to unite their two countries.[19] New institutions (such as a joint parliament) were created on paper, but neither side was willing to cede any real power to the union structures. In 2002, President Putin poured cold water on the idea of a union by pointing out the obvious—that Russia could never allow a union with Belarus to proceed at the expense of Russia's economic or political interests. Since then, talk of union has subsided considerably.

The same point applies to the numerous agreements that have been signed by interministerial committees of the CIS, which have largely remained dead letters. It may be that at some point in the future, some subset of former republics of the Soviet Union may achieve meaningful integration, but for the time being the main task for all of them is establishing new post-Soviet political and economic institutions and new identities as national states.[20]

On December 25, 1991, Gorbachev announced that he was resigning as president of the Soviet Union, and turned state powers over to Yeltsin. The Russian Federation was recognized internationally as the legal successor to the Soviet Union; Russia inherited the USSR's seat as permanent member on the Security Council of the United Nations as well as the sovereign debt owed to the Soviet Union by a number of its former client states. In effect, the inept organizers of the August coup, who plotted to take over the state in order to restore the Soviet state, had brought about precisely the opposite. Russia could now chart its own destiny without reference to the larger union state.

Very soon, however, opinion polls in Russia were registering a wave of public disillusionment over the failure of popular hopes for rapid improvement of their lives. An obvious target for their blame was the dissolution of the union. Already by late 1993, a large majority of Russian citizens were inclined to condemn the breakup of the Soviet Union as harmful.[21] Two-thirds of Russians blamed the breakup of the Soviet Union for their current economic woes. With each passing year, the proportion of Russians who give a favorable evaluation of the old, communist regime goes up. By early 2000, 70 percent of the population rated the pre-Gorbachev regime positively, while 48 percent rated the current system negatively.[22] A majority was even willing to agree with the proposition that the West was trying to weaken Russia with its economic advice.[23]

Each year since 1990, Russia has commemorated its independence of the Soviet Union on June 12. June 12, 1990, was the day when the newly elected Russian legislature adopted its "Declaration of Sovereignty" and exactly one year later, Boris Yeltsin was elected president for the first time. Since then, each year on June 12 the government seeks to recapture the optimistic mood of 1990 and 1991 by commemorating Russia's hopes for a bright future as a sovereign nation. Yet the attitude of many Russians toward the holiday is one of irritation and indifference: Independence has brought few perceptible benefits. A survey taken in June 2000 revealed that 28 percent of the Russian population did not know what the June 12 holiday was supposed to celebrate. Another 51 percent of the respondents did know that the day was "Independence Day," but few were in a mood to celebrate: 57 percent of the respondents said that independence had brought Russia nothing but harm.[24]

Toward Democratic Government

Concurrent with the breakup of the Soviet Union, Russia undertook the revolutionary task of remaking its political institutions. The first steps in democratizing the communist system were taken by Mikhail Gorbachev, who came to power as General Secretary of the Communist Party of the Soviet Union (CPSU) in 1985. Although Gorbachev did not intend for his reform policies to bring about the dissolution of the Soviet Union, he did push for a far-reaching and radical set of changes in the economic and political institutions of the regime. These changes, in turn, led to demands for still more autonomy by regional leaders and to the mobilization of protest against the existing regime by large segments of the population in many republics. In Russia, Boris Yeltsin and other political leaders successfully challenged Gorbachev and the union government for power by championing the cause of liberal democracy, the market economy, and national sovereignty for Russia. After the breakup of the Soviet Union, President Yeltsin and his government continued to press for market-oriented economic reform. In doing so Yeltsin sometimes resorted to undemocratic methods, most spectacularly in 1993, when he dissolved parliament. Yet there can be no question about the fact that Russia enjoys significantly more political freedom today than it did for nearly the whole Soviet period or, for that matter, at almost any time in its history. Democratization in Russia, although neither complete nor secure, has brought about fundamental changes of at least three kinds.

Individual Rights. First, the barriers to individual political liberties which the communist regime imposed have largely been lifted: The intrusive Communist Party mechanisms for enforcing ideological discipline in public discourse are gone and with them, political censorship; persecution of religious practice has ended and the state has instead embraced religion, particularly the Russian Orthodox Church, as an ally in strengthening public morality; citizens are now free to organize independent political parties and associations; and, gradually, the courts have been gaining independence in the enforcement of individuals' legal rights. A large body of research suggests that commitment to democratic principles of individual rights is widely shared although not uniformly practiced.[25] Around two-thirds of the public support the idea of democracy, but about 80 percent are dissatisfied with the way democracy is developing in Russia.[26] On the other hand, Russians value the political freedoms that democratization has brought them. Over 85 percent consider freedom of expression, freedom of convictions, and freedom to elect their leaders to be important to them.[27] Citizens' ability to defend their rights against encroachment by central or local authorities remains tenuous, however. In a number of regions, governors have imposed their own authoritarian regimes.

Associational Freedom. A second type of change that advances democracy is the emergence of autonomous social and civic organizations. Under the old regime, public organizations were monitored and sometimes directly controlled by the Communist Party. In the Stalin era (1928–1953), the major public organizations, such as trade unions and youth leagues, were considered to be "transmission belts" linking society to the political authorities. Transmission belt organizations provided regime-sponsored outlets for organized collective action and ensured that they would serve the regime's political goals. In the Gorbachev period, a huge number of new, autonomous social organizations sprang up under the influence of the regime's political reforms, some with avowedly political purposes, others for cultural or philosophical pursuits.[28] After the demise of the communist regime, many of these vanished. With time, however, a more stable set of interest groups began to develop. Among these are organizations defending the interests of regions, collective and state farms, state industrial firms, new entrepreneurs, private farmers, bankers, and industrial workers, not to mention a shifting array of political parties and movements competing for attention.

Contested Elections. The third aspect of the democratic process is that elections have become competitive and regular. Between the first contested elections of USSR deputies in 1989 and the presidential election of March 2000, Russian voters went to the polls ten times in nationwide elections:

- 1989: election of USSR deputies
- 1990: election of RSFSR and local deputies
- 1991: March: referenda on preserving union and creating Russian presidency
- 1991: June: election of RSFSR president
- 1993: April: referendum on approval of Yeltsin and government
- 1993: December: election of deputies to new parliament and referendum on draft constitution
- 1995: December: election of deputies to parliament
- 1996: June/July: election of president
- 1999: December: election of deputies to parliament
- 2000: March: election of president

In addition to these nationwide elections, there have also been numerous regional and local elections of executive and legislative officials. These elections varied in the degree to which they were honest, open, and fair. But the principle of democratic elections as a means of conferring legitimate power on political leaders is now well established, in both political practice and public opinion.

Many political scientists have warned that the holding of elections is no guarantee that a political system is democratic: In many countries, elections are no more than a means of giving the aura of democratic legitimacy to rulers who otherwise trample on democratic principles; they do not give voters an effective instrument for holding leaders responsible for their actions. However, while elections are not a *sufficient* condition of democracy, certainly they are a *necessary* condition for it.[29]

In other respects Russia's political system remains authoritarian. One result of the democratic movement of 1989–1991 was the creation of a powerful state presidency invested with enormous power to overcome resistance to reform. The new constitution ratified in the nationwide referendum in December 1993 embodied President Yeltsin's conception of the presidency. Under it, the president has wide powers to issue decrees with the force of law and faces few constraints on the exercise of his powers. In practice the president directly oversees foreign policy and national security. Presidents Yeltsin and Putin have interpreted this power, reinforced by the constitutional provision that the president is the supreme commander-in-chief of the armed forces, to authorize him to order armed forces into action to preserve order.

In December 1994 and again in September 1999, President Yeltsin ordered the army and security troops to defeat the armed forces fighting for the independence of the separatist Chechen Republic, an ethnic enclave within the Russian Federation. In neither case did the president seek parliamentary approval for the action. The military campaign by the federal forces in 1994–1996 and again in 1999–2000 resulted in massive destruction of Grozny, the capital city, and of many other cities and towns in the republic. Tens of thousands of people have been killed, hundreds of thousands of people have fled the republic, and hundreds of thousands more have been left homeless by the fighting. A group of legislators challenged President Yeltsin's use of his decree power to wage war in Chechnia by appealing to the Constitutional Court, but the Court found that Yeltsin had acted constitutionally in dealing with a threat to national security.

President Yeltsin sometimes used the powers of the presidency to take unconstitutional action. In September 1993, Yeltsin issued a decree summarily dissolving parliament and ordering the holding of elections for a new parliament to be held in December of that year. When a group of hard-line parliamentarians resisted and barricaded themselves in the parliament building, Yeltsin ordered the army to shell the building. Under Yeltsin, television broadcasters also came under pressure to support the Kremlin's candidates in elections. For example, state media coverage of the 1999 parliamentary elections was severely biased in favor of the pro-Kremlin parties.[30] Under President Putin, media freedom has been eroded further, as independent news organizations have been shut down or reorganized.

The concentration of political power in the president and the executive agencies he oversees is reinforced by the weakness of checks on its use. The institutions that could monitor and expose malfeasance by the president and government, such as parliament, the mass media, and interest groups, are hampered by the cloak of secrecy that surrounds the executive and by the fact that the executive controls many of the material and informational resources that they depend on for their activity. For instance, the government can deny licenses to opposition-minded broadcast companies and newspapers. On several occasions President Putin has professed to be completely unaware of actions taken by law enforcement officials against individuals whose opposition to his policies went too far. The presidential administration controls a wide array of material resources and administrative levers with which to check the independence of both the legislative and judicial branches.

The tendencies toward a reconcentration of authoritarian power in the executive are echoed in many regions of the country where powerful local bosses rule. Often individuals who have successfully survived the upheavals of the past several years, these regional chief executives have established strong political machines that make them relatively independent of both federal power and accountability to the local citizens. In a few cases, local officials have suppressed political opposition and arrested their opponents. At both the federal and regional levels, then, the outcome of the struggle for democracy remains in doubt.

Economic Transformation

In addition to the wrenching change in state structure and the uneven movement toward liberal democracy, a third and equally momentous change has been under way in Russia. This is the transformation from the state-owned, centrally administered economy to one approximating a market system. In a market economy, the right of private ownership of productive resources enjoys legal guarantees, decisions on production and consumption are made by producers and consumers, and coordination of the myriad activities of individuals and organizations is accomplished primarily through their interaction in a competitive environment. Russia remains far from having reached this point—in fact, no economy in the real world completely matches this description. But in Russia the state has gone very far to dismantle the former socialist system in favor of a rudimentary market framework. Russia's method of enacting economic reform—rapid, radical price liberalization, combined with sharp decreases in state spending and increases in taxation—was called "shock therapy." Russia's version of shock therapy was a very crude policy instrument, but it was never fully implemented and was often quietly sabotaged in practice. It may have been the only means available to policy makers for making rapid and irreversible changes in the behavior of economic actors, but it created many unwanted side effects and did not succeed in setting Russia onto a path where market incentives would stimulate economic growth.[31]

Among the several painful side effects of the reforms, which included the decontrol of most prices, was a huge jump in prices in 1992 and uneven but slowly declining inflation thereafter. Another consequence was a deep and protracted depression. A mounting dependence by the government on borrowed money to finance current expenditures led to a major financial crisis in August 1998, when the government defaulted on its domestic and international obligations and let the ruble's value against the dollar plummet. By the end of the

1990s, Russia's gross domestic product had fallen to roughly half of its 1989 level. Only in 1999 and 2000 did the economy begin to recover and show evidence of sustained growth in output.

On the other hand, the reforms did succeed in making some crucial changes in the economy. One was to create a rudimentary system of market institutions, such as banks, stock exchanges, and property rights, which provide the rough underpinnings of an open, competitive economy. Another was to end most shortages of goods and services in major cities. The public's demand for basic consumer needs could be satisfied, and both domestic and imported food and other goods became widely available throughout the country.

The most striking consequence of the economic reform has been the sharp rise in rates of poverty and inequality. The depression has driven around 30 percent of the Russian population into poverty.[32] Both poverty and inequality have grown sharply since the end of the Soviet era. Moreover, public health indicators show a shocking decline. There are now roughly twice as many deaths as births per year in Russia.[33] After 1998, inequality and poverty began falling, and incomes rose. But the deterioration in social well-being brought about by the economic and political dislocations remained acute. Chapter 7 discusses these changes and their causes in more detail.

The attempt to stabilize state finances was one prong of economic reform in Russia. The other was a shift to private ownership of productive resources through the privatization of state enterprises and the growth of independent businesses.[34] By 1999, the private sector had grown to the point where it exceeded the state sector in share of employed workers.[35] The results of these policies have been mixed. Market forces now play a far greater role than in the past. But control over real economic assets of factories and farms often remains in the hands of the same managers and officials who held them in the past, with the difference that now they have acquired legal ownership.[36] As a result of the legacy of communist rule, many of those who held power under the old system wound up in positions of wealth and power in the new system.

The Question of Identity: Imperial Russia—USSR—Russian Federation

The breakdown and reconstruction of Russia's state structure, political institutions, and economic system created enormous uncertainty for Russians. The uncertainty also affected the way Russians defined themselves as a people. Although today's Russian Federation is the direct successor of a thousand-year-old tradition of statehood, the political forms and boundaries of the state as it exists today differ from any that Russia has known. From the late fifteenth century until the early twentieth century, Russia's state was constituted as an imperial monarchy ruling a contiguous expanse of territories and peoples. As a result, Russia's political evolution differed from the typical path taken by Western countries.[37] In Western Europe, nations formed as social communities in territories defined through contests and treaties among state rulers. In Russia, by contrast, the state created a territorial empire spanning a huge landmass and populated by a diverse array of European and Asian peoples, who differed profoundly among themselves in religion, way of life, and relationship to Russian authority. Russian national consciousness was less based on ethnicity, therefore, than on identification with a powerful imperial state. Russia's history lacks a model of a nation-state to serve as a precedent for the postcommunist period.

Then, in the period of Soviet rule, Russia was transformed further and became the core of a communist-rule union of national republics. Russia lent its language and much of its political culture to the Soviet Union, but in the process it lost its own character as a distinct national entity. In effect, the Soviet Union was a new kind of empire, one whose culture was partly Russian but that pretended to be a higher type of political organization. Following its demise, Russians were once again called upon to form attachments to a redefined state, the Russian Federation. As had been the case for much of Russian history, Russia's leaders generally have chosen not to base the identity of the newly independent state on an *ethnic* principle. No doubt this was partly out of the practical consideration that some 20 percent of the population was not ethnically Russian, but it also reflected the historical tradition of defining Russia as a multi-ethnic state rather than a national state. Generally Russia's leaders have characterized the state as a multinational federation in which the major ethnic communities have territorial units within the federation. To build loyalty to the new Russia, the leaders have emphasized Russian and Soviet historical achievements in war, industry, science, technology, and the arts, but they have also sharply differentiated the new post-Soviet Russia from either its communist-era or tsarist predecessors. They aim at creating a set of overlapping identities for citizens, including the sense of belonging to a particular ethnic community while at the same time being a citizen of the multiethnic Russian state.[38]

Of course the collapse of the multinational Soviet state did not restore the prerevolutionary status quo: Instead, the fifteen union republics that constituted the nominal federation of equal republics each acquired formal independence. Thus, although the Soviet state was the heir of the Russian imperial state, contemporary Russia is only one of fifteen successor states of the Soviet Union. Some had possessed national statehood before being annexed to the Soviet Union, but others gained the institutional infrastructure of nationhood in the course of Soviet rule. The Soviet regime's policies affected different nationalities in the union differently: Some small peoples assimilated into larger groups; in many cases the national culture of a people was severely restricted; in yet others, the formal features of national existence that the federal model of the Soviet state provided tended to stimulate the rise of a national consciousness. Therefore the breakup of the Soviet Union has not simply restored the status quo ante. Many of the newly independent states are now engaged in the difficult task of constructing new national identities for themselves.[39]

Although in this book we will focus on Russia's political system, we should note that the dissolution of the centrally run union state has resulted in a wide variety of paths of development in the successor states with respect to their domestic political and economic orders.

The three Baltic states, Lithuania, Latvia, and Estonia, have established stable democracies and market-dominated economies that are increasingly being integrated into the larger European economy. These states do not belong to the CIS and their relations with Russia range from correct to frosty. It is worth noting, in passing, that of the former Soviet states, only the Baltic states have parliamentary political systems and only they are securely democratic. The other twelve successor states all have presidential systems, and only a few adhere consistently to basic democratic principles.

For instance, the Central Asian states—Tajikistan, Kyrgystan, Turkmenistan, and Uzbekistan, and their huge neighbor Kazakhstan—have become *less* democratic since the union's breakup. Their presidents have claimed sweeping powers and restricted citizens' rights, although they all also seek foreign capital investment in their economies. Most have also sought close relations with Russia. Indeed, Tajikistan, which has suffered from a violent civil war between Islamic fundamentalists and government forces, has accepted a status akin to that of a protectorate of Russia.

Russia has also gained a dominant strategic position with respect to the security and energy interests of other former Soviet republics, including the three trans-Caucasian states of Armenia, Azerbaijan, and Georgia. These states differ in the degree to which democracy and the rule of law are honored, but each has had to accept a degree of Russian domination as the price for political peace and stability. Each has also been the site of several conflicts. Georgia has suffered three civil wars since the late Soviet era, and Armenia and Azerbaijan have had to deal with the consequences of a bloody war over the status of the Armenian ethnic enclave located physically within Azerbaijan, Nagorno-Karabakh. The Armenians of Nagorno-Karabakh fought successfully to break free of their administrative subordination to Azerbaijan, but so far no framework for a peaceful settlement of the conflict is simultaneously acceptable to Armenia, Azerbaijan, and Nagorno-Karabakh, despite intensive efforts at mediation by the Organization of Security and Cooperation in Europe (OSCE). All have evolved toward quasi-authoritarian rule.

Belarus has already been mentioned. Its post-Soviet history has been difficult: Politically Belarus is less democratic than it was in the late Soviet period, and its economy has been declining. It has not been constructing a new national identity around its independence, but its attempts to form an equal partnership or union state with Russia have failed as well, and under its dictatorial president it has remained locked in a rigid state-socialist economic system. Moldova, another state on the southwest border of Russia, has been more successful in constructing a new political identity for itself as an independent state despite the fact that it was created by Stalin as a Soviet republic out of a slice of eastern Romania. However, its sovereignty is threatened by the fact that the Russian-speaking population on the east bank of the Dniester River refuse to concede to Moldova's sovereignty and have constituted themselves as their own separate state, unrecognized by any other country in the world.

Ukraine's political stance will be critical to determining whether the future will bring about any restoration of a new union of former Soviet states. Its leadership has been united in the aim of maintaining independence from Russia politically and economically. Ukraine's political and economic development has lagged behind Russia's both in the consolidation of democratic institutions and in the spread of market-oriented relations: To a considerably greater extent than in Russia, the old Soviet-style, state-centric social order remains intact in Ukraine, propped up in large measure by the appeal to anti-Russian Ukrainian nationalism. Russia and Ukraine have nonetheless succeeded in keeping their relations on a reasonably harmonious track despite recurrent tensions over issues such as the disposition of the old Soviet Black Sea fleet and the status of the naval port Sevastopol. Politically, however, Ukraine remains stuck between communism and democracy; the president rules in a quasi-authoritarian fashion and a handful of oligarchs wield disproportionate power.[40]

The diversity of political and economic interests of the successor states has so far limited the capacity of the institutional framework created by the CIS to exercise any real authority. Such capacity as the CIS has is the product of Russia's military, economic, and political clout, which it has exercised on occasion with all the bluntness of a nineteenth-century imperial hegemon. Yet at the same time, democratic and market reforms have proceeded further in Russia than in nearly any other CIS state.

In retrospect, the breakup of the Soviet Union into its constituent republics may appear to have been the logical culmination of the Soviet state's development, but until 1991, most observers considered breakup to be highly unlikely. The reason is that the communist rulers were committed to a long-term goal of eradicating differences among peoples based on ethnic or linguistic characteristics, and instead building a new Soviet national identity based on the Soviet socialist way of life. As a practical matter, though, they recognized that harmony in the Soviet state required preserving some cultural rights for territorially based national groups. Therefore they provided territorial political institutions for larger nationalities through which the traditional languages and cultures could be maintained.

In nearly every case, the national minorities in the Soviet Union were the same groups occupying the same lands that the tsarist Russian empire had conquered in previous centuries. But denying that the multinational, communist state was in any way a Russian empire—the very name was meant to show that the state was neither Russian by national identity nor an empire politically—the communist regime imposed a common socialist model of economic ownership and administration on the entire territory of the state. Although Soviet ideology held that in the long run, national differences would be subsumed in a common Soviet national identity, during the late 1980s, leaders in the fifteen republics pursued demands for greater autonomy for their republics.

In many republics, mass movements for national independence grew powerful. This was even true in Russia: The structures of the union itself were so firmly associated with a conservative, exploitative political arrangement that both nationalist conservatives and democratic reformers in Russia were firmly convinced that progress for Russia was possible only if Russia escaped the USSR's political straitjacket.

Many Russians believe that that the Russian state requires a great national mission as a foundation for its values, goals, and legitimacy. They cite the fact that the tsarist political order had regarded itself as the preserver of the true Christian faith, and that the Soviet regime considered itself to be the base of a worldwide revolutionary struggle for socialism. In 1996, shortly after his reelection as president, President Yeltsin called for the formulation of a "new national idea." He observed that previous eras of Russian history had been characterized by overarching political ideologies, such as monarchy, totalitarianism, or perestroika. The new Russian state demanded a new national idea, he declared. However, the team he charged with discovering such a unifying ideology in a year's time reported a year later that they had been unsuccessful in devising one. Perhaps, as Georgii Satarov, the coordinator of the effort, commented at the time, it was impossible to frame a single idea that could encompass the full range of contradictory realities of the new political situation. Rather, perhaps the never-ending *search* for a national idea was itself the idea.

CHOICES AND CHANGES IN RUSSIAN POLITICS

These have been huge changes—breakup of the Soviet Union, dismantling of the communist political system, a shift toward market capitalism, and the change in the very national identity of the state. How have they affected Russian citizens? How much have they changed the distribution of *real* power in the country?

The political changes in Russia in the 1990s have not brought the country into the "rich, bright, and civilized future" that Yeltsin spoke of in his resignation speech: Many of the same political elites remain in place and the breakdown of the old regime has brought less democracy, and more disorder and corruption, than anyone had hoped. Still, the degree of change has been significant. The upheavals of the last decade are equivalent to a revolutionary break with the past, comparable to the formation of the Soviet regime in 1917.[41] True, it is easy enough to detect the persistence of older patterns of political life, such as the dual executive of autocrat and government, the impotence of legal institutions and pervasiveness of corruption, the proliferation of centralized state agencies together with the inability to accomplish stated policy purposes, the power and autonomy of the security police, and the survival of the former regime's ruling elite in positions of power. Looking at these phenomena, we might jump to the conclusion that nothing essential has changed, except that social disorder and distress have grown. People are even more likely to say this when they have personally been caught up in hopes and expectations that were subsequently betrayed. Many Russians today say that the apparent democratic revolution in Russia was a fraud and illusion that simply allowed a new group of greedy, power-hungry elites to win a share of control of the country's property and power.

However, it would be as wrong to exaggerate the degree of continuity with the past as it would to overlook the ways in which the transition from communist authoritarianism to a democratic system is incomplete. The dismantling of the old Communist Party mechanisms for exercising its monopolistic power means that political processes are more open. The pluralistic diversity of political interests has now moved from the arena of behind-the-scenes bureaucratic politics to a more open competition of interest groups and parties for influence over policy. Individual rights are more strongly protected than in the past. Contact between Russia and the outside world has expanded enormously. There is far more freedom for economic activity. Overall, these changes in national identity, political institutions, and economic system amount to a revolution. When we remember the level of violence required to carry out the communist revolution and establish the Soviet system in Russia, the peaceful nature of the transition from the old regime is astonishing.

In the following chapters, I shall argue that the reason that change has been largely peaceful is twofold. First, the Soviet regime's modernizing policies had the effect of creating a much more conducive environment for pluralistic democracy than existed before the October Revolution. Second, many of the powerful elite groups that persisted from the Soviet period into the post-Soviet system found ways to take advantage of the new conditions. In doing so, however, they manipulated the new system to their benefit, creating a political system that is not fully democratic and an economy where property rights are not always secure and market competition is often overridden by rent seeking.[42] Although some believe that the democratic promise of the transition was betrayed by powerful insiders who took advantage of the change in institutions to entrench themselves in positions of power and wealth, the mutual adaptation of elites and institutions may have been the price paid for averting more serious social conflict during the passage from communism to democracy.

At a more basic level, the Russian case offers us a powerful test of the effects of institutional engineering. To what extent is democracy a product of long-term social and economic processes that produce conducive economic and cultural conditions, and to what extent can democracy be created by constructing new democratic institutions? This issue has been the subject of intense research by political scientists in recent years.[43] Some political scientists believe that certain social conditions are prerequisites or facilitating factors in the establishment and consolidation of democracy. These include a political culture dominated by democratic values, a flourishing network of civic associations, and a reasonable level of economic prosperity and equality.[44] Other scholars argue that there is a very wide range of different social conditions in which democracy may be created and that there is no clear causal relationship between a particular set of social conditions and a particular type of political system. They believe, instead, that a democratic system can result from the willingness of rival sets of political leaders to abide by a common set of rules and procedures to govern their competition for power.[45]

Russia will not conclusively prove one side or the other right in this debate. Whatever the final outcome of Russia's transition, people will disagree over its causes. If democracy fails, some will say that Russia's postcommunist constitution was poorly designed (for instance, that it granted too much power to the president and too little to other institutions), while others will say that the political culture or the economy were still too powerfully influenced by the communist system to permit a democratic experiment to succeed. If it succeeds, some will say that democracy was the product of long-term changes in the domestic and international environment that created a more demanding, individualistic populace that could no longer be ruled by autocratic methods. Others will say that radical reforms made it possible for Russia to escape its authoritarian past, and to create a new path of political development for itself. In the study of politics, unlike the study of the natural world, we do not have laboratory conditions for isolating and testing the effects of causal agents. We draw our analytical judgments from observations of a sometimes murky, confusing reality, so our generalizations are inevitably tentative. We can show, however, that the choices political actors made at certain important turning points had major consequences. Much of Russia's contemporary political system is the cumulative product of the day-to-day actions of millions of ordinary citizens under enormous uncertainty.

PLAN OF THE BOOK

The premise of this book is that Russia's future is still open. There is no assumption here that having departed the station of "communist authoritarianism," the train will reach the station of "liberal democracy." Many stops and detours in between are possible, and the train can reverse direction numerous times. History suggests that political systems can remain trapped in intermediate zones in which some democratic institutions coexist with strong elements of authoritarianism for decades or longer. Our task, therefore, is to see whether there is some overall direction to the development of Russia's political system.

The rest of the book explores the institutions and processes of Russia's political system in greater detail. Chapter 2 provides a brief overview of the political history of the last decade, when the old Soviet regime collapsed and a new political order in Russia took shape. The chapter details the main changes in the structures and processes of rule in the Soviet period, describing the Communist Party–dominated regime and showing how power was organized and used. Then it discusses the Gorbachev reforms, their objectives, and the succession of schemes he advanced to reorganize the political system. The chapter shows that the reforms had unanticipated effects that resulted in Gorbachev's loss of control over political developments. When the Soviet regime collapsed in 1991, it was succeeded by newly independent regimes in the former republics. Already, however, the Russian republic had initiated its own major reforms that culminated in a political crisis in 1993 and the adoption of a new constitution, which is in force today. In Chapter 3, we discuss the 1993 constitution of the Russian Federation, describing its institutional structures and processes.

In Chapter 4, we look at how the public participates in the political system. The nature of popular participation in politics has greatly changed since the Soviet era. In the old regime participation tended to be ceremonial, regimented, and controlled. Today the prevalent pattern is one of political disengagement and mistrust of government, along with high levels of turnout at elections. Many of the informal organizations that sprang up during the late Soviet period have become the basis for political parties and interest groups in the present period, and we inquire into the forms and nature of their activity. We look at the place of elections in the system of participation.

The second part of the chapter takes up the subject of elite recruitment. In every political system, popular participation in politics is closely related to the process of elite recruitment: Through elections, organizational activism, and the exercise of influence over policy makers, some individuals grow particularly active and interested in politics; of them, some become full-time political professionals. Of considerable interest in this connection is the question of the relation between the old political elite in Russia and the contemporary political elite. Is it true, as some charge, that the same crowd is still running things? Is there new blood, and what has happened to the old communist elite? We will also inquire into the close, sometimes collusive, relations between the political and business elites.

Chapter 5 assesses the findings of public opinion surveys about the values and beliefs of Russians. It observes that although typical Russian citizens value political rights and freedoms, they also expect the state to provide basic social equality and welfare for its citizens. Although most rate the old regime favorably, not many would actually wish to restore it; and most people are deeply disappointed with the way political and economic reforms have worked out in practice. Confidence in the institutions of the new order is low.

In Chapter 6 we ask how Russians voice their political demands and interests through interest groups and political parties. We review several categories of actors—industrial managers, women's groups, organized labor, the Orthodox Church, and the new "oligarchs"—to see how the social changes of the last five years have altered the balance of power and interest among different kinds of social groups.

In the second part of the chapter we ask how political parties are developing. How do they tie different groups of the population to the national political arena? The chapter argues that a system of national, competitive political parties is essential for balancing power and accountability in a democratic political system. Yet Russia's party system seems to be little more than a handful of elite political teams that form at election time to bid for votes.

Chapter 7 examines the remaking of the economy. It tries to solve some of the puzzles of the transition, such as why production fell so catastrophically, why the economy came to depend so heavily on barter and other forms of nonmoney exchange, why the financial system collapsed in August 1998, and how much the economy has recovered from that collapse.

Chapter 8 assesses the legal system, asking whether Russia is moving toward the rule of law. The chapter discusses the problem of law and legal institutions at two levels: the task of putting the activity of state officials and private citizens securely under the rule of law, and the effectiveness of legal institutions in enforcing constitutional and legal rules. The chapter reviews the major institutions of the judicial system and the reforms that are being made in it. Of particular interest is the emergence of a mechanism for judicial review of the acts of other government institutions. We discuss the obstacles toward the rule of law, including the power of organized crime, pervasive corruption, and the abuse of power by executives.

The last chapter offers an overview of Russia's emerging role in the world and emphasizes the close link between Russia's political and economic development and its relationship to the international community. The chapter shows that Russians continue to face insecurity about their place in the world and discusses the difficulties it faces in integrating itself into the community of democratic, market-oriented industrial powers. It argues that Russia's history imposes a severe but not insurmountable constraint on the prospect for democracy.

REVIEW QUESTIONS

1. Most communist regimes have undergone changes. Some have become fully democratic, others have become dictatorships, and others have become mixed regimes combining elements of democracy with authoritarianism. Why do we see such a variety of successor regimes?
2. What are the implications of Russia's regime change for its role in the international system, including the nuclear-arms race with the United States?
3. Sometimes it is said that free and fair elections are a *necessary* condition for democracy, but not a *sufficient* condition. Is this true? If so, what other conditions need to be met for a political system to be democratic?
4. Why has Russian had to *rebuild* the state following the demise of the communist regime and the Soviet Union?

ENDNOTES

1. Studies of Yeltsin and his leadership include Leon Aron, *Yeltsin: A Revolutionary Life* (New York: St. Martin's Press, 2000); George W. Breslauer, *Gorbachev and Yeltsin as Leaders* (Cambridge, England: Cambridge University Press, 2002); and Lilia Shevtsova, *Yeltsin's Russia: Myths and Reality* (Washington, D.C.: Carnegie Endowment for International Peace, 1999).
2. Quoted from text of speech as posted to CNN Web site, **www.cnn.com**, December 31, 1999.
3. For an examination of some of the parallels, see Eugene Huskey, *Presidential Power in Russia* (Armonk, N.Y.: M. E. Sharpe, 1999). Huskey points out that both the tsars and the general secretaries chose not to exercise executive authority directly, as the president of the United States does, but rather to use their powers to provide political direction, legitimacy, and energy to the system as a whole, while leaving the actual management of the executive branch to a prime minister—who could always serve conveniently as a scapegoat when things went badly. Russia's presidency is organized in the same way, with a huge bureaucracy parallel to that of the government, enabling the president to oversee and guide the government without having to take direct responsibility for the consequences of policies.
4. A thorough discussion of the problem of defining democracy and authoritarianism is offered in Larry Diamond, *Developing Democracy: Toward Consolidation* (Baltimore and London: Johns Hopkins University Press, 1999), pp. 1–23.

5. For example, the Khmer Rouge regime in Cambodia, which was probably the bloodiest regime in history in per capita terms, killed as many as one in six or seven of the people of the country between 1975 and 1979 through starvation, forced labor, or executions. The numbers of victims of political violence, politically engineered famine, and forced labor in the Soviet Union and China were far higher in absolute terms: perhaps 25 million in the Soviet Union and 65 million in China. For a broad, devastating overview of the destructiveness of communist regimes in the twentieth century, see Stephane Courtois et al., eds., *The Black Book of Communism*, trans. Jonathan Murphy and Mark Kramer (Cambridge, Mass.: Harvard University Press, 1999).

6. Political scientists have devoted considerable attention to theories of transition from authoritarian to democratic regimes and the consolidation of newly democratic regimes. See, for example, Juan J. Linz and Alfred Stepan, *Problems of Democratic Transition and Consolidation: Southern Europe, South America, and Post-Communist Europe* (Baltimore and London: Johns Hopkins University Press, 1996); Adam Przeworski, *Democracy and the Market: Political and Economic Reforms in Eastern Europe and Latin America* (Cambridge, England: Cambridge University Press, 1991); Samuel Huntington, *The Third Wave: Democratization in the Late Twentieth Century* (Norman, Okla.: University of Oklahoma Press, 1991); Diamond, *Developing Democracy*.

7. Mikhail Gorbachev became General Secretary of the Communist Party of the Soviet Union in 1985 and quickly launched a program of economic and political reform. In 1990 he became president of the USSR, the first and last individual to hold this post. On December 25, 1991, he resigned as president and turned the formal powers of his office over to Russian President Boris Yeltsin. Gorbachev continued to play an active role in public life after his resignation.

8. Larry Diamond defines civil society as "the realm of organized social life that is open, voluntary, self-generating, at least partially self-supporting, autonomous from the state, and bound by a legal order or set of shared rules." It "involves citizens acting collectively in a public sphere" for a variety of purposes. Diamond, *Developing Democracy*, p. 221.

9. Among the critics arguing this way is Joseph Stiglitz, formerly the World Bank's chief economist. Joseph Stiglitz, *Globalization and Its Discontents* (New York: Norton, 2002), especially the chapter "Who Lost Russia?" Other works in this vein include Stephen F. Cohen, *Failed Crusade: America and the Tragedy of Post-Communist Russia* (New York: W.W. Norton, 2001); and Peter Reddaway and Dmitri Glinski, *The Tragedy of Russia's Reforms: Market Bolshevism against Democracy* (Washington, D.C.: The United States Institute of Peace, 2001).

10. Stiglitz, *Globalization*, pp. 137–38, 183–84; Jerry F. Hough, *The Logic of Economic Reform in Russia* (Washington, D.C.: Brookings Institution, 2001), pp. 245–48.

11. Figures taken from the Web site of the Carnegie Endowment for International Peace: "Nuclear Numbers," **www.ceip.org/files/nonprolif/numbers/default/asp**, October 4, 2002. The Carnegie Endowment estimates that Rusia has about 5,800 nuclear warheads, and the United States around 5,900 warheads, in deployment.

12. For example, despite signing the 1972 treaty banning all biological weapons, the Soviet Union pursued a large-scale program for research on and production of a number of biological weapons, including smallpox, anthrax, and plague. It is believed that this program employed some 60,000 people. A former top scientist in the Soviet bioweapons program who now lives in the United States has written a memoir of his experiences. Ken Alibek and Stephen Handelman, *Biohazard* (New York: Delta, 2000).

13. Studies of Soviet foreign policy include Peter Zwick, *Soviet Foreign Relations: Process and Policy* (Englewood Cliffs, N.J.: Prentice Hall, 1990); Joseph L. Nogee and Robert

H. Donaldson, *Soviet Foreign Policy since World War II*, 4th ed. (New York: Macmillan, 1992); and Alvin Z. Rubinstein, *Soviet Foreign Policy since World War II: Imperial and Global*, 4th ed. (New York: HarperCollins, 1992). A magisterial study of Soviet foreign policy is Adam Ulam, *Expansion and Coexistence: Soviet Foreign Policy, 1917–1973*, 2nd ed. (New York: Praeger, 1974).

14. World War II ended in 1945, and the postwar era of antagonism between the United States and its allies and the Soviet Union and its allies began in 1947–1948. Mikhail Gorbachev, the last leader of the Soviet Union, assumed power as General Secretary of the Communist Party of the Soviet Union in March 1985. In 1990 he created and assumed the position of President of the Soviet Union. He resigned formally from this position in December 1991. The USSR (Union of Soviet Socialist Republics; also known as the Soviet Union) formally dissolved as a legal entity on December 31, 1991. Since the Bolshevik Revolution in 1917, when the Soviet regime was established, the Soviet leaders and the dates of their rule were as follows:

   1. Vladimir Lenin (1917–1924)
   2. Iosif Stalin (1924–1953)
   3. Nikita Khrushchev (1953–1964)
   4. Leonid Brezhnev (1964–1982)
   5. Yuri Andropov (1982–1984)
   6. Konstantin Chernenko (1984–1985)
   7. Mikhail Gorbachev (1985–1991)

15. Coit D. Blacker, *Reluctant Warriors: The United States, the Soviet Union, and Arms Control* (New York: W. H. Freeman & Co., 1987), p. 25.

16. Carnegie Endowment for International Peace: "Nuclear Numbers," **www.ceip.org/files/nonprolif/numbers/default/asp**, October 4, 2002.

17. The hair-trigger alert status of Russian nuclear forces means that an erroneous indication of a missile attack could result in a disastrous response. For example, in January 1995, Russia mistook the launch of a scientific rocket in Norway for an attack by an American missile from a Trident submarine. President Yeltsin immediately convened a conference of top advisers. With only two or three minutes to spare before the counterattack order would have been given, Russia determined that the missile was heading away from Russia and was not a threat.

    See Stephen I. Schwartz, "U.S. Tells Russia: Let's Keep Nukes Forever. An Introduction to ABM Treaty 'Talking Points,'" *Bulletin of the Atomic Scientists*, May/June 2000, as posted to the Web site of the *Bulletin of Atomic Scientists*, **www.thebulletin.org/issues/2000/mj00/mj00schwartz.html**.

18. The treaty did not require the dismantling of all the weapons, however. It left open the possibility that either side might simply put the weapons into storage, where they might be vulnerable to theft or could be placed back into deployment.

19. Agreements or treaties of union were signed by the two presidents on April 2, 1996; April 2, 1997; May 23, 1997; December 28, 1998; and December 8, 1999.

20. On the challenge of building legitimate national states in the former constituent republics of the USSR, see Pàl Kolstø, *Political Construction Sites: Nation Building in Russia and the Post-Soviet States* (Boulder, Colo.: Westview, 2000). On the difficulty of establishing sovereignty in post-Soviet states facing their own ethno-territorial secession movements, see Charles King, "The Benefits of Ethnic War: Understanding Eurasia's Unrecognized States," *World Politics* 53:4 (July 2001), pp. 524–52.

21. Jerry F. Hough, "The Russian Election of 1993: Public Attitudes Toward Economic Reform and Democratization," *Post-Soviet Affairs* 10:1 (January–March 1994), p. 13.

22. From the New Russian Barometer series for 2000. The New Russian Barometer series is a regular public opinion survey conducted by the Center for the Study of Public Policy of the University of Strathclyde under the direction of Richard Rose, in cooperation with the All-Russian Center for Public Opinion Research (VTsIOM), a respected survey organization based in Moscow. The Center and VTsIOM maintain a Web site (**www.russiavotes.org**) publishing survey data concerning Russian electoral dynamics. The April 2000 data were posted to the **www.russiavotes.org** Web site on June 2, 2000.

23. Hough, "The Russian Election of 1993," p. 6.

24. Results of a survey of a nationally representative sample of 1,600 adult Russians conducted by VTsIOM. Cited on the Web site of **www.polit.ru** on 12 June 2000. However, a survey in 2002 found that a slight majority of Russians now believed that Russia's independence was a positive development. See RFE/RL Newsline, 11 June 2002.

25. James L. Gibson, Raymond M. Duch, and Kent L. Tedin, "Democratic Values and the Transformation of the Soviet Union," *Journal of Politics* 54:2 (May 1992), pp. 329–71; James L. Gibson, "A Mile Wide But an Inch Deep (?): The Structure of Democratic Commitments in the Former USSR," Paper delivered at the 1994 meeting of the American Political Science Association, New York, September 1994; William Zimmerman, "Markets, Democracy and Russian Foreign Policy," *Post-Soviet Affairs* 10:2 (April–June 1994), pp. 103–26; and Stephen Whitefield and Geoffrey Evans, "The Russian Election of 1993: Public Opinion and the Transition Experience," *Post-Soviet Affairs* 10:1 (January–March 1994), pp. 38–60.

26. Timothy J. Colton and Michael McFaul, "Are Russians Undemocratic?" Carnegie Endowment for International Peace, Working Papers no. 20 (June 2001), pp. 5, 8.

27. Colton and McFaul, "Are Russians Undemocratic?" p. 11.

28. Jim Butterfield and Marcia Weigle, "Unofficial Social Groups and Regime Response in the Soviet Union," in Judith B. Sedaitis and Jim Butterfield, eds., *Perestroika from Below: Social Movements in the Soviet Union* (Boulder, Colo.: Westview, 1992), pp. 175–95; Marcia A. Weigle, *Russia's Liberal Project: State-Society Relations in the Transition from Communism* (University Park, Pa.: Penn State University Press, 2000).

29. See the discussion of the conditions of democracy in Diamond, *Developing Democracy*, chs. 1–2.

30. Sarah Oates, "Television, Voters and Democracy in Russia: The Development of the 'Broadcast Party,' 1993–2000," in Vicki L. Hesli and William M. Reisinger, eds., *Elections, Parties, and the Future of Russia* (Cambridge, England: Cambridge University Press, forthcoming 2003). Also see the report on media bias in the 1999 elections on the Web site of the European Institute for the Media, **www.eim.de**.

31. Among the studies of the economic transformation of Russia and its consequences are Andrei Shleifer and Daniel Treisman, *Without a Map: Political Tactics and Economic Reform in Russia* (Cambridge, Mass.: MIT Press, 2000); Thane Gustafson, *Capitalism Russian-Style* (Cambridge, England: Cambridge University Press, 1999); and Anders Aslund, *Building Capitalism: The Transformation of the Former Soviet Bloc* (Cambridge, England: Cambridge University Press, 2002).

32. The Russian State Statistics Committee estimates that as of 2000, 29.1 percent of the population had incomes lower than the subsistence minimum (which was 1,210 rubles per month, or about $41 U.S.). Goskomstat Rossii, *Rossiiskii statisticheskii ezhegodnik 2001: Statisticheskii sbornik* (Moscow: Goskomstat Rossii, 2001), p. 171.

    Note that using different methods, the European Bank for Reconstruction and Development estimated that as of 1998, 38 percent of the Russian population lived below the poverty line. European Bank for Reconstruction and Development (EBRD), *Transition Report 1998: Financial Sector in Transition* (London: EBRD, 1998), p. 187.

33. RFE/RL Newsline, 23 March 2000, citing Russian State Statistics Committee figures reported by the Russian news service, Interfax.

34. A valuable analysis of the economic reform program is the book by Shleifer and Treisman, *Without a Map: Political Tactics and Economic Reform in Russia*. Shleifer, a Harvard economist, helped advise the Russian government on the reforms.

35. The remainder work in joint ventures or for public organizations or in other forms of mixed public–private enterprises. Figures drawn from *Rossiiskii statisticheskii ezhegodnik: 1999* (Moscow: Goskomstat Rossii, 1999), p. 114. This publication is the official statistical annual published by the State Statistics Committee of Russia.

36. A useful study of ownership and control of privatized enterprises is Joseph R. Blasi, Maya Kroumova, and Douglas Kruse, *Kremlin Capitalism: Privatizing the Russian Economy* (Ithaca, N.Y., and London: ILR Press/Cornell University Press, 1997).

37. Roman Szporluk, "The Imperial Legacy and the Soviet Nationalities," in Lubomyr Hajda and Mark Beissinger, eds., *The Nationalities Factor in Soviet Politics and Society* (Boulder, Colo.: Westview, 1990), pp. 1–23; and idem, "Dilemmas of Russian Nationalism," in Rachel Denber, ed., *The Soviet Nationality Reader: The Disintegration in Context* (Boulder, Colo.: Westview, 1992), pp. 509–43.

38. Valery Tishkov and Martha Brill Olcott, "From Ethnos to Demos: the Quest for Russia's Identity," in Anders Aslund and Martha Brill Olcott, eds., *Russia after Communism* (Washington, D.C.: Carnegie Endowment for International Peace, 1999), pp. 61–90.

39. Ronald Grigor Suny, *The Revenge of the Past: Nationalism, Revolution, and the Collapse of the Soviet Union* (Stanford, Calif.: Stanford University Press, 1993); Kolsto, *Political Construction Sites: Nation-Building in Russia and the Post-Soviet States.*

40. For overviews of political development in the former Soviet states, see the volumes of essays edited by Karen Dawisha and Bruce Parrott, *Democratic Changes and Authoritarian Reactions in Russia, Ukraine, Belarus, and Moldova* (Cambridge, England: Cambridge University Press, 1997) and idem, *Conflict, Cleavage, and Change in Central Asia and the Caucasus* (Cambridge, England: Cambridge University Press, 1997).

41. Political scientist Michael McFaul has argued that we should view Russia's transformation since the end of the Soviet Union as a peaceful revolution. See Michael McFaul, *Russia's Unfinished Revolution: Political Change from Gorbachev to Putin* (Ithaca, N.Y.: Cornell University Press, 2001).

42. Rent seeking refers to activity by individuals, bureaucrats, firms, or other economic actors to use or obtain control rights to assets that allow them to receive above-normal gains from the exploitation of the assets. This problem will be discussed in more detail in Chapter 6.

43. See, for instance, Przeworski, *Democracy and the Market: Political and Economic Reforms in Eastern Europe and Latin America*; Giuseppe DiPalma, *To Craft Democracies: An Essay on Democratic Transitions* (Berkeley: University of California Press, 1990); Guillermo O'Donnell, Philippe C. Schmitter, and Laurence Whitehead, eds., *Transitions from Authoritarian Rule: Prospects for Democracy* (Baltimore: Johns Hopkins University Press, 1986); and Huntington, *The Third Wave: Democratization in the Late Twentieth Century.*

44. Seymour Martin Lipset, "Some Social Requisites of Democracy: Economic Development and Political Legitimacy," *American Political Science Review* 53 (1959), pp. 69–105; Larry Diamond, "Economic Development and Democracy Reconsidered," *American Behavioral Scientist* 35 (1992), pp. 450–99.

45. The seminal statement of this view is Dankwart Rustow, "Transitions to Democracy: Toward a Dynamic Model," *Comparative Politics* 2:3 (April 1970), pp. 337–64.

2 The Soviet System and Its Demise

ussia's present-day political institutions are the product of a series of political struggles that began in the late 1980s when Mikhail Gorbachev first began his attempts to reform the Soviet regime. The battles that he set in motion ultimately brought down the regime and continued into the early 1990s. The struggle over state power in Russia subsided once the 1993 constitution came into force. The adoption of the constitution settled the problem of how power should be formally organized in the Russian state and bears the strong imprint of Yeltsin's own political objectives. In particular, the powerful presidency embodies his vision of a president holding paramount power to set national policy. Likewise the design of the parliament, the Constitutional Court, and nature of federalism all were shaped by his tactical and long-term goals. While a large number of leaders and experts participated in drafting the constitution, Yeltsin had the final say on most points.[1]

In a longer-term perspective, today's political order has been shaped by a thousand-year history of state building, as Russia's rulers have sought to create the means for extending central control over a vast and thinly populated land. The drive to establish instruments for exercising power has been far more brutal than in most Western societies: Russian rulers have had to struggle with the immense territorial expanse of the country, its generally harsh and inhospitable climate, and its location on the borders of several European and Asian civilizations and empires. Over time, these pressures have intensified Russia's rulers' demands for absolute power over their society and pushed their ideological doctrines to take on extreme and dogmatic forms. This historical legacy helps to explain why Russians place a particularly high value on state power and why their efforts to accumulate and manage state power have been so difficult.

Before we review the basic elements of the current constitutional order, therefore, we need to know something of its historical origins. This chapter therefore describes the Soviet system and its breakdown. Chapter 3 discusses the creation of the current Russian regime.

THE SOVIET REGIME BEFORE GORBACHEV

From October 1917 until 1991, Russia was a communist regime, meaning that the Communist Party held a monopoly on political power (see Close Up 2.1: Socialism,

Communism, Marxism, Leninism). Originally, the Communist Party was a revolutionary movement aimed at overthrowing the tsarist state. Indeed, its ambitions went much further than that. The communists' long-range goal was the overthrow of capitalism throughout the world and the establishment of a worldwide socialist system. In the end, the communist movement succeeded in establishing communist regimes in Russia, Eastern Europe, much of Asia, and a few isolated countries in other regions (among them Cuba). But the worldwide communist revolution never arrived, and Russia's communists devoted most of their energies to building up the power of the Soviet state. They constantly invoked the language of class war as they sought to portray their drive for economic and military power, and for moral unity and loyalty, as a struggle against the capitalist world.

To the Russian communists, socialism meant a society without private ownership of the means of production, where the state owned and controlled all important economic assets, and where political power was exercised in the interests of the working people. *Vladimir Ilyich Lenin* (1870–1924; in power 1917–1924) was the leader of the Russian Communist Party and the first head of the Soviet Russian government.[2] In keeping with Lenin's model of the Communist Party as a "vanguard party," the Soviet regime divided power between the *soviets,* which were elective councils through which workers and peasants could voice their desires, and the Communist Party, which would lead the soviets. The Bolsheviks saw the soviets as vehicles of mass participation in the state by the workers, but ensured that they would be dominated by the more tightly organized and disciplined Communist Party. The party, as the bearer of the guiding vision, would direct the soviets and their executive organs, but it would remain organizationally separate from them.[3]

Lenin's successor, *Joseph Stalin* (1879–1953; in power 1924–1953), consolidated the institutional underpinnings of Lenin's model of rule, but also took its despotic impulses to extremes: Stalin's regime employed mass terror against large categories of the population, killing millions of Soviet citizens through executions, induced famine, forced labor under inhuman conditions, and deportations.[4] Stalin's regime expanded Soviet state power, and defended it in World War II; it carried out a crash program of forced industrialization and agricultural collectivization. Stalin was a state builder, in the sense that under his rule the Soviet state extended its capacity to rule over all regions of the country and in all aspects of society. Under Stalin the vast state hierarchies of military and police power were built up, together with factories, mines, power stations, highways, canals, and railroad lines; vast numbers of schools, clinics, and cultural and scientific institutions were built; whole cities were constructed, and Moscow itself was remade. Soviet society was penetrated with networks of informers, and millions of people were arrested on charges of "anti-Soviet" activity. Yet there was also a profound strain of hope and pride running through Soviet culture, as many people believed that they were building the bright socialist future.

Stalin may have been a state builder, but he also left a legacy of very weakly institutionalized power because political authority was heavily dependent on fear, suspicion, and an abject dependence on Stalin himself. Stalin's power was as close to being absolute as any leader in history has ever come: He set the country's

Close Up 2.1   Socialism, Communism, Marxism, Leninism

Terms such as *socialism* and *communism* can be confusing because they have been used in a number of different ways, and often by people with strongly held ideological visions of what they *want* these concepts to mean. But there is a coherent core of meaning to each of these terms, and it is helpful to recognize the distinctions.

Socialism has a very broad range of meaning. Generally it refers to the elimination of private property in some or all of the means of production of a society—that is, those forms of wealth that can be used to produce more wealth (including land, factories, natural resources, banks, and so on). Instead, society or some agent of society such as the state would be the owner of the wealth, and would use its control of resources to eliminate poverty, exploitation, and inequality in society as well as to build up the productive potential of the society to a higher level. Socialists disagree over how comprehensive state ownership of productive property should be: Some advocate that the state own only certain basic industries and natural resources, while others want to end private property altogether. Some link socialism with political freedom and popular democracy, while others would allow the state to suppress some freedoms for the sake of a larger collective goal. Some advocate immediate action, while others prefer to allow society to evolve gradually from capitalism to socialism. In recent decades, socialism in advanced industrial democracies has turned into "social democracy," a system where the state uses its power not to eliminate private property but rather to use its taxing and spending power to promote equality of opportunity and provide for basic social well-being, all the while seeking to encourage the incentives of a market economy to promote economic growth, productivity, and national competitiveness.

Communism has a more specific meaning. It can be used to refer either to an economic system or to a type of political regime. As an economic system, communism refers to a society where there is no private property in the means of production. Most communists would subscribe to the view that the ultimate goal of communism is the elimination not only of private property but also of the state itself. They would argue that the state should take ownership and control of society's wealth from the capitalists, but should gradually give way to a system of self-organized, self-managed communal life—the kind of society that is to be found in a commune, where all share and share alike both in producing and in consuming. However, no large-scale society has ever been able to operate in the way that small communal societies operate. And even small communal societies have generally been short-lived. Communists are therefore always socialists, in that they want to do away with capitalism (the system comprising a market

(continued)

Close Up 2.1 *(continued)*

economy and private-property rights). But not all socialists are communists, since not all socialists would want to eliminate all private property and dismantle the institutions of political democracy.

In the political sense, communism refers to the type of regime in which a communist party—meaning a party devoted to the communist doctrine—holds power. In fact, no communist regime has ever taken any serious steps to dismantle the machinery of state power. To the contrary, communist regimes always expand the power of the state over individuals, not merely taking control of all or some of the means of production, but also intervening to different degrees in social and private life, suppressing political opposition, and sometimes putting society on a quasi-military footing. In the twentieth century, some communist regimes turned into extraordinarily violent and bloody dictatorships. Communist regimes continued to promote the vision that one day everyone would live as in a commune and that the state would at some very distant point "wither away," but in practice they placed heavy emphasis on building up the power of the state to control society, so they demanded absolute loyalty to the state, its principles, and its goals. As a regime type, nearly all communist regimes have collapsed. As of this writing, North Korea remains communist, as does Cuba; Vietnam and China combine capitalism with political monopolies by their communist parties. But no serious observer now believes that communism as a regime type has a future.

Marxism is a form of communist doctrine, developed by Karl Marx and Friedrich Engels, which holds that the end of capitalism will come about when the working class seizes control of the means of production from the capitalists and uses it to establish socialism, and eventually communism. Marxists are therefore communists. *Leninism* refers to the brand of Marxism developed by Lenin: Lenin emphasized the need for political revolution even before all the economic conditions for socialism were met, and he was especially insistent about the need for an iron dictatorship over society to be exercised by the Communist Party "in the name of" the working class. Through most of the Soviet period, the official doctrine taught to all citizens was called "Marxism-Leninism," because it was officially regarded as a system of thought originated by Marx and Engels and subsequently developed by Lenin and his successors. Over time, the doctrine became rigid, hollow, formulaic, and dogmatic—no longer of any relevance to Soviet leaders faced with the realities of the world in the twentieth century, where capitalism proved itself considerably more dynamic than the Soviet system.

priorities in every sphere; intervened in any issue he cared to take up (whether deciding whether a particular movie or play should be released or suppressed; whether—as in the case of the famous linguistics dispute—human language belonged to the Marxian "base" or "superstructure" or editing the words to the new Soviet national anthem); he personally approved lists of "enemies of the people" who were to be arrested and shot. His own tendencies toward paranoia only intensified the climate of fear and mistrust that permeated official life. Moreover, the pattern of personal despotism was repeated in many subordinate organizations, where smaller-scale "little Stalins" ruled with an iron fist in their own organizations. Little wonder that upon Stalin's death in 1953, there were no agreed rules and procedures for transferring power to another leader nor was there a clear division of authority between the leader at the top, the party, and the state.

Therefore Stalin's successors, beginning with *Nikita Khrushchev* (1894–1971; in power 1953–1964), grappled with the challenge of defining a new and more institutionalized framework for ruling the state. Lacking Stalin's unchallengeable power, they agreed on the need to make the regime less dependent on fear and more on popular consent without relinquishing their power.[5] They made the system less personalistic and more rule governed, with power in the party exercised more collectively. They ended the use of mass terror and raised living standards somewhat, but they retained the basic Leninist tenets of state ownership of the means of production and the Communist Party's role as the source of political direction for state and society. Under Khrushchev and Brezhnev, then, the outlines of the mature Communist Party–state became more firmly defined and less subject to the caprices of any one leader.

A key to understanding the institutional basis of the Soviet regime is the theory of the "leading role" of the Communist Party. The theory demanded that the Communist Party penetrate and control government without itself replacing government. The party would set goals, resolve conflicts, and monitor political socialization, elite recruitment, and bureaucratic performance. It would coordinate the many agencies of the state and ensure that they worked together to maintain the system and achieve its goals. But the party was not supposed to usurp the actual functions of government, such as managing the economy, policing the society, or running schools, hospitals, and television stations. The Soviet model was a strategy for building state power in a society at a low level of development: It created opportunities for mass participation and the recruitment of leaders, and gave experience in government to ordinary working people. It presented a democratic facade to the Soviet population and the outside world, while concealing the enormous brutality and wastefulness of its methods. With time, the model also demonstrated its incapacity to respond to new kinds of political imperatives that arose from the immobilism and self-interest of its powerful bureaucratic components.

The model incorporated a federal element. Formally, the state comprised fifteen sovereign national republics, but centralized political control over them was guaranteed by the Communist Party's hierarchical chain of command that stretched across all governmental and societal organizations. Soviet citizens learned to switch back and forth between a world of fictions proclaimed in Soviet doctrine, taught in schools, and repeated endlessly in the mass media, and a world of everyday realities. The fictions concerned the shining ideals of Soviet communism, the nominally democratic political institutions in which citizens were said to be the masters of the state, and the progress the society was making toward a life of abundance and justice. The realities reflected the stagnation in living standards, the acceptance of endless venality and cant in public life, and the gap between the majority of the population and those whose political status entitled them to lives of privilege.

The word *soviet* means council, and the Soviet model of government revolved around a system of soviets. These were elected bodies symbolizing the principle of democratic self-government. There were soviets in every territorial unit of the country—village, town, county, province, and so on, all the way up to the Supreme Soviet of the USSR itself. In theory, the soviets exercised all state power in the Soviet Union, but in reality it was understood that the soviets had no real policymaking power. The USSR Supreme Soviet, for instance, met only twice a year, and then for a few days each time, in order to hear official reports and approve motions proposed by the leadership. Generally, everyone accepted that the soviets served the function of creating a formal appearance of representative democracy, while in fact the party and the executive organs of government made all the major decisions. The only sense in which the soviets "represented" the public was descriptive, in that the candidates were selected by the party to ensure the presence of fixed quotas from each major demographic category by occupation, sex, age, ethnic group, and party status. This allowed the regime to boast that large proportions of particular groups of the population were serving as elected representatives (called *deputies*). Usually only one candidate ran for a given seat, so that the elections offered voters only the opportunity to vote for or against the candidate offered. Elections were not an institution for making officials accountable to voters for their actions, but they were treated as grand national ceremonies in which the nearly universal voter turnout demonstrated the unity of the people and their state.

Formally, the deputies of a soviet elected a set of executive officials to manage government in its jurisdiction, making the executive arm of each soviet accountable to the soviet for its actions. In reality, the soviet simply ratified a choice that had been made by the Communist Party authorities. Nonetheless, executive officials had real bureaucratic power, and together they formed an executive-branch chain of command that stretched all the way from the lowest level of government up to Moscow. Meantime, the Communist Party supervised and directed—but was not supposed to usurp—the work of government executives. At the highest levels, those at the level of union republics and the all-union central government, there was a Supreme Soviet, which had the power to enact laws. Executive power was invested in the Council of Ministers. The USSR Council of Ministers was thus formally equivalent to the cabinet of a parliamentary government in a Western democracy and its chairman was the functional equivalent of a prime minister. As the person in charge of the executive branch for the entire Soviet Union, the chairman of the Council of Ministers was in fact a very powerful figure—but never as powerful as the head of the Communist Party of the Soviet Union.

A second feature of the Soviet regime was its use of ethnic federalism. Soviet federalism was designed to give symbolic rights to ethnic minorities, especially those located on the outer perimeter of Russia's territory that had traditions of national autonomy or statehood. So, unlike federalism in the United States or Germany, the constitutional form that federalism took in the Soviet Union was linked to the goal of giving ethnic-national populations a means to maintain their national cultures but to do so without challenging the center's power. In Soviet federalism, fifteen nominally sovereign republics were considered to be the constituent units of the federal union. Each republic gave a particular ethnic nationality a certain formal opportunity for representation. Most structures of power at the central level were replicated in the fifteen union republics; of course, the army and the money supply were exclusively central functions.

Power was so highly centralized in the Soviet regime that the federal structure of the state was largely a formality. Yet the effect of organizing the state around ethnic territories, each with its own trappings of statehood, proved to have powerful cumulative effects on Soviet political development. The development of "national" educational systems, cultural institutions, and mass media reinforced ethnic-national identities in all fifteen republics, even in those where there was only a weak sense of national consciousness before Soviet rule. At the same time, the centralization of political and economic power in Moscow prevented the national leaders of the federal republics from making any serious claims on the union government for greater autonomy. As time passed, members of the indigenous nationalities in the republics came to take certain rights for granted, including tolerance for national cultural traditions to the extent that these did not directly contradict Soviet ideological doctrine. The stability of these informal rules and understandings about how far each nationality could go in preserving its national identity fostered a tendency for leaders and peoples in the republics to think of the territory and institutions of the republic as "theirs," a kind of collective national property. Coupled with the steady rise in the population's educational levels over the decades of Soviet rule, this tacit but powerful assumption contributed to the growth of ethnic self-consciousness in each republic among the indigenous nationality.[6]

The Soviet state was federal in form, unitary in fact. In federalism, the constituent regions of the state possess a constitutionally protected domain of power in which they are autonomous and can make policy so long as they do not violate constitutional rules.[7] In the Soviet Union, the central government (the Communist Party leadership and central executive authorities) had ultimate control over the political, economic, and cultural life of the republics, choosing how much autonomy the republics could exercise at any given time. Each jurisdictional unit was treated as subordinate to the higher-level unit within which it was located, in keeping with the chain-of-command principle. The union center controlled major productive resources throughout the country, including land, natural resources, industry, and human capital, while the constituent republics were given the right to manage lesser assets on their territories. Strategic decisions about economic development in the republics were determined by the center. The pattern resembled colonial imperialism in that a dominant metropolitan state developed the economies of peripheral territorial possessions for its benefit.

Yet reality and perception diverged. The fact that the Soviet regime was dominated by Russians did not mean that the Russian Republic benefited from the arrangement. The Russian Republic (RSFSR) was by far the largest of the fifteen union republics in territory and population, and its language and culture dominated the entire union. Yet the republic itself lacked even the weak instruments of statehood that the other republics possessed, such as its own republic-level Communist Party branch, KGB (Committee on State Security—the secret police), trade union council, Academy of Sciences, and the like. The reason of course is that if these organizations had had branches at the level of the Russian Republic, they would have threatened the power of the union-level structures. Union-level party and state organs thus doubled as Russian ones. One could say that Russia used the Soviet state to rule a quasi-imperial state.

But empires are costly. In the USSR, the balance of trade among republics was not always favorable to the Russian Republic, even though Russia dominated the union politically. In many respects, because of the deliberately low prices set for energy and other industrial inputs supplied by Russia, Russia ended up subsidizing the development of other republics. By 1991, Russia was providing the equivalent of one-tenth of its gross domestic product to other republics in the form of implicit trade subsidies.[8] Centralized planning and controlled prices made it impossible to judge who was exploiting whom, and within each republic people became convinced that the union was exploiting their republic.[9] Meantime, ethnic federalism enabled republican party and state leaders to build up political machines and expand their own political control. Many of the leaders in the union republics were keen to win greater control over state resources, not necessarily to put them to better or more productive use, but in order to build up their own political power by distributing the stream of benefits they yielded to their favored constituents. Thus when the political leaders in the union republics demanded the *decentralization* of economic administration, often what they wanted was to capture control over state resources for their own political benefit rather than to make more productive use of them—to transfer the *union's* bureaucratic control over the economy to control by the *republic-level* bureaucracy. Decentralization in this sense was neither democratic nor market oriented. Often republic-level leaders played the ethnic card in behind-the-scenes bureaucratic bargaining, demanding greater economic autonomy for their territories on the grounds that the ethnic nationalities residing in those territories needed more opportunities for development.

This point is a clue to the struggle for power between the union and Russian republican levels of the Soviet system. The demand for decentralization was one on which both democratic forces and bureaucratic officials in the republics could agree: The democrats wanted to break the hold of the Communist Party and the central government over citizens' political rights, while the republic-level officials were eager to claim a share of control over Soviet state assets located in their republics. They found common cause in the desire to weaken the central government. Thus to a large extent, the struggles over sovereignty in 1989–1991 resulting in the breakup of the union were a contest for control over state resources between elites whose institutional position was at the union level and the political forces at the next level down who sought to gain autonomy within their territorial jurisdictions. As far as the Russian Republic was concerned, this strategy meant that when the Russian leaders won sovereign power over the Russian territory, they had to give up their power over other republics.

After all, the fight for national sovereignty had a strong economic component since the state owned and controlled the means of production: land, natural resources, factories and farms, and wealth in all its forms. The struggle for power in the old regime was a struggle for the right to control the immense wealth of the country. Political and economic power were closely intertwined in the Soviet system. The relationship between these two domains is a key to understanding the difference of the Soviet system from liberal democracies, even those where the state has a large ownership stake in the economy. Even the most strongly social democratic polity in Europe differs sharply from the state socialism of the Soviet-type system. In contrast to societies where there is private ownership of productive property, in the Soviet system an individual's power, prestige, and wealth depended on his or her position in the political hierarchy. Productive wealth could not be passed on through inheritance to others.[10] State ownership of productive resources meant that political and social status derived from the same source; even the most powerful leaders depended on the favor of party officials because all lines of advancement and opportunity converged in the Communist Party. The "new class"—those who rose to power and privilege in the system—sought to use the Communist Party to protect their interests, but the absence of firm political rights or popular legitimacy created insecurity, which they compensated for by the use of propaganda and repression that fended off political challenges to their positions.[11]

In the planned economy, output growth was a constant obsession. The heads of enterprises were under intense pressure to fulfill their plan targets, and generally the authorities gave them substantial autonomy in choosing how to meet their output goals. Managers could generally get by with cutting corners, for instance, reducing quality, so long as they met the basic target for raw output set by the planners. Managers had little incentive to innovate or modernize, since the risk that a new technology might fail outweighed the potential benefits of increased productivity. In short, the incentives faced by enterprise managers tended to militate against flexibility, adaptiveness, entrepreneurship, and innovation. With time, as a result, the economy tended to grow stagnant and unable to compete in the global market. Its abundant natural resources (minerals, oil, timber, and many other goods) gave it the capacity to export and earn foreign exchange, but by the 1960s it was experiencing chronic shortfalls in agricultural production and the quality of its manufactured goods (apart from the defense industry) was appallingly low.

Stalin's strategy of industrializing Russia rapidly brought about another important feature of the state socialist model—the reliance on the enterprise as a source of noneconomic benefits to the populace. Goods such as housing, child care, subsidized meals, groceries, scarce durable goods such as cars, and subsidized vacations have long been allocated through enterprises alongside the ordinary retail distribution system. In the late 1970s, when the economy's performance began slipping seriously and food rationing had to be introduced in many cities, enterprise "social funds" assumed a greater political importance. As the supply of housing, food, and ordinary services fell ever further behind demand, enterprise managers exercised still more leverage over the state. Workers and managers were tightly bound to one another in mutual need. Managers needed a large and cheap labor force to enable them to fulfill their plan targets, and workers needed a secure position in a state enterprise in order to obtain a range of social benefits that were unavailable except through the enterprise. This created a bond of reciprocal dependence between workers and managers, which some have termed an implicit "social contract." Under the social contract, the regime committed itself to providing job security, social benefits, and relative income equality, in exchange for quiescence and compliance from workers.[12]

The social contract tended to weaken trade unions. In the Soviet model, trade unions were organized around entire economic branches, so that the managers of a firm were members of the same trade union as the engineers, the bench workers, and the cafeteria staff. Their common dependence on the state for the well-being of their workplace gave both managers and workers an incentive to pressure the state to maintain a steady stream of orders and financing regardless of whether the enterprise was profitable and productive or a wasteful drain on society's resources. Just as the economy created little incentive for entrepreneurship or innovation, it also discouraged the restructuring or closing of loss-making firms. Indeed, since the price system was set according to political criteria rather than being set by the play of demand and supply, it was next to impossible to know whether a given enterprise was operating profitably or not. Some, in fact, were subtracting value from the economy by producing goods that were worth less than the materials that went into making them.

Moreover, the weakness of financial constraints on enterprises' appetites for resources created a chronic syndrome of excess demand, shortages, and repressed inflation.[13] Low efficiency and failure to innovate on the part of enterprises did not incur economic penalties. To some extent enterprises were able to conceal the facts of their performance, and to some extent the center simply lacked the clout to improve productivity through administrative pressure. The center itself was constantly pressured to satisfy the needs of powerful industrial and regional interests. As a result, the system settled into inertia and decay. Each year the plan represented a modest incremental change over the previous year. Any serious attempts at reform were defeated by the combination of weak central power and inertial resistance by those who were called upon to carry out the reform. A very powerful latent coalition of interests—ministries, regional officials, enterprise directors, and workers—shared an interest in the preservation of the status quo since any serious change threatened them. Yet continuation of the status quo allowed the economy to reach the point where it had essentially stopped growing. But that meant that competing with the United States on military spending placed an ever-heavier burden on the economy. By the time Gorbachev came to power, defense expenditures were running at about a quarter of gross domestic product, and the share was still increasing.[14]

The deadweight economic loss caused by high military expenditures was one of the major reasons Gorbachev undertook his program of radical reform.

The deteriorating performance of the economy in the 1960s, 1970s, and 1980s placed a greater burden on the regime's ability to meet social expectations. It meant that fewer jobs were opening up in managerial and professional positions. Yet the stream of graduates with specialist degrees kept growing. More and more people occupied jobs below their educational qualifications. This affected both manual and specialist social strata. Many groups considered themselves underpaid and undervalued. Many of the grievances voiced in the early years of glasnost centered around the low professional autonomy and esteem of managerial and professional groups, including the administrative staff of the Communist Party itself. These strains were in part the consequence of the Brezhnev leadership's policy of leveling by raising the wage levels and educational qualifications at the lower end of the social hierarchy without achieving a corresponding transformation of the structure of labor. As a result, a sizable part of the work force occupied jobs for which they were significantly overqualified.

Economic stagnation exacerbated popular resentment of the privileges of the political elite. Crucial to understanding the explosive quality of social protest in the late 1980s is the accumulation of popular alienation, which often took nationalist forms, but which also arose from other issues, such as environmental degradation, the perception that the ruling *nomenklatura* was indifferent and parasitic, anger over shortages in the economy, and the conviction on the part of nearly every region and republic that it was being economically exploited by a distant, bureaucratized center.

In addition to the use of the soviets as the building block of the state, the principle of ethnic federalism, and the centralization of economic power, the political dominance of the Communist Party was the fourth defining characteristic of the old regime. Lenin's model of rule ensured that the organizational structure of the Communist Party maximized central control over all levels of government. The party itself was kept rather small, emphasizing that membership was a privilege and an obligation, and taking pains to admit only individuals whose political loyalties and social backgrounds passed stringent review. At its peak, the Communist Party had around 20 million members, around 9 percent of the adult population.[15] In many professions the membership rate was higher, and generally membership was higher among the more highly educated strata of the population. Among individuals in positions of high political and administrative responsibility, party membership was nearly obligatory. Indeed, for most individuals with high career ambitions, Communist Party membership was not just useful, it was a requirement.

The party's own organization paralleled that of the government, which it supervised and directed. In every territorial jurisdiction—district, town, province, and so on—the party maintained its own full-time organization. For instance, each city had a city CPSU organization with its own governing committee, a more powerful inner body called *bureau*, a set of functional departments overseeing industry, agriculture, and ideology, and personnel with their own full-time staff, who were overseen by managers called *secretaries*. The first secretary of the party organization of the city was always the city's most powerful official. The top party official was not the chief executive of the city: That was the chairman of the local executive committee of the city soviet. The first secretary of the party organization worked closely with the chairman of the executive committee of the city, but the party official was superior in status. Directives and advice from the party secretary were binding on executive-branch officials, but, by the same token, if the city government needed special help from Moscow, the party represented a direct channel of access to the highest levels of power in the country.

At the top, final power to decide policy rested in the CPSU Politburo. The Politburo was a small committee made up of the country's most powerful leaders that made decisions in all important areas of policy at its weekly meetings. Supporting the Politburo was the powerful Secretariat of the Central Committee of the Communist Party. The Secretariat ran the party's central headquarters, which was linked to all lower party organizations. Here the party monitored the political and economic situation throughout the country and around the world, and determined which problems needed to be addressed, developing policy options for the Politburo. Here the party managed the political careers of thousands of top political officials. Here it determined the ideological line that was to be reinforced and echoed throughout the country through the channels of party propaganda and the mass media. And here it supervised the vast government bureaucracy, the army, the police, the law enforcement system, the KGB, and the governments of the republics and regions. The description of the Communist Party's political role given in the 1977 Soviet Constitution, to the effect that the party was "the leading and guiding force of Soviet society, the nucleus of its political system of [all] state and public organizations"—was reasonably accurate.[16] Three of the party's most important powers were deciding policy, recruiting officials, and policing the ideological doctrine of the country. All major policy decisions were made by the party, at every level of the political system. All responsible officials were chosen with the approval of the party. And the ideas discussed in the media, the arts, education, or any public setting had to meet with the approval of the party's ideological watchdogs.

Sweeping as the party's powers were, they were undermined by bureaucratic immobilism. This problem grew more severe in the 1970s and 1980s for many reasons, among them the growing complexity of the political system, the loss of social cohesion, and the declining capacity of the aging leaders to manage the system coherently. The role that fear of arrest had played in reinforcing central power in the Stalin era gradually diminished and gave way to the certainty on the part of many officials that they could behave incompetently or even criminally with impunity. Certainly it is true of hierarchical organizations everywhere that overcentralization brings its own pathologies of control, through distortions of information flow, tacit resistance to the center's orders by officials at lower levels who have their own agendas, and the force of inertia.[17] By the time Mikhail Gorbachev was elected General Secretary of the CPSU in 1985, the political system of the USSR had grown top-heavy, unresponsive, and muscle-bound.[18]

The old regime appeared stable, but in fact its institutions were weak. More than in political systems where legal rules and traditions govern the way power is exercised by those holding political office, Soviet politicians had to struggle for power constantly, even when they occupied an important position. Behind the surface unity and consensus of Soviet politics, Soviet political leaders were engaged in a continuous competition for power. Naturally, Soviet leaders did not advertise their moves in this game. Nonetheless, by close examination of the public record, it is possible to identify the political alliances and commitments formed by top political leaders of the CPSU. Contenders for power consolidated power by showing that they could solve policy problems: Successes in policy tended to strengthen their hand in attracting supporters and eliminating opponents, while failures weakened the incentives that other officials had for supporting them.[19] The contest was not carried out in the electoral realm since there was no electoral link between the desires of the public and the policy choices considered by the regime. Nonetheless the contest was real and was played for high stakes. It resembled games of bureaucratic politics played out in other complex hierarchical organizations but with lower agreement over the rules and with a high risk factor: Failure in the political arena could lead, at best, to forced retirement and disgrace, and at worst to arrest and imprisonment—in Stalin's time, to the concentration camps.

For example, the transfer of power from one leader to another often set off an intense struggle for power. Once a leader climbed to the top, however, and won the office of General Secretary of the CPSU, he could normally use the powers of the office to stay in power for the rest of his life. Nikita Khrushchev was removed from power by a successful conspiracy in 1964; he spent the rest of his life as a pensioner out of the public eye.[20] The ringleader of the conspiracy, *Leonid Brezhnev* (1906–1982; in power 1964–1982), quickly consolidated his own power. He built a base of support that allowed him to remain in that office, despite obviously worsening health, until his death in November 1982. Brezhnev learned the lessons of Khrushchev's fall only too well. He owed his success at holding power for eighteen years to avoiding any serious attempts at political reform that might have upset the balance of ministerial and regional power centers that dominated the regime. There was relatively little turnover of political officeholders and even less policy innovation. The result was drift in policy, worsening government performance, and a gradual aging of the entire ruling elite of the USSR, during which the political system grew increasingly unresponsive to the imperative of economic and political reform.

Brezhnev was succeeded by *Yuri Andropov* (1914–1984), who had served as Chairman of the KGB and as a secretary of the CPSU Central Committee. Although Andropov initially launched a policy program to reverse the decline in national economic performance, it soon turned out that he was gravely ill and could only rule from his hospital bed. When he, in turn, died in February 1984, he was succeeded by another aging, ailing member of the Brezhnev generation, *Konstantin Chernenko* (1911–1985). Chernenko had been a loyal member of Brezhnev's personal clientele and tried to hold on to power by allying himself with the remnants of the old Brezhnev political machine. This meant halting the limited reform programs launched under Andropov and returning to the conservatism and drift of the Brezhnev era. But Chernenko, too, was fatally ill, and died in March 1985. At this point, the senior leadership was evidently concerned by the impression of debility and weakness created by this rapid succession of deaths, and agreed to turn to a much younger, more dynamic, and open-minded figure as the new General Secretary. The youngest member of the Politburo at the time he was named its leader—born in 1931, he was only fifty-four when he took over—*Mikhail Gorbachev* quickly grasped the levers of power that the system granted the General Secretary, and moved both to strengthen his own political base and to carry out a program of economic reform.

Gorbachev Comes to Power. One of the enduring mysteries about Gorbachev is how so radical a reformer could ever have reached the pinnacle of power under the old regime. One explanation lies in the fact that he could appeal not only to groups who wanted to liberalize the regime, but also to conservatives alarmed at the deterioration of discipline and morals in state and society. These conservatives could accept a certain amount of administrative reform in the interests of strengthening socialism. They, and pro-reform elements in the party apparatus and intelligentsia, were therefore a natural base of support for an ambitious and ingenious political leader such as Mikhail Sergeevich Gorbachev. At the same time, probably few within the party leadership realized how radical Gorbachev was until it was too late for them to remove him: His youth, self-confidence, intelligence, exposure to the West, and personal instincts all helped fuel his drive to carry out far-reaching changes in the Soviet system, aimed at transforming it into some version of a socialist democracy. Shortly before he was made General Secretary of the Communist Party of the Soviet Union, Gorbachev and his future Foreign Minister Eduard Shevardnadze (who later became president of post-Soviet Georgia) chatted while walking along a beach at a resort on the Crimean Sea. They agreed, according to their recollections of the conversation, that "everything was rotten" and "we cannot go on living this way."[21] At that point, although he knew that the system was deeply dysfunctional, neither the model of the change he intended to bring about nor the means of achieving it was clear to Gorbachev. He possessed enormous confidence, energy, ambition, and zeal for reform, but would he have launched his reforms had he known how they would turn out?

Gorbachev's remarkable rise began in the late 1970s. In 1978 he was named Secretary of the Central Committee; in 1979 he became candidate member, and in 1980 full member of the Politburo. In March 1985, upon Chernenko's death, Gorbachev was named General Secretary of the party. He needed to build a broader base of support in the Politburo for a policy of reform. To help persuade his colleagues to embark on real reform, Gorbachev needed to generate an elite perception of impending crisis in order to overcome his colleagues' reluctance to accept the risks of major reform.

Emphasizing the need for greater openness—glasnost—in relations between political leaders and the populace, Gorbachev stressed that the ultimate test of the party's effectiveness lay in improving the economic well-being of the country and its people. By highlighting such themes as the need for market relations, pragmatism in economic policy, and less secretiveness in government, he identified himself as a champion of reform.[22] The party amplified his modestly unorthodox message through its propaganda machine, disseminating to officials and citizens everywhere the new leader's appeals for glasnost, modernization, and intensification of economic development. Gorbachev called his program for reforming the Soviet system perestroika, which means a restructuring. He meant by this that he wanted to overhaul the entire structure of the Soviet economy and state system, but to leave its foundations intact.

Gorbachev moved rapidly to consolidate his own power using the General Secretary's power over the appointment of ranking elites. Acting cautiously at first, and then with increasing decisiveness, Gorbachev removed opponents and promoted supporters. Gorbachev not only stripped power away from the Brezhnev-era old guard, but he began transferring power away from the Communist Party altogether. Gorbachev also made use of the party's control of national policy to set new directions in domestic and foreign policy. In the economic sphere, he demanded "acceleration" of technological progress and economic growth through an infusion of capital, including stepped-up foreign investment. He also promised to loosen the suffocating bureaucratic controls that discouraged innovation on the part of enterprise managers. He called for breathing new life into the desiccated democratic forms of Soviet political life by making elections and public debate real and meaningful. In the sphere of foreign policy he pursued a new, active diplomacy in Europe and Asia, served up a series of disarmament proposals, and promised greater flexibility in relations with the West.

Gorbachev not only called for policy reform, he also made far-reaching institutional changes. He pushed through a reform bringing about the first contested elections for local soviets in many decades.[23] He sponsored a Law on State Enterprise that was intended to break the stranglehold of industrial ministries over enterprises through their powers of plan setting and resource allocation. He legalized private, market-oriented enterprise for individual and cooperative businesses and encouraged them to fill the many gaps in the economy left by the inefficiency of the state sector. He called for a "law-governed state" (*pravovoe gosudarstvo*) in which state power—including the power of the Communist Party—would be subordinate to law. He welcomed the explosion of informal social and political associations that formed. He made major concessions to the United States in the sphere of arms control, resulting in a treaty that, for the first time in history, stipulated the destruction of entire classes of nuclear missiles.

In 1988, he proposed still more far-reaching changes at an extraordinary gathering of party members from around the country, where in a nationally televised address he outlined a vision of a democratic, but still socialist, political system. In it, legislative bodies made up of deputies elected in open, contested races, would exercise the main policy-making power in the country. The Supreme Soviet would become a genuine parliament, debating policy, overseeing government officials, and adopting or defeating bills. Moreover, the judiciary would be separated from party control, and at the top of the system there would be a body called upon to adjudicate the constitutionality of legislative acts. The party conference itself was televised, and treated the Soviet public to an unprecedented display of open debate among the country's top leaders. Using to the full the General Secretary's authoritarian powers, Gorbachev quickly railroaded his proposals for democratization through the Supreme Soviet, and in 1989 and 1990 the vision Gorbachev laid out before that party conference was realized as elections were held, deputies elected, and new soviets formed at the center and in every region and locality. When nearly half a million coal miners went out on strike in the summer of 1989, Gorbachev declared himself sympathetic to their demands.

Gorbachev's radicalism received its most dramatic confirmation through the astonishing developments of 1989 in Eastern Europe. All the regimes making up the socialist bloc collapsed and gave way to multiparty parliamentary regimes in virtually bloodless popular revolutions (Romania was the only country where the ouster of the ruling communist elite was accompanied by widespread bloodshed)—and the Soviet Union stood by and supported the revolutions![24] The overnight dismantling of communism in Eastern Europe meant that the elaborate structure of party ties, police cooperation, economic trade, and military alliance that had developed since Stalin imposed communism on Eastern Europe after World War II vanished. Divided Germany was allowed to reunite, and, after initial reluctance, the Soviet leaders even gave their sanction to the admission of the reunited Germany to NATO. In the Soviet Union itself, meantime, the Communist Party was facing massive popular hostility and a critical loss of authority. Gorbachev forced it to renounce the principle of the "party's leading role" and to accept the legitimacy of private property and free markets. Real power in the state was being transferred to the elective and executive bodies of government—marked, above all, by the new office of state president that Gorbachev created for himself in March 1990.[25] The newly elected governments of the national republics making up the Soviet state were one by one declaring their sovereignty within the union; and the three Baltic Republics had declared their intention to secede altogether from the union. Everywhere, inside and outside the Soviet Union, Communist Party rule was breaking down.

POLITICAL INSTITUTIONS OF THE TRANSITION PERIOD: DEMISE OF THE USSR

Gorbachev's inability to overcome resistance to his economic programs by the party and state bureaucracy undoubtedly prompted the radicalization of his reforms. He was careful not to go too far, however. His design for the democratization of the soviets had clear roots in the Leninist past, and, not incidentally, also served to reinforce his own power at the top. In introducing his political reforms in 1988, Gorbachev made it amply clear that he was not endorsing a move to a multiparty system as well. Parliamentarism was all very well and good as a further extension of glasnost, Gorbachev seemed to think, but it must be kept firmly in its place. The power to make major decisions on domestic and national policy was to remain with the Communist Party leadership. Gorbachev sought to play the new parliamentary structures off against the party bureaucracy, bringing pressure to bear on party officials to carry out his reform policies, while ensuring that the newly elected deputies would not overstep the boundaries of their power. Gorbachev's political reforms had both direct and strategic purposes. Gorbachev did want to open up the system to more democratic participation. But he intended for the new channels of mobilization to expand his base of support for the reforms he wanted to make: He calculated that if he created new political arenas in which supporters of liberal reform could gain influence, they would pressure the bureaucracy for more perestroika. But by creating these new arenas of participation, including media glasnost, elections, and democratized soviets, Gorbachev made it possible for a wide variety of political tendencies—radical democrats, hard-line communist conservatives, and nationalist movements—to seize the initiative. Many of these groups had entirely different aims from his own.

In retrospect it is clear that Gorbachev underestimated the centrifugal force of demands for national sovereignty and independence in a number of the union republics. As the liberalization of political life enabled new autonomous political movements to press for changes going far beyond what he was then prepared to tolerate, he concluded that the two posts he held—General Secretary of the CPSU and Chairman of the Supreme Soviet of the USSR—did not give him enough power. Although he had initially opposed the idea of creating a state presidency, he changed his mind and declared early in 1990 that only as president would he be able to control the executive branch. Accordingly, in March 1990, he railroaded constitutional amendments creating a presidency through the Congress of People's Deputies. He coupled this with a change in the constitution that had the effect of legalizing multiparty competition. Both of these reforms, needless to say, seriously threatened the Communist Party's power. Now Gorbachev would set policy and oversee the bureaucracy in his capacity as president, not as general secretary; even worse from the Communist Party's standpoint was the fact that the party would be forced to compete for popular support in competitive elections against legal rivals.

Once again, Gorbachev's reforms had consequences he clearly did not intend. Although he was readily elected president of the Soviet Union, he was elected by the Congress of People's Deputies, not in a direct popular election (which he might have lost). Elimination of the long-standing provision that assigned the Communist Party the "leading role" in government and society authorized opposition movements to contest the party's mandate to rule. Therefore the 1990 elections of deputies both to the Supreme Soviets in all fifteen republics and for soviets in regions and towns all across the country, stimulated competition among political movements and parties. In Russia, a coalition of democratic reformers ran under the banner of a movement called "Democratic Russia," which sought to form caucuses in each soviet to which its candidates were elected. In the March 1990 elections, the Democratic Russia movement succeeded in winning a majority of seats in both the Moscow and Leningrad (a year later the city took back its old name of St. Petersburg) soviets. And in the races for the Russian Congress of People's Deputies, the Democratic Russia contingent claimed as many as 40 percent of the newly elected deputies as adherents. (Of course, as events later showed, many of these deputies had only a very weak, opportunistic commitment to the radical democratic tenets of its program.) A roughly equal number of the new Russian deputies identified themselves with the conservative, antireform, prosocialist ideology of the communists of Russia. Under the influence of the democratic aspirations and national self-awareness that the electoral campaign stimulated, the Congress narrowly elected Boris Yeltsin chairman of the Russian Supreme Soviet in June 1990. As chief of state in the Russian Republic, Yeltsin was now well positioned to challenge Gorbachev for preeminence in the country.[26]

A course of developments then followed in the Russian Republic that paralleled those occurring at the level of the USSR federation during the previous year. Like Gorbachev a year earlier, Yeltsin, too, decided in early 1991 to create a state presidency in Russia. Unlike Gorbachev, Yeltsin put the matter to a national referendum. But he did so in such a way as to counter Gorbachev further. When Gorbachev held a USSR-wide referendum in March 1991 on whether the populace desired to preserve the Soviet Union in some new, vaguely defined form, Yeltsin added a question to the ballot distributed in the Russian republic. This asked whether voters approved the idea of instituting a national presidency for the Russian republic. Both measures—the preservation of the union and the introduction of a Russian presidency—passed by wide margins (71 percent of Russian voters supported preservation of the union, 70 percent a Russian presidency), but the popularity of the principle of a Russian presidency effectively undercut Gorbachev's desire to win a national mandate for his efforts to defend central power.

Moreover, Yeltsin linked his power and the cause of Russian national freedom with a program of radical market-oriented economic reform. In the spring of 1990, Yeltsin had endorsed a program of rapid, uncompromising economic transformation intended to dismantle the old system of state ownership and planning and set loose the forces of private enterprise. The strategy discussed by Yeltsin's economic advisers had much in common with the programs of stabilization being adopted in Poland and Czechoslovakia. First, the central government would relinquish many of its administrative controls over the economy, allowing prices to rise to meet demand and freeing producers to determine their own production goals. Second, the government would launch a massive effort to privatize state assets and create a broad base of property owners who would help ensure that communism would never return. In Russia, the "500 Days" program that was developed embodying these ideas had the added feature of allowing the republics to claim sovereign control over the assets on their territories. This provision helped make the program palatable to republic leaders and publics, but would have eliminated most remaining controls that the union center still had to regulate the economy. Little wonder that Gorbachev, pressured by conservative elements in the Politburo, military, government, and KGB, rejected the plan after having initially considered it; and little wonder that Yeltsin embraced it in his struggle with Gorbachev.

The winter of 1990–1991 saw an intense political struggle between Gorbachev and Yeltsin. Gorbachev fought to hold on to his power in the central leadership while maneuvering to defeat Yeltsin. By April 1991, Yeltsin had defeated the conservative forces in the Russian parliament and Gorbachev had failed to bring Yeltsin down. Gorbachev was forced to accept Yeltsin's power and that of Russia's sovereign status within the federal union. Gorbachev then sought to find terms for a new federal or confederal union that would be acceptable to Yeltsin and the Russian leadership, as well as to the leaders of the other republics. He initiated negotiations with the republic leaders aimed at drafting a new constitutional framework for the Soviet Union. In pursuing these talks, though, he was negotiating from a position of weakness: He lacked the support of the conservative, bureaucratic elements of the union government, and democratic forces were shifting their support to Yeltsin and the cause of a sovereign Russia.

Nonetheless, in April 1991 Gorbachev succeeded in reaching agreement on the outlines of a new treaty of union with nine of the fifteen republics, including Russia. The agreement would have established a new balance of power between the federal union government and the constituent republics. The union government would have preserved its responsibility for defense and security, energy and transportation, money and finance, and other coordinating functions. The member republics would have gained the power to make economic policy and control productive assets within their territories. Most of the power of the union bureaucracy would have been transferred to the republics. Gorbachev once again underestimated the strength of his opposition, based in the great bureaucracies of the union government. On August 19, 1991, his own vice president, prime minister, defense minister, KGB chief, and other senior officials moved to prevent the signing ceremony of the treaty by forming the "State Committee on the State of Emergency" and seizing power in what became known as the August putsch. They put Gorbachev (then vacationing in the Crimea) under house arrest and attempted to restore the shaken power of the Soviet regime. The coup organizers made some critical errors, however. Evidently they counted on widespread public support for their actions, but instead, the tide of public sympathy in Moscow and Leningrad was against them. Thousands of people came out to defend the "White House," the building where Russia's parliament met. The organizers failed to arrest Boris Yeltsin, who rallied mass opposition to the coup. After three days, the coup collapsed, the organizers were arrested, and Gorbachev returned again as president of the Soviet Union. But Gorbachev's power was now fatally compromised. Neither union nor Russian power structures heeded his commands. Through the fall of 1991, the Russian government took over the union government, ministry by ministry. In November 1991, President Yeltsin issued a decree formally outlawing the Communist Party of the Soviet Union. One by one, the union republics declared their independence and on December 9, 1991, the leaders of the Russian, Ukrainian, and Belorussian republics met to issue a declaration that the Soviet Union was dissolved and replaced by the Commonwealth of Independent States. Gorbachev became a president without a country. On December 25, 1991, he resigned as president of the USSR and turned the powers of his office over to Boris Yeltsin.

As his nemesis Yeltsin would do eight years later, Gorbachev appeared on national television to announce his resignation. Bitterness alternated with self-justification in his speech. He explained the necessity of his attempt to reform the system, even though his efforts had led to the country's dissolution, by arguing that it would have been wrong for him simply to win office and then cling to power as long as possible (as Brezhnev, he was implying, had done). He had no alternative but to initiate major reforms: "All the attempts at partial reform—and there were any number of them—suffered failure one after the other. The country lost its vision of the future. It was impossible to live like that any longer. What was needed was a radical change. That is why I have never, ever regretted not taking advantage of the post of general secretary merely to reign for a number of years. I would have viewed that as irresponsible and amoral. I realized that it was an extremely difficult and even risky business to begin reforms on that sort of scale and in our sort of society. Even today I am convinced of the historical correctness of the democratic reforms begun in the spring of 1985."[27]

Mikhail Gorbachev's reputation stands considerably higher in the West than it does in his own country. He attempted to overcome the paralysis of the Soviet political system by introducing partial measures toward a market-oriented economy and a democratic political system while retaining the essential features of Communist Party domination, state ownership of productive property, and a centralized union state. The wave of demands that his reform awakened stimulated political leaders to make still more far-reaching demands for democratization, decentralization, and market capitalism. These demands provoked a backlash in the form of the August 1991 coup attempt, which in turn fueled a wave of independence movements in all the union republics—even Russia. With the collapse of the union itself each former republic became a nominally independent, sovereign state. Their leaders were each faced with the challenge of finding a new basis for legitimate rule and adapting the Soviet institutional legacy to new tasks. In Russia, the struggle between the defenders of the old communist order and the advocates of a Western-oriented democratic and capitalist system now grew intense.

REVIEW QUESTIONS

1. Did Lenin and Stalin achieve the goals of communism as Marx understood it? If not, in what ways did they betray or distort Marxism?
2. What were the most important means by which the Communist Party of the Soviet Union exercised its power in state and society?
3. What were the stakes of the competition between Gorbachev and Yeltsin in the period from 1989 to 1991? What were the main political resources each possessed?
4. Why was the Soviet system able to achieve high rates of growth in the 1930s but not in the 1980s?
5. What were the goals of Gorbachev's perestroika program? What were its main results?
6. What were the effects of glasnost on the Soviet political system and why were these effects so far-reaching?
7. What was the August 1991 coup? Why did it occur? Why did it fail?
8. Looking back, do you think that Gorbachev's reforms could have succeeded had he pursued different policies, created different institutions, or carried out his reforms in a different order?

ENDNOTES

1. Michael McFaul, *Russia's Unfinished Constitution: Political Change from Gorbachev to Putin* (Ithaca, N.Y.: Cornell University Press, 2001).
2. Vladimir Ilyich Lenin (1870–1924) was the leader of the wing of the Russian Marxist movement that insisted that socialism in Russia would only be possible if the revolutionaries seized state power and used it to construct a modern, industrial, and socialist economic base in Russia, as well as to launch similar revolutions elsewhere. This wing, which later became a separate party, was called the Bolsheviks. Still later it was renamed the Russian Communist Party, and finally the Communist Party of the Soviet Union. Lenin and his fellow Bolsheviks carried out their plan after seizing power in October 1917 in the name of the workers and peasants, and establishing a government formed around state socialist principles. As de facto leader of the Bolshevik (later Communist) party, and chairman of the new Soviet Russian government, Lenin established the basic governing institutions of the new Soviet regime. Throughout Soviet history, Soviet citizens were taught to revere Lenin as the infallible source of guidance about ideological doctrine and his teachings were codified, systematized, and joined to official versions of Marxist theory. Together, these bodies of official teachings were given the name *Marxism-Leninism*. In the Soviet Union and throughout the communist world, Marxism-Leninism had the status of dogma.
3. Two useful recent historical surveys of the Soviet regime are Sheila Fitzpatrick, *The Russian Revolution: 1917–1932* (New York: Oxford University Press, 1984); and Mary McAuley, *Soviet Politics: 1917–1991* (New York: Oxford University Press, 1992).
4. For an authoritative biography of Stalin that explains much of his behavior in psychological terms, see Robert C. Tucker, *Stalin as Revolutionary, 1879–1928: A Study in History and Personality* (New York: Norton, 1973); and Robert C. Tucker, *Stalin in Power: The Revolution from Above, 1928–1941* (New York: Norton, 1990).
5. On Khrushchev, see William J. Tompson, *Khrushchev: A Political Life* (New York: St. Martin's Press, 1995).
6. Ronald Grigor Suny, *The Revenge of the Past: Nationalism, Revolution, and the Collapse of the Soviet Union* (Stanford, Calif.: Stanford University Press, 1993). On early Soviet policies toward ethnic nationalities aimed at building ethnic national identities within a common multinational Soviet state, see Terry Martin, *The Affirmative Action Empire: Nations and Nationalism in the Soviet Union, 1923–1939* (Ithaca, N.Y.: Cornell University Press, 2001).
7. Peter Ordeshook, Olga Shvetsova, and Mikhail Filippov, *Federalism* (Cambridge, England: Cambridge University Press, forthcoming).
8. Anders Åslund, *How Russia Became a Market Economy* (Washington, D.C.: Brookings Institution, 1995), p. 108.
9. Stephen White, Graeme Gill, and Darrell Slider, *The Politics of Transition: Shaping a Post-Soviet Future.* (Cambridge, England: Cambridge University Press, 1993), p. 85.
10. A person could leave "personal" property to his or her heirs, including money, but not property that was used to create other forms of wealth or income.
11. The famous theory of the "new class" was devised by Yugoslav dissident Milovan Djilas to explain how there could be a ruling class in a supposedly classless society.
12. Linda Cook, *The Soviet Social Contract and Why It Failed: Welfare Policy and Workers' Politics from Brezhnev to Yeltsin* (Cambridge, Mass.: Harvard University Press, 1993).
13. Janos Kornai, *The Socialist System: The Political Economy of Communism* (Princeton, N.J.: Princeton University Press, 1992).

14. Ibid.
15. On the Communist Party, see Ronald J. Hill and Peter Frank, *The Soviet Communist Party*, 3rd ed. (Boston: Allen & Unwin, 1986); Graeme J. Gill, *The Collapse of a Single Party System: The Disintegration of the CPSU* (Cambridge, England: Cambridge University Press, 1994).
16. From Article Six of the USSR constitution as given in Robert Sharlet, *The New Soviet Constitution of 1977: Analysis and Text* (Brunswick, Ohio: King's Court Communications, 1978), p. 78.
17. Anthony Downs, *Inside Bureaucracy* (Boston: Little, Brown, 1967).
18. Philip G. Roeder, *Red Sunset: The Failure of Soviet Politics* (Princeton, N.J.: Princeton University Press, 1993).
19. George W. Breslauer, *Khrushchev and Brezhnev as Leaders: Building Authority in Soviet Politics* (Boston: Allen & Unwin, 1982).
20. He did dictate his memoirs into a tape recorder. The tapes were smuggled out and published under the title *Khrushchev Remembers* (Boston: Little, Brown, 1970) and *Khrushchev Remembers: The Last Testament* (Boston: Little, Brown, 1974). Both volumes were translated and edited by Strobe Talbott.
21. Archie Brown, *The Gorbachev Factor* (New York: Oxford University Press, 1996), p. 81.
22. Brown, *The Gorbachev Factor*.
23. Stephen White, "Reforming the Electoral System," *Journal of Communist Studies* 4:4 (1988), pp. 1–17.
24. The eyewitness reports by Timothy Garton Ash, *The Magic Lantern* (New York: Random House, 1990), are exceptionally valuable firsthand accounts as well as brilliant political analysis of the revolutions of 1989 in Eastern Europe. A thorough history of this period is Gale Stokes, *The Walls Came Tumbling Down: The Collapse of Communism in Eastern Europe* (New York: Oxford University Press, 1993).
25. On Gorbachev's autocratic methods in forcing through the constitutional amendments needed to create a powerful presidency, see David Shipler, "Between Dictatorship and Anarchy," *The New Yorker*, 25 June 1990.
26. On the 1989 and 1990 elections and the new representative bodies they formed, see Yitzhak M. Brudny, "The Dynamics of 'Democratic Russia,' 1990–1993," *Post-Soviet Affairs* 9:2 (1993), pp. 141–170; Giulietto Chiesa, with Douglas Taylor Northrop, *Transition to Democracy: Political Change in the Soviet Union, 1987–1991* (Hanover and London: Dartmouth College; University Press of New England, 1993); Robert T. Huber and Donald R. Kelley, eds., *Perestroika-Era Politics: The New Soviet Legislature and Gorbachev's Political Reforms* (Armonk, N.Y.: M. E. Sharpe, 1991); Brendan Kiernan, *The End of Soviet Politics: Elections, Legislatures and the Demise of the Communist Party* (Boulder, Colo.: Westview, 1993); Michael E. Urban, *More Power to the Soviets: The Democratic Revolution in the USSR* (Aldershot, England and Brookfield, Vt.: Edward Elgar, 1990); and Thomas F. Remington, ed., *Parliaments in Transition: New Legislative Politics in Eastern Europe and the Former USSR* (Boulder, Colo.: Westview, 1994).
27. "Gorbachev Resigns as USSR President," *FBIS-SOV*-91-248 (26 December 1991), pp. 20–21.

3

Russia and the Post-Soviet Constitutional Order

THE RUSSIAN REPUBLIC IN THE TRANSITION PERIOD

The last chapter showed that the Soviet regime established a highly centralized political order where power flowed from the center and political institutions formed a hierarchy of repeating structures. Each of the fifteen union republics was a smaller-scale replica of the whole union in its political organization. Each had its own Supreme Soviet, its own government with its own ministries (even a foreign ministry!), and its own republic-level branch of the KGB. Each had its own republic-level branch of the Communist Party. A uniform, centrally planned economic system and political ideology kept the system closely knit. In each national republic, the language of the dominant ethnic nationality could be taught in schools and used in the cultural sphere, but Russian served as a lingua franca across the union, and was the language of politics, science, diplomacy, and security.

Russia differed somewhat from the other republics, however, and not only because its language was the language of the country or because it comprised half the population and three-quarters of the territory of the whole union. In Russia there was no republic-level Communist Party, no republic-level KGB, no Academy of Sciences. Many of the structures that would have given the Russian Republic the semblance of independent statehood simply did not exist, and for good reason. If Russia itself had possessed the instruments of state power, these would have inevitably competed with the union-level structures. Instead, Russia's provinces were directly ruled by the federal bodies of power.

Russia did have, however, a Supreme Soviet and executive branch corresponding to the republic. When Gorbachev introduced the new two-tiered parliamentary structure consisting of a Congress of People's Deputies and Supreme Soviet for the USSR, the Russian Republic dutifully followed suit one year later and created its own Congress and Supreme Soviet. These became the political base for the radical democratic movement and Boris Yeltsin. Over the period 1990–1993, Yeltsin mounted his challenge to Gorbachev for preeminence in Russia by building support in the Russian legislative branch for a directly elected presidency, running for and winning the office of president, and then defying Gorbachev by demanding a program of radical economic reform. When the Soviet Union broke up at the end of 1991, these executive and legislative bodies of the Russian Republic became the supreme organs of power in a sovereign state.

Boris Yeltsin clearly understood that if he had the mantle of legitimacy that comes from being a directly elected president, he would have a political advantage over Gorbachev and an asset he could use in dealing with the executive bureaucracy of the Russian Republic. Once he succeeded in being elected president of Russia in June 1991, he was able to outflank Gorbachev every time Gorbachev attempted to assert the power of the union government over the republics.

But Yeltsin's political strategy also contained a weakness. When he ran for president in June 1991, he held the office of chairman of the Supreme Soviet. As chairman, he was effectively both the chief officer of the legislature and, because state power was constitutionally seated in the legislature rather than divided between legislative and executive branches, he was also the highest official in the state. But as soon as he was elected president of the Russian Federation, he left his position as chairman of the Supreme Soviet to assume the new office of president. The legislature's deputy chairman, Ruslan Khasbulatov, replaced him as chairman. At that point Yeltsin no longer could directly control the Supreme Soviet. Over the next two years, Khasbulatov and the legislature moved from a posture of support for Yeltsin and his policies to one of sharp opposition. The conflict reached a bloody climax in September and October 1993 when Yeltsin dissolved parliament by decree, and the opposition forces launched an armed uprising against him, which he suppressed. Yeltsin demanded that the legislature adopt a new constitution giving him sweeping authority as president; the legislature refused. The growing confrontation between Yeltsin's allies and his opponents in the period between August 1991 and October 1993 very nearly resulted in civil war.

1990–1993: Deepening Constitutional Conflict

In the fall of 1991, with the union government losing power, economic shortages were spreading and prices rising; some regional authorities even erected roadblocks to prevent the sale of foodstuffs from their territories. Tax collections were plummeting. Invoking the very real danger of a breakdown of state authority, Yeltsin demanded that the Russian legislature grant him extraordinary powers to cope with the country's economic crisis. Yeltsin made it clear that he believed that only a decisive program of dismantling state controls on production and prices would restore economic activity again. In October 1991, he was given the power to carry out his radical economic program by decree. The Congress also consented to his demand that he be authorized to appoint the heads of government in each region of the country, rather than holding local elections for heads of the executive branch. Yeltsin then named himself acting prime minister and proceeded to form a government led by a group of young, Western-oriented leaders determined to carry out a decisive economic transformation. Charged with planning and carrying out the program was his deputy prime minister, Egor Gaidar.

Under the program—widely called "shock therapy"—the government undertook several radical measures simultaneously that were intended to stabilize the economy by bringing government spending and revenues into balance and by letting market demand determine the prices and supply of goods. Under the reforms, the government let most prices float, raised taxes, and cut back sharply on spending in industry and construction. These policies caused widespread hardship as many state enterprises found themselves without orders or financing. The rationale of the program was to squeeze the built-in inflationary pressure out of the economy so that producers would begin making sensible decisions instead of chronically wasting resources. By letting the market rather than central planners determine prices, output levels, and the like, the reformers intended to create an incentive structure in the economy where efficiency would be rewarded and waste would be punished. Removing the causes of chronic inflation, the reform's architects argued, was a precondition for all other reforms: Hyperinflation would wreck both democracy and economic progress; only by stabilizing the state budget could the government proceed to restructure the economy. A similar reform program had been adopted in Poland in January 1990, with generally favorable results.

In every country where it is applied, radical economic stabilization affects many interests and causes acute hardship for society, at least in the short run. Groups that are particularly hard-hit, including those dependent on state subsidies that are being cut, make their voice heard through the political process. In Russia's case, the program caused particularly deep distress and led to a bitter collision between the president and the parliament, each representing a powerful coalition of organized political interests. Each claimed to represent Russia's true interests, the president backing the cause of liberal reform and the parliament demanding a return to state socialism.

The reform program took effect on January 2, 1992. The first results were immediately felt as prices skyrocketed, government spending was slashed, and heavy new taxes went into effect. A deep credit crunch shut down many industries and brought about a protracted depression. Quickly a number of politicians began to distance themselves from the program: Even Yeltsin's vice president, Alexander Rutskoi, denounced the program as "economic genocide."[1] The chairman of the Russian Supreme Soviet, Ruslan Khasbulatov, also came out in opposition to the reforms, despite still claiming to support President Yeltsin's overall goals. Through 1992, opposition to the reform policies of Yeltsin and Gaidar grew stronger and more intransigent. Increasingly, the political confrontation between Yeltsin and the reformers on the one side, and the opposition to radical economic reform on the other, became centered in the two branches of government. President Yeltsin expanded the powers of the presidency beyond constitutional limits in carrying out the reform program. In the Russian Congress of People's Deputies and the Supreme Soviet, the deputies refused to adopt a new constitution that would enshrine presidential power into law. They refused to allow Yeltsin to continue to serve as his own prime minister and rejected his attempt to nominate Gaidar. They demanded modifications of the economic program and directed the Central Bank, which was under parliament's control, to continue issuing credits to enterprises to keep them from shutting down. The Central Bank's liberality wrecked the regime of fiscal discipline that the government was attempting to pursue: The money supply tripled in the third quarter of 1992 and for the year, prices rose more than 2,300 percent.[2] Through 1992, Yeltsin wrestled with the parliament for control over government and government policy.

In March 1993, Yeltsin threatened to declare a regime of special emergency rule in the country and to suspend parliament, but then backed down. The Congress of People's Deputies immediately met and voted on a motion to impeach Yeltsin. The motion failed by a narrow margin. Yeltsin countered by convening a large conference to hammer out a constitution that would give him the presidential powers he demanded. On September 21, shortly before the deputies were to meet to adopt a law that would have lowered the threshold for decisions in the congress and thus would have made it easier for them to impeach the president, Yeltsin declared the parliament dissolved and called for elections to a new parliament to be held in December. Yeltsin's enemies then barricaded themselves inside the White House, as the building where the parliament was situated was popularly known. Refusing to submit to Yeltsin's decrees, they held a rump congress, which declared Alexander Rutskoi president. After ten days, during which Yeltsin shut off electric power to the building, they joined with some loosely organized paramilitary units outside the building and assaulted the building next to the White House where the Moscow mayor's offices were located. Then they tried to take over the television tower where Russia's main national television broadcast facilities are housed, driving trucks through the entrance, smashing offices, and exchanging gunfire with police. Rutskoi and Khasbulatov evidently hoped their action would set off a national revolt against Yeltsin or win the army over to their side. Finally, the army decided to back Yeltsin and suppress the uprising. Khasbulatov, Rutskoi, and the other leaders of the rebellion were arrested. The army even lobbed artillery shells against the White House, killing an unknown number of people inside.

In subsequent decrees soon afterward, Yeltsin dissolved local (city, district, and village) soviets and called for the formation of new kinds of local representative bodies. He also called upon regional soviets to disband and hold new elections to new assemblies under guidelines that he also issued. Yeltsin was in fact ending the system of soviet power. He had made his views on this issue amply clear the previous June when, at the constitutional assembly that he convened, he declared that the system of soviet power was intrinsically undemocratic because it failed to separate legislative from executive power. In place of soviets he decreed that there be small, deliberative bodies at the local and regional levels, and a national parliament called the Federal Assembly representing Russia as a whole.

Yeltsin's plan for the parliament was embodied in the draft constitution that he put before the country in December 1993. According to it, the Federal Assembly would have two chambers. The upper house, the Federation Council, would give equal representation to each of Russia's eighty-nine regions and republics (called *subjects of the federation*). As in many other parliaments, it would be weaker than the lower, or popular, chamber. The latter, called the State Duma, would be formed in a manner entirely new to Russia. It was to have 450 seats. Half were to be filled in proportion to the share of votes that parties received for their party lists.[3] The other 225 seats were to be filled in traditional single-member district races. Each voter in December 1993 therefore cast four votes for the Federal Assembly: two for the seats from his or her region in the Federation Council, and two for the deputies of the State Duma. One of these was for a candidate running for the local district seat and one was for a party list.[4]

In the national referendum on December 12, 1993, Yeltsin's constitution was approved. According to the official figures, turnout was 54.8 percent, and of those who voted, 58.4 percent voted in favor of the constitution.[5] The constitution therefore came into force. Figure 3.1 presents a schematic overview of the main structures of the current constitutional order.

The 1993 Constitution and the Presidency

The new constitution was designed to establish a dominant presidency: Yeltsin referred to the model as a "presidential republic." We can call the Russian system "presidential-parliamentary." In such a system there is both a president and a prime minister. The president appoints the prime minister and other cabinet ministers, but the cabinet must also have the confidence of parliament to govern.[6] In Russia, the president does have the power to make law by decree, and to dissolve parliament, although he is subject to several specific constitutional constraints. His decrees may not violate existing law and can be superseded by laws passed by parliament. The president appoints the prime minister (who is formally termed the chairman of the government), subject to the approval of parliament. The Duma can refuse to confirm the president's choice, but if after three attempts, the president still fails to win the Duma's approval of his choice, he dissolves the Duma and calls for new elections. Likewise the Duma may hold a vote of no confidence in the government. The first time a motion of no confidence carries, the president and government may ignore it, but if it passes a second time, the president must either dissolve parliament or dismiss the government. The president's power to dissolve parliament and call for new elections is also limited by the constitution. He may not dissolve parliament within one year of its election, once it has filed impeachment charges against the president, once the president has declared a state of emergency throughout Russia, or within six months of the expiration of the president's term.[7] The president can veto legislation passed by parliament, but parliament can override the veto by a two-thirds vote in each chamber. Thus although the constitution gives the president the upper hand in relations with parliament, it is not an entirely free hand.

Moreover, the president cannot bypass parliament and put an issue to a popular referendum on his own authority, nor may he block one. Only once a citizens' initiative has gathered 2 million signatures can a ballot proposition be put before the country as a national referendum.

The constitution calls the president *head of state* and *guarantor of the constitution*. He "ensures the coordinated functioning and collaboration of bodies of state power" (Article 80, paragraphs 1 and 2). He is not made chief executive.

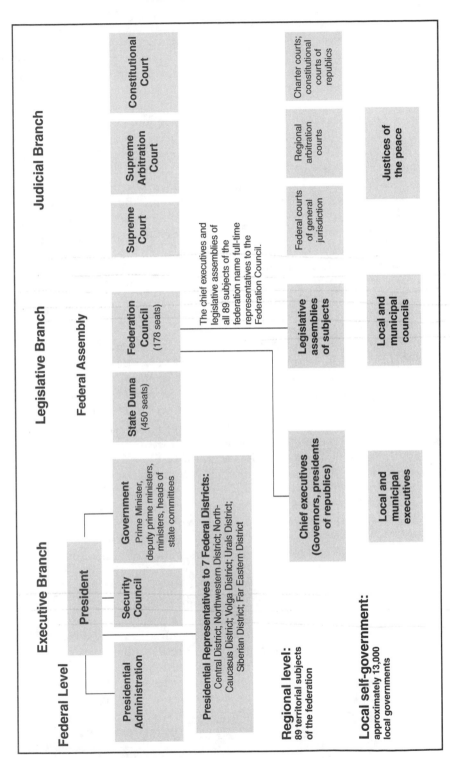

Figure 3.1 Russian Political System under the 1993 Constitution

Although the president's nominee for prime minister must be confirmed by parliament, the president can appoint and remove deputy prime ministers and other ministers without needing parliamentary consent. These decisions are, nonetheless, to be made "upon the proposal" of the prime minister. On this point the president's power is the same as that of the French president, and the language of the relevant provisions of the two constitutions is the same.[8] As in France, therefore, the Russian Constitution seems to allow a good deal of room for variation in the possible relationship between a president and a prime minister, depending on the personalities and political tendencies of each. A powerful and popular president is likely to dominate policy making in all spheres, with his prime minister serving as an executive in charge of formulating specific policy options and administering the machinery of government. But the system could accommodate a different relationship between president and parliament, if the president were weaker and the prime minister enjoyed a strong base of support in parliament. The great difference between Russia's system and that of France, however, is that Russia's government is not formed from a party majority in parliament. The president appoints the government based on calculations about the relative power of different bureaucratic and personal factions, taking care to balance competing interests. The weakness of institutional authority is offset by the strength of the leader's personal power.

The Russian president has far-reaching formal and informal powers at the center and in the regions. The president exercises his power through a staff structure called the *administration of the president.* This is an immense organization. The French president, for example, gets by with a staff of forty to fifty people; the American president has a White House Staff with more than 400 people and another 1,300 in the Executive Office of the President. In Russia, the presidential administration comprises around 2,000 people, and as often as presidents may try to trim it, the number keeps creeping upward. It is made up of many units, such as the press office, divisions for liaison with other bodies of power and with the regional governments, a division overseeing law making and judicial institutions, even a unit that owns and manages the properties belonging to the presidency, among which are apartment buildings, office buildings, hotels, health resorts, and other facilities—even the buildings of parliament itself.

To some extent, the presidential administration duplicates the ministries of government. Some units of it work to ensure that governments in the regions carry out federal policy. The "power ministries"—the Foreign Ministry, Federal Security Service (formerly the Committee on State Security, or KGB), Defense Ministry, and Interior Ministry—now answer directly to the president. There are, in addition, a large range of official and quasi-official commissions and administrations that are funded and directed by the president that carry out a variety of supervisory and advisory functions. The president also directly oversees the Security Council, which consists of a full-time secretary, the heads of the power ministries and other security-related agencies, the prime minister, and, more recently, the president's representatives to the seven federal "super-districts" through which he keeps tabs on the eighty-nine federal regions of the country. The president can appoint other officials to the Security Council as well. Its powers are broad but shadowy. President Putin has relied on it to develop policy initiatives directed at strengthening the power of the central government vis-à-vis the regions, and he has appointed senior generals from the FSB (security police) and military as its top staff.[9] Since there is still no legislation establishing the rights and obligations of the Security Council, its structure, role, and power at any given time depend on the president's discretion.[10]

Beyond the purely formal powers of the president are the symbolic resources at his disposal. The president's offices are in the Kremlin. The *Kremlin*—a term that means fortress or citadel—was the symbolic seat of the Russian state under Ivan the Terrible in the sixteenth century. It remained the center of Russian state power until Peter the Great moved the capital of the country to the new city of St. Petersburg that he founded on the Baltic Sea at the beginning of the eighteenth century; the Bolsheviks moved the capital back to Moscow in 1918 and again made the Kremlin the physical and symbolic center of the Soviet state. Thus in the postcommunist era, Russian presidents deliberately identify themselves with Russian rulers of the tsarist and Soviet eras in order to underline the continuity of state power.

More than Yeltsin did, Vladimir Putin has quietly fostered a cult of personality through such methods as the use of official portraits that officials are encouraged to hang in their offices and signals to the mass media to portray him in a flattering light. In keeping with the old tradition by which notable officials from the tsar down to local dignitaries are expected to listen to the complaints of ordinary people, President Putin's staff annually receives over half a million letters from Russian citizens. Putin's staff have also promoted a media image of Putin as a straightforward, accessible figure, who shares the thoughts and feelings of his fellow citizens and even allows himself to use profane language on occasion. Occasional televised clips of Putin arm wrestling or engaged in a martial arts contest reinforce the official message that he is youthful, energetic, and in charge.

The personalization of state power is not confined to Putin and the presidency. Many state structures in Russia's postcommunist system are closely tied to the personalities of their chief executives: The leader's personal priorities often define the rights and responsibilities of the office. Rules remain undeveloped and fluid. There is still no regular civil service in Russia protected from political pressure.[11] The consolidation of a more law-governed political process will take some time. Still, a slow process of institutionalization of power is under way. For the first time in Russian or Soviet history, there is a Constitutional Court to adjudicate jurisdictional disputes among branches of government and levels of state authority, and parliamentary debate allows for an open and vigorous airing of many policy issues. Generally the struggle for political power takes more open forms than it did during the communist or tsarist era, when there was no open party competition or legal constraints on the state's sovereignty.

On the other hand, the new Russian political system bears many similarities to the tsarist and communist regimes that preceded it. The historical patterns of weak institutions, the drive for concentrated, centralized power at the top, the hierarchical organization of political life—all have left a strong mark on the present regime. First of all, the Russian presidency has come to resemble the central Communist Party organs of the Soviet era. The president is a kind of General Secretary, his administration something like the machinery of the Central Committee.[12] Both in structure and function, the comparison is apt. The reason that a similar pattern of organization has emerged in the post-Soviet period is the same dilemma that the communist authorities faced. In the absence of a rational-legal foundation for bureaucratic authority and of a professionally oriented civil service, direct political supervision from above seems to be the only means Russian rulers know for controlling the sprawling state bureaucracy.[13] Yet no president wants to relinquish the enormous formal and extraconstitutional powers he can exercise over the state.

Many observers have called the Russian system "superpresidential" because the president's powers are so broad.[14] There are three dangers in this arrangement: The regime depends heavily on the person of the president, who may be (or become) unfit for the job; president and parliament have competing electoral mandates and so may well come into conflict; and the government is in an ambiguous position since it must serve both president and parliament.[15] Any of these design features can readily contribute to a constitutional deadlock or breakdown. One other weakness of such a system should be noted. In a system that relies so heavily on the president's power for making and carrying out policy, the president's power inevitably turns out to be inadequate to achieve large-scale policy goals that require extensive coordination, persuasion, and public support. Even a strong president soon discovers how limited are the resources at his disposal for changing the behavior of large state bureaucracies across a large range of policy issues simultaneously. The real problem with presidentialism is not that presidential power is too strong—it is that it is too *weak*.

The Government

Successful performance under a dual executive system requires a constructive working relationship between president and prime minister. This comes about either through the prime minister's clear subordination to the president, or they work out a mutually acceptable division of labor between them. Russia has shown examples of several different types of relationship beween president and prime minister. For example, Prime Minister Chernomyrdin and President Yeltsin achieved a surprisingly harmonious working relationship that lasted more than five years. First appointed by Yeltsin as head of government in December 1992 and finally dismissed in March 1998, Viktor Chernomyrdin had a comparatively long tenure as head of government. His successors as prime minister under Yeltsin did not hold on to power so long.[16] The relationship between president and prime minister is variable. When Yeltsin was ill and removed from much day-to-day policy making, his prime minister could exercise a considerable degree of autonomy in running the government. Under President Putin, however, it is clear that the president has the major say in setting policy direction and sees the government as the executive machinery for achieving his goals. And as in other dual executive systems, the president finds it very convenient to be able to use the government as whipping boy for failures of policy and to claim credit for successes.[17]

The prime minister (formally, the chairman of the government) has overall responsibility for the work of the executive branch. Constitutionally, the president is head of state but not chief executive. The prime minister manages the government through an intermediate layer of deputy prime ministers, each of whom supervises a particular bloc of ministries and state committees. The organization chart of the government changes often, as ministries are consolidated or split and as the president chooses to elevate or demote government officials in rank. Generally, however, there are some sixty to seventy government ministries, state committees, and other agencies that together form the government. President Putin chose to streamline the structure of the government as one of his first acts. Under the plan he put into place in May 2000, the government consisted of the prime minister, five deputy prime ministers, twenty-four ministers, and thirty-three heads of state committees and other cabinet-rank agencies of government.

Deputy prime ministers outrank ordinary ministers, and ordinary ministers outrank chairs of state committees. As has been true in Russia for centuries, the fine gradations in administrative rank are acutely important to the individuals concerned, because they determine how other material and political privileges are allocated. Each deputy prime minister supervises a particular bloc of ministries and state agencies, coordinating their work and serving as liaison between the ministers in charge of particular ministries and the head of government.

In Russia the makeup of the government is not directly determined by the party composition of the parliament, as it would be in a parliamentary system. The relationship between the distribution of party forces in the Duma and the political balance of the government is extremely loose. Most members of the government are career administrators rather than party politicians. Both President Yeltsin and President Putin have sometimes brought particular members of parliament into the government, seeking to take advantage of their substantive expertise and their political influence. This path of recruitment remains the exception, however. Most ministers are chosen for their expertise in a particular sphere or their links to particular patron–client networks, but not as representatives of parties.

Of course, the president forms the government with a view to reflecting the dynamics of political life in the country. Typically the president seeks to balance the influence of different political "clans" by bringing their representatives into the cabinet, as well as by rewarding loyal friends and supporters. The composition of the cabinet is thus a reflection of both the president's political needs and policy intentions. It is striking in Russia how *small* a role parties play as channels of recruitment into government. For example, only one representative of the political party that Putin backed in the December 1999 parliamentary elections (then called *Unity* and now called *United Russia*) holds a seat in the government. By and large, the heads of government and other ministers under Yeltsin and

Putin have not been party politicians. Even when the president has encouraged the formation of a propresidential party, such as Our Home Is Russia and, more recently, Unity, their leaders are not given responsibility for policy making.

The Parliament

The parliament—Federal Assembly—is distinctly inferior to the president in power but does have a measure of independent influence. Several features make it a meaningful player in the political process. One is the important role played by party factions in collectively managing decision making in the lower house, the State Duma. Another is its bicameral nature; the two chambers differ markedly in their makeup and operations. Finally, the president is eager to put his policy decisions into legislative form, which increases their credibility and legitimacy.

State Duma. The State Duma has the constitutional right to originate legislation except in certain categories of policy that are under the jurisdiction of the upper house, the Federation Council. Upon passage in the State Duma, a bill goes to the Federation Council. If the upper house rejects it, the bill goes back to the Duma, where a commission comprising members of both houses may seek to iron out differences. If the Duma rejects the upper house's changes, it may override the Federation Council by a two-thirds vote (see Figures 3.2 and 3.3 on the Duma and the legislative process).

When the bill has cleared parliament, it goes to the president for signature. If the president refuses to sign the bill, he returns it to the Duma, outlining his objections. The Duma may pass it with the president's proposed changes by a simple absolute majority, or override the president's veto, for which a two-thirds vote is required. The Federation Council must then also approve the bill, by a simple majority if the president's amendments are accepted, or a two-thirds vote if it chooses to override the president. On rare occasions, the Duma has overridden the president's veto and it has overridden Federation Council rejections several times. In other cases, the Duma has passed bills rejected by the president after accepting the president's amendments. Even when parliament and president have been at odds over policy—as happened frequently during Yeltsin's presidency—the two sides avoided provoking a conflict that could trigger a major constitutional crisis. Even under Yeltsin, around three-quarters of the laws passed by parliament were eventually signed into law by the president. Under President Putin the relationship between parliament and president is far friendlier. The parliament almost never opposes the president. Instead, deputies typically bargain to see how many concessions they can get from the Kremlin over the details of spending and regulatory bills to win benefits for key interest groups and local constituents.

The steering committee of the Duma is the Council of the Duma. The Council of the Duma makes the principal decisions in the Duma with respect to legislative agenda and proceedings, and sometimes forges compromises to overcome deadlocks among the political groups represented in the Duma. It is made up of the leaders of each party faction or registered deputy group regardless of

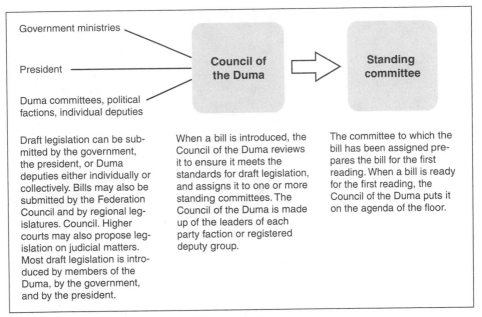

Figure 3.2 The Legislative Process: Bill Introduction

Government ministries

President

Duma committees, political factions, individual deputies

Council of the Duma

Standing committee

Draft legislation can be submitted by the government, the president, or Duma deputies either individually or collectively. Bills may also be submitted by the Federation Council and by regional legislatures. Council. Higher courts may also propose legislation on judicial matters. Most draft legislation is introduced by members of the Duma, by the government, and by the president.

When a bill is introduced, the Council of the Duma reviews it to ensure it meets the standards for draft legislation, and assigns it to one or more standing committees. The Council of the Duma is made up of the leaders of each party faction or registered deputy group.

The committee to which the bill has been assigned prepares the bill for the first reading. When a bill is ready for the first reading, the Council of the Duma puts it on the agenda of the floor.

size.[18] Every party that has won at least 5 percent of the party list voting in the proportional-representation half of the ballot is entitled to form a faction in the Duma made up of its elected deputies, together with any of the deputies elected in single-member districts who care to join. Moreover, any group of deputies that can assemble thirty-five members has the right to register as a recognized deputy group in order to obtain exactly the same rights and benefits as the party factions obtain. These benefits are valuable to deputies: They include funds for staff, office space, and procedural rights. Moreover, the factions and groups divide up all the leadership positions in the chamber, including the committee chairmanships, among themselves. The factions and groups see the Duma as a means for showcasing their pet legislative projects, giving their leaders a national forum, obtaining crucial organizational support for their party work, and providing service to their constituents. Not surprisingly, nearly all deputies join one of the factions or groups.

The Duma also has a system of standing legislative committees—twenty-eight in the Duma that convened in January 2000—whose leadership and membership positions are distributed to factions in accordance with an interfactional agreement. Each deputy is a member of one committee. The work of drafting and developing legislation goes on in the committees. However, only a few committees do much active legislative work: In the second Duma, which sat from 1996 to 1999, 70 percent of the bills that came to the floor were handled by just seven committees.[19] The most important of these are the committee on legislation, which handles matters concerning the judicial system, federal relations,

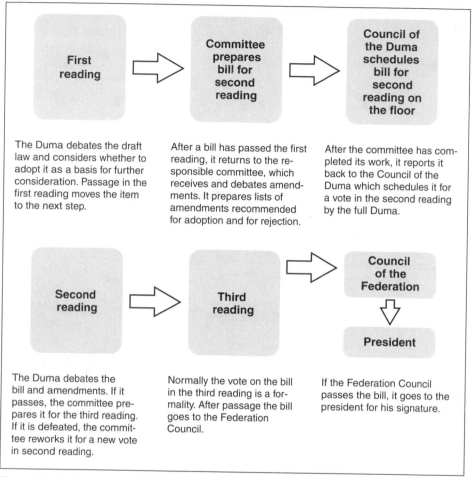

Figure 3.3 The Legislative Process: Three Readings

and other constitutional questions; the budget committee; and the committee on labor and social policy.

Bills are considered in three readings. In the first reading, the Duma simply decides whether or not to approve the basic conception of a piece of legislation. If so, then the bill goes back to the committee, which then sifts through the amendments that are offered to the bill by deputies (sometimes thousands of amendments are offered to a single bill). When the committee has agreed on its recommended version of the bill, it reports it out again to the floor for a second reading, and the whole chamber decides on which amendments to approve and which to reject. At that point the floor votes on the bill in its entirety, and sends it back to the committee for a final editing and polishing. The third reading then gives the Duma's final approval to the bill and it goes to the Federation Council.

Since the new constitution came into force in 1993, parliament has passed and the president has signed a vast body of legislation providing the legal underpinnings for a modern, democratic, and market-oriented society. Among them are laws expanding parliament's control over the federal budget; laws regulating federal relations, including the structure of government power in the territorial units of the federation (including a bitterly contested provision limiting governors to two terms in office); an extensive set of laws on elections including standards regulating elections in all regions; major laws on reform of the judicial system; a number of market-oriented laws, including laws regulating taxation, banking, securities trading, mortgage lending, bankruptcy, foreign investment in natural-resource development, and property rights; and numerous laws providing social benefits to the population. To be sure, many of these laws were greatly watered down in the course of being passed, and others have had to be repeatedly revised. Some are clearly passed under the pressure of powerful and wealthy interest groups. Many laws are vague and invite extensive interpretation by bureaucratic agencies. But taken as a whole, the legislative record reflects a parliament that is a significant player in the policy-making process.

Federation Council. The upper house is called the Federation Council. It has certain important prerogatives in addition to its role as a check on the actions of the lower house. It approves presidential nominees for high courts such as the Supreme Court and the Constitutional Court. It approves presidential decrees declaring martial law or a state of emergency, and any actions altering the boundaries of territorial units in Russia. It must consider any legislation dealing with taxes, budget, financial policy, treaties, customs, and declarations of war. The Federation Council has defied the president's will on a number of issues, rejecting some of his nominees for the Constitutional Court, as well as his candidates for Procurator-General.[20] On matters of ordinary legislation, however, where the Federation Council does not have exclusive jurisdiction, the State Duma can override a veto by the Federation Council with a two-thirds vote. The president can then choose whether to support the Duma's position and sign the law, or to uphold the Federation Council and veto it.

The Federation Council is designed as an instrument of federalism in that (like the U.S. Senate) every constituent unit of the federation is represented in it by two members. Under the constitution, they must come from the executive and legislative branches of the regional governments. As in the United States, equal representation from territories of unequal population means that the populations of small territories (which in Russia are often ethnic-national units) are greatly overrepresented compared with more populous regions. Members of the Federation Council were elected by direct popular vote in December 1993 but since the constitution was silent on how they were to be chosen in the future, a law was passed in 1995 governing the formation of the chamber. Under that law, the heads of the executive and legislative branches of each constituent unit of the federation were automatically given seats in the Federation Council.

However, in 2000, President Putin chose to change this procedure as part of a package of reforms intended to strengthen the power of the federal government vis-à-vis the regions. Under the law that he proposed, each region's chief executive would name a full-time representative to serve as a member of the

Federation Council, and each regional legislature would name another. This bill passed by a wide margin in the Duma (whose deputies had often complained that the members of the upper house were not full-time) and was rejected by a wide margin in the Federation Council. After intense three-way bargaining among the Duma, the Federation Council, and the president, a compromise version was worked out and passed by both chambers. The compromise phased in the new system over an eighteen-month period, and gave regional executives the right to recall their delegates to the Federation Council (so long as the regional legislature did not block the recall by a two-thirds vote). The right of recall meant that governors would be able to keep their representatives in Moscow on a short leash.

The new members named in 2000 and 2001 were a diverse group. Many had extensive experience in regional and federal politics. Many had no previous ties to the regions that sent them. About a quarter of the new members were high-level business executives. One, for instance, was formerly the deputy CEO of one of Russia's largest oil companies. In its new composition, the Federation Council has consistently supported President Putin and his program, and has passed nearly every law he has proposed even when the legislation directly countered the interests of the regions. The members have found the credentials (and immunity from all criminal prosecution) that go with parliamentary membership to be useful to them in lobbying for the interests of the regions that delegated them. But among both members and the political elite generally there continues to be a great deal of dissatisfaction over the current role of the chamber and most observers believe that the current law on the composition of the chamber should be replaced by one providing that the members of the upper house are popularly elected. This must be reconciled in some way, however, with the constitutional requirement that the two members of the chamber from each of Russian eighty-nine territorial subjects represent the executive and legislative branches.[21]

Executive-Legislative Relations

The president's powers vis-à-vis parliament are great but should not be exaggerated. Certainly the constitution makes it extremely difficult for the parliament to remove the president. As in the United States, the legislature's sole device for forcing out the president is the drastic means of impeachment. The Russian procedure is even more cumbersome than the American.[22] (See Close Up 3.1: Impeachment Russian-Style.) Parliament's power to check the president has little to do with the threat of impeachment, however. Rather it stems from two constitutional facts: first, that any piece of legislation must have parliament's approval, and, second, the requirement that the government must enjoy the confidence of parliament. A president who ruled by decree could not be certain that the government would comply with his directives; a law has greater credibility and longevity than a decree.[23] Of course there are large swaths of executive power—particularly those relating to foreign policy and national-security policy—where the parliament's influence is diminished because it is directly overseen by the president.

Close Up 3.1   Impeachment Russian-Style

The 1993 Constitution provides for removal of a president through impeachment. The procedure consists of four basic steps. The State Duma must vote by a two-thirds majority (or 300 affirmative votes) in favor of impeachment; the Supreme Court must affirm that the president's actions constitute grave crimes or treason; the Constitutional Court must rule that no procedural violations were committed in the Duma's approval of the decision to impeach; and the Federation Council must vote by a two-thirds majority to remove the president. Initiating impeachment proceedings gives the Duma leverage over the president, in that once the Duma has approved (by the required two-thirds majority) the motion to impeach, the president may not dissolve the Duma and call new elections.

The communists in the Duma finally succeeded in placing impeachment on the agenda in 1998. The Duma voted to form a commission to examine five charges against Yeltsin: that he had committed treason by signing the agreement in December 1991 to dissolve the Soviet Union; that he had illegally initiated the war in Chechnia in 1994; that he had illegally dissolved the Russian Congress and Supreme Soviet in 1993; that he had destroyed Russia's defense capacity; and that he had committed genocide against the Russian people through the effects of the economic policies of his government since 1992. In March 1999 the commission approved all five charges and submitted them to the full chamber for its consideration. The Duma began debate on impeachment on May 13, 1999, and on May 15 voted on the five charges. None of the charges gained the required 300 votes, although the charge that Yeltsin had illegally initiated and conducted military operations in Chechnia came close, receiving 284 votes. Yeltsin used the full range of carrots and sticks at his disposal to avert impeachment, promising material rewards to some deputies in return for their support, and reminding the Duma, as he replaced Evgenii Primakov with Interior Minister Sergei Stepashin as his new prime minister on the eve of the vote, that he still had other trump cards in his hand. Days after the impeachment vote failed, the Duma turned around and approved Stepashin's appointment by the margin of 301 votes to 55.

The Constitutional Court

The Yeltsin constitution also provided for a Constitutional Court to exercise judicial review. The Court is empowered to consider the constitutionality of actions of the president, the government, the parliament, and lower level governments based on actions that are brought to it; it has no right to seek out cases on its own. Through 2002, the Court had not issued any decisions restricting the president's powers in any significant way but it had decided several thorny constitutional issues, including the relations between the two chambers of parliament and the delineation of powers between the central and regional governments. Generally its decisions have upheld the authority of the federal constitution and of federal law over separatist actions on the part of regional governments, and it has tried to expand the ability of citizens to defend their constitutional rights in ordinary courts.

A crucial question for Russia's political development will be how the balance among president, government, parliament, and Constitutional Court evolves. At present, the president, once he has won an electoral mandate, has enormous freedom to rule as he chooses; he is not bound by accountability to a party and constitutional restraints on his power are weak. He can dominate the government and put pressure on the courts, the governors, the mass media, and business leaders to support his policies. Oversight by the legislative branch over the executive is weak. But by the same token, the president's ability to implement his preferred policies is also weak, because of how weak are the institutions for aggregating the wishes and views of ordinary citizens and for coordinating the efforts of politicians and officials throughout the system. With a relatively meager array of interest associations, independent media outlets, national political parties, and other means of linking state officials and citizens across regions and sectors of society, the president tends to fall back on traditional methods of personal rule—building personal support networks and playing them off against one another, intimidating political rivals and coopting potential allies, and making tactical concessions to powerful and organized opposition groups. If, on the other hand, Russia develops a system of nationally competitive, programmatic political parties, reinforced by a fabric of civic associations that can articulate and aggregate social interests, then it is likely that executive power will flow from a party majority in parliament. The president can then allow the government to formulate policy and build support for it and can confine his role to that of general strategic leadership. A strong state supported by a strong civil society would increase the president's ability to accomplish his objectives. And, to the extent that power is in fact balanced between the executive and legislative branches, the Constitutional Court will be able to exercise its mandated role as arbiter of the constitutionality of the actions of the other branches. At present, however, the president tends to act as previous Russian rulers have done, by diverting power from other state and social institutions to build up his own power.

The birth of the new constitutional order in 1993 was marked by extraconstitutional coercion. Yeltsin decreed that national elections were to be held for a legislature that did not, constitutionally, yet exist. Moreover, the government imposed severe limitations on party competition during the electoral campaign, outlawing some parties and disqualifying others from running candidates. Senior officials tried to impose press censorship (which was quickly lifted) and to prohibit public criticism of the constitution by candidates.[24] Observers inside and outside Russia were further alarmed at the electoral success of antidemocratic forces.

Nevertheless, the new constitutional order did resolve some of the tensions and conflicts of the early 1990s. As president, Yeltsin's strategy was to remain above the arena of party politics. He sometimes lent tepid support to one or another party, but generally preferred to preserve his autonomy, balancing, and arbitrating among contending forces according to the needs of the moment. But he also used the powers of the presidency to push for policy and institutional reforms that would make Russia's turn from communism irrevocable.[25] It may be that history will judge that he should have built a lasting political organization that united a following throughout the country and gave reform-minded politicians a common cause. On the other hand, a party affiliation might have made it more difficult for Yeltsin to maneuver politically in order to preserve his power and win support for his policies. Putin, too, has repeatedly declared that he favors the development of a strong party system to help aggregate and channel demands from populace to state leaders, but he has pointedly avoided committing himself to a political party.

The constitutional order remains subject to change. Reacting to President Yeltsin's habit of arbitrarily dismissing his government whenever he grew dissatisfied with it, a number of politicians have called for constitutional amendments restricting the president's powers. Others have called for amending the constitution so as to give some of the constitutional powers currently possessed by the Federation Council to the State Duma. Yet most political tendencies active in politics remain committed to bringing about change only by constitutional means. Both Yeltsin and Putin have been casual about political institutions, creating new structures when it was politically expedient to do so, then forgetting about them just as quickly when they were no longer useful. The history of the 1990s is full of institutional improvisation; some of the new forms proved viable, many others fell by the wayside. Yet constitutional structures such as parliament, the Constitutional Court, and popular elections are important institutions in shaping the exercise of state power, even if central and regional leaders continue to wield a great deal of extra-constitutional power.

Russia bears some similarities to other political systems where the presidency is invested with enormous power and legal checks on its exercise are weak.[26] In such a country, the presidency is the greatest prize in politics, and the struggle to win it provokes intense political struggle. Yeltsin's preterm resignation, by which he turned over presidential power to his appointed successor, and received full legal immunity for himself in return, falls considerably short of a clean turnover of power following a competitive presidential election. Therefore Russia is only a partial democracy. The stakes in the contest for state power are so high that those determined to keep or win control of the Kremlin are strongly tempted to resort to undemocratic means. In March 1996, for example, at a point when he was convinced he would lose the upcoming election, President Yeltsin decided to cancel the election, suspend parliament, and outlaw the Communist Party. He even drafted a decree to this effect. As he explains in his memoirs, he was persuaded to abandon this plan by his adviser Anatolii Chubais, who convinced him that in the current environment, whoever resorted to unconstitutional action first would ultimately lose the ensuing struggle for power.[27] A peaceful transfer of power from an incumbent to a challenger following a free and fair election would be the single greatest impetus to democracy that could be made at present. Equally important is the observance of constitutional principles by the winner of the election. Violation of them before, during, or after the election by the incumbent or a challenger would gravely compromise democracy.

THE FEDERAL DIMENSION

Notwithstanding the two wars fought in Chechnia since 1991, Russia's path of development during the transition period has not culminated in the state's dissolution along national-territorial lines like that which ended the Soviet Union's existence. As was true of the USSR under Gorbachev, Yeltsin's government confronted the twin crises of relations between the central government and the constituent members of the federation and of carrying out deep economic reform in the face of powerful opposition. The breakdown of the Soviet order both eroded the central government's power to enforce its power in the regions and limited the carrots it could offer regional governments to induce their compliance with federal law. Since both Gorbachev and Yeltsin had made liberal offers of autonomy to the subnational governments of Russia as part of their rivalry in 1990–1991, Russia found it particularly difficult to reestablish the primacy of its own central authority. Through the Yeltsin period, subnational governments fought with the Russian federal authorities over the appropriate spheres of powers. This was particularly true for several of the ethnic-national territories, which enjoy a privileged constitutional status in Russia. Under Putin, however, there has been a strong reassertion of the center's power over the regions.

By far the most intractable case is that of the Chechen Republic, whose leaders declared independence in 1991. (See Close Up 3.2: The Chechen Quagmire.) Nevertheless, the Chechen war proved to be the sole case where the federal government had to resort to force to preserve the unity of the state. Unlike the union government, the Russian state preserved itself despite centrifugal pressures from the regions. Several factors distinguishing Russia's situation from that of the USSR help to explain the different outcomes.

One is the demographic factor. The Soviet population was more ethnically fragmented than was that of the Russian Republic. Whereas half of the Soviet population was ethnically Russian and the other half was a diverse array of smaller national groups, Russia's population is 80 percent Russian. As Table 3.1 indicates, its ethnic minorities thus form a very small proportion of the total. The Soviet population, moreover, was never an ethnic nationality, whereas Russia's national culture provided a historic identity, which encouraged (and sometimes required) other national groups to assimilate to it. Finally, the national republics of the Soviet Union were all located on the perimeter of the country, and thus bordered other countries. The national territories of Russia are mainly internal to the Russian Republic and therefore have had less direct interaction with the outside world.[28]

A second factor has to do with Russia's internal administrative structure. In Russia, only around 17 percent of the population lives in territories designated

Close Up 3.2   The Chechen Quagmire

Chechnia, or the Chechen Republic, is located in the mountainous region of the North Caucasus, between the Black and Caspian Seas, amid a belt of ethnic republics that includes several other predominantly Muslim republics. (Note that Dagestan is a kind of "dormitory" republic providing a common homeland to several small mountain peoples.) The Chechen people were subjugated by the Russian imperial army in the nineteenth century but continued to resist Russian, and later Soviet, rule. In 1944 the entire Chechen people were deported by Stalin to Kazakstan on suspicion that the entire nation was disloyal and would collaborate with the Germans. The Chechens were allowed to return to their homeland after the war, after suffering terrible hardships, but harbored deep grievances against Moscow. In 1991, with the USSR breaking up, the leader of the republic declared independence of Russia. Yeltsin rejected the declaration as invalid but did not initially attempt to force the republic to rescind it. However, in December 1994, following unsuccessful efforts to restore federal authority in Chechnia through back-channel negotiations and covert armed intervention, Russia launched a large-scale military assault, employing heavy and often indiscriminate force. Fighting between Russian federal troops and the forces fighting for Chechen independence continued for nearly two years, punctuated by mass hostage-taking raids by Chechens on Russian soil, and unsuccessful cease-fire declarations. Tens of thousands of civilians fled their homes. Finally, in October 1996, when both sides had had enough, the Chechen authorities and the federal government signed a treaty permitting the withdrawal of federal troops and granting Chechnia wide de facto autonomy.[1]

The agreement only led to a pause in the fighting, however. The government in Chechnia was unwilling or unable to impose basic civil and political order. Quasi-independent paramilitary forces continued to operate with impunity from Chechen soil. Kidnappings for ransom and drug trafficking flourished. In the summer of 1999 armed guerrilla forces (said to have been supported by radical international Islamist groups) crossed the border from Chechnia into the neighboring republic of Dagestan and attempted to seize power in several villages, as the opening blow of what they called a crusade to liberate the entire North Caucasus region. Federal forces pushed them back into Chechnia. Soon afterward, bombs exploded in apartment buildings in several Russian cities. The federal authorities immediately claimed that Chechen terrorists were responsible, and began a new ground operation in Chechnia intended to destroy all the rebel units. However, neither the massive aerial bombardment of cities and suspected

(continued)

Close Up 3.2

rebel bases nor the massive federal intervention succeeded in wiping out all of the resistance, and hostilities continued with hit-and-run raids and suicide car bomb attacks on federal troops. Federal forces used brutal tactics to pacify the population, including massive round-ups of civilians accompanied by interrogations and torture to identify supporters of the rebels. The harshness of federal military tactics aroused worldwide condemnation. Although the federal government appropriated funds for rebuilding the republic, nearly all the funds were pilfered. Chechens continued to live in misery, many in squalid refugee camps outside the republic. Russian news coverage of the Chechen war was subject to drastic censorship, so that most Russians received a distorted picture of the war.

At the same time, international sympathy for the Chechen cause was weakened by the rebels' use of terrorism to achieve their goals. In one of the most shocking episodes of the war, a group of Chechens seized an entire theater in Moscow during a performance of a play in October 2002, holding the audience and cast hostage. Demanding the immediate withdrawal of federal forces from Chechnia, they threatened to kill the hostages and blow up the theater if their demands were not met. After sixty hours, federal security forces infiltrated a powerful sleeping agent into the ventilation system, then stormed the theater. Killing all the terrorists, they freed most of the hostages. However, the gas killed well over 100 of the hostages, who had been weakened by exhaustion, hunger, and thirst, and the Russian authorities refused to disclose to health workers the identity of the gas used or how to treat its effects.

President Putin emphasized that the incident proved yet again that the Chechen rebels were part of the international terrorist movement and must be dealt with as uncompromisingly as the Al Qaeda network. Public opinion is divided about how to handle Chechnia. Frustrated by the high number of casualties on both sides (experts estimate that as many as 40,000 to 160,000 people have been killed in the fighting on both sides since 1994) and the inability of federal forces to quash resistance, many Russians favored finding a negotiated political solution. At the height of the hostage taking at the Moscow theater, a national survey found that 46 percent of the populace supported continuing the war in Chechnia, but 44 percent wanted Russia to begin peace talks to end the war. Eighteen percent agreed with the view that the solution to the Chechen crisis is to "wall Russia off from Chechnia and give the republic its independence."[2] The authorities, however, adamantly rejected Chechen independence as an outcome, and continued to look for ways to give Chechnia a special status

(continued)

Close Up 3.2 *(continued)*

within the federation. The prospects for a peaceful settlement in the short term were remote, however, because of the absence of any unified leadership on the Chechen side to accept and enforce any binding agreement.

[1]On the first Chechen war, see John B. Dunlop, *Russia Confronts Chechnya: Roots of a Separatist Conflict* (Cambridge, England: Cambridge University Press, 1998); Carlotta Gall and Thomas de Waal, *Chechnya: Calamity in the Caucasus* (New York: New York University Press, 1998); Anatol Lieven, *Chechnya: Tombstone of Russian Power* (New Haven, Conn.: Yale University Press, 1998).

[2]RFE/RL Newsline, 30 October 2002, citing a VTsIOM survey of the Russian population during the hostage crisis.

---

as ethnic homelands.[29] In the Soviet state, by contrast, all territory was included in one or another of the ethnic-national republics. The republic of Russia took up three-quarters of Soviet territory and half its population. In the Soviet state, most of the national groups giving their names to the republics had lived in the territory of their republics for centuries and had some reason to consider them national homelands. In most cases, these peoples had a national history and had been subjugated by the Soviet Russian state. Like the USSR, the Russian Republic was also formally considered a federation and had internal ethnic-national

--- **TABLE 3.1** ---

Population of Major Nationalities of the Russian Federation (in thousands)

	1970	1979	1989
TOTAL	130,079	137,410	147,022
Russians	107,748	113,522	119,866
Tatars	4,755	5,006	5,522
Ukrainians	3,346	3,658	4,363
Chuvash	1,637	1,690	1,774
Bashkirs	1,181	1,291	1,345
Belorussians	964	1,052	1,206
Mordva	1,177	1,111	1,073
Chechens	572	712	899
Germans	762	791	842
Udmurts	678	686	715
Mari	581	600	644
Kazazh	478	518	636
Avar	362	438	544
Jews	792	692	537
Peoples of the north	168	170	199

subdivisions. But in contrast to the larger union, only some of its constituent members are ethnic-national territories. Most are pure administrative subdivisions, populated mainly by Russians. In the past, Russia's internal ethnic-national territories were classified by size and status into autonomous republics, autonomous provinces, and national districts; today all the former autonomous republics are simply termed republics. In many, the indigenous ethnic group comprises a minority of the population. Since 1991, the names and status of some of the constituent units in Russia have changed. As of 2002, Russia comprises eighty-nine constituent territorial units; in Russian constitutional terminology, these are called the "subjects of the federation." Of these, twenty-one are republics, six are *krais* (territories), ten are autonomous districts (all but one of them located within other units), one is an autonomous oblast, two are cities, and forty-nine are oblasts. (See Table 3.2.) Republics, autonomous *okrugs* (districts), and the one autonomous oblast are units created specifically to give certain political rights to populations living in territories with significant ethnic minorities. Autonomous *okrugs* are located within larger territorial entities, although they are treated as constituent members of the federation along with republics, the single autonomous oblast, oblasts, *krais,* and the two great cities of Moscow and St. Petersburg. Republics, on the other hand, have inherited certain special rights. They may adopt their own constitution so long as it does not contradict the federal constitution. They may maintain state symbols, such as a flag. In contrast, oblasts and *krais* are simply administrative subdivisions with no special constitutional status. Not surprisingly, therefore, between the oblasts and *krais,* on the one hand, and the republics on the other, there is constant rivalry. Leaders of oblasts and *krais* complain of the special privileges that republics are given that enable them to circumvent federal law but receive benefits such as federal subsidies.

Republics, in turn, jealously guard their special status. During 1990–1992, all the republics adopted declarations of sovereignty and two made attempts to declare full or partial independence of Russia, Chechnia, and Tatarstan. Tatarstan, situated on the Volga, is an oil-rich and heavily industrialized region. Eventually Russia and Tatarstan worked out a special treaty arrangement satisfactory to both sides, and the separatist movement in Tatarstan gradually subsided. This treaty then served as a precedent for subsequent bilateral agreements signed by the federal executive branch with the executives of forty-five other subjects during the period from 1994 to 1998. These treaties delineated the rights and obligations of the federal government and government of the region, and in some cases granted special privileges and exemptions to the region under which it is exempt from certain taxes, permitted to retain a higher share of earnings from the exploitation of regional resources, or even relieved of having to contribute soldiers to the army.

Under the old regime, federalism was largely nominal; it served symbolic purposes but did not provide any actual autonomy on the part of the constituent regions of the country. In recent years, Russia's constitutional order has evolved toward a more meaningful form of federalism, where constituent units of the

—————————— TABLE 3.2 ——————————
Territory and Population of Constituent Members of the Russian Federation, January 1, 1999

Name of unit	Territory (thous. sq. km.)	Population (thous.)	Name of unit	Territory (thous. sq. km.)	Population (thous.)
Russian Federation	17,075.4	146,693	**Central-Black Earth Region**		
Northern region			Belgorod oblast	27.1	1,492
Republic of Karelia	172.4	722	Voronezh oblast	52.4	2,475
Komi Republic	415.9	1,149	Kursk oblast	29.8	1,327
Arkhangelsk oblast	587.4	1,479	Lipetsk oblast	24.1	1,245
includes:			Tambov oblast	34.3	1,282
Nenetsk auton. okrug	176.7	47	**Volga Region**		
Vologda oblast	145.7	1,333	Republic of		
Murmansk oblast	144.9	1,000	Kalmykia		
Northwestern region			(Khalmg Tangch)	76.1	316
St. Petersburg (city) l	85.9	4,728	Republic of Tatarstan	68.0	3,780
Leningrad oblast l		1,681	Astrakhan oblast	44.1	1,026
Novgorod oblast	55.3	736	Volgograd oblast	113.9	2,694
Pskov oblast	55.3	812	Penza oblast	43.2	1,542
Kaliningrad oblast*	15.1	951	Samara oblast	53.6	3,308
Central region			Saratov oblast	100.2	2,721
Briansk oblast	34.9	1,456	Ulyanovsk oblast	37.3	1,477
Vladimir oblast	29.0	1,623	**North Caucasus Region**		
Kaluga oblast	29.9	1,090	Adygei Republic	7.6	450
Kostroma oblast	60.1	793	Dagestan Republic	50.3	2,121
Moscow (city) l	47.0	8,630	Ingush Republic** l	19.3	318
Moscow oblast l		6,547	Chechen Republic l		785
Orel oblast	24.7	904	Kabardino-Balkar		
Riazan oblast	39.6	1,296	Republic	12.5	792
Smolensk oblast	49.8	1,148	Karachaev-Cherkess		
Tver oblast	84.1	1,621	Republic	14.1	436
Tula oblast	25.7	1,769	North Osetian SSR		
Yaroslavl oblast	36.4	1,426	(Alania)	8.0	664
Volga-Viatka Region			Krasnodar krai	76.0	5,070
Mari-El Republic	23.2	761	Stavropol krai	66.5	2,689
Mordova SSR	26.2	938	Rostov oblast	100.8	4,384
Chuvash Republic	18.3	1,360	**Urals Region**		
Kirov oblast	120.8	1,602	Republic of		
Nizhnii Novgorod oblast	74.8	3,682	Bashkortostan	143.6	4,117

*Kaliningrad oblast is physically separate from Russia. Before World War II it was part of Eastern Prussia. It is situated on the Baltic Sea and borders on Lithuania and Poland.
**Territory for the Chechen and Ingush Republics is reported as if they were still a single republic but population figures are reported separately. Since 1992 they have been separated into two republics.

(continued)

—————————————— **TABLE 3.2** ——————————————

(Continued)

Name of unit	Territory (thous. sq. km.)	Population (thous.)	Name of unit	Territory (thous. sq. km.)	Population (thous.)
Udmurt Republic	42.1	1,636	Krasnoyarsk krai	2,339.7	3,063
Kurgan oblast	71.0	1,103	includes:		
Orenburg oblast	124.0	2,229	Taimyr (Dolgano-		
Perm oblast	160.6	2,979	Nenetsk aut. okrug.)	862.1	43
includes:			Evenki aut. okrug	767.6	19
Komi-Permyak aut.			Irkutsk oblast	767.9	2,764
okrug	32.9	153	includes:		
Sverdlovsk oblast	194.8	4,641	Ust'-Ordyn Buryat		
Chelyabinsk oblast	87.9	3,684	auton. okrug	22.4	144
			Chita oblast	431.5	1,269
Western Siberian Region			includes:		
Altai Republic	92.6	204	Agin-Buryat aut. okrug	19.0	79
Altai krai	169.1	2,664			
Kemerovo oblast	95.5	3,008	**Far Eastern Region**		
Novosibirsk oblast	178.2	2,752	Republic of Sakha-		
Omsk oblast	139.7	2,178	Yakutia	3,103.2	988
Tomsk oblast	316.9	1,072	Jewish autonomous		
Tiumen oblast	1,435.2	3,226	oblast	36.0	203
includes:			Chukotka autonomous		
Khanty-Mansiisk			okrug	737.7	77
auton. okrug	523.1	1,370	Primorsk krai	165.9	2,197
Yamalo-Nenetsk			Khabarovsk krai	788.6	1,584
auton. okrug	750.3	498	Amur oblast	363.7	1,015
			Kamchatka oblast	472.3	390
Eastern Siberian Region			includes:		
Republic of Buryatia	351.3	1,041	Koryak auton. okrug	301.5	30
Republic of Tuva	170.5	311	Magadan oblast	461.4	240
Republic of Khakassia	61.9	583	Sakhalin oblast	87.1	608

Source: State Committee on Statistics of the Russian Federation, *Rossiiskii Statisticheskii ezhegodnik 1999* (Russian Statistical Annual 1999) (Moscow: 1999).

federation possess a defined sphere of autonomy. Even so, the 1993 constitution failed to specify a particular set of rights and powers where the subjects of the federation possessed exclusive jurisdiction. Instead, after defining those powers where the federal level has exclusive jurisdiction (such as providing for the national defense and a money system), the constitution defines a set of rights in which the federal and regional governments *share* responsibility, among them regulation of the use of natural resources. The constitution thus leaves it to laws and agreements to work out how they are to share power. Still the new constitution went some way to make federalism real by ensuring that each of the eighty-nine federal subjects had an equal number of representatives in the Federation

Council. The Federation Council has strongly defended the prerogatives of the regions, which has helped to mitigate some of the intensity of the problem. With time, some of the nationalist passions that helped to drive the movements for separatism in the republics have subsided as populations have concluded that their economies are not likely to benefit from independence.

The relations between the central government and the governments of regions and republics continue to evolve. President Putin made it clear that the reform of federal relations was a top priority for him. Among his first steps as president were several measures intended to impose greater uniformity in the relations of regions with the central government and to ensure that regional governments adhered to federal law. As he put it in his message to parliament in July 2000,[30]

> In adopting the 1993 Constitution of Russia, a federative state was seen as a worthy goal which it would be necessary to work for painstakingly. At the beginning of the nineties the center gave away a lot to the regions. This was a conscious, although sometimes forced, policy. But it helped the leadership of Russia achieve the main goal and, I think, it was justified. It helped hold the federation together within its borders. We have to recognize this; it's too easy to criticize that which went before.

Putin was referring to Yeltsin's strategy of appeasing regional leaders with grants of power and bilateral treaties as a way of obtaining their support for his battles with his communist opposition. For example, there was an especially intense phase of treaty making when President Yeltsin was out on the hustings during his 1996 presidential election campaign. Typically, as part of a visit to a region, he would ceremoniously sign a treaty on power sharing with the governor or head of state, clearly using the occasion of a treaty between the federal government and a region as a means of appealing to the regional authorities for their electoral support.[31] After the election the pace of treaty making slowed down considerably.

Putin made clear his intention to reassert the authority of the federal government. His proposed law reforming the makeup of the Federation Council was one step toward this end: By stripping the regional governors[32] and parliamentary speakers of their seats in the upper house, he was explicitly demoting them in political status. Another law that Putin pushed through parliament gave him the ability to remove a sitting governor if a court found that the governor had refused to bring his actions into line with the federal constitution and law. Needless to say, the governors strongly opposed these changes. But the Duma overrode the upper house's veto and, with some modifications, the law was passed and signed by the president.

One of the most dramatic actions taken by Putin to recentralize control over the regions was his decree on May 13, 2000, creating seven new "federal districts," each with a special presidential representative whose task was to monitor the laws and actions of the governments of a set of regions. The purpose of the new districts was to strengthen central control over the activity of federal bodies in the regions; often, in the past, local branches of federal agencies had fallen under the de facto influence of powerful governors. The new structure was intended to ensure that federal revenues were not diverted into local coffers and to supervise and coordinate federal law enforcement bodies, which had sometimes developed cozy relations with local interests. That the new presidential representatives were to rely more on military style than political methods was underscored by the fact that five of the seven individuals whom Putin appointed had made their careers in the army, the security police, or the Interior Ministry. Critics of Putin's reform complained that it was a step in the direction of creating a hyper-centralized, authoritarian system of rule. Defenders argued that many regions had effectively become dictatorial fiefdoms and that decisive steps were needed to bring them back under central control. In practice, the impact of the presidential representatives has been modest. They have succeeded in bringing many regional laws into conformity with federal law and have increased federal supervision of regional government. On the other hand, they have not made the performance of regional government appreciably more efficient or transparent and they have frequently clashed with the federal ministries whose branch offices they try to coordinate.

At the local level, Russia's constitutional order remains unsettled. The respective powers of regional and local governments still have not been fully worked out in law and practice. Under the constitution, local government is called local *self-government,* signifying that it is not formally subordinate to the hierarchy of state executive power. But fixing a sphere of authority in which local self-government is autonomous has proven difficult. After protracted battles, parliament passed a law recognizing certain powers for local self-government. However, the law remains largely an empty shell because there are still no clear legal guidelines specifying the taxing and spending powers of local governments. The problem arises from the fact that *regional* governments resist allowing local governments to exercise any significant powers of their own, and regional governments have a great deal of clout through their representation in the Federation Council. In many cases, the mayors of the capital cities of regions are political rivals of the governors of the regions. Moscow and St. Petersburg are exceptional cases because they have the status of regions. Therefore they are treated as subjects of the federation along with the other republics and regions, with their chief executives and the chairs of their legislative assemblies serving as members of the Federation Council. (The mayor of Moscow, Yuri Luzhkov, in fact wields a great deal of political power at the level of the federal government.) Other cities lack the power and autonomy of Moscow and St. Petersburg, and must bargain with their superior regional governments for shares of power. President Putin has called for a thorough restructuring of the relations among the federal government, governments of the federal subjects, and local government, but the governors have bitterly resisted any effort to redistribute powers from the regions to either the central or local levels.

At present, executive power in Russia's regions is a good deal more powerful than the legislative bodies. Regional assemblies are generally very weak and in most cases are dominated by regional chief executives. For the most part, most deputies work in regional assemblies on a part-time basis and only a few are full-time employees of the assembly. Often, in fact, staff officials of the executive branch form the largest contingent of representatives to the local assemblies. There is little separation of powers at the regional and local level.[33] A report by the Central Electoral Commission found that of the deputies elected to representative bodies in the regions in 1996, 20 percent were employees of commercial firms and banks, 25 percent were employed in municipal enterprises, and 25 percent were government employees and others on government payrolls, such as teachers.[34] Surveys have also found that the public has little confidence in the legislative branch of regional government but considerably more in the executive branch.[35]

Regional chief executives are elected in direct popular elections in their regions. Under a 1999 law, they cannot serve for more than two consecutive terms.[36] Many governors' races are hotly contested, and the central government usually chooses a candidate to back whom it thinks will be sympathetic to its interests. Some races involve a contest between two or three opposing parties or political coalitions. In nearly every case, however, the winner puts aside any party ties and seeks to develop cooperative relations with the Kremlin. Party leanings or affiliations have little to do with how they govern their regions.[37] More important than party leanings are the connections between particular governors or challengers and powerful industrial and financial interests. For instance, the gubernatorial race in the vast and mineral-rich territory of Krasnoyarsk in September 2002 was regarded as a contest between competing financial-industrial empires, demonstrating how important it was to big business to have direct influence over the government of major regions. (See Close Up 3.3: The Krasnoyarsk Governor's Race.)

The twenty-one ethnic republics have the constitutional power to determine their own form of state power so long as their decisions do not contradict federal law. All twenty-one have established presidencies. In many cases, the republic presidents have constructed personal power bases around appeals to ethnic solidarity and demands to preserve the cultural autonomy of the indigenous nationality. Often they have used this power to resist the expansion of political and economic rights. In the 1990s, the central government's power to enforce federal law in the republics tended to be weaker than in ordinary regions, and hence relied more on a combination of fiscal sticks and carrots.

Relations between the federal government and the governments of regional republics reveal a considerable degree of conflict. Many regions have passed laws that violate the Russian constitution. For instance, several republics have declared that the republic has sovereign control—in effect, ownership—over the natural resources located in the republic. However, most of these disputes are coming before the Constitutional Court rather than being resolved by force. The Court has shown itself to be politically shrewd in defending the prerogatives of the federal government, trying to reconcile the interests of the center and the regions while reinforcing its own legitimate authority as an arbiter in intergovernmental disputes. It has struck down several laws adopted in republics and in

Close Up 3.3   **The Krasnoyarsk Governor's Race**

In September 2002 an election was held for governor of the vast and mineral-rich Krasnoyarsk territory. One candidate for the post was Alexander Khloponin, who at the time was governor of the Taimyr autonomous ethnic district, located within Krasnoyarsk. He had previously headed the huge Norilsk Nickel metallurgical complex, which was part of the financial-industrial conglomerate Interros, headed by the prominent oligarch Vladimir Potanin. Khloponin was supported by Interros, which poured resources into the campaign. His principal rival, Alexander Uss, was chairman of the Krasnoyarsk regional legislature. Uss was supported by Oleg Deripaska, who controls most aluminum production in Russia. The election was unusually dirty and the outcome provoked a major national scandal. Initially Khloponin was declared the winner by a 48.52 percent to 42.25 percent margin, but the regional election commission declared the election invalid due to massive irregularities. A local court ruled that the election commission's decision was invalid and demanded that it rescind it. The federal election commission also demanded that the regional election commission overturn its decision. When the regional election commission refused to comply, President Putin intervened and appointed Khloponin acting governor. In turn, the federal election commission annulled the decision of the regional commission and declared Khloponin the official winner. At no point was there a recount of the votes; President Putin rather disingenuously observed, in naming Khloponin acting governor, that the dispute was not about the fact that Khloponin had won more votes than Uss, but only about "the way the election was held." The entire episode embarrassed the president and the election commission, and some observers even speculated that the scandal had been deliberately arranged in order to discredit the very institution of regional elections.[1] Observers interpreted the outcome as a victory for Vladimir Potanin and his Interros financial-industrial group, and an indication of the immense influence it wielded not only in the regions, but over the federal government as well.

[1]RFE/RL Newsline, reports 30 September, 1–8 October 2002; RFE/RL Russian Political Weekly, 2 October 2002; and Polit.ru, reports 26 September – 8 October 2002.

ordinary territorial subjects that it found to conflict with the federal constitution, but it has also upheld several appeals from the regions against the unconstitutional intrusion of the federal government into the sphere of their legal power. The court has been cautious in treading too far out into the open waters of political disputes, but in June 2000, it took advantage of President Putin's tough stance against regional separatism to strike down the claims to sovereignty that were asserted in the constitutions of several ethnic republics. Now no region may claim that it has sovereignty in any area of law, even areas that are not under federal jurisdiction.

The fears that Russia would split apart much as the Soviet Union did proved to be exaggerated despite the tragic case of Chechnia. Although Russia also underwent a wave of ethnic-national mobilization within its national republics, separatism never brought Russia itself to the brink of dissolution. The different demographic and administrative makeup of Russia, and Moscow's willingness to negotiate special arrangements with some of the national republics, have preserved Russia's integrity and begun the process of establishing a meaningful form of federalism. On the other hand, the central government's power over regional governments is very weak, and in many areas, local authorities wield arbitrary power much as they did before communism fell. Reversing the central government's loss of control over the country in turn became President Putin's first great policy priority.

REVIEW QUESTIONS

1. In what ways did the political institutions of the Russian Republic mirror those of the USSR during the Soviet period? How did the Russian Republic differ from the Union in the makeup of its political structures? What significance did these similarities and differences have in the Gorbachev period?
2. Why did Yeltsin's "shock therapy" program lead to the constitutional crisis of 1993?
3. What effects did the constitutional struggles of 1992–1993 have on the features of the 1993 constitution?
4. Under Presidents Yeltsin and Putin, what have been the typical working relations between president and prime minister? How does this relationship differ from the relations between president and premier in France?
5. How do the two chambers of parliament differ in the ways they are formed and in their organization?
6. Describe Russia's mixed electoral system. How does the combination of two ways of electing members of the Duma affect the system of parliamentary factions in the Duma?
7. What are the defining features of Russia's form of federalism? How is it similar to or different from federalism in systems such as the United States or Germany?
8. How has President Putin gone about strengthening the power of the central government at the expense of regional governments? What are his reasons for shifting the balance of power in this way?
9. Both the USSR and the Russian Federation were ethnically diverse and nominally federal systems, but the USSR dissolved whereas the Russian Federation stayed intact. What are the main reasons for the different outcomes in the two cases?

ENDNOTES

1. Celestine Bohlen, "Yeltsin Deputy Calls Reforms 'Economic Genocide,'" *New York Times*, 9 February 1992.
2. See Table 3 in Chapter 6.
3. To receive any seats, however, a party or electoral association had to have been legally registered and to have won at least 5 percent of the party list votes. For the 225 proportional-representation (PR) seats, the entire Russian federation was considered a single district. Votes for each party's list were added, and the sum was divided by the total number of votes cast to determine the share of PR seats that each party would receive. Certain parties further divided their lists into regional sublists to determine which of their candidates would win parliamentary mandates.
4. On the new parliament and the manner of its formation, see Thomas F. Remington, *The Russian Parliament: Institutional Evolution in a Transitional Regime, 1989–1999* (New Haven, Conn.: Yale University Press, 2001).
5. Serious charges of fraud in the vote counting were made by a team of Russian analysts. Combining individual reports of irregularities from a number of regions with statistical modeling techniques, they estimate that actual turnout may have been as low as 46 percent and that, as a result, the constitution did not pass. They also claimed that the results of the vote for parliamentary candidates were extensively falsified as well. Although these accusations created a stir, all sections of the political elite tacitly agreed not to challenge the validity of the referendum or the elections.
6. Matthew S. Shugart and John M. Carey, *Presidents and Assemblies: Constitutional Design and Electoral Dynamics* (New York: Cambridge University Press, 1992) (chap. 2, pp. 18–27). An alternative type of system is "premier-presidential" where the president lacks the power to appoint and dismiss cabinet ministers unilaterally.
7. The restriction on dissolving the Duma within one year of its election applies to the no-confidence procedure but not to the requirement of parliament confirmation of the president's nominee for prime minister. Thus while the president may not dissolve the Duma twice within one year of its last election in the case where it votes no confidence in the government twice within three months or defeats a motion of confidence in the government, he is not so limited if the Duma rejects the candidates he nominates for prime minister three times in a row.
8. The French Constitution, Article 8, says that "On the proposal of the Prime Minister, he [the president] shall appoint and dismiss the other members of the Government."
9. Ilia Bulavinov and Elena Tregubova, "Druz'ia, prekrasen nash Sovbez!" *Kommersant Vlast'*, 13 June 2000, pp. 14–17.
10. Article 83 of the Constitution provides that the president forms and heads the Security Council but stipulates that its powers and duties are to be prescribed by law. To date, however, no such law has been passed.
11. Eugene Huskey, "Democracy and Institutional Design in Russia," *Demokratizatsiya: The Journal of Post-Soviet Democratization*, no. 4 (1996), p. 459. One of the reforms promised by President Putin is a major overhaul of the civil service. A first step in this direction was a presidential decree in 2002 establishing an ethical code for state employees. Attempts at more significant reform, however, are meeting strong but quiet resistance by the bureaucracy.
12. Eugene Huskey, *Presidential Power in Russia* (Armonk, NY: M. E. Sharpe, 1999), p. 59.
13. The size of the Russian state bureaucracy is now estimated at around 1 million employees, which represents a doubling since the end of the Soviet era. (Polit.ru, No-

vember 21, 2002.) Only about a third of these work at the federal level, however. The rest are employed at the regional or local level.

14. In his review of the powers of presidents in twenty-four postcommunist countries, Timothy Frye observes that Russia's president has the largest number of formal and residual powers of all of them. Timothy Frye, "A Politics of Institutional Choice: Post-Communist Presidencies," *Comparative Political Studies*, 30:5 (October 1997), pp. 523–52. By formal powers he means powers exercised under a grant of authority where the exercise of power is specified by law or constitution. By residual powers he means the right to exercise power under circumstances that the law does not specify.

15. Stephen White, "Russia: Presidential Leadership under Yeltsin," in Ray Taras, ed., *Postcommunist Presidents* (Cambridge, England: Cambridge University Press, 1997), pp. 57–61.

16. President Yeltsin appointed Viktor Chernomyrdin, an experienced state official who had run Russia's natural-gas monopoly, as prime minister in December 1992. However, as economic difficulties mounted, Yeltsin suddenly dismissed Chernomyrdin in March 1998 and appointed a young reformer named Sergei Kirienko to take his place. Under heavy pressure from Yeltsin, the Duma confirmed the nomination on the third vote. Kirienko's government proved unable to prevent a financial collapse in August 1998. Yeltsin then dismissed Kirienko and tried to bring back Chernomyrdin again as prime minister. This time the Duma, incensed at the president's actions, balked. Twice the president submitted Chernomyrdin's candidacy, and twice the Duma rejected it. Another constitutional crisis loomed. But this time Yeltsin yielded. Instead of nominating Chernomyrdin a third time, he proposed Foreign Minister Evgenii Primakov to head the government. Primakov, a pragmatist with long diplomatic and foreign intelligence service experience, enjoyed good relations with both the progovernment and the opposition factions in the Duma. He was quickly confirmed, and the political crisis was, for the moment, resolved.

    Primakov did not remain in his post long, however. Yeltsin grew suspicious that Primakov was gaining in strength and popularity and dismissed him in May 1999, after only eight months in office. Yeltsin named *Sergei Stepashin*, who had formerly been head of the FSB and later been Interior Minister, to replace him. The Duma confirmed the appointment on the first ballot by a wide margin.

    However, Stepashin's tenure was even shorter than Primakov's. In August 1999, Yeltsin once again abruptly dismissed the government, and named Vladimir Putin as his candidate to head the new government (see Close Up 1.1: Who Is Mister Putin?). The Duma narrowly voted to confirm Putin and Putin quickly established himself both in public opinion and in Yeltsin's estimation as a competent and trusted head of government. After the success of the political forces close to Putin in the December 1999 parliamentary elections, Yeltsin decided to resign from the presidency in order to make Putin the acting president and thus give Putin the advantages of incumbency in running for president in his own right. Putin handily won the election in March 2000 and named Mikhail Kas'ianov as his prime minister. Kas'ianov has continued in this office since then.

17. The same game applies in the United States as well, of course. President Kennedy once commented of a particular foreign policy initiative that if it failed, it would be another State Department failure, whereas if it worked, it would be another White House success.

18. Any party that has won at least 5 percent of the party list vote and thus obtained seats through the proportional-representation vote is entitled to form its own political

faction in the Duma and is given full rights to maintain a staff and participate in the legislative process. Groups of deputies from outside parties may also organize. If a group has thirty-five members, it may register as a recognized parliamentary group and enjoy the same rights and privileges as party factions. Each faction and registered group is entitled to have one representative—generally its leader—on the Council of the Duma, which steers the chamber. It is important to note that the Russian Duma therefore does not favor a majoritarian structure, such as the U.S. House and Senate use, or the British House of Commons uses. Every party and group has an equal voice in setting the agenda and managing the proceedings.

19. Federal'noe Sobranie—parlament Rossiiskoi Federatsii. Gosudarstvennaia Duma. Analiticheskoe upravlenie, Analiticheskii vestnik, vyp. 3 *Statisticheskie kharakeristiki zakonodatel'noi deiatel'nosti Gosudarstvennoi Dumy vtorogo sozyva (1996–1999)* (Moscow: 2000), pp. 28–9.

20. The Procurator-General oversees the Procuracy, a branch of the legal system somewhat similar to government prosecutors in the American system, but with far broader powers. For more details, see Chapter 8.

21. The stipulation that the two members from each region had to represent the executive and legislative branches—which creates a good deal of confusion and rigidity—was added at the last minute by President Yeltsin and sent out for publication before his aides could stop him.

22. The constitution provides that the president can only be removed in case of serious crime or high treason and specifies the sequence of procedures required: One-third of the members of the Duma must initiate the process; the decision must be considered by a special commission of the Duma; the Duma must approve the action by a two-thirds vote; the Supreme Court must issue a ruling finding that the president's actions constituted a grave crime or act of treason; the Constitutional Court must find that the parliament acted properly; and the Federation Council must finally approve removal by a two-thirds vote.

23. During 1994–1995, the Duma passed 461 laws, and of them 282 were signed by the president. About 100 of the latter were major regulatory or distributive policy acts in areas such as budget appropriations, social welfare, reform of state political institutions, and reform of law enforcement and the judicial system (*Segodnia*, 23 December 1995). Over the same period, the president issued approximately 4,000 decrees *(ukazy)*, most of them of minor significance—such as appointments of individuals to state positions or the awarding of honors for merit. A few, however, were highly important because they attempted to shape major national policy. These included the terms of privatization of shares of the state television and radio company, the powers that law enforcement bodies would have to prosecute organized crime, and decisions on which enterprises were subject to privatization in the current cash phase of the privatization program. In the case of the cash privatization program, the president's decree was modified to accommodate some of parliament's concerns, and in the case of the decree on fighting organized crime, the president invited parliament to pass its own more sweeping crime-fighting legislation.

24. A good account of these events is Michael Urban, "December 1993 as a Replication of Late-Soviet Electoral Practices," *Post-Soviet Affairs* 10:2 (1994), pp. 127–58, esp. pp. 129–39.

25. A biography of Yeltsin emphasizing his attempts to transform Russia from communism to democracy is Leon Aron, *Yeltsin: A Revolutionary Life* (New York: St. Martin's Press, 2000).

26. The political scientist Guillermo O'Donnell has termed such systems "delegative democracies." Guillermo O'Donnell, "Delegative Democracy," *Journal of Democracy* 5 (1994), pp. 55–69.

27. Boris Yeltsin, *Midnight Diaries* (trans. Catherine A. Fitzpatrick) (New York: Public Affairs, 2000), pp. 23–4; see also Stephen White, Richard Rose, and Ian McAllister, *How Russia Votes* (Chatham, NJ: Chatham House, 1996), pp. 253–54.

28. Ian Bremmer and Ray Taras, eds., *New States, New Politics: Building the Post-Soviet Nations* (Cambridge, England: Cambridge University Press, 1997).

29. Note that some of these territorial units are huge in physical terms: Sakha (formerly Yakutia) alone constitutes 17 percent of the territory of Russia. Altogether a little over half of Russian territory is located in ethnic republics and regions.

30. V. Putin, "Vystuplenie pri predstavlenii ezhegodnogo Poslaniia Prezidenta Rossiiskoi Federatsii Federal'nomu Sobraniiu Rossiiskoi Federatsii [speech in presenting the annual Message of the President of the Russian Federation to the Federal Assembly of the Russian Federation]," 8 July 2000, p. 7. (Taken from Russian president's Web site: **http.president.kremlin.ru/events/42.html**.)

31. OMRI Russian Regional Report, Vol. 2, No. 9, March 6, 1997.

32. All the chief executives of the subjects of the federation are commonly referred to as governors, whether they are the head of a regular oblast or *krai,* or the president of one of the ethnic republics. All are conventionally referred to as "the governors."

33. L. Smirnyagin, "Razdeleniia vlastei na mestakh bol'she ne sushchestvuet [Separation of Powers in the Localities No Longer Exists]," *Segodnia,* 2 August 1994. Leonid Smirnyagin is a distinguished Russian geographer and in the Yeltsin period was a member of the presidential advisory council.

34. *Segodnia,* February 22, 1997.

35. Ibid.

36. There has been a fight over the application of this law. Governors argued that since the law took effect as of October 1999 and could not have retroactive force, no service before October 1999 could be counted toward the two-term limit. A ruling by the Constitutional Court upheld their position. As a result, several governors were eligible to serve a third and fourth term.

37. Kathryn Stoner-Weiss, "The Limited Reach of Russia's Party System: Underinstitutionalization of Dual Transitions," *Politics and Society* 29:3 (September 2001), pp. 385–414; Debra Javeline, "Does It Matter Who Governs? The Effects of Partisanship on Leadership Behavior in Russia's Regions," Paper presented to 1998 Annual Meeting of the American Political Science Association, Boston, MA, 3–6 September 1998.

4

Political Participation and Recruitment

POLITICAL PARTICIPATION AND SOCIAL CAPITAL

In a democracy, citizens take part in public life through both direct forms of political participation, such as voting, party work, organizing for a cause, demonstrating, lobbying and the like, and more indirect forms of participation, such as membership in civic groups and voluntary associations. Both kinds of participation influence the quality of government. By means of collective action citizens signal to policy makers what they want government to do, and activists rise to positions of leadership through channels of participation. But, despite the legal equality of citizens in democracies, individuals' political engagement in any society varies with differences in resources, opportunities, and motivations. The better-off and better-educated tend to be disproportionately involved in political life everywhere, but in some societies the disproportion is much greater than in others.[1]

Political scientists have shown that the pattern of political participation in a society is structured by two factors. One is the way resources such as time, money, and civic skills are distributed among citizens. The other is the way the political system provides institutional channels for active involvement in politics.[2] In democratic societies, the tendency for policy makers to be more responsive to powerful, wealthy, and well-organized private interests than to weaker or more diffuse interests is offset, to some extent, by the ability of parties and elections to mobilize large masses of citizens into participating at the voting booth.

Parties and elections also offer channels to bring politically motivated individuals into politics, including individuals from outside the established circles of wealth and privilege.[3] Parties and other civic associations such as community organizations, trade unions, and religious groups give opportunities to individuals to gain civic skills, such as the ability to stand up in front of a group of people and persuade them to take action on an issue and to manage a collective undertaking. In the United States, churches and other religious institutions have been an especially important setting where individuals, regardless of their incomes or education, have been able to acquire civic skills.[4] Participation therefore does not only have to be directly political activity, such as campaigning and voting, to affect government. Even indirect forms of participation in public life affect the effectiveness and responsiveness of democracy.

The Importance of Social Capital

A strong fabric of voluntary associations has been recognized since de Tocqueville's time as an important component of democracy. Recently, political scientist Robert D. Putnam has offered an influential theory explaining why this should be so. Fair, honest, responsive government, Putnam argues, is a public good.[5] Everyone is interested in obtaining its benefits but few are willing to invest much time and effort to provide it. In this dilemma, individuals are strongly tempted to let others bear the costs of informing themselves about issues, getting involved in politics, running for office, monitoring the actions of officeholders to make sure that they do not misuse their power, and so on. If everyone cooperated in getting involved, no one person would bear a disproportionate share of the costs of keeping government responsive. And no one would have a disproportionate amount of influence in government. As with other public goods, therefore, providing good government is a collective action problem: If everyone cooperates, everyone is better off. But each individual is better off individually by free riding on others' efforts.

The stock of cooperation in a community or a society varies, Putnam shows. In some societies, people are convinced that even if they themselves are willing to act in accordance with the public interest, others will look out for their own interest at the expense of others, for instance, by cheating on their taxes, avoiding civic responsibilities, and even bribing officials to get something done. Since no one wants to play a sucker's game, everyone is tempted to cheat first. What can induce members of a community to be willing enough to trust one another to engage in collective activity for the common good? Putnam calls this quality of a society *social capital.* Social capital refers to the network of ties that keep people engaged in various kinds of cooperative endeavors. These do not need to be political. Putnam finds that one can predict the quality of government by counting how many people in the society belong to all sorts of voluntary associations—whether church choirs or bird-watching clubs or softball leagues or parent–teacher associations.[6] A key to the importance of social capital is that when there is a strong likelihood that people who have a relationship in a community also know some of the same people, they know that they have a reputation that depends on their behavior. The fact that each person's circle of acquaintance is part of a larger network of social ties reinforces the propensity for trust and cooperation in social relations.

Social capital therefore rests on a set of mutual understandings about the kinds of behavior that people can expect from one another and is reinforced by an actual fabric of social relations in which people encounter one another frequently—and their friends and family encounter one another as well. The denser the accumulated social capital, the likelier it is that members of society will be able to cooperate for the collective good in the public realm. This applies equally to politics and economics. Remarkably, in societies where social capital is thick, both the quality of government and the spread of economic opportunity are greater than in societies where the absence of trust, cooperativeness, and social capital impedes people's ability to hold government accountable and to take advantage of opportunities for economic development.[7]

A society with a low level of social capital and correspondingly poor quality of government can persist over long periods of time, as a result of the stability of mutually reinforcing expectations. In a society where social capital is weak, people come to expect that nothing will change, at least for the better, and fall into what Richard Rose calls a "low-level equilibrium trap" where people adjust their *demand* for better conditions downward as they grow discouraged and frustrated with the quality of government. As a result, the *supply* of good government and economic development stays low:

> The lowering of popular demands to the actual behaviour of government can create a low-level equilibrium trap. Citizens can adopt what the French describe as *incivisme*, a preference for government leaving people alone and a refusal to make it better. This can be stable, in so far as reform is off the political agenda and both the people and political elites tolerate a very imperfect democracy as a lesser evil by comparison with undemocratic alternatives.[8]

In such a case, people may prefer a "strong hand" in the form of a harsh, unresponsive central government to supply public order, since they cannot rely on society to provide it. They may be convinced that only an authoritarian state can prevent anarchy and that democratization will only make government vulnerable to the pressures of powerful and wealthy interests. Where there is low trust and low social capital, people are likelier to seek *private* favors through *vertical* relations with bosses and patrons rather than to work for good *public* policy through *horizontal* institutions of self-government.

The Problem of "Dual Russia"

Putnam developed his theory of the importance of social capital for effective democracy in the context of Italy, but it offers a powerful insight on many other societies, including Russia. In Russia, indeed, an enduring pattern of political life has been the social distance and political alienation between state and society: State authorities have rarely been integrated into the fabric of social relations, but rather stood above society, extracting what resources they needed from society but not cultivating ties of reciprocity or obligation to it. In a famous essay, Robert C. Tucker characterized this problem as the "image of dual Russia." He quotes the Russian liberal statesman and historian, Pavel Miliukov, who wrote that in Russia the state had traditionally been:

> an outsider to whom allegiance was won only in the measure of [its] utility. The people were not willing to assimilate themselves to the state, to feel a part of it, responsible for the whole. The country continued to feel and to live independently of the state authorities.[9]

To a large extent, the gap between state and society still remains today, in both Russians' attitudes and behavior. Mass participation in voting is at a high level. But participation in other forms of political activity is very low. Public-opinion polls show that most people believe that their involvement in political activity is futile, and few believe that government serves their interests.

In the late 1980s, political participation in Russia saw a brief, intense surge followed by a protracted ebb. But tens of thousands of voluntary associations do exist, reflecting a wide range of interests and causes. Although participation in public life is low compared with European or North American societies, it is higher than in most periods of Russian history. Certainly there is more participation in voluntary associations today than there was in the Soviet period despite what appeared to be extremely high levels of mass participation in state-sponsored political organizations.

In the Soviet period, the authorities devoted tremendous efforts to urging people to take part in the regime-sponsored forms of mass participation. For instance, they placed huge emphasis on achieving extremely high turnout levels in the uncontested, single-candidate elections of deputies to the soviets. The facade of mass participation served the needs of Soviet propaganda, which promoted the idea that the state was the instrument of the people's collective will. But most mass participation in Soviet times was purely nominal. People joined mass organizations because it took an active effort *not* to be a member. Today, although most Russians are not members of formal associations and are rather skeptical about their ability to influence government through political participation, all the evidence suggests that Russians today *do* take elections seriously, highly value their new political freedoms including the freedom *not* to participate in public life, and are involved in a dense set of social networks with family and friends. But unfortunately for democracy's prospects, these networks are largely outside the sphere of state power; often, in fact, they reinforce antidemocratic patterns of behavior.

Participation in voluntary associations in contemporary Russia is extremely low: According to 2001 survey data, 91 percent of the population do not belong to any sports or recreational club, literary or other cultural group, political party, local housing association, or charitable organization. Only half a percent report being a member of a political party. Four percent are members of sports or recreation groups. About 9 percent report attending church at least once a month, and about 20 percent report being members of labor unions.[10] Compare these figures with the United States: In the 1990s, even after several decades of steadily declining civic involvement, around 70 percent of Americans belonged to one or more voluntary associations and half consider themselves *active* members.[11] To be sure, the United States is still distinctive in the world for the high degree to which citizens actively take part in voluntary associations. But Russia stands out for the severe disengagement of its citizens.

This is not to say that Russian citizens are *psychologically* disengaged from public life. Half of the Russian adult population reports reading national newspapers "regularly" or "sometimes" and almost everyone watches national television "regularly" (81 percent) or "sometimes" (14 percent). Sixty-nine percent read local newspapers regularly or sometimes. Sixty-four percent discuss the problems of the country with friends regularly or sometimes and 48 percent say that people ask them their opinions about what is happening in the country. A similar percentage of people discuss the problems of their city with friends.[12] Seventy-nine percent of Russians in a survey conducted just after the 1999 elections responded that they do favor an election system that has a wide choice of candidates and parties for parliament and president.[13] Moreover, Russians accept that voting is a civic duty. Asked whether it is important to vote in national elections, 46 percent responded that they should make every effort to vote (31 percent responded that there is no need to vote if it is not convenient to do so, and only 23 percent responded that there is no point in voting because it doesn't do any good).[14] Indeed, Russians do vote in high proportions in national elections—higher, in fact, than their American counterparts.[15]

Moreover, Russians prize their right to participate in politics as they choose, including the right *not* to participate. Asked to compare the present regime to the old regime before Gorbachev, large majorities of Russians regard the present system as better in providing political freedoms: With respect to the right to say what one thinks, 73 percent think the present situation is "better" or "much better" than previously; concerning the right to join any organization one pleases, 75 percent consider the present regime "better" or "much better" than the old regime. On freedom of religion, 79 percent rate the present regime as better or much better, and 66 percent regard the present as better or much better in allowing individuals to choose whether to participate in politics or not.[16]

But Russian citizens rate government's performance itself very negatively: Concerning whether "people like me" have any ability to influence government, only 9 percent rate the situation as better than before perestroika; 45 percent say that it is unchanged; and 46 percent say that the present situation is "worse" or "much worse" than before. And concerning whether government treats everyone equally and fairly, only 8 percent think the situation has improved, 42 percent think it is much the same, and half respond that things have gotten worse.[17] Evidently Russians value their political rights, including the right not to take part in politics, but are convinced that these rights do not afford them any influence over government. In one late 2000 survey, 85 percent of the respondents expressed the opinion that they have no influence to affect the decisions of the authorities.[18] In another survey, 60 percent said that their vote would not change anything; only 14 percent of the respondents thought that Russia was a democracy while 54 percent said that "overall" it is not a democracy.[19] The political authorities are viewed very negatively (except for Putin). Fifty-five percent of the respondents in a survey in late 2000 said that the authorities are concerned with only their own material well-being and career. Another 13 percent regarded them as honest but weak, while another 11 percent considered them honest but incompetent.[20]

The evidence suggests that Russians regard their regime with deep mistrust although valuing their political rights. Part of the reason for this may be the fact that the reforms of the Gorbachev period and the revolutionary breakdown of the old regime raised people's hopes to unrealistically high levels about how quickly conditions would improve. In the late 1980s there was a great surge of popular mobilization in Soviet society. It took multiple forms, including mass protest actions such as strikes and demonstrations, as well as the creation of tens of thousands of new informal organizations. But following the end of the Soviet regime, this wave subsided. The disengagement and skepticism reflected in public opinion today certainly reflects deep disillusionment with how conditions have turned out after the wave of public enthusiasm and mobilization in the late 1980s.

Another reason for the alienation of citizens from the regime, however, has to do with the fact that the old mechanisms of participation and recruitment have not been replaced with an effective system of democratic institutions that would allow voters to exercise influence over public policy and hold officeholders accountable to the public for their actions. The old regime did have a system for holding officials to account, but it worked hierarchically, as in a military organization. Government officials answered up the chain of command to their administrative superiors and to the party for their actions, not to the voters. Officials by the same token often had the discretion and the ability to get around the rules, for instance, to grant a favor, to speed up the processing of a bureaucratic transaction, to ignore a rule, or to forgive an offense. Social capital in the sense of thick horizontal ties among people may have been lacking, but vertical ties compensated for this to some extent. Today, even these have broken down. Most people think that the new system is run for the benefit of a few wealthy and powerful interests, leaving most ordinary citizens without much opportunity to exert any influence through the political process.

In the old system, citizens who had a problem often sought the intercession of an influential individual, someone placed high in the hierarchy of power. They turned to party and government officials, newspaper editors, soviet deputies, managers at their place of work, or other influential individuals. Or they could trade favors with people. In a centrally planned economy, where many items were in short supply, it required using connections to obtain scarce goods and services.[21] Now, however, Russians believe that it takes money to buy things that are available but expensive or to bribe an official for a routine service. Russians believe that the level of corruption in the country has increased: Asked whether bribe taking and corruption have increased or decreased since the Soviet period, 52 percent of respondents say that it has increased "a lot" and another 21 percent say that it has increased "a little." Twenty-three percent say that it has remained at the same level, and only 4 percent think that it has declined at all. Eighty-nine percent believe that "most" or "almost everyone" of the officials of the national government in Moscow are corrupt.

In short, connections, political influence, and informal networks used to be critical to coping with daily life in the old system. Now it appears that money is replacing personal connections as the way to get around bureaucratic difficulties and greedy officials. Richard Rose's New Russia Barometer survey in 1998 asked respondents whether they agreed with the following pair of propositions: "Some people say that in Soviet times to get anything done by a public agency you had to know people in the Party" and "Some people say that nowadays to get anything done by a public agency you have to pay money on the side." Sixty-eight percent agreed with the first statement and 90 percent agreed with the second. The problem is that in the old system, more people had access to influential connections than have access to money today. As a result, the sense of powerlessness and alienation from the state is pervasive.

Since participation and recruitment are closely related processes, it is not surprising that the breakdown of the old system of participation has been accompanied by the breakdown of the old system's mechanism for elite recruitment. Elite recruitment refers to the set of institutions in a society by which individuals enter careers giving them access to influence and responsibility. Educational institutions, voluntary associations, civil-service examinations, political-party work, and elections are all means by which societies' need for officials and leaders are met. In the Soviet system, the formal channels of mass participation were closely linked to its method for grooming officials and placing them in positions of responsibility. Since the old system has not been replaced by an open, transparent, democratic system of participation and recruitment, a closer look at how the old system operated will help explain why its breakdown has produced so pronounced a sense of disengagement of the public from the political system today. It will also shed light on why Russians today report that money, rather than democratic politics or bureaucratic connections, is the new medium of exchange in public life.

PARTICIPATION AND RECRUITMENT UNDER THE SOVIET REGIME

Channels of Mass Participation

For most rank-and-file citizens of the old Soviet regime, participation in membership organizations was mainly formal—a matter of attending required meetings, paying the monthly dues, and obtaining the benefits these organizations distributed. Virtually everyone who was employed belonged to a trade union, if only because trade unions administered social-insurance funds and subsidized vacations. Youth groups provided recreational opportunities as well as political indoctrination, and nearly all youth belonged to the organization appropriate for their age group. Millions of people were members of voluntary public associations. For most people, membership in such organizations was largely nominal. For some individuals, however, and especially those who were keen on making political careers, mass organizations were an essential rung on a career ladder through which energetic activism, coupled with political reliability, could bring ambitious individuals to the attention of the party's personnel managers, who in turn could ensure that the individual received the right combination of political education, volunteer assignments, and job opportunities to allow him or her to rise through the ladder of promotions.

A good example of mass participation was the soviets, the elected councils that served as representative and law-making bodies. Elected deputies were expected to help their constituents with various individual problems, but they were not able to make policy decisions in their jurisdictions without the guidance of the Communist Party. In every territorial subdivision of the state—every town, village, rural district, city, province, ethno-territory, and republic—there was a corresponding soviet. (In the case of the union and autonomous republics, and at the level of the union government itself, it was called Supreme Soviet.) Soviets tended to be quite large: In 1987, 2.3 million deputies were elected to 52,000 soviets across the country. A deputy's calling was not full-time; soviets usually met on a quarterly or biannual basis, for a day or two at a time, hearing reports and approving the proposed budget and plan. Soviets were not deliberative, policy-making bodies, but were means of acquainting deputies and citizens with the policies and priorities of the regime at each level of the state, for giving deputies a feeling of personal responsibility for the well-being of the system, and for showcasing the democratic character of the state. This last function was particularly evident in the care taken to ensure a high level of participation by women, blue-collar workers, youth, nonparty members, and other categories of the populace who were severely underrepresented in more powerful organs. To this end, the party employed a quota system to select candidates to run, controlling the outcome of the nomination process to obtain the desired mix of social characteristics among the elected deputies.[22] Generally speaking, the party tried to select as candidates people who could serve as role models to society, leading citizens from all walks of life who were politically reliable and socially respectable. Virtually all prominent Soviet citizens were deputies to soviets at one level or another.

In addition to service as deputies, Soviet citizens were brought into the work of local government and administration in other ways as well. Many served as volunteer members of the standing committees of local soviets monitoring government's performance in housing, education, trade, catering, public amenities, and other sectors of community life. Still others joined residential committees and neighborhood self-help groups. These activities were not entirely ceremonial. Often they gave public-spirited citizens an outlet for community service.[23]

Parochial Contacting. The habit of turning to deputies for help with private problems is characteristic of a pattern called "parochial contacting," which is a form of citizen participation focused on obtaining private benefits rather than influencing public policy. The Soviet authorities encouraged citizens to transmit their grievances, hopes, and petitions to a wide range of official institutions. The volume of letters and personal visits was huge. For 1983 alone, it was estimated that Central Television received about 1.7 million letters; all-union radio more than 600,000; Moscow radio, more than 170,000; the central newspapers, around half a million each; provincial newspapers, 30,000 to 35,000 letters each; the trade unions, 2 million letters and personal visits; and party organizations, 3.3 million letters and visits.[24] At the local level, ordinary citizens had some opportunity to influence government administration, pushing for improvements in the condition and availability of housing, for example, or for better provision of stores and cultural amenities. But these demands were generally nonpolitical in nature, not aimed at influencing basic policy or challenging the incumbents' right to rule.[25] Often this kind of contact between citizen and state generated a pattern of individualized, clientelistic participation, in which individuals became adept at "working the system" for their own private benefit rather than changing the allocation of resources for whole classes of people.[26] The regime in fact encouraged the *demobilization* of society. That is, they gave people numerous opportunities to pursue particularistic demands but repressed any effort by people to get involved in the political system to satisfy general policy-related demands, whether by organizing independent political movements or by taking to the streets in protest.[27]

Voting. Voting for deputies to soviets was another example of the directed, formal aspect of political participation in the old system. The regime went to great lengths to ensure that everyone cast a ballot and treated the massive turnout and near unanimous endorsement of the candidate as a sign of the unshakeable unity of regime and people, despite the fact that virtually every race was uncontested.[28] The act of voting was a matter of dropping a ballot with a single, preprinted name into a ballot box at a polling station, where, after the polls closed, officials would count the number of ballots cast for the candidate and duly announce the candidate's election by an overwhelming majority. The campaign emphasized the ideological solidarity of society—there was no room for an "opposition platform"—but voters were encouraged to see the deputies they elected as go-betweens who could intercede with the bureaucracy for their particular needs. Soviet elections illustrate the ritualistic quality of much participation under the old regime. For the authorities, the *appearance* of mass support was evidently of great importance, while for much of the population, participation in such ceremonies was regarded as part of the harmless pageantry of everyday life.

Party Control of Social Organizations. As time went on, the growth of repressed popular grievances far exceeded the slow growth of regularized opportunities for Soviet citizens to voice their demands. As a result the gap between approved gestures of participation and the actual realities of power widened. Those new public organizations that formed with official approval quickly grew into branches of the state rather than autonomous expressions of a public interest.[29] Even the Russian Orthodox Church had a quasi-official status, despite the constitution's declared separation of church and state. The KGB had a large network of informers and agents working within the Church for surveillance of believers and to guide the Church's social and political activity in directions congruent with the regime's purposes.[30] The party, in short, claimed a "licensing" power over organized social bodies through which it ensured control over their choice of leaders and the direction of their activity.[31] Because the nominally public (*obshchestvennye*—meaning formally nonstate) organizations in fact carried out state-set goals and operated under close political control, the boundary lines between state and society were never distinct. However, precisely because social organizations were so heavily controlled by the party, they did not foster much usable social capital in the form of generalized social trust and autonomous collective action. Until the end of the Soviet regime, people continued to rely much more heavily on personal networks of family and friends to exchange information and favors than in democratic societies, and much less on voluntary participation in public life.[32] At home and at work, in the intimate company of trusted family and friends, Soviet citizens swapped information and opinion. Such networks were necessary for coping with the bureaucratized Soviet system, but at the same time they undermined both its basic ideological premise—that the people and the state were one—and its centralized control over resources.[33]

Informal social networks remain a powerful and important feature of Russian society today as well. Surveys show that around 90 percent of Russians can name at least one person (a family member or a friend) with whom they can discuss serious personal matters, including politics. Most Russians can name at least two such people.[34] Most Russians feel confident that they can ask their family and friends for help, for example, by borrowing money or asking someone to look after them if they are ill. Such relationships are also an important source of political information and opinion. For instance, 11 percent say that talking with family and friends is an important source of guidance to them in deciding how to vote in Duma elections.[35]

But is the continuing strength of such informal social ties a sign that Russia has a civil society supportive of democratic values and institutions? There is a lively debate on this point. Political scientist James Gibson finds that Russian social networks are characterized by a high degree of exchange of political information and opinion and that there is a high level of trust among such networks, even outside immediate family members. He argues that such networks can therefore help to transmit information and values consistent with democratization. Richard Rose draws exactly the opposite conclusion, for three reasons. First, he points out that in Russia, informal social networks for many years have been means of surviving in an environment where the state was remote, harsh, and corrupt. They therefore reflect the alienation between state and society. Second, the density of social ties is not accompanied by high levels of associational membership. They may reinforce bonds of personal reciprocity, but they do not contribute to the capacity for cooperation in collective action. They are therefore not useful social capital for democracy. Finally, individuals are extremely mistrustful toward state authorities, particularly those who are supposed to represent them and be accountable to them. Therefore social networks do not serve as vehicles for keeping government responsive or honest. Freedom, argues Rose, is valued because it allows people to keep their distance from a corrupt and exploitative state.[36]

Dissent and the Intelligentsia. During the Soviet period, some groups operated outside the state and, as a result, risked being repressed. Overt dissent from the official doctrines was treated by the authorities as a criminal offense. Beginning in the mid-1960s, various small, unofficial groups pressed the regime to respect the civic and political rights that were granted by the Soviet constitution but were denied whenever the authorities found that a particular act violated the limits of permitted expression.[37] Those individuals who stepped outside the limits of permissible public expression—called *dissenters* or *dissidents*—were harassed, arrested, or even incarcerated in mental hospitals; a few were forced to emigrate. Many more people, particularly members of the cultural and scientific intelligentsia, chose not to take actions that could provoke their arrest, but shared similar democratic values. Working in institutions such as theaters, labs, research institutes, universities, the mass media, and professional bodies, many of these individuals formed strong ties of mutual trust. Some of them later came to lead the movements for democratic, national, and religious rights that blossomed in the Gorbachev period.

Some prominent dissident and nondissident intellectuals became leaders of new political movements in the late 1980s, such as Andrei Sakharov, the most famous of the democratic dissidents, who became the moral leader of the democratic group of USSR deputies elected in 1989. Another dissident-turned-politician is Sergei Kovalev, a close friend and collaborator of Sakharov's in the democratic movement who became chairman of the human rights committee of the Russian Republic's parliament in 1990 and was a member of the Russian parliament throughout the 1990s. Another intellectual—a nondissident, who remained within the system—who entered politics in 1989 was Anatolii Sobchak. Sobchak was a law professor at Leningrad State University (Vladimir Putin was a student of his) who rode the wave of democratic ideals to election to the Leningrad city soviet in 1990 and then went on to become mayor of Leningrad (later St. Petersburg). In Russia and a number of other republics of the union, scientists, professors, and cultural figures, some with dissident backgrounds, others not, comprised the first wave of leaders when the opportunity for democratic politics opened up in 1989–1990. They drew upon their networks of friends and acquaintances for support and could articulate coherently the principles on which they based their opposition to the Soviet system—ideals such as liberal democracy and an open, market-oriented economy; in many republics, these were linked to the cause of national sovereignty.

Generally speaking, however, as a result of the pattern of state-directed mass participation in the old regime, most civic associations developed in opposition to the state (and were therefore illegal) or were extensions of the state's power.[38] Elimination of most forms of private property, the suppression of opposition, and the spread of state control over social organizations left a vacuum of non-state structures when the political regime fell apart. This vacuum in turn created opportunities for a surge of radical politics, particularly radical nationalism, because of the destruction of class and other cleavages that cut across national divisions.[39] Ties among intellectuals cemented in the post-Stalin era enabled figures from the scientific and cultural elite to assume leading roles in the wave of political activism that crescendoed at the end of the 1980s and beginning of the 1990s.

Participation and Recruitment in the Old Regime: Interlocking Directorates

Why did the communist regime place such emphasis on mass participation? One reason is that it contributed directly to the recruitment of leaders.[40] The numerous governing bodies of social organizations created positions for activists and leaders who directed mass participation. Leaders in these organizations, in turn, belonged to the governing bodies of other organizations. The Communist Party likewise formed its own party committees at every level: Its members always included the ranking full-time party officials in the given jurisdiction, as well as the heads of government and social organizations. For example, the party committee for a city typically included, besides the city party organization's own top party secretaries, the heads of the city government, the chairman of the trade union council, the first secretary of the Komsomol (Communist Youth League) branch, directors of major enterprises, the editor of the local newspaper, and other notables. Serving as the hub from which a series of membership ties extended into a locality's organized institutions, the party committee at each level of the hierarchy was a vehicle for the *horizontal integration* of elites by drawing together the key government and societal leaders in any given jurisdiction. At the same time such channels provided for the *vertical integration* of elites through the inclusion of heads of subordinate organizations on nominally elective collective bodies at higher levels. A good example would be the membership of the first secretaries of the most important regional party committees on the Central Committee of the Communist Party of the Soviet Union.

Integration of elites through organizational cross-representation helped cement ties among the members of different elite groups in the Soviet system and thus helped preserve central control and coordination throughout the political system. Although in practice, the old regime vested actual decision-making authority in administrative bodies, it also preserved elements of the old Bolshevik model of *democratic centralism* and *soviet democracy*. These were embedded in the system of soviet elections as well as within the party. Party members cast ballots for representatives to governing bodies that were supposed to oversee the work of its own executive organs. These governing bodies included the Central Committee at the summit of the party hierarchy, as well as party committees at each level of the party organizational ladder. But, as in elections of deputies to soviets, elections within the party were noncompetitive and the act of voting was purely ceremonial. Likewise the authority of party committees that were "democratically elected" in this way was understood by everyone to be a formality. The entire system was regarded as lip service to the party's claim to be democratic and representative. It was considered unthinkable to demand that the party actually behave as if it were democratically accountable to its members.[41]

By comparison with many present-day failed states, the Soviet system had a high level of organizational capacity. It had institutions for the recruitment of elites, the coordination of policy makers, and the participation of the population in political routines that acquainted them with the basic institutions of the state. It enabled central policy makers to communicate their goals and priorities down to lower-level elites, and provided political leadership throughout the state. By comparison with more developed political systems, however, the Soviet state demonstrated serious failings. It did a poor job of holding officials accountable either to central authorities or to the citizens at large. Its reliance on self-nominating, closed procedures for appointing and "electing" officials made it vulnerable to pathologies such as corruption, favoritism, and incompetence. Perhaps most fatally, the system became rigid and immobile, so that it could not modernize the economy without upsetting powerful and well-entrenched political interests. Ultimately the system proved incapable of adapting itself to pressures for better performance and greater international competitiveness.

Participation and Recruitment in the Old Regime: Conclusions

Reviewing the patterns of state-sponsored mass political participation and elite recruitment under the old regime, we can draw three conclusions. First, the high volume of formal civic involvement reflected the mobilizing impulses of a political regime that was born in revolution and that sought to impose comprehensive controls on public attitudes and behavior. However ritualized and formalistic these forms of participation became, they demonstrated a massive effort by the regime to control society. Second, they generated little social capital that could be made the basis for a democratic regime following the collapse of communism. For the most part, citizens continued to rely heavily on networks of family, friends, and coworkers for communication and on parochial contacting in their dealings with state authorities. The webs of voluntary overlapping social association that are the base of support for democratic societies were replaced in the Soviet system by a series of interlocking state hierarchies. As a result, officials were accountable to their superiors rather than to their constituents, and there was a wide gap between the political elite and ordinary citizens.

Finally, there were some important exceptions to this generalization. Some arts organizations, research institutes, universities, and other institutions fostered ties of generalized trust and social cooperation through the long decades after Stalin's death. When Gorbachev finally opened the doors to freer public communication and political action, intellectuals based in these institutions initiated new forms of collective action. In some republics, these movements were aimed at winning national independence for their republics. In several major cities of Russia, these groups spearheaded political movements for democratic reform and became the nucleus of new democratic coalitions and parties that competed in the elections of 1989 and 1991. Intellectuals in alliance with some radicalized members of the ruling elite mobilized popular pressure for democratization, linking populist demands for an end to elite power and privilege with the longing for a more prosperous, open, "civilized" way of life. These aspirations were quickly succeeded, however, by disillusionment with the outcome of the transition.

SURGE AND EBB IN POLITICAL PARTICIPATION

The Mobilization of Discontent

In a famous comment on the fact that the minor reforms under Louis XVI in France not only failed to relieve the revolutionary pressure of mass discontent, but actually seemed to stimulate it, Alexis de Tocqueville noted that "the most dangerous time for a bad government is when it starts to reform itself." In our time there have been many examples when authoritarian regimes attempted to release the pressure of popular discontent by holding elections or legalizing opposition groups, only to find that the public's desire for radical, fundamental change was more powerful than they calculated.

The process of democratization results in a peaceful transition if the leadership is willing to concede power without suppressing its opponents. But its ability to do so depends on the civilian leadership's ability to preserve the support of the military and secret police *and* the ability of the opposition to remain sufficiently united as it pushes the regime to prevent popular demands from spilling out and provoking large-scale repression. Often in such revolutionary settings, mass frustrations and grievances, having accumulated over a long period, sweep away the more moderate elements of the leadership that could mediate between regime and opposition, and instead thrust forward maximalist leaders, with the result that confrontation results in new violence. Both sides need to be willing and able to compromise if the transition is to result in a peaceful and democratic outcome.

In the case of the Soviet Union, new channels of participation and recruitment quickly sprang up in response to the opening that Gorbachev's democratic reforms provided. In 1986 and especially 1987 and 1988, an explosion of associational activity in society occurred.[42] Much of this was not explicitly political in character, and took the form of rock music groups, body-building and martial arts clubs, loose associations of pacifists, hippies, and religious mystics, and cultural and environmental preservation movements. But even many groups without an explicit political agenda were expressions of "identity politics" as they joined in asserting the right to a public voice.[43] They were *implicitly* political, because they challenged party controls over ideology and personnel selection. They could therefore become nuclei of opposition ideas and organization. Moreover, in a rapidly changing environment, the clash between groups seeking to preserve their independence and the party-state bureaucracy tended to politicize and radicalize society. With time, therefore, and particularly as opportunities opened up for forms of political expression, such as mass demonstrations, publication of independent newsletters and leaflets, and electoral campaigning, more and more groups were drawn into politics. This process of politicization of the informal groups reached a peak in the 1988–1989 period, as society was drawn into the debate over democratization.[44] Broadly speaking, two processes occurred simultaneously over the 1987–1989 period: the proliferation of independent social associations (Soviet authorities estimated that 30,000 unofficial groups had formed in 1988, and perhaps as many as 60,000 by 1989) and the aggregation of smaller groups into larger movements and organizations.

Popular Fronts. One of the most common forms of independent, organized political activity in the 1988–1989 period was the popular front. Typically the popular front was a broad popular movement with a democratic orientation that aggregated several overlapping causes: environmental preservation, the expansion of political freedoms, and, for those operating in national republics, greater autonomy for the national homeland. The first to form were those in the Baltic Republics, where during the 1988–1989 period they quickly grew from loose groupings of the cultural and scientific intelligentsia into broad movements with mass followings and organized branches in every town. The strength and cohesiveness of the popular-front organizations in all three Baltic Republics—in the face of economic and other forms of pressure from Moscow—were important factors in Gorbachev's willingness to negotiate with the republican leaderships on republican independence from the Soviet Union.

Strikes. Another important form of spontaneous collective action was strikes. Usually strikes by industrial workers were motivated by a set of grievances revolving around degrading living and working conditions, demands for meaningful workplace and regional autonomy, and resentment at the privilege and power of the ruling elite. In many regions, however, strikes were vehicles of ethnic-national protest, beginning in 1988 with strikes in Transcaucasia and the Baltic Republics.[45] The largest labor action was the strike by coal miners in July 1989, when at its peak, the strike was joined by 300,000 to 400,000 workers. The strikes ended when the government promised to make substantial concessions to the workers' demands for better living and working conditions and greater economic control over their mines and cities. In turn the miners' frustration with the government's failure to make good on these promises led to a new, smaller, but far more politically directed strike wave in November. Generally, nationalism mobilized more strikes than did the labor movement. The evidence from the count of workdays lost to strikes and protest in 1989 indicates that far more downtime was caused by ethnically related movements than from economically inspired protest.[46]

The strike movements helped to generate new organizations and new leaders independent of the old party-state. In the coalfields, the strike movement of 1989 created a cadre of grassroots leadership as strike committees turned into permanent workers' committees. In turn, in May 1990, these workers' committees created an independent confederation of labor to compete with the official trade union structure for the loyalty of workers. However, it failed to rally the workers of other industries to its fold. Soon afterward, coal miners created an independent trade union.[47] These were not the only workers' organizations formed out of the great strike wave of 1989. In addition to efforts by the regime to coopt the movement, regional organizations emerged as well, such as the Union of Kuzbass Workers, which sought to unite workers with peasants and intellectuals, as well as purely local workers' organizations.[48]

In 1991 a new wave of strikes erupted, again centered in the coalfields. Although it embraced fewer workers than the 1989 strikes, at its height, labor leaders estimated that around a third of the mines were out.[49] Coordination across regions was managed by a council formed of representatives of the major regional strike committees, which drafted a list of demands supported by all the striking workers. Besides the demands for a general wage agreement and meaningful improvements in living conditions, the program included radical political points, including demands for the resignation of the entire structure of central power—including Gorbachev's resignation as president, the dissolution of the USSR Congress of People's Deputies, the resignation of the USSR Cabinet of Ministers, and the transfer of power to the republics. Moreover, smaller-scale work actions in other industries suggested that workers outside the coal industry were sympathetic to the miners and unwilling to be used by the government to oppose them. The strikes ended only after the central government agreed in early May to transfer control of the coal mines to the Russian Republic's jurisdiction. The miners trusted Yeltsin and mistrusted Gorbachev.

Anomic Protest.   The strike committees, popular fronts, and other grassroots political organizations that sprang up in the 1987–1990 period were generally peaceful channels of informal mass participation, even when they exceeded the limits of what the authorities were willing to tolerate. Some events, however, resulted in violence and bloodshed. A shocking incident occurred in Tbilisi, capital of the Georgian republic, in April 1989, when a peaceful rally for Georgian independence and sovereignty was broken up with brutal force by Soviet troops, leaving at least nineteen people dead. The Tbilisi killings in turn fortified Georgian determination to achieve independence from the Soviet Union. A similar incident occurred in Kazakhstan in December 1986, in one of the first nationality related mass political demonstrations of the Gorbachev period. Some interethnic grievances were so intense that they spilled out into warfare, especially in the Transcaucasian region where Armenia, Azerbaijan, and Georgia are located. Undoubtedly the bloodiest is the dispute between Armenians and Azerbaijani over Nagorno-Karabakh. The conflict between Armenians and Azerbaijani over the status of this enclave inside Azerbaijan turned into full-scale war, which has tapered off into a low-intensity war of attrition.

The informal, often anomic, character of much popular political participation in the late Gorbachev period had important effects on the subsequent development of Russian politics. The explosiveness of demands for decent living conditions, ending bureaucratic privilege, autonomy for the national culture, and redress of other broad popular grievances substantially raised the costs to the regime of using force to suppress protest. They therefore helped to bring about radical change, such as the acknowledgment of the right to strike, the legalization of opposition parties, and ultimately the breakup of the union. Since the Soviet regime had suppressed almost all forms of organized participation except those it controlled and directed, there were few independent associations able to channel popular protest in the perestroika period. Many informal organizations sprang up but quickly faded away. The regime attempted to coopt others by drawing them under state sponsorship. Most organizations found it very hard to survive since the economy continued to be overwhelmingly state owned and state administered: New informal organizations struggled simply to obtain office space and equipment. In contrast to Central Europe, Soviet society lacked a network of civic associations that could assume responsibility for mobilizing and managing popular pressure for democratic change. In the Soviet case, the mass outpouring of popular protest in 1989–1991 therefore tended to be followed by a rapid demobilization. Still, the surge of popular participation in this period left two lasting institutional changes: regular democratic elections and the nuclei of a number of political parties and interest groups. In the next section we discuss electoral participation before turning to the relationship between participation and the formation of the political elite. Then in the next chapter we take a closer look at the dynamics of Russians' attitudes and values.

Electoral Participation

Yeltsin and Electoral Politics. The mobilization of popular political participation had the effect of generating new leadership and new organizations voicing a variety of populist, democratic, and nationalist demands. In many areas it forced former Communist Party and government executives to adapt themselves to a pluralized political environment that they could no longer control. Some were swept away, but most managed to hold on to their power and a few emerged as champions of reform. A prominent example of the latter was Boris Yeltsin. (See Close Up 4.1: Boris Yeltsin—Patriarch of Postcommunist Russia.)

Radical Democratic Populism. The elections to the all-union Congress of People's Deputies in 1989 and the republican and local soviets in 1990 illustrate the turn from the directed political participation characteristic of the old system to the new politics of competitive elections. The 1989 and 1990 elections were conceived by Gorbachev as ways of giving the wave of popular political participation stimulated by glasnost a constructive outlet, one that would help weaken Gorbachev's conservative opposition while at the same time enabling him to continue to set the country's basic policy direction. But the elections had much more far-reaching effects than he anticipated, by activating popular movements and generating new opposition leaders with large popular followings. Although the elections of 1989, 1990, and 1991 were not organized around competing parties for the most part, proto-partisan tendencies formed as candidates aligned themselves with competing political causes—some emphasizing liberal democracy, others hard-line communism, still others ethnic nationalism.

The surge of electoral participation in 1989–1990 had a strongly populist impulse. Campaigns were not organized around political parties as much as they focused on antiestablishment causes and personalities. In many cases they were a referendum on the system rather than a choice between alternative political programs. The 1989 elections to the USSR Congress of People's Deputies enabled the populace to register their opposition to the old party and government elites, resulting in some dramatic upsets. Dozens of leading party and government officials were defeated, and a group of 300 to 400 deputies identified with liberal democratic views were elected to the Congress. In some republics,

Close Up 4.1   Boris Yeltsin—Patriarch of Postcommunist Russia

Boris Yeltsin was Russia's first president and the architect of its breakaway from the USSR. As a leader he embodied all the contradictions of the stormy passage from the communist to postcommunist era. He alternated between taking radical steps toward democracy and retreating toward opportunistic alliances with wealthy and powerful interests that could keep him in power. Gifted with a brilliant instinct for political strategy, he was also prone to fits of depression, heavy drinking, and passivity. Ill for much of his presidency with serious heart disease, he was also capable of summoning enormous energy when battling against his enemies. Most of the breakthroughs as well as the fatal compromises of Russia's transition are the direct result of decisions he made.

Yeltsin rose through the ranks as a Communist Party leader in the heartland industrial region of the Urals. Born in 1931, he graduated from the Urals Polytechnical Institute in 1955 with a diploma in civil engineering, and worked for a long time in construction. From 1976 to 1985 he served as first secretary of the Sverdlovsk oblast (provincial) Communist Party organization. He was known there as a hard-driving, imperious leader, blunt and impatient with subordinates who failed to measure up to his standards, but genuinely devoted to improving the well-being of his region.

Early in 1986 he became first secretary of the Moscow city party organization but was removed in November 1987 for speaking out against Gorbachev. Positioning himself as a victim of the party establishment, Yeltsin made a remarkable political comeback. In the 1989 elections to the Congress of People's Deputies, he won a Moscow at-large seat with almost 90 percent of the vote. The following year he was elected to the Russian republic's parliament with over 80 percent of the vote. He was then elected its chairman in June 1990. In 1991, he was elected President of Russia, receiving 57 percent of the vote. Thus, he had won three major races in three successive years. He was reelected as president in 1996 in a dramatic, come-from-behind race against the leader of the Communist Party.

In foreign policy, Yeltsin generally regarded maintaining good relations with the United States as being of paramount importance, despite a growing set of serious policy differences over issues such as Russia's brutal war in Chechnia, the admission of new members to NATO, American military actions against Serbian aggression in Bosnia and in Kosovo, and Russia's squandering of IMF loans and credits through corruption. It was extremely important to Yeltsin that the West grant Russia the status of an equal partner in great-power deliberations, and he recognized how important Western trade and investment were for the future revival of the

(continued)

Close Up 4.1 *(continued)*

economy. Russia's methods for fighting Chechen rebel forces provoked worldwide condemnation because of the massive civilian destruction and refugee flight they brought about, but it was also Yeltsin who, in 1996, accepted the need for a peaceful political resolution of the conflict and signed a truce agreement with the Chechen leadership providing for a withdrawal of federal forces.[1]

Yeltsin's last years in office were notable for his lengthy spells of illness and for the carousel of prime ministerial appointments he made. The entourage of family members and advisers around him, dubbed colloquially "the Family," seemed to exercise undue influence over him on behalf of a clique of powerful state bureaucrats and financial tycoons. He became preoccupied with finding a successor who would protect his security and his political legacy and in 1999 settled on Vladimir Putin as the right candidate. Following the success of the hastily concocted pro-Kremlin party, Unity, in the Duma elections of December 1999, Yeltsin decided to resign six months ahead of the expiration of his term in order to give Putin an edge in running for president. Upon his retirement, Yeltsin became a private citizen and generally stayed out of the public limelight. He resurfaced with his old rival Mikhail Gorbachev to attend President Putin's inauguration on May 7, 2000.

[1]For a firsthand account of U.S.–Russian relations during the 1990s, see Strobe Talbott, *The Russia Hand* (New York: Random House, 2002). Talbott was President Clinton's senior policy adviser on Russia policy, and offers fascinating firsthand accounts of meetings with Yeltsin. For a detailed biography of Yeltsin, see Leon Aron, *Yeltsin: A Revolutionary Life* (New York: St. Martin's, 2000). George Breslauer, in *Gorbachev and Yeltsin as Leaders* (Cambridge, England: Cambridge University Press, 2002), provides a systematic comparison of the leadership styles of Gorbachev and Yeltsin.

however, particularly in Central Asia, the entrenched political elite was able to maintain its control in much the same way as it had done in the past. The same pattern was apparent in the 1990 elections as well: Candidates who were state officials managed for the most part to win their races by avoiding direct confrontation with well-organized opposition movements, but, especially in major cities, new political movements succeeded in electing democratically minded candidates to the republican and local soviets.

Democracy and the End of "Descriptive Representation." The results of the new, open elections differed considerably from the old system in social makeup of the elected deputies. For one thing, voters generally rejected the social tokenism of the old system. This is reflected most dramatically in the sharp decline in the number of women, workers, and collective farm workers among the new deputies. Women fared poorly in the 1989 all-union elections, where they comprised only 17 percent of the candidates and an equal percentage of the winners. They were still more disadvantaged in the 1990 elections to the Russian Republic parliament, where they comprised 7.2 percent of candidates and 5.4 percent of winners. Workers suffered a similar drop in their representation. Table 4.1 illustrates the sharp decline in the rates of representation of two of the social groups affected by the old system of quotas in the soviets, women and workers.

Second, these early elections were not structured by party. Broad political coalitions with ideological identities did form, but they were informal, loose movements based on shared ideological outlooks rather than organized parties capable of turning out loyal followers. Only in the 1993 and 1995 parliamentary elections did voters have a choice among actual parties. For the first time parties

TABLE 4.1
Workers' and Women's Representation in USSR and Russian Federation Assemblies
(as percentage of elected deputies)

	Manual Workers	Women
1. USSR Supreme Soviet (1970) (N = 1,500)	31.7	30.5
2. USSR local soviets (1971) (N = approx. 2 million)	36.5	45.8
3. USSR Supreme Soviet (1984) (N = 1,500)	35.2	32.8
4. Russian Republic Supreme Soviet (1985) (N = 975)	35.8	35.3
5. USSR Congress of People's Deputies (1989) (N = 2,250)	18.6	17.1
6. USSR Supreme Soviet (1989) (N = 542)	24.7	18.4
7. Russian Republic Congress of People's Deputies (1990) (N = 1,026)	5.9	5.4
8. Local Russian Republic soviets (1990) (N = 702,268)	24.9	35.0
9. State Duma of the Federal Assembly (January 1994) (N = 450)	1.3	13.5
10. State Duma of the Federal Assembly (January 1996) (N = 450)	n.a.	10.2
11. State Duma of the Federal Assembly (January 2000) (N = 450)	.65	7.7

Note: N refers to the number of seats or mandates in the given assembly.

begin to link the preferences of segments of the electorate with the policy-making processes of the state. Yet the process of developing a system of nationally competitive parties remained painfully slow.

As in other countries undergoing a transition from communism to democracy, members of the "prestige" elite formed a large share of the first generation of elected politicians as voters looked to turn out the existing political establishment.[50] Candidates' prior political experience was often a liability in the voters' eyes. Later elections, however, witnessed a backlash against the antiestablishment politics of the 1989–1990 period. This is because of the sharp disappointment that most people felt over the results of the change of regime. The very label of *democrat* became a pejorative name, often coupled with the term, *so-called*. The intellectuals who entered politics in 1989–1991 either turned into career politicians, or left the political arena.

Disillusionment with the early wave of democratic populism resulted in a sharp decline in electoral turnout. In 1989 total turnout for elections of deputies to the new all-union Congress of People's Deputies was 90 percent. In 1990, turnout for the elections of deputies to the new Russian Congress of People's Deputies was 76 percent. Seventy-four percent of the electorate took part in the 1991 presidential election in Russia. Sixty-nine percent voted in the Russian referendum of April 1993 on approval of President Yeltsin and his government.

At the end of 1993, after Yeltsin forcibly dissolved the parliament and demanded new elections to a parliament whose structure he instituted by decree, turnout fell further. Anticipating that turnout would be low, Yeltsin decreed that elections of representatives to the parliament would be valid if turnout in a district was at least 25 percent, and that a candidate would be elected if he or she received more votes than any other candidate. For passage of the constitutional referendum, however, Yeltsin decreed that at least half of the registered voters in the country would have to take part in the voting and that at least half of them would have to have approved it. President Yeltsin and his administration went to considerable lengths to ensure the constitution's passage. Regional heads of administration were placed under heavy pressure by President Yeltsin to achieve a 50 percent turnout and a majority for the constitution. In the end, the government declared that some 54.8 percent of the electorate had voted and that of these, 58.4 percent cast their ballots in favor of the constitution. However, these official figures may overstate the actual level of turnout. According to estimates by a respected team of researchers, actual turnout was probably closer to 46 percent, which implied that the constitution had, in fact, not been adopted.[51] While these charges were stoutly refuted by election officials,[52] the precipitous decline in electoral participation was a warning to all sides that many citizens no longer considered voting worth the effort. Turnout in many regional and local races was still lower in the 1990s.

However, turnout, at least in national elections, began to rise again in the mid-1990s. Perhaps because of the efforts by parties to mobilize voters for their leaders, voter turnout in the December 1995 parliamentary elections was almost

---

TABLE 4.2

Voter Turnout in Russian Parliamentary and Presidential Elections (official figures)

Election	Turnout (%)
Presidential election 1991	74.7
Duma election 1993	54.8
Duma election 1995	64.8
Presidential election 1996	
First round	69.8
Second round	68.9
Duma election 1999	60.4
Presidential election 2000	68.8

---

65 percent and it was still higher for the two rounds of the presidential election in 1996. Table 4.2 shows the figures for electoral participation in parliamentary and presidential elections in the 1990s.[53] It may be that the vigorous campaigns mounted by the parties in the elections, including heavy—but heavily biased—television news coverage and advertising, have had the effect of persuading voters that their interests were at stake in these elections.[54] Evidently no matter how disillusioned voters may feel with democratic politics, they see a link between their participation in the electoral process and the country's future. A survey in 1995 found that 53 percent of respondents agreed with the proposition that elections could "change something in the life of our country."[55] Yet many Russians in 1993 and 1995 were not so much voting for particular parties, programs, and candidates as they were voting *against* them.[56] Few Russians feel any sense of loyalty to or identification with a party, and fewer still trust parties in general. Only around 22 percent of Russian respondents in a 1994 survey reported feeling close at all ("very close," "somewhat close," or "not very close") to a political party, and only 7 percent reported that they could trust political parties to look after their interests.[57] According to Timothy Colton, who conducted a systematic study of partisanship in Russia, only about 40 percent of Russian voters in 1995 both expressed a feeling of attachment to a particular party and also voted for it: The rest either voted for a different party or had no particular feeling of identification with any party.[58] The low level of attachment between voters and parties helps explain the fact that small but significant shares of the electorate choose the "against all" box on the ballot form or cast an invalid ballot (see Table 4.3).

Backlash against Democratic Populism.   Besides the ebbing turnout in elections in the early to mid-1990s, another effect of the disillusionment with radical democratic expectations was a backlash against democratic candidates and parties. This trend was worrisome to President Yeltsin and his supporters. Yeltsin's

——————————————————————— TABLE 4.3 ———————————————————————
"Against All" Votes and Invalid Ballots

As percentage of all valid ballots cast	Against all (%)	Invalid ballots (%)
1993 Duma election (party list vote)	4.36	3.10
1995 Duma election (party list vote)	2.8	1.9
1996 Presidential election		
First round	1.5	1.4
Second round	4.8	0.7
1999 Duma election (party list vote)	3.3	1.29
2000 Presidential election	1.99	0.94

political successes had always come about through his ability to appeal to the public at large for support. The results of the April 1993 referendum showed that his faith in his popular support was not misplaced: Whatever the missteps and failures of the democratic reformers who came to power in 1990 and 1991, the public preferred Yeltsin to his communist opponents in parliament. He and his administration evidently underestimated, however, the extent of public dissatisfaction with the government. Both the December 1993 parliamentary elections and a series of regional and city elections in 1993 and 1994 showed that the day when democratic reformers could win elections with a platform calling for rejection of the old communist regime had passed. In several regional races in 1993, candidates running for the post of chief regional executive (governor) won who were former party and government officials. In the parliamentary elections of December 1993, the reorganized Communist Party and its Agrarian Party ally together took 20 percent of the party list vote, while the extremist Liberal Democratic Party of Vladimir Zhirinovsky, running on a demagogic and xenophobic platform, won 23 percent of the party list vote. The party associated with the radical economic reforms carried out by the government, Russia's Choice, won only 15.5 percent of the party list vote.[59] Most observers were surprised at the degree to which democratic reformers had been repudiated and disturbed at the strength of support for antidemocratic parties.

The December 1995 elections produced an even higher share of votes for antireform parties, although the total proportion of votes cast for reform-oriented parties remained roughly similar to the 1993 results. Now, instead of Zhirinovsky winning 23 percent and the communists 12 percent of the party list vote, the communists won 22 percent and Zhirinovsky 11 percent. Most analysts concluded that the opposition parties were mainly competing for the same constituency while the pro-reform electorate tended to hold its own.[60] The core constituencies for basic ideological alternatives may therefore be relatively stable even though the party system is in flux. Moreover, the June–July 1996 presidential election, where Gennadii Ziuganov's support could not rise beyond a ceiling of about 40 percent, suggested that however unpopular President Yeltsin and the current postcommunist leadership was, the majority of voters were unwilling to endorse a return to communist rule. Only 35 percent of the respondents in 1996 agreed with the statement that it would be better to restore the communist system.[61]

Thus since the late 1980s political participation in Russia has undergone enormous change. Perestroika upset the old model of directed participation—where the rituals of lip service to communist ideals were complemented by a modest undercurrent of unlicensed activity and a great deal of parochial contracting between citizens and state. Initially Gorbachev's reforms stimulated a great surge of popular involvement in new forms of participation. This wave of activism brought a generation of democratic political leaders to power, some of them intellectuals from outside the political establishment, others young and ambitious politicians. A few, like Yeltsin, were ranking officials of the old regime who became champions of change. Then this wave passed, leaving many fewer informal organizations behind but still giving citizens numerous opportunities to cast ballots in local and national elections. In its wake was widespread disillusionment with the promise of reform and a broad withdrawal of the populace from political participation except for voting in elections.

At the high point of democratic mobilization in the late 1980s and early 1990s, levels of some kinds of political participation in Russia approached those in North American and European political systems. Surveys taken in 1990, 1991, and 1992 found that around 15 percent of Russian citizens reported having contacted a newspaper or magazine at least once; around 20 percent had contacted an elected official; 30 percent had participated at least once in a rally or demonstration; and a third had signed a petition.[62] These rates were comparable to, and in some cases, higher than, those found in Western Europe and North America. On the other hand, levels of membership in voluntary associations in Russia were far lower than in other democracies. Only 6 percent of Russian respondents in the 1992 survey reported having joined a social organization or initiative group and only 2 percent reported belonging to a political party or movement.[63] Moreover, the surveys showed a tendency for participation to fall off in 1992. As the researchers put it, "the 'defeat' of the old regime and the beginning of a new political phase occurs at the end of 1991."[64]

Summing up, the evidence indicates that apart from voting, there is little popular participation in organized political activity in Russia, and the sense of powerlessness is widespread. This discourages efforts to organize for collective benefit. This situation replicates a much older pattern of political disengagement by the Russian people from the authorities, one that survived even the Soviet regime's strenuous efforts to turn the masses out in a variety of forms of state-sponsored channels of activity. For a brief time in the late 1980s, there was an upsurge of voluntary participation in a variety of political and social efforts. But it subsided quickly once the old regime fell and was replaced by the new system, with its difficulties and disappointments. The low expectations that people held of the government were matched by government's poor performance, forming a "low-level equilibrium trap" in which the low level of actual demand for good government was matched by an equally meager supply of it.

The alienation of the populace from public life is reinforced by the high level of inequality in income and wealth, which has widened as a result of the economic changes occurring in Russia since 1991. As in other societies with high disparities in economic resources, the political system may act so as to deepen inequality rather than to offset it. As we saw, in most countries, people with higher levels of education and income tend to be more active in politics.[65] However, in most societies *voting* reflects a somewhat different pattern than other forms of participation, such as joining political associations or taking part in campaigns. Voting requires much less effort than many other forms of political activity and so tends to be more readily accessible to poorer, less mobile, and more marginal strata of a society. Participation in elections, therefore, for individuals with low education and income levels depends on the success of parties and interest groups in motivating them to take part. A competitive party system thus offsets some of the effects of inequality in social status that are reflected in other forms of political participation. Therefore although participation in Russia lacks a sturdy foundation in organizational membership, the relatively high partipation in elections contested by opposing parties is at least one bridge across the gap separating the populace from the regime. But, given the skepticism and mistrust with which Russians view both parties and elections, it is a frail bridge at best.

ELITE ADAPTATION AND REPLACEMENT

Political Recruitment, Old and New

Like other features of the pre-Gorbachev Soviet political system, the method by which political elites were chosen was carefully regulated by the Communist Party. The filling of any position that carried important administrative responsibility or that was likely to affect the formation of public attitudes was subject to party approval. The system for recruiting, training, and appointing individuals for positions of leadership was called the *nomenklatura* system, and those individuals who were approved for the positions on *nomenklatura* lists were informally called, the *nomenklatura*. Many citizens thought of them as the true ruling class in Soviet society.

Members of the *nomenklatura* did enjoy certain privileges, minor ones in the case of lesser posts, substantial ones for positions carrying greater status and authority. For much of the post-Stalin era, their careers were relatively secure: Only in cases of severe incompetence or malfeasance were they likely to be removed entirely from the ranks of the privileged. Some organizations, such as the trade unions, were considered "retirement homes" for older or less able officials, while postings to others were considered necessary stepping-stones for political advancement. Many officials, for instance, spent a tour of duty as a full-time functionary for the Communist Party itself before reentering jobs in government or economic management.

The party used the *nomenklatura* system to enforce lower officials' accountability for their actions, although it was a relatively inefficient mechanism. Among other effects, the *nomenklatura* system fostered the formation of patron–client relationships: A leader was often more interested in subordinates' political loyalty in party power struggles than in their merits as administrators. These networks evidently contributed to elite cohesion and coordination and thus helped stabilize the political regime in much the same way that corruption, to which patronage was often linked, helped to redistribute resources and therefore iron out certain rigidities in the centrally planned economy. But this flexibility came at a very high price, which was ultimately paid by the political regime as a whole. The undermining of party policy and principles by the pursuit of private ends, the ubiquity of mediocrity and incompetence, and the impunity of corruption all corroded the foundations of the regime. Finally, as the entire Brezhnev-era political elite entrenched itself into power, growing older and older through the 1960s, 1970s, and 1980s, upward mobility ground to a near halt, blocking the opportunities for advancement by succeeding cohorts of elites. Not the least of the reasons for the collapse of the Soviet system was the frustration of their aspirations for a larger share of power.[66]

Changing Patterns of Elite Recruitment. The democratizing reforms of the late 1980s and early 1990s made two important changes in the process of elite recruitment. First, the old *nomenklatura* system crumbled along with other Communist Party controls over society. Second, although most members of the old ruling elites adapted themselves to the new circumstances and stayed on in various official capacities, the wave of new informal organizations and popular elections brought about an infusion of new people into elite positions. Thus the contemporary Russian political elite consists of some people who were recruited under the old *nomenklatura* system together with a smaller share of individuals who have entered politics through new democratic channels. The political elite has not simply reproduced itself from the old regime to the new; nor has it been completely rejuvenated.[67] It would be fairer to say that it has been expanded to accommodate the influx of new, often younger, politicians who have come in to fill positions in representative and executive branches. In numerous cases, the old guard have successfully adapted themselves to the new conditions, and, drawing upon their experience and contacts, have found different high-status jobs for themselves. But the new wave of young politicians who have come up through elections to local and national soviets have also found positions in the political elite in both the legislative and executive branches. And a large number of both old-guard officials and new-wave entrepreneurs have become part of a new business elite.

The Russian public opinion research institute VTsIOM studies Russia's contemporary social and political elite.[68] In one survey, VTsIOM compared a sample of more than a thousand people who had held senior *nomenklatura* jobs in

1988 with an equivalent group holding leading positions in the state administration, politics, science, culture, and economic management in 1993. The results showed that the great majority of the 1993 elite either had held *nomenklatura* jobs in 1988 or came from positions that were in the "reserve *nomenklatura*"— positions such as deputy director of important institutions rather than director. Only 16 percent had entered elite positions without having had any administrative experience at all. By the same token, 57 percent of the old *nomenklatura* group had been able to stay in administrative positions in the state or economy; another 18 percent found reasonably high but not top-level positions. Most of those who failed to stay in the elite were over 60 years of age. Clearly the old elite has managed to survive in positions of power and influence.

One major reason for their success in staying in power was the value of their social connections. Among those of the current elite who were former Communist Party members, former full-time party officials made up three-quarters, suggesting that their personal networks had helped them withstand the collapse of communist rule. Other factors, however, are education and youth. The new elite, on average, was ten years younger than the old one, reflecting a generational turnover that had probably been over long in coming. Over 20 percent had never been Communist Party members.

Turnover was least among the economic managers and greatest among those in politics. Seventy percent of those in economic elite positions in 1993 had held *nomenklatura* jobs in 1988 as enterprise managers or ministerial officials. But of those holding top government positions, only one-third had been in *nomenklatura* jobs in 1988. Still, even those holding jobs in the state and Communist Party bureaucracy in 1988 were often able to hold on to their elite status: One-third of state bureaucrats in 1988 were still in the state bureaucracy in 1993. Of party officials in 1988, 20 percent had taken top-level positions in the state bureaucracy and 40 percent were in high managerial jobs, such as executives in state firms and holding companies.

Continuity through adaptation thus accounts for a larger share of the members of the new Russian political elite than does turnover through democratic renewal. This is perhaps logical in view of the largely peaceful nature of the transition from communist rule in Russia. Quite clearly, the old *nomenklatura*—which comprised most of the people who possessed leadership and administrative experience at the time that the old system fell apart—had to be the principal pool from which political and bureaucratic officials in the post-1991 period were drawn. In this connection the variations in the degree to which various elements of the new political elite come out of the old *nomenklatura* are telling.

There are two major differences between elite recruitment in the old system and the present. The closely integrated *nomenklatura* system of the Soviet regime meant that in every walk of life, those who held positions of power and responsibility were cleared or appointed by the party. They thus formed different sections of a more or less integrated political elite, whose members owed their positions to their political loyalty and usefulness. But today, there are multiple, albeit overlapping, elites (political, business, scientific, cultural, diplomatic, and so on), with no one overarching mechanism for grooming and selecting their members. Second, multiple streams of recruitment form the elite. Some old-guard party and state officials have found niches for themselves in state adminis-tration in the present regime. But many new-wave politicians have climbed the ladder of success in elections or have entered the political elite after careers in business or science. Therefore, depending on which elite group we examine, we see a mixture of old and new channels of recruitment. The officials in the exec-utive branch and the presidential administration, for instance, come overwhelm-ingly out of careers in state administration.

Regions also differ in the degree to which the political elite is open to out-siders. Some regions have political regimes that have tended to preserve the old patterns of elite recruitment and the old political elite. In others, democratiza-tion and economic reforms have brought an intake of new people into the polit-ical elite.[69]

Finally, one of the most marked changes since the fall of the Soviet regime has been the formation of a new business elite. To be sure, many of its mem-bers come out of the old Soviet *nomenklatura*, as old-guard bureaucrats discov-ered ways to cash in on their political contacts, "turning power into money," as a Chinese expression puts it. Some people estimate that money from the Com-munist Party found its way into the establishment of as many as a thousand new business ventures, including several of the first commercial banks. (Party officials diverted money into overseas investments as well, creating several hun-dred firms outside the former Soviet Union.)[70] As early as 1987 and 1988, officials of the Communist Youth League (Komsomol) began to see the possi-bilities of cashing in the assets of the organization and started liquidating them in order to set up lucrative business ventures, such as video salons, banks, discos, tour agencies, and publishing houses.[71] They benefited from their insider contacts, obtaining business licenses, office space, and exclusive con-tracts with little difficulty.

But many other members of the new business elite rose through channels outside the state. Many, in fact, entered business in the late 1980s, as new oppor-tunities for legal and quasi-legal commercial activity opened up. A strikingly high proportion of the first generation of the new business elite comprised young scientists and mathematicians working in research institutes and universi-ties.[72] The new commercial sector sprang up very quickly: By the end of 1992 there were nearly 1 million private businesses registered, with some 16 million people working in them.[73]

We will come back to the private sector in Chapter 7. Our purpose here is to make two points. First, as we have already seen, there has been a major shift in the pattern of recruitment of political elites. The formation of the political elite has become much more diverse than in the old regime, and the old *nomenklatura* elite has accommodated itself successfully to the new system. Some of the old elites have gone on to high positions in the state bureaucracy in the new regime, but others have entered the business elite. Second, the new busi-ness elite is closely tied to the state. Powerful financial-industrial conglomerates have formed close and often collusive relations with ranking state administrators and legislators. The same pattern is evident at the regional and local levels as well, as political leaders and business elites form close relations of mutual dependence. Businesses need licenses, permits, contracts, exemptions, and other benefits from government; political officials in turn need financial contributions to their campaigns, political support, favorable media coverage, and other benefits that business can provide. The climate of close and collusive insider relations between many businesses and many political leaders has nurtured widespread corruption and the meteoric rise of the business tycoons popularly known as *oligarchs*. This atmosphere has created a situation where money has replaced connections as the way to get things done. The old system was constructed around the party's monopoly on political power, including its control of participation and recruitment: People could not freely organize to change policy, but they could turn to influential officials to get a policy modified, ignored, or enforced to serve a pressing personal need. Now the rise of a new business elite has created numerous opportunities for government officials to enrich themselves.

Thus there has been a considerable change in the patterns of political elite recruitment in Russia, just as there has been in the forms of participation. Gone is the centralized control exercised through the *nomenklatura* system, which used the channels of mass participation as recruiting pools for ruling elites. In the old regime, to make an official career, an individual had to stay in the good graces of higher-level party officials. Today alternative routes to power and influence are available through electoral politics and business. Even though the largest share of the present-day political elite is drawn from the old *nomenklatura*, today elections play an important part in bringing fresh political forces into power. In turn, election to representative bodies is often a springboard into other elite positions. With time, therefore, fewer new officials will have risen through the *nomenklatura* system and more will have entered local and national politics through competitive elections. Yet even though the political elite is itself more diverse, and there is a greater diversity of elite groups, business and political elites often share common origins in the old Soviet elite as well as a common interest in preserving their privileges by shutting the doors to competition from outsiders.

Summing Up. In this chapter we have seen that the pattern of mass alienation and disengagement that characterizes Russia in the 1990s followed a surge of popular mobilization in the late 1980s and early 1990s, much of it motivated by radical democratic, populist, and nationalist aims. This wave then ebbed and left widespread disillusionment and mistrust toward government in its wake. At the same time survey research consistently finds that Russians value their democratic freedoms, including the freedom to vote (or *not* to vote), to practice religion, and to criticize the regime.

We noted that the current alienation of citizens from the state echoes an older model of Russian political life, which some have called the image of *dual Russia,* while looking very different—on the surface, at any rate—from the picture of mass participation in public life that the Soviet regime presented. In the Soviet period, everyone belonged to a trade union; participation in youth activities was nearly universal; a massive vote turnout effort got nearly all citizens to the polls to elect deputies to soviets in uncontested elections; 2 million people served on a part-time basis as deputies to soviets at different levels; and membership figures in huge, state-directed public associations were enormous.

Yet actual participation was much lower than the reported figures suggested and public associations did not result in the formation of much usable social capital that could help people cooperate in bearing the burden of providing good government. In today's Russia, the low level of demand for good government is matched by the correspondingly low supply of it. The rise in political rights may have been accompanied by the massive withdrawal of citizens from involvement in direct political participation and in public associations more generally, but society was deprived of the foundation of public-spiritedness, cooperativeness, and reciprocal trust that encourages government officials to be responsive, honest, and fair-minded.

The breakdown of the Soviet system of state-directed political participation had another set of effects as well. In the old regime, as in any political system, participation was closely tied to the mechanisms for generating political leadership. In the Soviet regime, this process was tightly regulated by the Communist Party, which used the *nomenklatura* system to ensure that the political elite was loyal and dependent on the party. No matter what sphere of state or society responsible officials worked in, they owed their positions and future careers to the party's favor. *Nomenklatura* officials came up through the ranks of mass organizations such as the party, youth leagues, trade unions, and so on, so the breakdown of party control over mass participation meant that elites in the 1990s became more diverse in their origins. Some entered politics through elections, others from business. Similarly, some of the old *nomenklatura* elite, having lost their former positions, readily found new jobs in the state administration or in business. Either way, ties between business and the state remain close and often collusive, reinforcing the widespread view that if in the old system, it took connections and influence to solve problems and get ahead, today it takes money.

REVIEW QUESTIONS

1. What is social capital? How can it affect the quality of democracy?
2. How would you explain the low levels of political participation in Russia today in light of the fact that formal mass participation in the Soviet system was very high?
3. What were the main forms of political dissent under the Soviet regime? In view of the fact that the regime was able to suppress dissidents, would you say that it had any effect on the political system?
4. Explain the mechanisms for horizontal and vertical integration of political elites under the old Soviet regime. How did they help keep the system stable? How did they contribute to the system's rigidity?

5. What were the main types of protest and popular mobilization in the late 1980s? Did they have any lasting impact on the post-Soviet Russian political system?
6. What were the elections of 1989, 1990, and 1991, and what was their significance for the end of the Soviet regime?
7. What was the *nomenklatura* system and why was it essential to preserving the Communist Party's political control under the Soviet regime? How might it have contributed to the downfall of the regime?
8. What are the main differences between the channels of elite recruitment under the old system and today? What are the continuities between the old political elite and the current elite?

ENDNOTES

1. Sidney Verba, Norman H. Nie, and Jae-on Kim, *Participation and Political Equality: A Seven-Nation Comparison* (Cambridge, England: Cambridge University Press, 1978).
2. Sidney Verba, Kay Lehman Schlozman, and Henry E. Brady, *Voice and Equality: Civic Voluntarism in American Politics* (Cambridge, Mass.: Harvard University Press, 1995). This volume presents a detailed examination of the way time, money, and civic skills affect patterns of political participation in the United States.
3. Joel D. Aberbach, Robert D. Putnam, and Bert A. Rockman, *Bureaucrats and Politicians in Western Democracies* (Cambridge, Mass.: Harvard University Press, 1981).
4. Verba, Schlozman, and Brady, *Voice and Equality*, pp. 313–33.
5. A public good, as opposed to a private good, is *nonrivalrous;* that is, it cannot be diminished in quantity as individuals consume it; one person's enjoyment of it does not lessen another person's opportunity to enjoy it. And it is *nonexcludable;* that is, one person cannot keep another from enjoying it. So, public goods typically tempt people to "free ride" on the efforts of others, since those who produce them cannot measure or meter others' use of them.
6. Robert D. Putnam, with Robert Leonardi, et al. *Making Democracy Work: Civic Traditions in Modern Italy* (Princeton,N.J.: Princeton University Press, 1993); Robert D. Putnam, *Bowling Alone: The Collapse and Revival of American Community* (New York: Simon and Schuster, 2000).
7. As Putnam and other scholars have pointed out, social capital can divide groups as well as link them. The members of an ethnic minority or religious cult may have dense social ties with another but these may serve more to isolate them from the rest of society than to integrate them. At their most extreme, divisive forms of social capital can foster extremism, intolerance, and exclusion.
8. Richard Rose, William Mishler, and Christian Haerpfer, *Democracy and Its Alternatives: Understanding Post-Communist Societies* (Baltimore: Johns Hopkins University Press, 1998), p. 14.
9. Quoted from Robert C. Tucker, "The Image of Dual Russia," in Robert C. Tucker, *The Soviet Political Mind: Stalinism and Post-Stalin Change*, rev. ed. (New York: W. W. Norton & Co., 1971), p. 122. Miliukov was a political leader in the late tsarist period who went into exile after the Bolshevik Revolution.
10. Richard Rose and Neil Munro, *Elections without Order: Russia's Challenge to Vladimir Putin* (Cambridge, England: Cambridge University Press, 2002), pp. 224–5. The sur-

vey data come from Richard Rose's New Russia Barometer. This is a series of opinion surveys of a nationally representative sample of adult Russians conducted by Russia's premier survey research organization, the All-Russian Center for Public Opinion Research. The most recent survey was conducted in summer 2001.

11. Putnam, *Bowling Alone*, p. 59.

12. Richard Rose, *Getting Things Done with Social Capital: New Russia Barometer VII*, Studies in Public Policy no. 303. (Glasgow: Centre for the Study of Public Policy, University of Strathclyde, 1998), pp. 32–33.

13. Richard Rose, Neil Munro, and Stephen White, *The 1999 Duma Vote: A Floating Party System*, Studies in Public Policy no. 331 (Glasgow: Centre for the Study of Public Policy, University of Strathclyde, 2000), p. 16.

14. Ibid., p. 39.

15. Turnout levels in American presidential elections in the 1970s, 1980s, and 1990s averaged 52–54 percent. Turnout for congressional elections was much lower.

16. Rose, *Getting Things Done with Social Capital*, pp. 35–36.

17. Ibid., pp. 35–36.

18. VTsIOM survey findings, as reported on Polit.ru Web site, 10 January 2001.

19. From a survey in *Novoe vremia*, no. 34, 2001, as reported in RFE/RL Newsline, 4 September 2001.

20. VTsIOM survey findings, as reported on Polit.ru Web site, 10 January 2001.

21. For a good study of the pervasive use of informal connections and means of exchange in the old Soviet system, see Alena V. Ledeneva, *Russia's Economy of Favours: Blat, Networking and Informal Exchange* (Cambridge, England: Cambridge University Press, 1998).

22. See Stephen White's discussion of this process in *Gorbachev and After* (Cambridge, England: Cambridge University Press, 1991), pp. 27–29.

23. Friedgut, *Political Participation*; L. G. Churchward, "Public Participation in the USSR," in Everett M. Jacobs, ed., *Soviet Local Politics and Government* (London: Allen & Unwin, 1983), pp. 38–39; and Jeffrey W. Hahn, *Soviet Grassroots: Citizen Participation in Local Soviet Government* (Princeton, N.J.: Princeton University Press, 1988).

24. Thomas F. Remington, *The Truth of Authority: Ideology and Communication in the Soviet Union* (Pittsburgh, PA: University of Pittsburgh Press, 1998), pp. 123–24.

25. On popular participation in local government, see Friedgut, *Political Participation in the USSR*, Hahn, *Soviet Grassroots*.

26. Wayne Di Franceisco and Zvi Gitelman, "Soviet Political Culture and 'Covert Participation' in Policy Implementation," *American Political Science Review* 78 (1984), pp. 603–21. These forms of *participation*, if that is the right term, included many kinds of parochial contacting (e.g., letters and visits to influential officials and organizations) as well as the use of networks of favor trading and influence peddling.

However, Donna Bahry and Brian D. Silver take issue with this view of Soviet citizen participation. In their article, "Soviet Citizen Participation on the Eve of Democratization," *American Political Science Review* 84 (1990), pp. 821–48, they argue that there is a higher degree of continuity between Brezhnev-era mass participation and the explosive informal associational activity under Gorbachev than is commonly supposed. Analyzing data about attitudes toward and forms of citizen participation from the Soviet Interview Project (SIP), the large U.S. government-funded study of 3,000 emigres to the United States during the 1970s, they show that some of the same attitudes (higher than average levels of interpersonal trust and a sense of personal political efficacy) characterize both within-system and extrasystemic ("dissent") political activists under the Brezhnev regime, and that citizen participation can be differentiated according to the types of individuals and types of activities in which people were engaged. They therefore refute the proposition that citizen participation was largely "for show" and devoid of all interest or benefit for ordinary citizens.

27. A particularly vivid example of the fate of labor protest in the Soviet period occurred in 1962. Following a government decision to raise prices on meat and butter and to lower wages, workers at a large locomotive plant in the city of Novocherkassk went out on a wildcat strike. The government arrested the leaders of the strike. In protest, large numbers of people from the city demonstrated peacefully. Government troops fired on the demonstrators, killing seventy or eighty people. Some of the leaders of the protests were sentenced to death. The state media kept silent about the episode, but news of it spread throughout the country by word of mouth.

See Donald W. Treadgold and Herbert J. Ellison, *Twentieth Century Russia,* 9th ed. (Boulder, Colo.: Westview, 2000), p. 383.

28. On elections, see Victor Zaslavsky and Robert J. Brym, "The Functions of Elections in the USSR," *Soviet Studies* 30:3 (July 1978), pp. 362–71.

29. On the Rodina Society, see John B. Dunlop, *The Faces of Contemporary Russian Nationalism* (Princeton, N.J.: Princeton University Press, 1983), p. 38. See also the article, published posthumously, by the great Soviet journalist Anatolii Agranovskii, "Sokrashchenie apparata," *Izvestiia,* 13 May 1984, which discusses the bureaucratization of Rodina and other nominally public organizations.

30. On the politics of the Church, see John Dunlop, "The Russian Orthodox Church as an 'Empire Saving' Institution," in Michael Bourdeaux, ed., *The Politics of Religion in Russia and the New States of Eurasia* (Armonk, N.Y.: M. E. Sharpe, 1995), pp. 15–40; and Dimitry V. Pospielovsky, "The Russian Orthodox Church in the Postcommunist CIS," Ibid., pp. 41–74.

31. John H. Miller, "The Communist Party: Trends and Problems," in Archie Brown and Michael Kaser, eds., *Soviet Policy for the 1980s* (Bloomington, Ind.: Indiana University Press, 1982), p. 2.

32. Soviet sociologists worked under severe political constraints, but were able to shed some light on how social communication and the formation of public opinion worked in fact. One major study found that despite the fact that the vast majority of the population watched Soviet television and read Soviet newspapers, half or more of the population still relied heavily on conversations with friends, family members, and coworkers for basic information and opinion. Until Gorbachev introduced glasnost, the relative lack of credibility of the mass media meant that people depended heavily on contacts with individuals whom they trusted for acquiring information and shaping opinion.

See Thomas Remington, "The Mass Media and Public Communication in the USSR," *Journal of Politics,* 43:3 (August 1981), p. 804.

33. This point is extensively documented in Ledeneva, *Russia's Economy of Favours,* p. 103 and passim.

34. James L. Gibson, "Social Networks, Civil Society, and the Prospects for Consolidating Russia's Democratic Transition," *American Journal of Political Science* 45:1 (January 2001), pp. 51–68; and Rose and Munro, *Elections without Order,* pp. 223–24.

35. Rose and Munro, p. 125.

36. Ibid., p227.

37. A comprehensive chronicle of such movements is Ludmilla Alexeyeva, *Soviet Dissent: Contemporary Movements for National-Religious, and Human Rights* (Middletown, Conn.:

Wesleyan University Press, 1987). See also Frederick C. Barghoorn, *Detente and the Democratic Movement in the USSR* (New York: Free Press, 1976).

38. Marcia A. Weigle and Jim Butterfield, "Civil Society in Reforming Communist Regimes: The Logic of Emergence," *Journal of Politics* 43:3 (August 1981), p. 804.

39. Zbigniew Brzezinski, "Post-Communist Nationalism," *Foreign Affairs* (Winter 1989/90), pp. 1–2.

40. See Bohdan Harasymiw, *Political Elite Recruitment in the Soviet Union* (New York: St. Martin's Press, 1984).

41. In a similar vein, Stalin once supposedly commented that every republic of the Soviet Union had the right to secede from the union under the 1936 constitution. But, he added, no republic had the right to exercise that right.

42. Vladimir Brovkin, "Revolution from Below: Informal Political Associations in Russia, 1988–1989," *Soviet Studies* 42:2 (April 1990), pp. 233–57; Judith B. Sedaitis and James Butterfield, eds., *Perestroika from Below: New Social Movements in the Soviet Union* (Boulder, Colo.: Westview, 1991).

43. Michael Urban, with Vyacheslav Igrunov and Sergei Mitrokhin, *The Rebirth of Politics in Russia* (Cambridge, England: Cambridge University Press, 1997), p. 115.

44. Brovkin, "Revolution from Below," p. 234.

45. Peter Rutland, "Labor Unrest and Movements in 1989 and 1990," in Ed A. Hewett and Victor H. Winston, eds., *Milestones in Glasnost and Perestroika: Politics and People* (Washington, D.C.: The Brookings Institution, 1991), p. 290.

46. Elizabeth Teague, "Soviet Workers Find a Voice," *Report on the USSR*, Radio Liberty 302/90, 13 July 1990, pp. 13–17.

47. Teague, "Soviet Workers."

48. Sarah Ashwin, "The 1991 Miners' Strikes: New Departures in the Independent Workers' Movement," Radio Liberty Research Report, RL 283/91, 7 August 1991.

49. Ashwin, "The 1991 Miners' Strikes."

50. Gerhard Loewenberg, "The New Political Leadership of Central Europe: The Example of the New Hungarian National Assembly," in Thomas F. Remington, ed., *Parliaments in Transition: The New Legislative Politics in the Former USSR and Eastern Europe* (Boulder, Colo.: Westview, 1994), pp. 29–53.

51. V. Vyzhutovich, "Tsentrizbirkom prevrashchaetsiia v politicheskoe vedomstvo," [The Central Electoral Commission Is Turning into a Political Agency] *Izvestiia*, 4 May 1994. While it is impossible to assess the validity of the charges, it is worth noting that the Central Electoral Commission (CEC) reported that the total number of voters on the registration rolls in December 1993 was lower by 1.14 million voters than the number in April 1993. The lower figure, of course, eased the task of declaring that a majority of voters had turned out for the election. How a million voters had vanished between April and December was not indicated. Moreover, the CEC refused to publish a full tally of election results by electoral district, confining itself to publishing only a list of winners. No independent verification of the CEC's own conclusions was thus possible.

See Vera Tolz and Julia Wishnevsky, "Election Queries Make Russians Doubt Democratic Process," *RFE/RL Research Report* 3:13 (1 April 1994), p. 3.

52. Iu. Vedeneev and V. I. Lysenko, "Vybory-93: Uroki i al'ternativy," *Nezavisimaia gazeta*, 28 June 1994.

53. Note that the Duma elections in 1993, 1995, and 1999 were held in December—when days are shortest and the weather cold. The 1991 presidential election was held on June 12 and required only one round. The 1996 presidential election required two rounds

because no candidate won an outright majority on the first round. These were held June 16 and July 3, respectively. The presidential election in 2000 did not require a second round because Vladimir Putin won an absolute majority of votes on the first round. It was held on March 26 rather than in June, because President Yeltsin's premature resignation forced new elections within three months of the resignation.

54. On the role of the media in the parliamentary elections of 1995 and 1999, see Sarah Oates, "Vying for Votes on a Crowded Campaign Trail," *Transition* (1996) 2: 26–29; and Sarah Oates, "The 1999 Russian Duma Elections," *Problems of Post-Communism* 47:3 (May/June 2000), pp. 3–14.

55. Cited in Stephen White, Richard Rose, and Ian McAllister, *How Russia Votes* (Chatham, N.J.: Chatham House, 1997), p. 190.

56. White, Rose, and McAllister, *How Russia Votes,* pp. 229–30.

57. Ibid., p. 135 (data for 1994); Rose, *Getting Things Done with Social Capital* (data for 1998), p. 58. In the United States, some 87 percent report feeling some level of identification with a political party; in Great Britain, 92 percent do.

58. Timothy J. Colton, *Transitional Citizens: Voters and What Influences Them in the New Russia* (Cambridge, Mass.: Harvard University Press, 2000), p. 130.

59. The December 1993 elections employed a new electoral system that Yeltsin decreed into law. Half of the 450 seats in the lower, popular chamber of the new parliament would be assigned to parties running candidates on national party lists. The other half would go to candidates who won a plurality of the vote in 225 individual districts. The upper house would be made up of two deputies from each of Russia's eighty-nine constituent federal regions (provinces as well as ethnic republics).

60. For example, see Michael McFaul, *Russia between Elections: What the December 1995 Results Really Mean* (Moscow: Carnegie Moscow Center, 1996), p. 4.

61. Richard Rose, *New Russia Barometer VI: After the Presidential Election,* Studies in Public Policy no. 272. (Glasgow, Centre for the Study of Public Policy, University of Strathclyde, 1998), p. 32

62. William M. Reisinger, Arthur H. Miller, and Vicki L. Hesli, "Public Behavior and Political Change in Post-Soviet States," *Journal of Politics* 57 (1995), pp. 941–70.

63. Ibid, p. 959.

64. Ibid, p. 966.

65. Verba, Nie, and Jae-on Kim, *Participation and Political Equality;* Samuel H. Barnes and Max Kaase, eds., *Political Action: Mass Participation in Five Western Democracies* (Beverly Hills, Calif.: Sage Publications, 1979).

66. Boris Golovachev, Larisa Kosova, and Liudmila Khakhulina, *«Novaia» rossiiskaia elita: starye igroki na novom pole? Segodnia,* 14 February 1996.

67. David Lane and Cameron Ross, *The Transition from Communism to Capitalism: Ruling Elites from Gorbachev to Yeltsin* (New York: St. Martin's Press, 1999).

68. Golovachev, Kosova, and Khakhulina, *«Novaia» rossiiskaia elita.*

69. Sharon Werning Rivera, "Elites in Post-Communist Russia: A Changing of the Guard?" *Europe-Asia Studies* 52:3 (2000), pp. 413–32.

70. Igor M. Bunin, ed., *Biznesmeny Rossii: 40 istorii uspekha* (Moscow: OKO, 1994), p. 373.

71. Steven L. Solnick, *Stealing the State: Control and Collapse in Soviet Institutions* (Cambridge, Mass.: Harvard University Press, 1998), pp. 112–24.

72. Bunin, *Biznesmeny Rossii,* p. 386.

73. Ibid., p. 366.

5 The Dynamics of Political Culture

C ontemporary Russian political culture has been strongly shaped by the long and turbulent history of Russian statehood. The Russian state has been transformed many times over the centuries, often through war or revolution. The very identity of the state—whether Russia was to be a nation-state, an empire, a communist republic, a crusade, or a democracy—has been bitterly contested and remains unsettled today. Many Russians believe that their country needs a national idea or spiritual calling to define its institutions and goals, which some still find in communism and others in the country's Russian Orthodox religious heritage. Still others argue that there is no alternative to adopting the universal values of human rights, individual freedom, and the rule of law. Russia's citizens are deeply conscious of being part of a cultural tradition that is neither entirely Western nor Asian, but that has absorbed elements of a number of neighboring civilizations with which it has come into contact.[1]

Broadly speaking, Russia's political culture has been shaped by four forces: the state's geographic location and huge territorial size; the tradition of patri-monial rule; its Orthodox Christian heritage; and, in the last century especially, modernization. These elements of Russia's development as a political commu-nity have influenced the values and beliefs of the population as well as the mu-tual expectations that rulers and populace hold toward one another.

The Russian state became the largest state in the world in territorial terms by the end of the seventeenth century through the centralization of the rule of the Muscovite princes and the expansion of their dominion southward and east-ward. Wars, both of defense and for conquest of new lands, strongly influenced the way the state structured its relations with the people. The challenge of rul-ing so large a domain always strained the resources of the state and encouraged it to place a premium on the development of a capacity for extracting human and material resources from the populace.

By comparison with European states, Russia's state was more absolutist and centralized, and its society weaker in independent resources for self-expression and organization. Russia did not experience the Enlightenment; doctrines of civic and human rights penetrated Russian intellectual culture long after they had been absorbed in Europe. As of the beginning of the twentieth century, four-fifths of Russia's population was still rural and illiterate. The growth of urban property-holding classes was very limited and late by comparison with Western Europe. The ideology of liberal democracy had a negligible following among Russians in the nineteenth century: Much more widespread, particularly among workers and peasants, were radical doctrines of revolutionary socialism. The rise of revolutionary ideologies focusing on the overthrow of the state reflected the long heritage of "dual Russia." For many Russians, the state was an alien and intrusive power that conscripted their young men into the army, enforced the institution of serfdom, rendered arbitrary justice, and sent opponents into exile or hard labor.

For centuries, the tsars symbolized the ideals of state power and glory. Tsarism also provided a focal point for a patrimonial pattern of rule that pervaded Russian political culture. In patrimonialism, the ruler considers his domain to be his private property rather than a community with sovereign rights and interests. A patrimonial ruler is not accountable to his subjects, but treats them as a landowner treats an estate—neglecting it or developing it, as the case might be, but never conceiving it as autonomous of his rule. Some tsars sought to expand the state, others to rationalize their rule, but none until the twentieth century thought it necessary to grant the country a constitution. The bureaucracy was secretive, riddled with corruption, and resistant to change. In neither the tsarist era nor the Soviet period were there institutions providing for the control of the bureaucracy by elected representatives or by courts of law: State officials were accountable to their superiors and ultimately to the tsar, but not to the people or to the law.

In turn the tsar was considered to be subordinate only to God; the people—nobles and commoners alike—were expected to submit to the tsar's absolute authority. The tsar sought to maintain an equal distance from all his subjects, because all classes and estates were equally bound in service obligations to the state. There was no conception of a public sphere or nation outside the state until late in the history of the empire. The idea that a strong state required a strong civil society was largely alien to Russian political culture until the late 1980s and the 1990s. Even when the tsar finally granted a constitution, following the 1905 revolution, the state did not evolve into a constitutional monarchy. Soon afterward, the First World War, which imposed insuperable strains on Russia's capacity to mobilize and supply a huge army, overwhelmed tsarism in the revolutions of 1917. First the tsar abdicated and was replaced by a short-lived provisional government. A half year later that government was pushed aside by the Bolsheviks in the October revolution.

Besides patrimonialism, Russia's cultural heritage was also marked by the close identification between state and church. Tradition holds that Grand Prince Vladimir of the Kievan city-state called Rus' (officially regarded by Russian historians as the predecessor of the contemporary Russian state) was baptized into the Eastern Orthodox faith in 988. By choosing the Byzantine or Eastern branch of Christianity for the spiritual ideology of his rule, Vladimir linked Russia with the Byzantine empire for trade and political relations. The impact of Orthodoxy has been felt strongly in Russian political culture, much as Roman Catholicism and Protestant Christianity have shaped West European legal and political traditions. Orthodox Christianity is organized into national churches, which are regarded as the spiritual patrimony of particular national communities, and in worldly matters each national church practices accommodation to the state authorities. In religious doctrine Orthodoxy values faithfulness to changeless forms of worship and resists new practices or ideas. Its doctrine emphasizes the distance separating the kingdom of heaven from the sinful world.

Orthodoxy in Russia nurtured the value of collectivism and communal harmony and opposed the West's individualism and materialism. It also fostered a sense of a special mission for Russia. In the sixteenth century, some writers went so far as to proclaim Russia the "Third Rome," arguing that with the fall of the two previous seats of Christianity's political power, Rome and Constantinople, Moscow was now destined to become the source of the message that would bring salvation to the world. The great nineteenth-century writer, Fedor Dostoevsky, had a similar conception of Russia's destiny, and echoes of the idea reappeared in the messianic ideology of Russian communism, which claimed to be a doctrine of universal force.

Contemporary Russians are deeply conscious of their distinctive political heritage, but they differ over what this legacy means for the future. We saw in the last chapter that the mistrust and alienation separating ordinary Russians from the state continue to be felt, but that Russians also value the democratic freedoms that have been won since the end of the communist regime. In this chapter we will explore some of the attitudes and values that underpin this contradictory pattern of democratic aspirations and deep skepticism among Russians about the quality of government they expect from the state. We will look at some of the enduring features of Russian political culture as well as ask what long-term and short-term forces are affecting it. And we will ask how political values and beliefs differ across social groups, by age, education, gender, and ethnicity.

One benefit of the opening up of Russia is the opportunity it presents to Russians and outside observers to study objectively the way people evaluate the tremendous changes their society has undergone. Survey research, carried out by Russian and outside teams, has gathered a great deal of information. To be sure, the findings are often contradictory. Perhaps in view of the rapid pace of the changes that have occurred in the last decade, it is not surprising to find that some popular attitudes about political and economic reform are inconsistent or volatile. Indeed, this century has brought overwhelming upheavals: two revolutionary changes of regime, one in the second decade, when the tsarist autocracy fell and gave way to communist rule, and the other in the last decade, when the communist regime in turn was replaced by a regime espousing liberal democratic and market principles. In between Russia experienced world war, famine, Stalin's industrialization and collectivization drives, and mass terror. These experiences have left their imprint on contemporary Russian political culture, as has the equally profound shift from a predominantly rural society with only a small educated stratum to a society that is overwhelmingly urban and highly educated.

Before we look at Russia's political culture more closely, however, let us explain what we mean by political culture and why it matters to understand it.

THE CONCEPT OF POLITICAL CULTURE

Political scientists define political culture as the distribution of people's values, beliefs, and feelings about politics in a particular society. Values are views about what is right or wrong, good or bad. Beliefs are conceptions of the state of the world. Emotions include pride, shame, desire, anger, or resentment felt toward objects in the political environment. A political culture is the totality of the values, beliefs, and emotions of the members of a society expressed about the political regime and about their own place in it.[2]

The subject of political culture has been the source of lively controversy in political science and in the study of Russia and the Soviet Union.[3] A major point of contention is how political culture is related to the structures and institutions of a political system. Political culture is never static, but culture tends to change gradually and incrementally, whereas political regimes sometimes undergo drastic and discontinuous changes. Therefore if political culture *directly* determined how a national political system operates, we could not explain some of the startling transformations in regimes that we have observed in our time. Some countries formerly considered to have deeply conservative, authoritarian political cultures have succeeded in sustaining viable and successful democratic polities after a major constitutional transition. Other countries considered to have had pro-democratic political cultures docilely accepted spells of authoritarian rule. Clearly there can be no simple causal path leading from the distribution of values and beliefs in a society to its form of government at any given point in time. Likewise we should not expect that any particular set of political and social institutions will transform the nature of a country's political culture. If so, we could not explain why so many regimes that have poured resources into shaping their populace's hearts and minds have had so little to show for their effort. Political culture may be malleable, but only up to a point. A country's institutions and its political culture interact and shape one another over time. Where institutions and culture stand in mutually reinforcing equilibrium, we expect change to occur without major ruptures. But in cases where institutions and culture are not congruent, the probability of discontinuities in political development is higher.

Differences across countries in the composition of political cultures are stable over time, but certainly not static. "Culture," political scientist Ronald Inglehart writes, "is not a constant. It is a system through which a society adapts to its environment: Given a changing environment, in the long run it is likely to change."[4] He provides evidence that the political culture of a country does influence its political and economic performance. In turn, the country's performance has a feedback effect on its political culture. For instance, where democracy is successful, its operation is likely to reinforce people's belief that democracy works better than the alternatives. A country locked in a low-level equilibrium trap, as we pointed out in the last chapter, may last for long periods of time because people have no faith that a different political system could work any better.

Still, political cultures can evolve, sometimes changing in significant ways. The succession of generations can bring about deep and lasting changes in the values and beliefs of a society. People in their late teens and early twenties are especially susceptible to formative influences in their political and economic environment. At that age people often come to adhere to orientations that continue to shape their outlook on politics and society for the rest of their lives. We shall see evidence of this phenomenon in Russia.

Political scientists believe that a country's political culture exerts an effect on the development of its political system through both direct and indirect pathways. The direct path is through the influence of people's values and beliefs on their political behavior, including their voting choices at election time. The second is the indirect influence of people's everyday habits, expectations, and values on their relations with the political environment. To the extent that people are able to sustain ties of mutual trust and cooperation in settings outside their immediate circles of family and friends, they are much likelier to be able to solve collective dilemmas, such as how to keep government honest, fair, and responsive. The direct and indirect routes by which political culture affects political life therefore parallel the kinds of political participation discussed in the last chapter: the participation that takes place directly in the political sphere, such as through voting and campaigning, and people's involvement in public life more generally.

The *direct* influence of political culture on the political system by means of voting can be compared to the relationship between consumers and producers in a market economy. In the abstract, consumer demand is supposed to guide the decisions of producers to offer the desired mixture of goods and services at competitive prices. But in the real world, individual consumers have little actual control over the economy because information about what consumers want and need may be hidden to producers and because consumers' knowledge about the quality and availability of what producers offer is never perfect. In a perfect market economy, consumers in the aggregate are sovereign, but no one consumer has much influence over what is produced or the price at which goods are sold. Matching demand and supply is a complex process that in the long run tends to yield an equilibrium between price and quantity. But at any one moment, there is likely to be a gap between what people want and what the economy provides.

The analogy between demand and supply in an economy and political culture and political institutions is useful, up to a point. A democracy will do a better job of matching what people demand and what politicians provide them than would a dictatorship, just as a market economy matches demand and supply for goods more efficiently than would a centrally planned economy. In a democracy, the distribution of people's preferences will influence the way parties and candidates compete for votes. Over time, as people's values and expectations change, leaders offer new policies that match the shifts in voter demand, keeping the demand for and supply of policies in a state of equilibrium.

But, just as there are many obstacles to the smooth matching of demand and supply in real-world economies, likewise political systems may suffer from a gap between the policies and institutions that people want and those that the political leaders offer them. In some societies, people give up expecting that government will supply them with fair and efficient administration, effective public order, or simple justice in the courts. The few brave souls who try to fight for an improvement may quit in discouragement when they fail to stir up their discouraged fellow citizens to join them in the cause. Observing the low demand for good government, rulers do not supply it and instead treat the state as a source of private plunder. Such situations can also become stable and last for long periods of time. In extreme cases, central government disappears altogether and is replaced by warlords or criminal rackets.

Although the influence of political values and beliefs on voting and other kinds of political action is important in guiding political elites about what sorts of promises to make at election time, probably the indirect path by which political culture influences the political system is still more important. Through their daily interactions, members of a society shape one another's values and expectations, including their expectations about government. The patterns of behavior that influence how government operates are established through these channels of association, many of them entirely outside the government sphere. In political cultures in which individuals harbor mistrust for one another, they fear that combining for the common good is a sucker's game: Reasoning that others will take advantage of them if they do not look out for themselves, they avoid committing themselves to any collective effort where the cost is known and immediate, and the payoff distant and uncertain—and dependent on the collective effort. Since good government requires collective effort on the part of citizens to keep officials responsive and effective, societies pervaded by norms of mistrust for those outside the immediate circles of family and friends are likely to be poorly governed. Where people discount the common interest in favor of private benefit, government is likelier to be both more oppressive and more corrupt. Therefore in studying political culture, we need to look at both people's values and beliefs about government as well as their expectations about social life more generally.

RUSSIAN POLITICAL CULTURE IN THE POST-SOVIET PERIOD

A good deal of survey research in the last decade has been devoted to analyzing the dynamics of Russian political culture. On some points, the findings of a large number of recent opinion studies converge. Survey researchers have found a sturdy core of commitment to democratic values in Russian society together with very high dissatisfaction with the current regime and very low levels of confidence in existing political institutions. Support for some features of a market economy is high but low for others, and dissatisfaction with the performance of the current economic system is even lower than that for the political regime. A number of studies have also found that a majority of the population supports the idea that the state should own heavy industry.[5] But generally speaking, surveys show that there is a high level of support for principles associated with liberal democracy, including support for the values of political liberty and individual rights, rights of opposition and dissent, independence of the communications media, and competitive elections.[6] Political scientist James Gibson sums up the findings of a number of studies by drawing three conclusions: There is rather extensive support in Russia for democratic institutions and processes so long as people see these as rights for themselves; there is much less support for extending rights to unpopular minorities; and the segments of the population who are the most exposed to the influences of modern civilization (younger people, more educated people, and residents of big cities) are also those most likely to support democratic values. This would suggest that as Russia becomes more open to the outside world, support for democratic values will grow.[7]

At the same time, as we have seen, dissatisfaction with the current political arrangements is very high: By a majority, Russians rate the present system negatively and by an even wider majority, they rate the pre-Gorbachev communist system favorably. Seventy-two percent of the respondents in Richard Rose's 1998 New Russia Barometer survey gave a positive rating to the pre-Gorbachev Soviet political system, and only 36 percent rated the current regime favorably. Yet these groups overlapped: 26 percent of the respondents evaluated *both* the old and the current regime positively. And almost half (49 percent) of the respondents were reasonably optimistic about the future, giving a positive rating to the political system that they thought would exist in five years.[8]

Democratic aspirations appear to be well established, although they create criteria by which people judge the current situation harshly and can be set aside as people reflect on the relatively higher degree of material security they had under the communist regime. Many more people remember the old regime in a positive light than would want to bring it back: Asked whether they would favor the restoration of the communist system, 41 percent agree (completely or somewhat) and 59 percent disagree (completely or somewhat), according to Rose's 1998 survey.[9] Eighty-five percent disagree with the notion that the army should rule the country, and 88 percent reject the idea that the tsar should be restored. Sixty-four percent disagree with the proposition that a tough dictatorship is the only way out of the current situation.[10] And optimism about the future is rising. Whereas in 1995, only 40 percent of the respondents gave a positive evaluation of the political system that they expected to exist in five years, by April 2000 some 72 percent rated the future political regime positively.[11]

The rather high levels of support found for basic democratic principles such as religious liberty, freedom of speech, competitive elections, and other rights challenge an impression that was widely held in the West, that Russian political culture was authoritarian, traditional, and influenced by decades of Soviet communist practice and indoctrination. Certainly Soviet propaganda reinforced some older values, such as the enormous emphasis placed on state power, the expectation that the state would provide for the material well-being of its citizens, and the priority of collective over individual needs. Consequently, it is not surprising to find a rather high degree of continuity in the level of support for values concerning the state's responsibility for ensuring society's prosperity and for providing individuals with material security.[12] More than in Western Europe or the United States, Russians continue to believe that the state is responsible for providing a just moral and social order, with justice being understood as social equality more than as equality before the law.[13] This pattern reflects the impact of traditional conceptions of state and society in Russian political culture. How prevalent are the older patterns of collectivism and statism in Russian political culture today?

A number of surveys find that there is broad support for the idea that the state has a responsibility for maintaining basic equality, cohesion, and security for members of society, while guaranteeing economic and political freedom to individuals to the extent consistent with society's well-being. Asked whether individuals or the state bore the basic responsibility for people's well-being, respondents in Richard Rose's New Russia Barometer in 1998 were rather evenly distributed, as Table 5.1 indicates.[14] Again, younger respondents were much likelier to choose the "individual" rather than the "statist" response; the older the age group of the respondent, the larger the proportion who chose the "statist" response.

These and other surveys find that the patterns of values differ significantly across generations and between social groups. Elites and the mass public differ; younger differ from older generations; men differ from women in their political outlooks; urban from rural residents; and the more educated differ from the less educated. People in elite positions and those who participate more in the culture of the modern world are significantly more likely to resemble people in Europe, North America, and other advanced industrial democracies in their values and beliefs.[15]

To be sure, Russians find it very difficult to define their ideological outlooks. Many fewer Russians find the conventional "left–right" political axis meaningful than do citizens of Western democracies; only 56 percent of Russian respondents in a 1996 survey could place themselves on a left–right spectrum and only

---
TABLE 5.1

Russian Views on Individual versus State Responsibility (in percent)

Individuals should be responsible for their own welfare	
Agree definitely	18
Agree somewhat	16

The state should be responsible for everyone's economic security	
Agree definitely	24
Agree somewhat	28
Don't know	13

40 percent could define those terms meaningfully. Yet of those who did have a notion of where they fit on a seven-point scale, where 1 represented the left-most position and 7 the right-most, over half placed themselves at point 4—the exact midpoint of the scale. Only 8 percent or fewer placed themselves at any other position. Evidently there is a strong tendency for Russians to wish to think of themselves as being middle-of-the-roaders.[16]

The strong support for liberal democracy among elites, the relative strength of support for democratic values among the general public, and the weakness of political awareness among the public are somewhat surprising in view of the extensive efforts by the old regime to mold political culture toward support for Soviet-style socialism. In order to understand how contemporary Russian values and beliefs are shaped, it is necessary to examine the old regime's system of political socialization. We need to ask how that system worked, in what ways it was effective and where it failed, how it related to older Russian political traditions, and what its legacy is for today.

SOVIET POLITICAL SOCIALIZATION

Throughout the regime's history, Soviet rulers placed a high priority on inculcating knowledge of and commitment to regime doctrine among the population. The system of formal political socialization embraced virtually every setting of education and communication in society—from schools and youth activity, to the mass media, the arts, and popular culture, and to collective activity in the workplace, place of residence, and avocational groups. As much as possible, influences that contradicted Marxist-Leninist doctrine were suppressed, while the rhetoric of public life constantly reaffirmed the doctrine of the leading role of the Communist Party, the superiority of socialism, devotion to the Soviet fatherland, and the correctness of the party's general policies at home and abroad. Because of the importance the regime assigned to the means of mass communications as agencies of political socialization and of mass mobilization, it saturated Soviet society with multiple channels of print and broadcast communications.[17]

The doctrine that guided political socialization—the doctrine called Marxism-Leninism—was based on the ideas of Karl Marx and Friedrich Engels as interpreted and applied by Vladimir Lenin and by the Soviet Communist Party's leaders. Each new leadership that came to power reinterpreted Marxist-Leninist ideas to serve its policy interests, often discarding concepts promulgated by the preceding leaders. The doctrine was highly flexible and was interpreted to justify the preferences and decisions of the party leadership. Ideological doctrine and political authority were always closely linked, because power and ideology legitimated one another. This pattern was a source of strength so long as there was no serious challenge to the leaders' power or policy. But it also gave rise to a dogmatic intolerance of any criticism of the tenets of the doctrine itself or of the leaders' interpretation of it. Dogmatism in the Brezhnev period, as under Stalin, stifled innovation and serious discussion of the trends affecting society.

The party's demand for political loyalty meant that no alternative political ideologies could be propagated publicly. Soviet leaders acknowledged that the two great ideological alternatives in the world, socialism and capitalism, might be able to coexist, and even cooperate, at the level of diplomacy, trade, and cultural and scientific contacts, but that at the fundamental level of ideas, the two ideologies were ultimately incompatible and that in the end socialism would triumph over capitalism because of its intrinsic superiority. Soviet leaders were hostile to any notion that the struggle between the world system of capitalism and the world system of socialism could lead to a convergence of ideologies. They often quoted Lenin to the effect that any weakening of socialist ideology would inevitably lead to a strengthening of bourgeois ideology. The state's propaganda system thus had a twofold purpose: to persuade Soviet people of the correctness of party doctrine and to prevent hostile ideologies from winning adherents.

The elaborate machinery for propagating and defending ideology included the following features:

1. Efforts to persuade parents to make the family an instrument for raising children steeped in communist morality, firm faith in the party and its leadership, a positive attitude toward labor, confidence in the socialist future, and intolerance toward hostile worldviews, such as religion. But, because the family was the least amenable to control by the party authorities, and because it tended to protect value systems at odds with the official ideology, the family was the most important agency of transmission of liberal democratic values, national awareness, and religious faith.

2. School. Schooling contributed to political socialization both through the curriculum, where lessons in history, social studies, literature, and other subjects were used to reinforce political doctrines, and through a system of youth groups that organized schooltime and after-school activities.

3. Youth groups. The regime maintained a set of organized youth leagues for different age categories that combined political indoctrination with organized activities such as field trips, hobby clubs, service activities, summer camps, and study circles. The system of organized youth activities was divided into three age-specific groups: Octobrists, for 7- to 9-year-olds; Pioneers, for 9- to 14-year-olds, and Komsomol (the acronym for the Communist Youth League) for 14- to 28-year-olds. Each combined play, recreation, and basic socialization with political indoctrination appropriate to the age level. Many youths who remained active in Komsomol into their twenties were admitted directly to the Communist Party from Komsomol on the strength of their good records as Komsomol members.

4. The mass media. Officially the broadcast and print media were to serve as instruments of political socialization in addition to their roles as conduits of needed information, exhortation to work hard and well, criticism of problems, and some feedback from the public through letters. They were thus called upon to mold the consciousness of the population while

at the same time combating the system's inefficiencies. All mass-media organizations were under the ideological authority of the party through its department of propaganda and similar departments charged with ideological oversight in every lower party committee.

5. Adult political education. The party oversaw a system of workplace talks and political study groups for various categories of the population—workers, managers, political executives, and so on. Party-run schools gave local party staff members up-to-date instruction on current party doctrine and policy and even gave graduate degrees in such topics as the theory of scientific communism.

Despite its immense scope, the Soviet political socialization machine never possessed, or even claimed, full control over all possible influences on citizens. Even in the darkest years of Stalinist tyranny, a sphere of private life survived, formed through powerful family and friendship links. So too did something of the legacy of Russian and Western humanism through the great classic works of prerevolutionary literature and art that generations of Soviet schoolchildren were taught to know and respect. Throughout the Soviet Union, intellectuals, artists, and teachers preserved more than a hundred different cultural legacies and national languages. The imperative of providing the Soviet regime with a powerful scientific and technological capability required the regime to accept a certain level of openness to outside influences: Scientific and cultural exchanges of people and ideas, though closely monitored and directed, nonetheless kept open channels through which the diverse influences of the world society filtered in and out of the Soviet Union. As the regime's own ideological machinery grew increasingly ossified and ineffectual in the 1970s and 1980s, these internal and external cultural influences assumed an ever greater importance in shaping Soviet political culture and public opinion.

A second point to remember is that the discrepancy between the beliefs and values that the regime preached, and the actual behavior of officials and citizens, tended to weaken the credibility of regime propaganda. Nearly universal was the understanding that in public certain forms and observances needed to be respected: Certain ritualistic words needed to be uttered and gestures made—one was to quote Lenin in a speech, article, or book. The vote taken at a meeting was to be unanimous; one would dutifully go to the polls to cast a ballot or attend a ceremony celebrating some official event. But these forms and observances had little bearing on one's ordinary, everyday life, both for officials and for citizens. They provided a certain stability and predictability in the forms of social interaction, which might have been comforting to people who had undergone the horrors of revolution, war, and terror in previous decades. These rituals and ceremonies also gave the authorities a convenient way to see whether anyone was bold enough to deviate from the accepted patterns. But few actually believed in the conventional doctrines and principles that were constantly echoed throughout the public domain. The actual rules governing behavior were quite different and diverged strongly among different groups of the population. Younger generations might be attracted to Western popular culture, while the thinning ranks of the older generation still wept each year at the ceremonies commemorating the Soviet victory in the Second World War. In Central Asia, traditional clan ties came to determine the real distribution of power and status, while in the Baltic states, citizens of all strata cherished the dream that they would once again regain national independence. Behind the ritual obeisances to Marxist-Leninist dogmas, Soviet political culture was extremely diverse. This diversity has contributed to the very different trajectories that the different republics have followed since the breakup of the union. Thus the incompleteness and weakening of the political socialization effort, combined with the sharp divergence between what was preached and what was practiced, meant that actual Soviet political culture was being shaped by a variety of home-grown and international influences.

Thus while the state expended substantial effort in the 1960s and 1970s to inculcate its increasingly hollow Marxist-Leninist doctrine, intellectuals in the arts, the sciences, the professions, and even in policy institutes of the party and state were coming to abandon many tenets of Soviet ideology. Elements of social democratic and liberal democratic thought, ethnic nationalism, and a kind of pan-human internationalism gained strength. Some thinkers explicitly rejected Soviet doctrine and clandestinely circulated their writings or those of other authors whose writings had been suppressed among friends.[18] Others tempered their dissent and remained within the system, while discussing their heterodox views in the intimate company of colleagues and friends and inserting cautious, indirect references to critical ideas in their published work.

By the time Gorbachev came to power, many intellectuals, including some in senior positions, were privately convinced that the old theory of an international "class struggle" between rival socialist and capitalist camps was leading the Soviet Union into a developmental dead end. The only way for the country to regain its economic and political strength was to adopt universal values of human rights and freedoms and to join in finding solutions to the challenges facing mankind as a whole. As Robert English has argued, this was a shift in the very conception of Russian national identity. Instead of seeing Russia as being defined by an ideological confrontation with the West, or even arguing that Russia must *cooperate* with the West, an influential body of intellectuals came to believe that Russia must become *part* of the liberal international community.[19] The philosophical ground was thus prepared for the leadership of Mikhail Gorbachev, who, remarkably, proved willing to embrace the radical new thinking that transformed Russia and the world.[20]

Why did the party persist in keeping its program of mass political indoctrination going despite the fact that its efforts were so unsuccessful? Various reasons have been proposed. One is inertia. The section of the party concerned with ideological propaganda and control justified its existence by ever greater quantitative displays of success, increasing the number of people reached and activists recruited. Another is fear. The leadership behaved as though it genuinely believed its claim that any weakening of socialist ideology must necessarily lead to a rise of hostile counterideologies. However ineffective the party's ideological effort may have been, it helped to combat the spread of ideas and values opposed to Marxism-Leninism. Ultimately, the reason ideological control over society was so important to the party was that it prevented the formation of opposition movements espousing alternative ideologies. In any event, no Soviet leader until Gorbachev was willing to relinquish the party's monopoly upon ideology, and even Gorbachev, when he first came to office, used the traditional powers of the general secretary to reprogram and redirect party propaganda, rather than to dismantle the system itself.

At first, Gorbachev's attempt to reform the Soviet economy and to introduce an element of freer debate under the slogan of glasnost (openness) hardly affected either the forms or content of "communist upbringing." Schoolteachers continued to teach children to revere Lenin as one who loved mankind and embodied its highest ideals. As in the past, basic moral education was identified with communist philosophy. Even in secondary school and higher educational institutions, until around 1989, the curriculum was little affected by the ideological ferment occurring in society. Students continued to be required to pass courses on Lenin's and the party's teachings. A scandal occurred in history education in the spring of 1988 when, all across the Soviet Union, history exams in secondary schools had to be canceled because the old history textbooks were considered inaccurate (they glossed over the magnitude of Stalin's terror) and new textbooks were not available. Yet on the whole, the old structures of ideological indoctrination and control continued to soldier on in a traditional spirit until 1989–1990, when the radical changes in the leadership's thinking and behavior finally provoked a crisis at all levels of the propaganda and socialization system.

The mass media also reflected the power of inertia and the slowness with which the ideological changes made at the top rippled out across the hierarchy of media organizations. Before Gorbachev the mass media had been under pervasive political control. The supply of newsprint was controlled by a state monopoly. All printing equipment had to be licensed by the government. The Communist Party selected all senior editors. The content of everything published or aired was subject to prior review by the party's ideological sector. Although unofficial, independent publications existed (called *samizdat*, or *self-publishing*), these were illegal and their publishers and distributors could be arrested and charged with spreading anti-Soviet propaganda.

But after a slow start, the glasnost campaign gained momentum.[21] Eventually it produced a significant feedback effect on the party's socialization program itself by revealing to people how widespread was the rejection of Marxism-Leninism. A poll of nearly 2,700 people throughout the Soviet Union in December 1989 found that 48 percent considered themselves religious believers, but only 6 percent thought that Marxism-Leninism had the answers to the country's problems.[22] Another countrywide survey in 1989 found that 61 percent of the respondents supported the principle of legalizing private property and only 11 percent opposed it.[23] During 1989 and 1990 there were many other indications of the power and speed of popular rejection of communist ideology. Close to 2 million members—one-tenth of the membership—quit the Communist Party before Yeltsin banned it in September 1991. A radical reform wing of the Communist Party itself threatened to break away from the party and form an alternative party.

At the same time, the policy positions taken by Gorbachev and the party leadership grew progressively more unorthodox, until by 1990 almost nothing of the old Marxist-Leninist doctrine remained. The theory of the international class struggle between capitalism and socialism was gone; the party's leading role had been abandoned in favor of support for multiparty competition and parliamentary politics; and Gorbachev called his domestic program a transition to a "social market economy." In the document adopted as a basis for economic policy for 1991 and 1992, Gorbachev himself declared that "there is no alternative to switching to a market. All world experience has shown the viability and effectiveness of the market economy."[24] Characteristic was the appeal to "all world experience" as the authority for the transformation of Soviet ideology.

By the end of 1990, Marxism-Leninism as such was essentially defunct. The doctrine had been abandoned in all essential points by the Communist Party, and the party itself had lost its power to rule the country's ideological life. Both among the leadership and among the populace, only a small minority remained willing to defend communist ideology.

As Marxism-Leninism declined, "bourgeois" political values gained strength—exactly as Lenin predicted. In particular, values associated with liberal democracy became widespread.

SUPPORT FOR DEMOCRATIC VALUES

As soon as survey researchers were able to start conducting objective, scientifically structured opinion surveys in Russia, beginning in 1989–1990, they reported surprisingly high levels of support for democratic rights. For instance, in 1990, James Gibson and a team of American and Soviet researchers conducted a survey of 504 residents of the Moscow oblast—that is, the region around the city of Moscow—to determine support for important values associated with liberal democracy. They found strong support for liberal values. For instance, on such issues as whether freedom of speech should always be respected, they found that Soviet respondents held roughly the same views as citizens of West European countries (77 percent in agreement for the Moscow province population, 78 percent for the West Europeans). On a series of items, measured by the percentage agreeing that a particular right ought always to be respected, Soviet citizens were extraordinarily similar to West Europeans.

In addition, Gibson et al. found that education was positively associated with rights consciousness, much as age (and being female) were negatively correlated with it; these were the only significantly associated variables they established from analysis of demographic factors. The impact of education was particularly strong: On average, the higher a person's educational level, the more likely he or she was to endorse the principle of individual political rights. By the same token, the older a person was, all else being equal, the weaker the support for individual rights. And women were on the whole slightly less supportive of individual rights than were men, even after controlling for the effects of education and age.

Gibson's group extended the survey to the entire Western portion of the USSR in May 1990 and found remarkably similar responses—that is, extremely high levels of support for liberal values with the single exception of the freedom of association, where fewer than half of the respondents agreed that the right must be respected always and around 40 percent believing that it depends on circumstances.[25] Once again, age and education were significantly correlated with rights consciousness, education positively, age negatively.

Given Russia's authoritarian history, it is reasonable to wonder whether findings such as these tap into deep and lasting value systems or capture the slogans and hopes of a particularly optimistic moment in time. As James Gibson puts it, "Like religion, Levis, and Snickers, democracy became fashionable in the USSR."[26] One way to examine this is to see whether Russians are reasonably consistent in their outlooks: For example, do supporters of freedom of the press and freedom of religion also tend to support freedom of association and competitive elections? Survey researchers find a high level of consistency among Russians' beliefs and values, with the exception that support for the political rights of disliked groups is much lower than support for political rights in the abstract. Moreover, surveyers have found that democratic values seem to hold up over time, while support for market institutions is more volatile. Gibson and his colleagues found, using panel data,[27] that between 1990 and 1992, respondents tended to maintain the same political views, while their views on economic institutions diverged sharply.[28]

Consistent with this theme of acceptance of democracy in general and sharp antagonism toward the actual present-day regime are the findings of many surveys that Russians have lower confidence in present-day representative political institutions than in such structures as the army and the Church. Surveys over the past few years have asked a battery of questions about how much Russians trusted various institutions to look after their interests. Table 5.2 reports the results of a 1998 survey.[29] The results suggest much higher levels of confidence in the army and Orthodox Church than in representative institutions. Parties and investment funds compete for the most-distrusted institutions prize.

Another recent survey illustrates the wide gap between trust in family and friends and trust in official institutions, as indicated in Table 5.3. (It also reveals a substantial body of confidence in President Putin.)

Thus surveys confirm the long-standing gap between the mistrust expressed by citizens toward the structures of national government and the representative institutions nominally designed to link them to government, and the trust in family and friends. The latter ties, in fact, remain vital for people who are trying to cope with the difficulties of the present. Rose found, for instance, that two-thirds of the respondents in his 1998 national survey believed that they could borrow up to a week's worth of wages from friends or relatives if they were in

—————————————————— TABLE 5.2 ——————————————————
Trust in Institutions, 1998 (in %) (N = 2,002)

	Trust	Neutral	Distrust
Army	34	22	44
Church	30	17	53
Courts	24	26	50
Television	23	24	53
Newspapers	22	25	52
Police	18	21	60
Local government	18	21	61
President of Russia	14	14	72
Trade unions	14	16	70
Duma	13	17	70
Private enterprises	11	17	72
Political parties	7	12	81
Privatization investment funds	5	9	85

great need.[30] At the same time, over half declared that the government in Moscow had little influence on their daily lives.[31] And 46 percent believed that "people like me" had even less influence on government than under the Soviet regime (with 45 percent responding that things were much the same in this regard); only 9 percent thought that they had *more* influence on government than before.[32] Thus there continues to be a dense, rich nexus of social relations at the primary level, where people interact in the setting of family, circles of friends, and the workplace, but neither is closely related to the great choices over national policy made at the level of the central government. Between the distant power of the state and the networks linking people with family and friends, there are few associational ties that would give people a sense of civic belonging or influence.

INFLUENCES ON RUSSIAN POLITICAL CULTURE IN THE SOVIET PERIOD

Earlier we pointed out that, along with geography, patrimonialism, and Orthodoxy, modernization exerted a substantial influence on Russian political culture in the last century. We can break down its effect into three components: the rise in society's educational attainments, the urbanization of society, and the turnover of generations. Cumulatively, these produced a far more diverse and demanding society by the late twentieth century.

Rising Educational Levels. A hallmark of the Soviet regime was its commitment to universal education. By the end of the 1980s, more than 60 percent of the So-

---
TABLE 5.3
"Whom Do You Trust Most?" (multiple answers possible)

Relatives	62
Friends	54
President Putin	28
Colleagues at work	24
Trade union	11
Army	11
Russian Orthodox Church or other religious organizations	8
Mass media	7
Managers at work	5
Organized crime bosses	4
Refuse to answer	3
Environmental organizations	3
Local government (town, district, village)	2
Procuracy and courts	2
State Duma	2
No one	1

(*Source:* Monitoring.ru, 30 September 2002. National representative sample. N = 1,600. From Web site **monitoring.ru/press-center/facts/article_1163.html**.)

viet population over 15 years of age had attained at least a complete secondary education, and more than 10 percent had higher educational degrees.[33] As many studies showed, education had the effect of reinforcing more critical and more demanding outlooks on the part of Soviet citizens.[34] Education, moreover, is closely linked to support for democratic principles: The more highly educated, the more likely an individual is to support values and principles associated with liberal democracy.[35] Consequently, over time, as Russian society comprised more and more people with secondary and higher educational degrees, levels of support for democratic principles grew.

Higher educational attainments were also related to rising skepticism about Soviet values. In the early 1990s, Arthur Miller and his colleagues from the University of Iowa identified a syndrome of alienation from the old regime, which consisted of low confidence in Soviet leaders and institutions and a sense of personal powerlessness. Significantly, they found that alienation from the old regime was associated with support for democratic values. Miller found that the alienated were four times as likely to join a political organization than were those low on the alienation scale. Other forms of nontraditional political activity were also significantly associated with high levels of alienation. Of course, as Miller observes, in some cases the organizations that the alienated joined were antidemocratic. Overall, however, one reason for the strength of democratic values in the Gorbachev period, therefore, is that they were associated with rejection of the old regime and its values. This tendency was stronger among the young and the better-educated.[36]

The Urbanization of Society. Although old village mentalities and habits have retreated only slowly, Russian society became predominantly urban in a relatively short span of time. By the late 1970s, more than two-thirds of the Russian population lived in cities; today, 73 percent of the population of Russia is classified as urban.[37] But as recently as the late 1950s, the society was half urban, half rural. From 1950 to 1980 the urban population of the Soviet Union increased by nearly 100 million people—most of them immigrants from the countryside, which suffers from a continuing flight of population. The growth of the urban population has had some significant but subtle effects on political culture, as the historian Moshe Lewin has argued. It has tended to focus the attention of policy makers on problems of individual personality and human needs more directly than when the society was composed of large, seemingly homogeneous social blocs such as "workers" and "peasants." Second, urbanization has facilitated the formation of informal and cross-cutting social ties that tend to nurture independent sources of public opinion and mediate the political messages sent out by the rulers.[38]

Generational Change. The effects of rising educational levels and of urbanization have been particularly important because each new generation of Soviet and Russian citizens has been more educated and urbanized than that of its parents. Political scientist Donna Bahry has compared surveys taken at different times to see how public opinion has evolved, and found that the single largest factor in the gradual change in political culture was the *turnover of political generations.*[39] The generation gap widened substantially by the time of the Brezhnev-era and Gorbachev-era studies. Those of the older generation might be critical of some features of the Soviet system, such as collectivized agriculture, but were more inclined to accept some of the political and economic values associated with state socialism. Not so the younger generations, which were significantly more critical of living conditions in the society and sympathetic to the loosening of political and economic controls. Thus, not age (and hence life-cycle effects), but generation, Bahry finds, affects the shift in public opinion: "Those born after World War II, and especially after 1950, had fundamentally different values from their elders."[40]

What were the differences in values? Later generations were more likely to see material shortages as unjust than had previous generations. More important, their standard of reference had shifted. They were less inclined to accept the egalitarianism characteristic of the Stalin-era generations, and more likely to express a resentment of *relative* deprivation. They were far more likely to express dissatisfaction with the same material conditions that the older generations had accepted. There was also a marked difference in views on political liberties. Stalin-era citizens tended to support a mixture of some liberties and some state limitations on individual freedom, while those from post-Stalin generations, "especially the ones with a college degree, were markedly more liberal across the board on individual rights."[41] The younger generations, and particularly those with higher educations, tended to be more consistent in their preference for more economic *and* political freedom, being more inclined to support private ownership of heavy and light industry and agriculture. In other words, while earlier generations might have supported a mixed economy and accepted a combination of state restrictions on liberty with some political freedom, later generations came to have a more ideologically consistent, individualistic, and liberal outlook on major policy questions. This important effect of changing generations was reinforced, in turn, by the cumulative effect of rising levels of educational attainment and other long-term social changes. And in turn, generational turnover and higher educational attainments generated a social base supporting political and economic reform.

The Soviet regime's strategy, then, of creating a modern urban, industrial, educated society had an entirely different effect from that which was anticipated. Rather than strengthening the hold of socialist ideology in the consciousness of the populace, modernization resulted in the formation of a critically minded, alienated, and democratically oriented constituency for radical reform.

The evidence shows that Soviet political culture developed in a way best predicted by the theory of social modernization: Support for individual rights and freedoms rose over the decades and was strongest among the youngest cohorts of society and among those with the greatest education and those living in the largest cities.

These changes in society made the political transformation wrought by Gorbachev both necessary and possible. They expanded the numbers of citizens with aspirations influenced by Western values and living standards. Certainly the modernization of Soviet society helped prepare the way for its democratization. But some of its effects were neither anticipated nor desired by Gorbachev: Having loosened central political controls, he could not prevent some republican leaders from employing police tactics and violence to shore up their political power or others from embracing the tide of anti-Russian nationalism that impelled popular movements for republic independence. His goal of preserving overall Communist Party control over the political system while democratizing it proved impossible, with the result that the political evolution of the fifteen successor states has varied significantly. Some, such as Uzbekistan, are far less democratic than was the Soviet system in the 1980s, and others, such as Lithuania, are much more so. These differences reflect both the different distributions of political values and beliefs in the societies of each former republic, as well as the commitment on the part of their national leaders to democratic practice.

CULTURAL DIVERSITY WITHIN RUSSIA

Much as the decay of the old regime combined with the modernization of society tended to stimulate alternative ideological movements in Russia and other national republics of the union, within Russia as well these changes affected the self-awareness among ethnic minorities living in Russia's national republics and autonomous territories. The revival of nationalism among Russians and other

Soviet peoples in the late 1980s, in response to the opening up of the media and the arts, gave this process a particularly strong impetus. Cultural centers, language revival movements, and political associations sprang up in many regions of Russia, including Tatarstan, Bashkortostan, Chechnia, Udmurtia, Tuva, and elsewhere.

A case in point is the Sakha Republic, formerly known as Yakutia.[42] Sakha occupies a huge territory in Northern Siberia, comprising 17 percent of Russia's landmass, an area three times the size of France. It is an extraordinarily rich area as well, containing vast reserves of gold, diamonds, and oil as well as other mineral resources. About 40 percent of the population is ethnically Sakha as of 1995, and about 50 percent is Russian. During the peak of ethnic political mobilization within Russia, in 1990, Sakha, like many other republics, passed a declaration of sovereignty, although signaling that it did not seek secession. Nonetheless, as in other ethnic republics, tensions between the republican leaders and Moscow increased, just as tensions increased between the Russian population of the republic and the population of the titular indigenous nationality. As elsewhere, these conflicts revolved around both redistributive economic issues (which side would get which share of the profits from the exploitation of native mineral wealth), as well as symbolic, cultural identity issues: What would be the language of instruction in the schools, and what would be the language of politics and administration?

In the case of Sakha, these tensions have been managed without reaching a critical point. The central Russian government has renegotiated the terms of profit sharing from the mining of gold and diamonds, and the Sakha government has encouraged the revival of Sakha language and culture without seeking to expel the Russian population in the republic. Mutual mistrust and hostility sometimes flare up, but in the absence of some new russifying campaign, the movement to make the Sakha Republic a cultural homeland for the Sakha people has been accommodated in the new model of Russian federalism.

The Sakha case is characteristic of a number of the ethnic republics in Russia in that demands for cultural autonomy and a greater share of economic sovereignty have been granted by the federal government in return for the preservation of Russia as a multicultural federal state. The center has shown a striking degree of flexibility, in fact, in handling the political implications of Russia's ethnic-cultural diversity. In Tatarstan, for example, a strong ethnic-nationalist movement (the leaders were not averse to citing the great victories of their illustrious forebear, Genghis Khan, over the Russians) subsided through adroit maneuvering by the republican and federal leadership, which granted the republic a sufficient share of economic and cultural autonomy to satisfy all but the most irreconcilable separatists.

Contemporary Russian political culture has thus been influenced by many factors, among them the thousand-year heritage of Russian statehood, the ambitious program of the Soviet communist regime to remake society, and the effects of social modernization that the communist regime generally encouraged but tried, with little success, to direct to its ends. We have noted the major lines of cleavage in society associated with generation, education, residence in city or countryside, and ethnic-national identity. The tumultuous events of Soviet history have affected different generations differently. Among the older generation, for instance, Stalin is viewed much more favorably than among the younger generations.[43] And to a large extent, these differences are mutually reinforcing: Members of the older generations tend to have lower levels of education and less exposure to the more cosmopolitan way of life of cities. Many individuals combine democratic values in the abstract with support for state ownership and control over much of the economy and a very negative evaluation of contemporary political and economic institutions.

The alienation from the authorities—Russia's characteristic pattern of reciprocal detachment, mistrust, and misunderstanding that separates state from populace—which helped to undermine the old regime, has returned again under the new regime. The disillusionment of many hopes that the gap would be closed has been filled, for many, not by hope for the future but by a bitter nostalgia for the past. There has also been a reaction against Western influence and models. Two 1993 surveys found a majority supporting the sentiment that the West has been trying to *weaken* Russia by meddling in its reforms.[44] These findings suggest that while democratic aspirations have been awakened, strongly shaping what Russians think *should* be in politics, they have also created standards of evaluation that existing institutions do not meet.

Russian political culture is a dynamic mixture of contradictory elements drawn from the prerevolutionary, Soviet, and post-Soviet periods, as well as from the interpenetrating medium of international influences. Even in Soviet times, behind the veil of apparent Marxist-Leninist solidarity, a variety of democratic, religious, and cultural values struggled for recognition. It is difficult to imagine how Russia's cultural diversity could ever be successfully reduced to the iron logic of a single ideology again.

Yet we have found that there are core tendencies in Russia's political culture. Support for democratic freedoms remains relatively strong, particularly among elite groups. Support for an economic system under which individuals would be responsible for their own well-being is less widespread than the belief that the state should ensure basic social justice and security. The former communist regime is regarded by a sizable majority in a generally favorable light, yet by a clear majority Russians would not wish to bring it back. Younger, more educated, and urban groups are significantly likelier to espouse liberal democratic positions than are older, more rural, and less educated people. As the passage of time brings about the turnover of generations and exposes more people to the outside world, therefore, it is likely that democratic values and beliefs will spread.

Will the spread of democratic values and beliefs lead to the consolidation of democracy? Our overview of Russian political culture suggests an answer. We have emphasized the persistence of thick networks of trust and communication linking Russian citizens with family and friends but that do not extend to a faith in representative political institutions such as parliament and parties. Involvement in civic associations is extremely low and mistrust of the state authorities extremely high. The result is that most citizens expect government to be indifferent to their interests and the quality of government drops to match their low expectations. Some in Russia believe that its progress depends on the country's reconstruction as a *national* state—where the nation is understood to mean a society of equal citizens, exercising the rights and responsibilities of citizenship and cooperating for the betterment of the country. Such a path of development would require rejecting both an imperial identity for the state as well as a view of the state as an ethnic nation—both would inevitably require the use of force to preserve state power. As the former chairman of the Foreign Relations Committee of the Federation Council of the Russian parliament, Vladimir Podoprigora, put it, in the past, for Russians "the phrases 'the great Russian people' and 'the great Soviet people' were readily interchangeable."[45] He went on:

> A large people and a large territory have always generated a sense of boundlessness and might, encouraged the illusion of the inexhaustibility of spiritual and physical forces, and a sense of national greatness. To maintain this perception, neither the Russian nor Soviet government spared the people. And the people themselves offered themselves up in sacrifice to this idea. But it did not justify itself. It exhausted the people's powers without bringing spiritual satisfaction. The aspiration to achieve recognition of national greatness, to win greater roles in solving world conflict situations, than we can allow ourselves, is not only fraught with new difficulties for the people, but also sometimes places us in a false and ridiculous position. Would it not be better to concentrate for a certain historical period on solving our own problems? Perhaps in this position there is not national greatness, but there is national honor. And that is the main thing.[46]

REVIEW QUESTIONS

1. What is patrimonial rule, and how has it affected the development of Russia's political system?
2. What are the main distinguishing features of Russian political culture? How deep an impact did the Soviet effort to remake political culture have on the values and beliefs of Russian citizens?
3. As we have seen, most Russians evaluate the pre-Gorbachev Soviet system favorably. Yet most Russians would prefer not to bring it back. How would you explain this apparent contradiction?
4. How would you explain the fact that support in Russia for liberal democratic values is very high despite seven decades of Soviet efforts to inculcate collectivist and statist values?
5. Although support for democratic values is high, Russians continue to vote for antidemocratic parties and politicians in large numbers. What explains this paradox?

6. We have seen that mistrust among the population for the authorities is very high. What explains this pattern, and what social or political changes might in time overcome it?

ENDNOTES

1. There is a vast literature on the history of Russian national identity. Two valuable recent contributions are Ilya Prizel, *National Identity and Foreign Policy: Nationalism and Leadership in Poland, Russia and Ukraine* (Cambridge, England: Cambridge University Press, 1998) and Vera Tolz, *Russia* (New York: Oxford University Press, 2001).

2. Gabriel A. Almond and Sidney Verba, *The Civic Culture: Political Attitudes and Democracy in Five Nations* (Boston: Little, Brown, 1965).

3. Gabriel A. Almond and Sidney Verba, eds., *The Civic Culture Revisited* (Boston: Little, Brown, 1980); Archie Brown, ed., *Political Culture and Communist Studies* (Armonk, N.Y.: M. E. Sharpe, 1985); Ronald Inglehart, *Culture Shift in Advanced Industrial Society* (Princeton, N.J.: Princeton University Press, 1990); Stephen White, *Political Culture and Soviet Politics* (London: Macmillan, 1979); Frederic J. Fleron Jr., "Post-Soviet Political Culture in Russia: An Assessment of Recent Empirical Investigations," *Europe-Asia Studies* 48:2 (1996), pp. 225–60; Harry Eckstein Jr., Frederic J. Fleron, Erik P. Hoffmann, and William M. Reisinger, eds., *Can Democracy Take Root in Post-Soviet Russia? Explorations in State–Society Relations* (Lanham, Md.: Rowman & Littlefield, 1998).

4. Inglehart, *Culture Shift*, p. 55.

5. Stephen Whitefield and Geofrey Evans, "The Russian Election of 1993: Public Opinion and the Transition Experience," *Post-Soviet Affairs* 10 (1994), pp. 46–49; William Zimmerman, "Markets, Democracy and Russian Foreign Policy," *Post-Soviet Affairs* 10 (1994), pp. 103–26; Donna Bahry, "Society Transformed? Rethinking the Social Roots of Perestroika," *Slavic Review* 52:3 (Fall 1993), pp. 511–54.

6. James L. Gibson and Raymond M. Duch, "Emerging Democratic Values in Soviet Political Culture," in Arthur H. Miller, William M. Reisinger, and Vicki L. Hesli, eds., *Public Opinion and Regime Change* (Boulder, Colo.: Westview, 1993), pp. 69–94; William M. Reisinger, Arthur H. Miller, and Vicki L. Hesli, "Political Values in Russia, Ukraine and Lithuania: Sources and Implications for Democracy," *British Journal of Political Science* 24 (1994), pp. 183–223; and Jeffrey W. Hahn, "Continuity and Change in Russian Political Culture," *British Journal of Political Science* 21(4) (1991), pp. 393–421.

7. James L. Gibson, "The Resilience of Support for Democratic Institutions and Processes in the Nascent Russian and Ukrainian Democracies," in Vladimir Tismaneanu, ed., *Political Culture and Civil Society in Russia and the New States of Eurasia* (Armonk, N.Y.: M. E. Sharpe, 1995), p. 57.

8. Richard Rose, *Getting Things Done with Social Capital: New Russia Barometer VII*, paper no. 303, Studies in Public Policy (Glasgow: Centre for the Study of Public Policy, University of Strathclyde, 1998), pp. 40–43.

9. Rose, *Getting Things Done*, p. 44.

10. Ibid., pp. 44–45

11. Reported on Web site **www.russiavotes.org**, 3 July 2002.

12. James R. Millar and Sharon L. Wolchik, "Introduction: The Social Legacies and the Aftermath of Communism," in James R. Millar and Sharon L. Wolchik, eds., *The*

Social Legacy of Communism (Washington, D.C., and Cambridge, England: Woodrow Wilson Press and Cambridge University Press, 1994), p. 16.

13. Marcia A. Weigle, *Russia's Liberal Project: State–Society Relations in the Transition from Communism* (University Park: Pennsylvania State University Press, 2000) pp. 432–41.

14. Rose, *Getting Things Done*, p. 30.

15. William Zimmerman, "Markets, Democracy and Russian Foreign Policy," *Post-Soviet Affairs* 10 (1994), pp. 103–26; William Zimmerman, "Synoptic Thinking and Political Culture in Post- Soviet Russia," *Slavic Review* 54 (1995), pp. 630–41; Judith S. Kullberg and William Zimmerman, "Liberal Elites, Socialist Masses, and Problems of Russian Democracy," *World Politics* 51 (April 1999), pp. 323–58.

16. Timothy J. Colton, *Transitional Citizens: Voters and What Influences Them in the New Russia* (Cambridge, Mass.: Harvard University Press, 2000), pp. 145–47.

17. On the impact of television in Soviet society, see Ellen Mickiewicz, *Split Signals: Television and Politics in the Soviet Union* (New York and Oxford, England: Oxford University Press, 1988); on propaganda and mass communications more generally, see Stephen White, *Political Culture and Soviet Politics* (London: Macmillan, 1979); and Thomas F. Remington, *The Truth of Authority: Ideology and Communication in the Soviet Union* (Pittsburgh, Pa.: University of Pittsburgh Press, 1988).

18. Comprehensive studies of Soviet dissent include Ludmilla Alexeeyeva, *Soviet Dissent: Contemporary Movements for National, Religious, and Human Rights* (Middletown, Conn.: Wesleyan University Press, 1987); Frederick C. Barghoorn, *Detente and the Democratic Movement in the USSR* (New York, Free Press, 1976).

19. Robert D. English, *Russia and the Idea of the West: Gorbachev, Intellectuals, and the End of the Cold War* (New York: Columbia University Press, 2000), pp. 5–8.

20. Mikhail Gorbachev himself portrayed his reform program not merely as applying to Russia, but as a doctrine for the whole world, as the title of the book he published in 1987 indicates: *Perestroika: New Thinking for Our Country and the World* (New York: Harper & Row, 1987).

21. Thomas Remington, "A Socialist Pluralism of Opinions: Glasnost' and Policy-Making under Gorbachev," *Russian Review* 48 (1989), pp. 271–304.

22. Yu. Levada, et al., "Homo Sovieticus: A Rough Sketch," *Moscow News*, no. 11 (1990), p. 11.

23. Tatiana Zaslavskaia, "Vesti dialog s liud'mi," *Narodnyi deputat*, no. 2 (1990), pp. 25–27. Zaslavskaia is a distinguished sociologist who was one of the most important theorists of reform in the pre-Gorbachev and early Gorbachev periods. A member of the Academy of Sciences and a deputy to the Congress of People's Deputies, she founded a new institute to conduct public-opinion surveys throughout the Soviet Union.

24. "Main Directions for the Stabilization of the National Economy and the Transition to a Market Economy," as published in the British Broadcasting System Summary of World Broadcasts (BBC SWB), SU/0900, 20 October 1990, p. C/1. This policy statement was adopted as the basis of national economic policy by the USSR Supreme Soviet on 19 October 1990. It is important mainly as a statement of goals and principles rather than as a working program of action.

25. Gibson and Duch, "Emerging Democratic Values," p. 79.

26. James L. Gibson, "'A Mile Wide and an Inch Deep' (?): The Structure of Democratic Commitments in the Former, USSR," *American Journal of Political Science* 40:2 (1994), p. 397.

27. A panel study is one that surveys the same sample of respondents at several different points over a given period of time. That way it is possible to judge whether the same people continue to hold the same views over time, or whether their opinions change.

28. Gibson, "'A Mile Wide but an Inch Deep' (?)."

29. Reported by Richard Rose, *Getting Things Done*, pp. 58–59. VTsIOM conducted the study in March–April 1998. The interviewers provided respondents with a seven-point scale with 1 indicating great mistrust and 7 indicating great trust. Anyone whose score was from 1 to 3 was coded as not trusting, and anyone with a score from 5 to 7 was coded as trusting. A score of 4 was coded as neutral.

30. Rose, *Getting Things Done*, p. 29.

31. Ibid., p. 36.

32. Ibid., p. 35.

33. These levels compare with those in the United States. In 1980, 66.3 percent of Americans aged 25 or over had completed secondary school and 16.3 percent had four or more years of college. See Andrew Hacker, *U/S: A Statistical Portrait of the American People* (New York: Viking, 1983), pp. 250–51.

34. Brian Silver, "Political Beliefs of the Soviet Citizen," in James R. Millar, ed., *Politics, Work, and Daily Life in the USSR* (Cambridge, England: Cambridge University Press, 1987), p. 127.

35. Gibson and Duch, "Emerging Democratic Values," p. 86; William M. Reisinger, Arthur H. Miller, Vicki L. Hesli, and Kristen Hill Maher, "Political Values in Russia, Ukraine and Lithuania: Sources and Implications for Democracy," *British Journal of Political Science* 24 (1994), pp. 216–18; Jeffrey W. Hahn, "Continuity and Change in Russian Political Culture," in Frederic J. Fleron Jr., and Erik P. Hoffmann, eds., *Post-Communist Studies and Political Science: Methodology and Empirical Theory in Sovietology* (Boulder, Colo.: Westview, 1993), pp. 319–22.

36. Arthur H. Miller, "In Search of Regime Legitimacy," in Miller, Reisinger, and Hesli, eds., *Public Opinion and Regime Change*, pp. 95–123.

37. *Rossiiskaia federatsiia v 1992: Statisticheskii ezhegodnik* [The Russian Federation in 1992: Statistical Annual] (Moscow: Republikanskii informatsionno-izdatel'skii tsentr, 1993), p. 88.

38. Moshe Lewin, *The Gorbachev Phenomenon*, expanded ed. (Berkeley: University of California Press, 1991), pp. 63–71; see also S. Frederick Starr, "The Changing Nature of Change in the USSR," in Seweryn Bialer and Michael Mandelbaum, eds., *Gorbachev's Russia and American Foreign Policy* (Boulder, Colo.: Westview, 1988), pp. 3–36.

39. Bahry, "Society Transformed?" Bahry reanalyzes data from three surveys taken at different times: the Harvard Project of refugees to Europe after World War II, which reflects attitudes shaped in the 1920s, 1930s, and early 1940s; the SIP data from the emigre survey in the United States in the late 1970s; and a Times-Mirror survey conducted in 1991. This method allows her to compare public opinion on comparable issues for the *same* generations across different surveys taken at different times, and to track change and continuity in opinion *across* generations. She finds that both the earlier and later studies found an essential consistency in the values of the prewar generations, even though members of those generations had grown much older by the 1970s and 1980s.

40. Bahry, p. 544.

41. Bahry, p. 540.

42. The discussion of the Sakha Republic that follows is based on the article by Marjorie M. Balzer and Uliana A. Vinokurova, "Nationalism, Interethnic Relations and

Federalism: The Case of the Sakha Republic (Yakutia)," *Europe-Asia Studies* 48 (1996), pp. 101–20.
43. Reisinger, Miller, Hesli, and Maher, "Political Values in Russia, Ukraine and Lithuania," p. 200.
44. Whitefield and Evans, "The Russian Election of 1993," p. 52; Hough, "The Russian Election of 1993," p. 6.
45. Vladimir N. Podoprigora and Tatiana I. Krasnopevtseva, "Russkii vopros kak faktor vnutrennei i vneshnei politiki Rossii" [The Russian Question as a Factor in Domestic and Foreign Policy of Russia], *Segodnia,* 18 October 1994.
46. Ibid.

6

Interest Groups and Political Parties

INTEREST ARTICULATION: FROM STATISM TO PLURALISM

Regime change in Russia has had a powerful impact both on the way political interests are defined and in the way they are organized. Decentralization, privatization, ideological liberalization, and the weakening of the state safety net have reshaped people's needs and desires. For most people, the changes have worsened living conditions.[1] At the same time, political liberalization has also allowed people to mobilize in defense of common interests, such as environmental protection and the rights of ethnic minorities, disadvantaged groups, business, and labor. Most people's lives are affected by the coexistence of elements of the old socialist system with new quasi-capitalist, semi-democratic institutions. Even in the same family it is common to find one wage earner who works in a private business and another who is employed by a state enterprise: The first is likely to earn higher wages but face greater insecurity, while the other receives paltry wages (and may go for months without receiving them at all) but can expect state benefits such as a pension upon retirement. In keeping with the more diverse array of interests in society, there is a far more differentiated spectrum of interest associations than there was under the old regime. But although there is much more organized interest articulation than there was in the past, inequality in the political clout of weaker and stronger groups has also increased. Even more than in Western democracies, the pluralistic environment of interest articulation has allowed the wealthy and powerful to dominate the policy-making process.

In Chapter 5, we saw that the provision of honest and effective government is a public good; people face a collective action dilemma in trying to obtain good government. Public goods are goods that anyone may enjoy whether they have expended any effort to obtain them or not, and the supply of which is not diminished as people use them. To explain where public goods such as honest and effective governance come from we must look both at demand and supply. As we know, public goods always tend to be undersupplied.[2] This occurs because few people are willing to take upon themselves the cost of organizing collective action for the common good of large groups of people if their own share of the benefit is worth less than the cost of the effort they make to achieve it. Those who do organize groups for collective benefit often are seeking some other private benefits for themselves by doing so. Some may have aspirations to become political leaders, for instance. By going to the trouble of mobilizing a group around a cause, they gain name recognition and followers.

How hard it is to organize a group of people around a common cause depends on what kind of organizational resources are already in place. If people are already members of an organization, or share ties through previous acquaintance, it is easier to reach them and communicate with them. If organizational entrepreneurs have to start from scratch, and go around to people one by one to persuade them to sign a petition or contribute dues or turn out for a demonstration, large-scale collective action is much harder to produce. Consequently, when a regime changes, we would expect that interests that can be mobilized through existing organizational channels will have an easier time being heard than interests that are not already organized.

The same logic applies to the political calculations of leaders. Leaders who can capture control of existing organizations, and make them vehicles for representing new groups of constituents, have an easier time winning influence than do leaders who must start a movement or party from scratch. Therefore, even in a time of deep change in society, the way political and organizational resources were structured in the past will affect the way interests are articulated in the new regime.

On the demand side, people's interests are strongly affected by a major change such as the shift from state socialism to market capitalism. In Russia, the demise of the old state-socialist economic system, where the state was the universal employer, has affected everyone. The crude and incomplete way in which the economic transition occurred in Russia has meant that a small minority of people have become immensely wealthy, while most people have grown poorer and more insecure. Inequality has grown among regions and within regions. Many cultural, social, and political groups have also organized and are making demands that would have been unthinkable under the Soviet regime.

Interest articulation is thus affected both by the degree to which people are able to organize for collective action and by the shift in their own definitions of what they want and need from government. People's interests and identities create a potential for mobilization in the political arena, but whether that potential is realized depends a good deal on the distribution of organizational resources and the strategies of leaders who hope to build popular followings. In this chapter, we will examine how the regime change has affected people's material and social interests. We also will discuss the change in the organizational structures by which people convey their demands to the policy makers.

Socialism and Bureaucratic Politics. The Soviet regime did not tolerate the open pursuit of any interests except those authorized by the state. Soviet doctrine did recognize that there were diverse interests in society and encouraged the formation of a number of public organizations, such as labor unions organized by branch of the economy, professional unions for creative artists, and associations for particular groups of the population, such as youths, women, and veterans. But the regime required that organizations articulating interests do so in a way compatible with its goals. As we have seen, the regime treated such organizations as means of directing and controlling the participation of the population in public life. Stalin defined public organizations as "transmission belts" by which the state drove society.[3]

Although it did not take the form of open, competitive politics, interest articulation went on through intense behind-the-scenes maneuvering for power and advantage, especially within the state bureaucracy. Bureaucratic agencies, regional governments, and leadership factions vied quietly but vigorously for influence over policy and appointments. They were not allowed to appeal openly to the public for support, so the public had no means of holding leaders accountable, but they used methods familiar to bureaucratic in-fighters throughout the world: building tacit coalitions, manipulating the flow of information, favoring clients with patronage benefits. And, as we have seen, sometimes the expression of demands and ideas took the form of clandestinely circulated contraband literature that the regime treated as subversive.[4]

There was constant bureaucratic lobbying by state actors, including the myriad agencies of the state. Like bureaucratic organizations everywhere, they developed a strong stake in their own organizational status and power. These included both the centralized branch agencies that managed the economy and society, as well as the leaders of the republics and regions of the union. Between the bureaucracy and the policy makers at the top, as political scientist Philip Roeder has argued, there was a relationship of mutual dependence. The party leadership needed the branch and regional structures to achieve their policy goals. In turn the heads of administrative agencies needed the support of top party leaders for their institutional and career interests. As the center grew weaker, and depended more on the support of the state officialdom, the idea of any serious reform of the system became more and more threatening.[5]

Since the articulation of interests was regulated by the Communist Party, and there could be no open competition among political parties or interest groups for support, the Communist Party was the major institution for weighing alternatives and deciding policy. In the Stalin era, party policies such as the collectivization of private farms were carried out using enormous coercion: Collectivization resulted in the loss of millions of lives through the killing, deportation, and starvation of peasants.[6] But in the post-Stalin era, as the system grew bureaucratized and corrupt, entrenched bureaucratic interests grew adept at manipulating the system. Any policy initiative that threatened to upset the existing distribution of resources was watered down before it was adopted, and often was further distorted or forgotten as it was implemented. Paradoxically, policy makers at the top of this seemingly centralized political system lacked the authority to break through the mass of bureaucratic inertia, and frequently lacked the information necessary for an accurate appraisal of the real state of affairs in many areas.

The statist model of interest articulation was upset by glasnost. Glasnost stimulated an explosion of political expression that in turn prompted groups to form and to make political demands and participate in elections. It is hard today to appreciate how profound was the impact of glasnost on Soviet society: Suddenly it opened the floodgates to a growing stream of startling facts, ideas, disclosures, reappraisals, scandals, and sensations. But if Gorbachev expected that glasnost would result in expression generally favoring his own strategy of perestroika, or restructuring, of Soviet socialism, he must have been surprised at the range and intensity of new demands and pressures that erupted. In loosening the party's controls over communication sufficiently to encourage people to speak freely and openly, Gorbachev also relinquished the controls that would have enabled him to limit political expression when it went too far.

Moreover, ideology and organization in the Soviet regime were so tightly intertwined that by releasing controls over the ideological limits of speech, Gorbachev was also giving up the party's traditional power to control public organizations. As people voiced their deep-felt grievances, others recognized that they shared the same outlooks, and made common cause with them. Thus a direct result of glasnost was a wave of participation in "informal"—that is, unlicensed and uncontrolled—public associations. Daring publications in the media allowed people with common interests to identify one another and encouraged them to come together to form independent associations. When the authorities tried to limit or prohibit such groups, they generated still more protest. Associations of all sorts formed: groups dedicated to remembering the victims of Stalin's terror; ultranationalists who wanted to restore tsarism; nationalist movements in many republics. The devastating explosion of the nuclear reactor at Chernobyl in 1986 had a tremendous impact in stimulating the formation of environmental protest, which also fed nationalist movements in Belarus and Ukraine.[7]

The mobilization of large-scale political activity led to the creation of new organizational outlets for popular participation in nationalist movements, independent labor unions, and electoral coalitions in 1990 and 1991. Some of these movements evolved into channels of interest articulation and aggregation in the post-Soviet era.[8]

Democrats, "Reds," and "Browns." In Russia, as new organizations espousing political goals proliferated in the late 1980s, two opposing ideological tendencies became distinct. One espoused principles of individualism, liberal democracy, market economy, and the rule of law—and generally a Western orientation for Russia. This group adopted the label "democrats" or "reformers." The other tendency voiced an inconsistent mixture of principles drawn from two not entirely compatible sets of values. One source was Marxism-Leninism, whose advocates made up for their limited base of popular support with flights of extravagant rhetoric. They yearned for strong leadership, centralized state power, an assertive foreign policy, a collectivist, centrally planned economy, and preservation of an imperial Soviet Union—for them Stalin was a heroic figure in Russian history.

The other forces in the opposition coalition appealed to traditional Russian and Slavophile conservative nationalism. Like the ultra-Marxists, they wanted Russia to have a hierarchical and imperial state and they also hated Western political and economic influences. For them, however, not Marxism but older Russian cultural values such as Orthodox religion should be the source for rebuilding society's exhausted moral fabric. At a deeper philosophic level, the conservative nationalists also rejected the rationalism and materialism associated with Marxism. But in more practical day-to-day politics, the conservative nationalists and the arch-Marxists have found it easy to make common cause in their hatred and contempt for the West's impact on Russia (and in other forms of xenophobia, such as anti-Semitism). Thus the "red" Marxist-Leninists have often allied with the "brown" nationalists in opposition to the democratizing trends in Russia over the past several years.[9] The "red-brown" strain of thought and feeling has continued to be powerfully felt in Russian politics to the present and is represented by extremist groups such as "Russian National Unity" and, in slightly diluted form, by the Communist Party of the Russian Federation. We shall say more about both of these groups below.

Toward Pluralism

The collapse of the Soviet regime ended the regime's ideological controls over political expression that Gorbachev's reforms had weakened. The transition created an opportunity for the rise of a variety of new groups that voiced a wide range of demands. But besides these fundamental political changes, the post-1991 period brought about another change of equal importance. The elimination of the state's monopoly on productive property resulted in the formation of new class interests, among them those of new entrepreneurs, commercial bankers, private farmers, and others interested in protecting rights of property and commerce. Another important category of interests was that of the managers of state-owned enterprises, who were facing a radically changed environment as state orders, credits, and sources of supply dried up, and as Yeltsin's privatization program took effect. Organized labor too found itself in a new position dealing with managers of privatized enterprises rather than, as in the past, with administrators of state property. Unions themselves were divided among competing labor federations. Also divided were the farmers: While private farmers were represented by an association pressing for legal guarantees and state support for private farming, the collective farmers formed a powerful association and political party. Meanwhile new associations representing banks, consumers, deceived investors, city governments, disabled persons, soldiers' mothers, defense industries, abused women, and a host of other interests began to form. No longer did the state demand that organized groups serve a single, state-defined political agenda, as was the case under the old regime. Now groups could form freely to represent a diversity of interests, compete for influence and resources, and define their own agenda. By 2001, there were more than 300,000 nongovernmental, noncommercial organizations registered with the government, of which around 70,000 were active.[10] More than 2 million people work in these organizations as activists and employees, and as many as 15 or 20 million people receive assistance in some form from them.[11]

Political scientists have observed that interest groups generally pursue either "inside" or "outside" strategies for influencing policy. That is, either they tend to concentrate their resources on cultivating close, friendly relations with key policy makers, or they seek to build large public followings and membership bases that can apply pressure on policy makers through elections, demonstrations, letter-writing campaigns, and media attention.[12] The effectiveness of insider strategies depends on establishing relations of trust, which generally requires that the group's representatives and the policy makers keep each other's confidences. For this reason it can be difficult to judge from the outside how powerful an "insider" group is. In the case of Russian groups, we see various combinations of strategies. Some older organizations that have survived into the new regime cling to their organizational assets and take advantage of their "insider" access to the state. Others that have sprung up from scratch also work closely with the authorities, but others play "outsider" roles, trying to influence government by mobilizing public support. Still others try to use both strategies.

The rapid changes in the structure of social relations have meant that both old and new organizations have had a difficult time keeping a firm base of support. Some organizations that appeared influential at first have turned out to be little more than an empty shell. Other interest groups have proven to be very strong politically even though they are not formally organized. Some formerly cohesive groups have split. The diversification of interests has generated a wide range of opportunities for activists. Interest articulation is therefore more pluralist than it is statist or corporatist, because the very rapidity with which new associations have formed has defeated efforts by both government and interest groups to form comprehensive umbrella organizations that the state could treat as the official voice of a particular interest. In most cases, interest associations are too numerous, too weak internally, and too competitive for corporatism to succeed. The prevalent pattern is one of differentiation and even fragmentation of interest representation.

But although the prevailing pattern of interest articulation is pluralist, it is important to remember what the political scientist E. E. Schattschneider observed of pluralism in the American context—that "the flaw in the pluralist heaven is that the heavenly chorus sings with a strong upper-class accent." This applies with particular force to Russia, where the postcommunist freedom to organize has allowed a handful of wealthy industrial and financial interests to acquire immense influence over government.

It will be helpful to illustrate the patterns of interest articulation in contemporary Russia by examining five groups in closer detail: the Russian Union of Industrialists and Entrepreneurs, the Committees of Soldiers' Mothers, the Federation of Independent Trade Unions of Russia, the Russian Orthodox Church, and the "oligarchs." These comprise both "old" and "new" types of interests and organization and will illustrate a range of strategies for collective action.

The Russian Union of Industrialists and Entrepreneurs. The case of the Russian Union of Industrialists and Entrepreneurs offers an excellent illustration of three points: Some inherited Soviet-era organizations have proven resilient in the face of the considerable changes that have taken place in politics and society; the interests of the state industrial managers have slowly adapted to the new market conditions in the economy; and the voice of big business in Russia today is far stronger than that of any other organized interest.

Privatization has sharply changed the environment for industry. Most formerly state-owned industrial firms are now wholly or partly privately owned. Gradually their directors have come to respond to the incentives of a market economy, rather than those of a state socialist economy. Under the old regime, managers were told to fulfill the plan regardless of cost or quality, and profit was not a relevant consideration.[13] Now, managers are increasingly motivated to maximize profits and to increase the productive value of their firms. Some firms continue to demand subsidies and protection from the state. More and more, however, firms are demanding that the state provide a level playing field for all businesses, that is, an environment where laws and contracts are enforced by the state, regulation is reasonable and honest, taxes are fair (and low), and barriers to foreign trade are minimized. As one consultant to a major firm explained, the CEO of the company at first did not understand why he should not simply "buy" a few government bureaucrats and members of parliament, and obtain the legislative and administrative decisions that he needed for his company through bribery. With time, however, he came to recognize that it was more efficient in the long run for him to work with other large companies in a business association to create a legal and regulatory environment that would favor growth and investment more generally. The association that is the vehicle for his lobbying efforts, and those of big business in Russia more generally, is the Russian Union of Industrialists and Entrepreneurs, or RUIE.

The RUIE is the single most powerful organized interest group in Russia. Its members are both the old state industrial firms (now mostly private or quasi-private) and the newer financial-industrial conglomerates headed by the "oligarchs." Its president is Arkadii Vol'skii, who used to be a senior CPSU official in charge of the Central Committee department overseeing industrial machine building. During the Gorbachev period, he headed a new association of the heads of state enterprises called the "Scientific-Industrial Union."[14] This organization sought to preserve economic ties among enterprises to offset the breakdown of the old system of central planning. After the dissolution of the Soviet Union, the organization was renamed the Russian Union of Industrialists and Entrepreneurs. Although the RUIE professed to have no explicit political goals, it did seek to defend the interests of state industry—including their interest in obtaining credits and production orders—as well as to prevent the interruption of supply and trade ties in the face of economic upheavals. Strongly opposed to the government's economic reform plans in 1992, RUIE threatened that unless the reforms were modified, "the directors would paralyze the country by calling their workers out on strike."[15] Like other interest groups, Vol'skii's organization was drawn into politics. In spring 1992, Vol'skii entered the field directly, first forming a political arm of the RUIE, then allying it with other parties and political groups in a coalition called Civic Union. Civic Union consistently declared that its political outlook was "centrist" and indeed it sought to stake out the center ground as opposing lines were hardening over the radical Yeltsin/Gaidar stabilization program.

For a time in 1992, Civic Union had a good deal of political clout. Its lobbying was one reason Yeltsin decided to bring some prominent industrial administrators into the government cabinet in the spring of 1992 and to modify the government's plans for privatization. Specifically, the government agreed that one of the forms that the privatization of state enterprises could take was to allow the work force of each enterprise to acquire 51 percent of its shares. Given the dominant position of the management within the workplace, this effectively meant that such a path to privatization turned a controlling share of ownership rights over to the managers. Not surprisingly, once this option was permitted, it became the most popular form: Around three-fourths of privatizing enterprises in 1992 and 1993 chose this option.[16] Of course, as always in trying to judge how powerful an interest group is, it is difficult to assess how much these decisions were made at the behest of Civic Union, as opposed to how much the government acted in *anticipation* of the interests of the industrial directors.

But the Civic Union's attempt to play outsider politics failed abysmally. In 1993 it put forward a list of candidates for the December 1993 parliamentary election. Civic Union campaigned as the party of moderation, gradualism, and experience. It received less than 2 percent of the vote, however, well below the 5 percent threshold required for representation of its party list candidates in parliament. Civic Union tried yet again to appeal for voter support in the 1995 Duma election. This time Vol'skii allied with the main official trade union federation in an electoral bloc called the "Trade Unions and Industrialists of Russia: the Union of Labor." Their appeal was pragmatic and centrist, calling for cooperation between industrial management and labor. But despite the seemingly huge social base for this alliance—the trade union federation claimed over 50 million members—it was crushed at the polls, receiving only 1.63 percent of the national list vote.

As an insider group voicing the interests of the state industrial sector, the RUIE has been far more effective. It has been an influential behind-the-scenes force for compromise between management and labor, and a source of policy advice for government and parliament. A measure of its stature is the fact that at its annual conference in June 2001, the prime minister, two deputy prime ministers, the minister of economic development, the head of the state pension fund, several governors, and officials from more than fifty regions attended. Vol'skii expressed satisfaction at the fact that the members of RUIE were responsible for producing over 80 percent of Russian GDP.[17]

With time, the RUIE's political interests have shifted and its role has expanded. For one thing, the Putin team institutionalized consultation with the RUIE in developing economic policy. For another, the oligarchs decided to join forces with the RUIE. (As Vol'skii put it, "the interests of the oligarchs are too diverse to create their own public association, and the RUIE can help them conduct civilized lobbying."[18]) And the improvement in economic conditions at the end of the 1990s made the RUIE's members themselves more interested in improving the business environment for Russia generally, rather than in capturing industry-specific privileges. The RUIE expanded its in-house capacity for working with the government and the parliament in drafting legislation. It maintains a number of specialized internal working groups that develop policy positions on a wide range of issues such as land reform; tax law; pension policy; bankruptcy legislation; reform of the natural gas, energy, and railroad monopolies; regulation of the securities market; and the terms of Russia's entry to the World Trade Organization (WTO). In September 2002, RUIE announced that it was planning a multi-million-dollar advertising campaign to improve the image of Russian business overseas.[19] By marshaling expertise, pooling the clout of its members, and maintaining friendly relations with policy makers in the government, both chambers of parliament, and the presidential administration, the RUIE has become a quietly powerful force in shaping policy on a wide range of economic issues.

The Committees of Soldiers' Mothers. The Soviet regime sponsored several official women's organizations, but these mainly served propaganda purposes. During the glasnost period, a number of unofficial women's organizations sprang up to voice the interests of groups who were otherwise unrepresented. One such group was the Committee of Soldiers' Mothers. It formed in the spring of 1989 when some 300 women in Moscow marched to protest the end of student deferments from military conscription. In response to their actions, Gorbachev agreed to restore the deferments. Since then the movement has grown, focusing its energy on pressing the military to eliminate the use of soldiers' labor in its construction battalions, ending the brutal hazing of recruits which results in the deaths of hundreds of soldiers each year, and helping young men avoid being conscripted.[20] The onset of large-scale hostilities in Chechnia in 1994–1996 and 1999–2000 stimulated a new burst of activity by the Committee. It helped families locate soldiers who were missing in action or captured by the Chechen rebel forces; it sent missions to Chechnia to negotiate for the release of prisoners and to provide proper burial for the dead; it collected fuller information about the actual scale of the war and of its casualties than the Russian military; and it continued to advise families on ways to avoid conscription and to lobby for decent treatment of recruits. It has even cooperated with Chechen women's groups in organizing antiwar protests. Through the 1990s, it became one of the most sizable and respected civic groups in Russia. Some 300 local committees sprang up in towns across the country and united into a nationwide League of Committees of Soldiers' Mothers that can call upon a network of thousands of active volunteers for its work. Its St. Petersburg branch alone reports that some 300 people visit its office every week seeking consultations and legal advice, and that it has helped 57,000 young people escape the draft.[21] They visit wounded soldiers in hospitals and help military authorities in identifying casualties. One of the movement's greatest assets has been its moral authority as mothers defending the interests of their children; this stance has made it hard for their opponents to paint them as unpatriotic or power-hungry.

The League has been active in lobbying parliament (for example, it joined with other civic groups to lobby for a liberal version of the law on alternative civil service for conscientious objectors, an effort that had only partial success), but for the most part it has concentrated its efforts on helping soldiers and their families deal with their problems. Thus it performs multiple functions, combining political goals with services to clients. Unlike many Russian associational groups, the League has chosen to remain independent of government, not seeking any special privileges or recognition. As Elena Vilenskaia, one of the founders of the Committee of Soldiers' Mothers in St. Petersburg, put it, "we realized we had to form an organization of a completely different type. Not a committee which is manipulated by someone, but something fundamentally new, constructive. From the beginning we separated ourselves from all central structures."[22]

Like many nongovernmental organizations (NGOs), the League of Committees of Soldiers' Mothers has cultivated ties with peace and women's groups in Europe and North America. It has won international recognition for its work. For some groups, such ties have become a source of dependence, as organizations compensate for the lack of mass membership with aid and know-how from counterpart organizations abroad. As Sarah Mendelson and John Glenn note of such organizations:[23]

> By creating a cadre of professional activists involved in their own networks, norms, and practices, Western assistance has in some ways widened the distance between the Russian women's movement and the rest of society. As civic associations become more institutionalized and professionalized, they are frequently transformed into more hierarchical, centralized corporate entities that value their own survival over their social mission. Their dependence on Western assistance often forces them to be more responsive to outside donors than to their internal constituencies. By selecting feminist organizations over other women's organizations, donors have ended up assisting organizations whose goals from the beginning were more firmly based in this transnational network than in Russian society.

Also, in a pattern familiar in many countries among many sorts of NGOs, the availability of Western funding support tends to stimulate fragmentation and competition among women's groups, as each seeks its own exclusive share of resources. With time, however, women's groups have become more conscious of the need to cooperate, pool resources, and broaden their own indigenous bases of support.[24]

However, these dilemmas of organizational development have not been a serious problem for the League of Committees of Soldiers' Mothers, which has developed a vital and self-sustaining base of support for its activity despite the sometimes-hostile attitude of the authorities. Still, the League's high international profile has made it vulnerable to the accusation that it is manipulated by foreign interests. In response, it has reduced its use of publicity-attracting public demonstrations and concentrated more on casework and lobbying through regular channels.[25]

The Federation of Independent Trade Unions of Russia. The cases of the RUIE and the Committees of Soldiers' Mothers illustrate the point that the old regime was rich in state-sponsored organizations but poor in autonomous social groups that could provide organizational resources to new interests seeking to organize and voice their demands. Official Soviet public organizations were mouthpieces of state policy and "transmission belts" for controlling society. Yet in some cases they served to foster skills and social ties that became important resources for interest organizations in the post-Soviet environment. The RUIE is an example of an organization that was built upon a Soviet-era association and that adapted itself successfully to the new postcommunist environment. The League of Committees of Soldiers' Mothers, in contrast, was an entirely new organization formed in the glasnost period, which has consciously chosen to keep its distance from the smothering embrace of the state. The first inherited networks of contacts and organizational resources from the old regime, whereas the second built itself up from scratch, taking advantage of the Internet to link branch organizations across the country as well as recognition from sympathetic organizations worldwide.

The Federation of Independent Trade Unions of Russia (FITUR) is the successor of the official trade union federation under the Soviet regime. Unlike RUIE, however, it has proven to be poor at adapting itself to the postcommunist environment although it inherited substantial organizational resources from the old Soviet trade union movement. In the Soviet era, virtually every employed person belonged to a trade union. All branch and regional trade union organizations were part of a single labor federation, called the All-Union Central Council of Trade Unions. With the breakdown of the old regime, some of the member unions became independent, while other unions sprang up as independent bodies representing the interests of particular groups of workers. Nonetheless, the nucleus of the old official trade union organization survived and is called the Federation of Independent Trade Unions of Russia. It remains by far the largest trade union federation in Russia; around 95 percent of all organized workers belong to unions that are at least formally members of FITUR. The independent unions are much smaller. By comparison with big business, however, the labor movement is fragmented, weak, and unable to mobilize workers effectively for collective action.

FITUR inherited valuable real estate assets from its Soviet-era predecessor organization, including thousands of office buildings, hotels, rest homes, hospitals, and children's camps. It also inherited the right to collect workers' contributions for the state social-insurance fund. Control of this fund has enabled the official trade unions to acquire enormous income-producing property over the years. These assets and income streams give leaders of the official unions considerable advantages in competing for members. But the FITUR no longer has centralized control over its regional and branch members. In the 1993 and 1995 parliamentary elections, for instance, member unions formed their own political alliances with parties. Thus internal disunity is another major reason for the relative weakness of FITUR as an organization. Much of its effort is expended on fighting other independent unions to win a monopoly on representing workers in collective bargaining with employers rather than in joining with other unions to defend the interests of workers generally.[26]

The ineffectiveness of the FITUR has also been illustrated by the tepid response of organized labor to the severe deterioration in labor and social conditions that occurred through the 1990s. There has been much less labor protest than might be expected. Unrest did increase through the 1990s, mainly because of wage arrears. Surveys find that in the 1990s, in any given year, three-quarters of all workers received their wages late at least once.[27] Teachers have been particularly hard-hit by the problem of unpaid wages and have organized numerous local strikes. Waves of strikes by teachers shut down thousands of schools in 1997, 1998, and 1999. During 1999–2000 teachers' protests subsided somewhat as wage arrears gradually were paid off due to the beginning of the economic recovery.[28]

We might wonder why there has not been more labor protest. One reason is workers' dependence on the enterprises where they work for a variety of social benefits that are administered through the enterprise, such as pension contributions, cheap housing, and access to medical clinics and day-care facilities.[29] Another, however, is the close, clientelistic relationship between the leadership of the FITUR and government authorities. Any time that FITUR considers any serious labor mobilization, the government threatens to take away its access to the distribution of social funds.

The Russian Orthodox Church. The great majority of the Russian people—as many as 89 percent, depending on how religious affiliation is measured—identify themselves with the Russian Orthodox Church. Another 9 to 10 percent identify with other faiths: 8 to 9 percent are Muslim, .5 to .6 percent are Buddhist, and .2 to .3 percent are Jewish.[30] The Russian Orthodox Church dates its origins to Prince Vladimir's baptism in 988 in the Kievan city-state, and considers itself to be the historic partner of the Russian state and people, providing spiritual guidance to society and sanctification of state authority in return for the state's protection. Its view of itself as a state church is at odds with the constitutional precept of the separation of church and state.[31]

During the communist era, the Russian Orthodox Church was not banned, but it was subject to persecution, at times violent, and to intense surveillance by the authorities. Young people were strongly discouraged from attending services, while party members and political officials understood that their careers would be jeopardized if they openly practiced religion. Appointments of senior clergy had to be cleared by the Communist Party, and some clergy were in fact police agents. The Church's public pronouncements had to be supportive of the state. For example, during the Cold War, church officials actively participated in the Soviet regime's propaganda campaign for "peace and justice" in the world, which was always directed against the "imperialist" world's policies, but not the communist bloc's. The Church never died out, as Soviet officials had once confidently predicted it would, but its public role was severely restricted.

The collapse of communism allowed the Church to regain much of its status and freedom.[32] Under legislation passed in 1990, the Church acquired the right of legal personhood, entitling it to own property and enter into contractual agreements. Many churches and monasteries that had been seized by the state were restored to the church, often in considerable disrepair. Religious education became legal and was even introduced in some schools. The Church also has benefited from the eagerness of the political elite to associate itself with the Church. Beginning with Gorbachev's celebration of the millenium of Russian Christianity in 1988 and continuing with President Yeltsin's attendance at major church events and Moscow Mayor Luzhkov's forceful drive to rebuild the Cathedral of Christ the Savior, torn down under Stalin, numerous Russian political leaders have found it expedient to embrace the Church as a symbol of Russian national unity and statehood. Although the 1993 constitution proclaimed the separation of church and state, state leaders have called upon the Orthodox Church to lend legitimacy to their actions. The Church, for its part, has welcomed its newly privileged status. The Patriarch, for example, attended the inaugurations of Russian Presidents Yeltsin and Putin.

The end of the Soviet regime also brought with it a religious awakening in Russia and other former Soviet republics. Many, including young people, sought to rediscover their religious heritage or to find a new religious identity. Thousands of foreign missionaries arrived to proselytize. Denominations and sects that had operated underground began to practice openly. New Protestant and Catholic churches were established. Muslim and Jewish organizations also gained strength. The Orthodox Church responded to the new activity by calling on the state to protect it against foreign competition. The Church drew a sharp distinction between those religions that had a long history on Russian soil, and hence posed less of a threat, and those that were new and alien to it. The Church pressured the president and parliament for protectionist legislation that would ban foreign missionary activity and would, in effect, require a state license for the exercise of the new religious freedom guaranteed under the Russian constitution.[33]

The idea of such a law was very popular among lawmakers, including the communists, who wanted to align themselves publicly with the moral authority of the Church. In 1997 the Duma passed and, after an initial veto and some minor revisions, President Yeltsin signed, a law that gave the Church much of what it wanted. The law was euphemistically called "On Freedom of Conscience and Religious Associations." Declaring that there were four religious communities that were historically indigenous to Russia—Orthodox Christianity, Islam, Judaism, and Buddhism—the law required that any other religious organization that wanted to operate on Russian soil would have to reregister with the state by the end of 1998. If it wanted to use the word "All-Russian" (*Rossiiskii*) in its name, an organization would have to demonstrate that it had operated in Russia for at least fifty years and had local branches in at least half the regions of the country. Alternatively, it could register if it could prove that it had a central organization and at least three regional branches and had existed in Russia for at least fifteen years. This would require that the regional authorities (many of whom were hostile to non-Orthodox faiths) provide it with a certificate that the organization had existed in that region for 15 years. Moreover, the law listed a number of grounds on which registration could be denied, including if they were harmful to the moral health and well-being of Russian citizens. Foreign missionaries would only be allowed to operate in Russia if they were invited by registered religious organizations.[34]

Many Russian and international religious groups were alarmed by this law. As experts noted, it was directed not against Islam, Judaism, or Buddhism, but against rival Christian groups that the Orthodox Church considered to be "destructive totalitarian sects," as the Patriarch termed them.[35] Several groups challenged the constitutionality of the law. In November 1999 the Constitutional Court upheld the main tenets of the law but struck down others in a decision involving congregations of Jehovah's Witnesses and Pentecostalists. It ruled that the state could restrict the activity of foreign missionaries and could ban those groups that violated human rights and Russian law. But it also declared that the clause that religious organizations had to prove they had existed for fifteen years did not apply to groups registered before the law was passed or to congregations that are part of centralized organizations. Therefore a local congregation of the Jehovah's Witnesses could be registered because the national organization had existed in Russia for more than fifty years.[36] A ruling several months later by the court went further and invalidated the other retroactive provisions.[37] Meantime, the deadline for registering religious organizations was extended, and several groups that were initially denied the right to register successfully defended their rights to registration in the courts.

The Orthodox Church holds that "the Russian people culturally, spiritually, and historically are the flock of the Russian Orthodox Church."[38] In contrast to the Western Christian doctrine of separation between the authority of the state and the authority of religion, Russian Orthodoxy regards church and state as interlocked elements of an organic national community.[39] It considers religious identification to be an attribute of a nationality, not simply a matter of individual taste, and it regards the Russian Orthodox Church as the patrimony of the Russians—whether they are believers or not. Therefore it is hostile to any efforts at conversion by outsiders, arguing that Western missionaries are trying to "buy" Russians' souls with promises of material prosperity. The Orthodox Church is amenable to coexisting with other religious communities in Russia, such as Muslims, Jews, and Buddhists, so long as the boundaries among the ethnic groups belonging to each religious community are respected. But it is deeply antagonistic to other Christian groups that believe Russia, like Western societies, should be religiously pluralistic. Because state leaders, both liberal and communist, have been solicitous of the Church for their own political interests, they have been unwilling to cross the Church on matters of religious politics. The Church's intense animosity toward the Catholic Church, for example, has made it impossible for the pope to pay a state visit to Russia.

In its political activity, the Church has formed a relationship of reciprocal dependence with state authorities, as in the prerevolutionary era: It looks to the state for protection and privileges, and in turn grants the state authorities moral sanction for their actions. If there is to be change in this symbiotic relationship, it will probably come from within the Church, as believers demand that the Church stop depending on the state for its power and status and instead draw its strength from the commitment of the faithful.

Rise of the Oligarchs. The term *oligarchs* has come to refer to a small group of wealthy and powerful individuals who succeeded in taking advantage of the opening of the Russian economy to acquire ownership of Russia's most lucrative industrial and natural resource assets.[40] Political contacts helped them win crucial licenses and monopolies early in the postcommunist period; by building up great economic empires they also became immensely powerful in the political realm.

The rise of the oligarchs was helped by Yeltsin's privatization policies, but in fact they got their start well before the Soviet regime fell. As the system of centralized administrative control over economic resources collapsed in the late 1980s, well-placed officials in the party, the KGB, and the Komsomol (Soviet Youth League) began cashing in on their power and privileges. Some quietly liquidated the assets of their organizations and secreted the proceeds in overseas accounts and investments.[41] Others created banks and businesses in Russia, taking advantage of their insider positions to win exclusive government contracts and licenses, and to acquire financial credits and supplies at artificially low, state-subsidized prices in order to transact business at high, market-value prices. Great fortunes were made almost overnight. Access to capital and contacts from the old regime helped these new "*biznesmeny*" considerably. Some called this wave of quasi-market activity "*nomenklatura* capitalism." By the time that the Soviet regime fell and the Yeltsin government began to try to establish a working market economy, some of the *nomenklatura* capitalists had already entrenched themselves as powerful players.

Privatization of state enterprises then gave many who had gained wealth in the late 1980s an opportunity to convert it into shares of privatized enterprises. The Yeltsin government hoped to use privatization to spread ownership of shares in formerly state enterprises as widely as possible, to create support for the market economy and to give as many people as possible a stake in it. The government used a system of free vouchers as a way to give mass privatization a jump start. But it also allowed people to purchase shares of stock in privatized enterprises with cash. As the government ended the voucher privatization phase and launched cash privatization, it devised a program that it thought would simultaneously speed up privatization and yield the government a much-needed infusion of cash for its operating needs. Under the scheme, which quickly became known in the West as "loans for shares," the government auctioned off substantial packages of stock shares in some of its most desirable enterprises, such as energy, telecommunications, and metallurgical firms, as collateral for bank loans. Under the terms of the deals, if the government did not repay the loans by September 1, 1996, the lender acquired title to the stock and could subsequently resell it or take an equity position in the enterprise. The first such auctions were held in the fall of 1995. The auctions themselves were usually held in such a way as to limit the number of banks bidding for the shares and thus to keep the auction prices conveniently low. By summer 1996, sizable packages of shares in some of Russia's largest firms had been transferred to a small number of major banks at bargain prices. Immediately there was public criticism of these deals for being, in effect, giveaways of valuable state assets to a few powerful, well-connected, and wealthy financial groups. For example, financing from the bank Menatep, which had been formed in 1990 by a group of young ex-Komsomol activists working in the Moscow city government, helped an affiliated company acquire control of the large oil firm Yukos; similarly, the bank Oneximbank acquired a 38 percent stake in the metallurgical giant, Norilsk Nickel, for a loan of $170 million. Oneximbank was headed by Vladimir Potanin, who, coincidentally enough, had designed the loans-for-shares scheme in 1995. In spring 1996, Parliament's Audit Chamber and the Procurator-General demanded that the courts reverse these deals, but by then the government had long since spent the cash proceeds from the auctions. And in September 1996, Potanin, whom Yeltsin had by now appointed first deputy minister in charge of the economy, declared that there was to be no rollback of the deals.[42] (See Close Up 6.1: The Norilsk Nickel Affair.)

The concentration of immense financial and industrial power, which loans for shares had substantially accelerated, extended to the mass media. One of the most prominent of the financial barons, Boris Berezovsky, who controlled major stakes in several banks and companies (including Aeroflot), acquired an 8 percent stake in the main state television company, ORT, when 49 percent of its shares were auctioned off; one of Berezovsky's banks was part of a banking consortium that owned 38 percent of ORT. Berezovsky himself became deputy director of the company and was considered to exert extensive influence over its programming. Berezovsky and the other ultrawealthy and well-connected tycoons who controlled these great empires of finance, industry, energy, telecommunications, and media became known as the "oligarchs." Yeltsin and his entourage had given them a royal opportunity to scoop up some of Russia's most desirable assets in return for their help in his reelection effort. The oligarchs returned the favor. In the spring of 1996, with Yeltsin's popularity at a low ebb, they agreed that they would cooperate in doing what they could to assure his reelection. How much money they poured into Yeltsin's reelection campaign is still a matter of dispute—some say the quantity was relatively insignificant—but there is no question about the fact that the media properties that they controlled were all turned to the service of ensuring Yeltsin's reelection. The media painted a picture of a fateful choice for Russia, between Yeltsin and a return to totalitarianism, directly serving Yeltsin's campaign strategy and unquestionably helping him win.

Are the "oligarchs" in any sense an interest group organized to serve collective interests? Boris Berezovsky was probably being more boastful than candid when he told the *Financial Times,* a few weeks after Yeltsin appointed him deputy secretary of the Security Council (October 1996), that there was now a group of seven individuals, with substantial influence over government, who controlled banks and

---

Close Up 6.1   Norilsk Nickel and the "Loans-for-Shares" Scheme

A notorious case of insider dealing was the privatization of Norilsk Nickel, a giant metallurgical firm in Russia's North that produces over 20 percent of the world's supply of nickel. An inefficient, debt-ridden behemoth of a company, it was also potentially one of Russia's most valuable assets. In 1995, with elections approaching and the government desperate for cash, a prominent entrepreneur named Vladimir Potanin proposed a deal to the government. His bank would bid on the right to manage a block of 51 percent of the shares of Norilsk Nickel in return for granting a loan to the government. If after a year's time the government failed to repay the loan, the bank would have the right to purchase the shares outright. He proposed conducting similar auctions for several other companies of strategic importance as well. Yeltsin and the government approved the plan despite the fact that it was clearly designed to turn over ownership of some of Russia's crown jewels to a small coterie of tycoons. Potanin's bank organized the auctions and banks he controlled were the sole bidders for Norilsk Nickel. Not surprisingly, his bid won. A year later, when the government failed to repay the loan, Potanin proceeded to acquire majority ownership in Norilsk Nickel. This was an astonishing bargain: For $170 million, Potanin bought a company whose output accounts for 1.9 percent of Russia's GDP.[1] Since Russia's GDP was estimated to be worth $323 billion in 2002, the company's production was worth over $6.4 billion. The case of Norilsk Nickel was only one example of the infamous "loans for shares" scheme. Controlling interests in several of Russia's largest oil companies were auctioned off to other oligarchs, also at dirt-cheap prices. The entire loans-for-shares program stands as one of the most flagrant examples of the cozy, collusive relationship between Russia's oligarchs and the Yeltsin regime.

[1]**www.nornik.ru/page.jsp?pageId=about**.

---

businesses that together controlled half of the economy. Berezovsky went on to justify this situation: "I think two types of power are possible. Either a power of ideology or a power of capital. Ideology is now dead, and today we have a period of transition from the power of ideology to the power of capital." Echoing the famous comment (by General Motors' chairman) that "what's good for General Motors is good for the USA," Berezovsky observed: "I think that if something is advantageous to capital, it goes without saying that it's advantageous to the nation. It's capital that is in a condition, to the greatest extent, to express the interests of the nation."[43] Berezovsky was surely exaggerating both the public-mindedness of the oligarchs and the degree to which they formed a coherent, coordinated group.

Yet for a moment in 1996, when Yeltsin's reelection hung in the balance, the oligarchs came close to forming a kind of board of directors for Russia; however, once Yeltsin was reelected they fell out and began feuding with one another. The 1998 financial crash hurt all of them and nearly wiped several out. But their power was real and proved extremely difficult to eradicate: A telling illustration of the point was the formation of a monopolistic giant controlling nearly the entire Russian aluminum industry in spring 2000. The new holding company was formed by Boris Berezovsky and Roman Abramovich (who through the Sibneft' oil company had purchased several aluminum-producing firms representing about 70 percent of Russian production), along with the Siberian Aluminum Company and Alfa Bank, with support from Anatolii Chubais, chairman of Unified Energy System. The holding group, called Russian Aluminum, was to act as a cartel, coordinating pricing among its constituent members. The head of the government's antimonopoly ministry declared that he saw no objection to the new entity, on the grounds that in view of international competition, the merger served Russia's national interests.[44] Thus the oligarchs proved that they were well able to cooperate when it served their common interest, although how much their common interest in fact served Russia's national interests was another matter entirely. Competitive as they are, the oligarchs were able to organize for collective action when it suited their needs. But their influence as a group depended on the unique environment of Yeltsin's presidency, when a weakening Yeltsin, faced with substantial political opposition and uncontrollable government deficits, gave them enormous assets at bargain-basement prices.

Putin's strength has meant that the oligarchs are no longer a collective force, although individually they remain extremely influential. In July 2000, Putin held a widely publicized meeting with several of the most influential oligarchs. There, according to later reports, he told them what the terms of their relations with the state would be under his rule. He promised that the oligarchs' property would be secure, no matter how dubious the manner in which it had been acquired, so long as they kept out of high politics and as long as they began investing in Russia rather than sending their money abroad.[45] Since then, most of the oligarchs have been content to abide by the new rules of the game. They have competed to build political machines at the level of regional government, but generally refrain from trading on connections with the Kremlin. Putin forced Berezovsky and another prominent oligarch, Vladimir Gusinsky, to relinquish their substantial media holdings (see Close Up 6.2: Putin and the Media). Both are now under indictment and living abroad. The lesson for the other oligarchs was clear: So long as they refrained from using their media holdings to advance their own political agendas, they were free to continue to amass wealth and power.

Moreover, there are at least suggestions that the oligarchs' interests themselves are changing. Much like American robber barons of the early twentieth century, Russia's oligarchs may be discovering that it is more profitable to live under the rule of law and enjoy social respect than it is to gain wealth through subverting the system. A significant case in point is Mikhail Khodorkovsky and his oil firm Yukos. Khodorkovsky is Russia's wealthiest person and is estimated to be worth $7–8 billion. Yukos is valued at nearly $20 billion; Khodorkovsky owns 36 percent of the firm. As we saw, in 1995 Khodorkovsky acquired around

Close Up 6.2   Putin and the Media

In 2000 and 2001, two Russian television companies, NTV and TV-6, were the targets of a takeover by the authorities using legal tactics of bankruptcy proceedings and civil suits. The companies were owned by two oligarchs, Vladimir Gusinsky and Boris Berezovsky, who had enjoyed considerable political visibility in the Yeltsin era but who had fallen out with the new Putin administration.

Gusinsky owned a sizable banking and media conglomerate. His media holding company, Media-Most, owned NTV, which was Russia's only fully private national television channel. NTV boasted a team of independent-minded journalists who were often critical of the authorities. In June 2000, Gusinsky was arrested on charges of embezzling funds from the state; Putin, who was traveling in Spain at the time, claimed to know nothing about the case: "If it's the procurator general [who arrested Gusinsky]," he said, "they are independent and make decisions on their own. I don't know anything about it."[1] Three days later, Gusinsky was released but the pressure on him continued to mount. The state-owned gas monopoly Gazprom, which had loaned Media-Most sizable amounts of money, filed suit against Media-Most, demanding repayment of the loans. Putin again claimed that the case had nothing to do with freedom of the press and re-fused to interfere on the grounds that he considered "it wrong to interfere in a conflict between two commercial organizations."[2] Gazprom went to court demanding that the company turn over a controlling stake in the company to repay the loans. The courts sided with Gazprom, which then proceeded to take over Media-Most. Gazprom installed new management and forced out a large number of the journalists working at NTV. NTV resumed broadcasting, but became a vehicle for tame entertainment and pro-Putin news. In May 2001, a court ordered the liquidation of the entire Media-Most company on the grounds that it was behind in its tax debt to the government. Gusinsky, now outside Russia, was indicted on fraud charges.

Meantime the authorities also moved against Boris Berezovsky. When Gazprom took over NTV, many of the journalists who worked there went to work for TV-6. Berezovsky was the majority shareholder in TV-6, but 15 percent of the shares were owned by an investment arm of the giant oil company, LUKoil, called LUKoil-Garant. As soon as the NTV team went over to TV-6, LUKoil-Garant filed suit to force TV-6 into bankruptcy. LUKoil claimed that it was acting out of purely commercial motives. This was hard to believe because TV-6 was beginning to be profitable after two years of operating losses. The courts upheld LUKoil-Garant's suit and de-clared TV-6 bankrupt. The government then auctioned off its broadcast li-cense to a new company that was politically reliable.

(continued)

Close Up 6.2 *(continued)*

The use of civil lawsuits against NTV and TV-6 allowed Putin to deny that there were any political machinations at work. But it is clear that in both cases, the courts were being used to end the independence of the two television companies that were owned by the two oligarchs most opposed to President Putin and that had been willing to pursue an independent editorial line. These actions not only tamed NTV and TV-6, but they sent an unmistakable warning to other media organizations to exercise considerable caution in how they covered the news. As one Russian parliamentarian put it, under Putin "there is freedom of speech, but not in prime time."[3]

[1]RFE/RL Newsline, 14 June 2000.
[2]RFE/RL Newsline, 27 September 2000.
[3]Quoted in Daniel Treisman, "Russia Renewed?" *Foreign Affairs* 81:6 (November/December 2002), p. 69.

---

80 percent of Yukos, which had been state-owned, by rigging the loans-for-shares program. With time, however, Khodorkovsky has found that by emulating Western business practices he could become far wealthier. He has made ownership and management of Yukos increasingly transparent in an effort to get his firm listed on Western stock exchanges. In turn, improving the efficiency and transparency of the firm has boosted share prices—and Khodorkovsky's net worth—substantially.

Meantime Khodorkovsky has created a foundation called Open Russia and launched several charitable initiatives in Russia, funding schools, hospitals, science, cultural exchange programs, and other worthy causes. He has recruited some distinguished international figures (among them Henry Kissinger) to his foundation's board and has actively worked to polish his reputation in Europe and the United States.[46] Many observers expect that other oligarchs will follow Khodorkovsky's example and reap the benefits of respectability.

New Sectors of Interest

We have seen that in a time when people's interests themselves are changing rapidly as a result of social change, both old and new organizations find it hard to stay united. As is true everywhere, smaller groups have an easier time acting collectively than do large, dispersed groups. Overall, the pattern is clearly one of a shift from a statist pattern of interest organization to pluralism. The statist inheritance remains significant, as shown by the cases of the trade unions and RUIE, which are built on Soviet-era organizations. But, for the most part, the prevailing pattern is pluralist, as is indicated further by the formation of new associations speaking for interests that had never been organized in the past, such as the Committees of Soldiers' Mothers and tens of thousands of other organized associations.

Among these are organizations that promote the interests of particular categories of officials, business, or social groups, such as associations for governors; associations of mayors of small towns and of mayors of closed cities; associations of small businesses and of entrepreneurs; associations for particular industries, such as the beer-brewing industry; and associations for particular categories of the population, such as the Association of Indigenous Peoples of the North and the Far East. There are many new professional associations, which act to set guidelines for professional practice, seeking to fend off onerous government restrictions and to regulate entry into their fields. For instance, three associations of defense attorneys (*advokaty*, who will be discussed further in Chapter 8) united in September 1994 under an umbrella association to press government to increase their autonomy to regulate legal practice.[47] Television broadcast companies founded a National Association of Television Broadcasters on August 31, 1995, to seek the expansion of private ownership of television facilities and tax relief for broadcasters.[48] In May 2000, representatives of 150 auditing and consulting firms formed their own national federation to set professional standards with which to regulate their own activity.[49] In January 2001, heads of publishing and media firms from twenty different regions formed an Association of Independent Publishers and Editors. Public relations firms created the Russian Association of Public Relations, which celebrated its tenth anniversary in October 2001.[50] Reindeer breeders have formed the Russian Union of Reindeer Breeders, which held a congress in Salekhard—located just south of the Arctic Circle, in the Yamalo-Nenets Autonomous Okrug—in March 2002, where they warned of the "tragic" consequences of the steep drop in the size of the reindeer herds.[51] One of the most recent interest groups to form is the Public Organization for the Defense of the Rights of Owners of Cars with Right-Hand Steering Wheels, which recently registered in Vladivostok. Press reports indicated that despite its name, the actual aim of the group was to lobby for a roll-back of new customs duties on imported cars (many Japanese cars imported to the Far East have right-hand steering wheels).[52]

Groups with charitable, social services, environmental, consumers' rights, and human rights interests have also formed by the tens of thousands. One of the most prominent is Memorial, which arose in the Gorbachev period to honor the memory of the victims of Stalin's repressions, and which has continued to work to protect human rights and democratic freedoms.[53] Most organizations are local. Examples are the Nizhnii Novgorod Society for Human Rights; the Center for the Support of Democratic Youth Initiatives in the city of Perm, which helps young men who want to do alternative service defend their legal rights; the Chukotka Ecology Society; the Magadan Center for the Environment; the Moscow Fellowship of Alcoholics Anonymous (AA started in Russia in 1987, and there are now some 300 AA groups around the country); and a group in Moscow called "the Circle," which offers special classes in music, dance, and theater to disabled children.[54]

Many local groups join together in national associations to amplify their clout. Examples include the All-Russian Society of Invalids; the Association of Help Hotlines (which represents 200 crisis helplines in sixty-eight cities); the Forum of Ecological Organizations; the Confederation of Consumers' Societies; and the Union of Charitable Organizations of Russia. Some groups act as facilitators of other nongovernmental organizations (an example is the Support Center for NGOs of Yaroslavl, which publishes directories with contact information for other organizations).[55]

Russian civic groups operate under very difficult circumstances, including unpredictable and sometimes hostile treatment by the authorities; scarcity of office space and other material resources; obstacles to communication with prospective members and with other groups; and habits of secretiveness and hoarding of information. Faced with economic and political pressure, many are dependent on foreign support, while others attempt to win official status and budget support from government. Some are simply fronts for commercial activity, and many are only sporadically active. Although only a very small number of citizens are members of such organizations, many more benefit from their activity (some NGOs claim that as many as 12 or 13 percent of the population receive assistance from civic organizations each year).[56] Taken together, they represent a substantial sector of independent civic activity.

The importance of these associations was recognized by the Putin administration, but its response has been to find a centralized, top-down method for aggregating the demands of civil society. Putin's administration pressed to create a comprehensive umbrella organization through which civic organizations could channel their demands. Representatives of civic organizations have been understandably wary of Putin's calls for "dialogue" on these terms, which they fear could lead to the imposition of state control. But they have cautiously welcomed Putin's expressions of support for the existence of civil society. In November 2001, a large assembly called the "Civic Forum" convened in the Kremlin's Palace of Congresses (where in the past, the Communist Party used to hold its congresses every five years). Some 5,000 delegates representing civic groups from all over Russia assembled. President Putin and most of the senior officials of the presidential administration and government attended the meeting. Addressing the assembly, Putin had warm words for the principle of civil society, observing that "civil society cannot be formed at the initiative of government officials" and disavowing any desire to subordinate civil society to the state. Rather, he noted that civil society "grows up on its own, feeding on the spirit of freedom" and cited the Internet as an example of the way state and society can work together for mutual benefit.[57] The meeting broke into a number of thematic working sessions, which drew up resolutions that were signed by members of the civic associations and the government.

Ultimately, little came of these documents, although one or two found their way into subsequent government policy planning on issues such as the problem of homeless children. Putin has not repeated the experiment and most observers said that it showed the failure of Putin's strategy for coopting civil society. Still, although the NGOs had little impact on national policy, they did succeed in fending off the clumsy efforts by state officials to bring them under state management. The event was noteworthy for the way it revived an old-fashioned, Russian and Soviet tradition—of convening a grand conclave to represent "society" under state-controlled auspices—for the purpose of performing an essentially post-Soviet function, that of aggregating the interests of society and transmitting them to policy makers. But if the Civic Forum was the last gasp of the old patrimonial, top-down style of coordinating and channeling society's demands, we might then ask how well other institutions perform the task of interest aggregation. In particular, what role do Russian political parties play in the political process?

INTEREST AGGREGATION: TOWARD A MULTIPARTY SYSTEM

Political scientists distinguish between the *articulation* of interests and their *aggregation*: Interest articulation is the voicing of demands by organized groups seeking to advance particular causes and interests. The major questions about interest articulation have to do with the nature of groups that have organized and what their political strategy is. Are they working inside the political establishment, or mobilizing popular pressure from outside it? Do they represent a broad or narrow constituency? How has the legacy of past organization influenced their current development as organizations? In the case of Russia, many present-day groups originated when old Soviet-era public associations began to adapt or collapse in the late 1980s and early 1990s, while others arose as independent groups in opposition to the Soviet regime. Although usable organizational resources were in short supply, some of the social capital created under the old regime played an important part in helping new groups to form.

Interest aggregation refers to the amalgamation of the demands of various groups of the population into programmatic options for government. Typically this is a by-product of the activity of political parties as they compete for voter support in elections and organize to assume responsibility for governing. Parties offer policy programs that they hope will attract wide support, generalizing the interests of the many in order to win a share of governing power. Although other political institutions also aggregate interests, among them the mass media, parliaments, and large interest groups, it is parties that are the quintessential agency performing this vital task of the political process. Indeed, most political scientists share the view that, as Seymour Martin Lipset put it, "modern democracy is unthinkable save in terms of parties."[58] This is because parties offer voters both choice and accountability: They give voters a choice over competing policy directions for government and make public officials responsible for their behavior in office. The question of whether and how well parties in Russia are serving to aggregate interests, define choices for voters, and hold politicians accountable for their use of power is therefore central to assessing the quality of democracy in Russia.

Russia today has around fifty organizations registered with the government as political parties but only a small number are electorally viable. There are around 150 more organizations registered as "social-political associations." Political associations are allowed to participate in politics, but—under a new law that took effect in 2001—only parties are allowed to compete in elections. Table 6.1 lists the most prominent political parties as of the end of 2002, together with an indication of their level of electoral support.

Some contemporary Russian parties grew out of the "informal" groups and movements that mobilized during the glasnost period.[59] Others emerged from the CPSU, as it fractured into hard-line and more liberal wings in 1989–1990. Still other parties are organizations formed by officeholding politicians who want to hold on to power by winning the next elections. Many politicians who belong to a party have only a weak attachment to their party (this is not true of the communists, however, nor of a few other parties). However, because the election law used to elect deputies to the Duma requires that half the seats in the Duma be filled from party lists, politicians who want to win or keep their parliamentary offices find it useful to affiliate themselves with a party. And once they are in the Duma, deputies affiliate themselves with parliamentary parties. Parliamentary elections are strongly influenced by party competition—it is executive power that avoids partisanship and thus weakens electoral accountability.

Russian parties usually adopt one of two political strategies. Some espouse a particular ideological outlook, while others avoid taking a clear policy stance and instead identify themselves with broad, vague appeals to support the status quo. Of those with a definable ideological stance, three main strains are apparent: democratic, communist, and nationalist. Although specific party names and organizational identities continue to evolve rapidly, the position of ideologically oriented parties can usually be identified in terms of support for a capitalist economy, liberal individualism, and a Western orientation (the democratic parties); support for a strong, centralized state-dominated economic and political system (the communist parties); and a proimperial or proethnic nationalist, anti-Western orientation (the nationalist parties). The nonideological parties offer a bland mixture of appeals to noncontroversial values, such as "centrism," "unity," "pragmatism," and "a strong state." Often such parties are simply political machines for officeholders, and are commonly termed "parties of power."

The greatest impetus to the development of political parties as electoral organizations has been the parliamentary elections of 1989, 1990, 1993, 1995, and 1999. Each round of elections stimulated a burst of organizational activity.[60] Presidential elections, on the other hand, held in 1991, 1996, and 2000, have not had a similar effect. Because Russia's presidential system encourages the president to avoid making commitments to parties, presidential elections have tended to concentrate attention on the candidates' personalities rather than their policy programs and therefore have even undermined party development. The same has been true of gubernatorial elections.

—————————————————— **TABLE 6.1** ——————————————————

Russian Political Parties and Electoral Support, November 2002 VTsIOM Survey Question: "If the Duma elections were to be held next Sunday, for which party would you vote?" (in percent)

	Oct-00	Jan-01	Apr-01	Jun-01	Dec-01	Jun-02	Nov-02
CPRF (Communist Party of the Russian Federation)	37	35	39	35	35	29	27
United Russia*	—	—	—	—	30	25	29
Unity	21	21	22	23	—	—	—
Fatherland	3	4	4	4	—	—	—
Yabloko	9	9	10	6	6	6	9
LDPR (Liberal Democratic Party of Russia)	6	6	7	8	5	9	5
SPS (Union of Right Forces)	11	11	7	8	6	8	10
Women of Russia	4	4	6	4	6	7	6
Russia/Seleznev (as of November 02 renamed "Party of Rebirth of Russia")	2	1	1	1	1	2	2
RNE (Russian National Unity)	1	1	1	1	2	2	2
Agrarian Party	—	—	—	—	1	3	1
People's Party	—	—	—	—	<1	<1	1
United Social-Democratic Party	—	—	—	—	1	2	1
Party for the Development of Entrepreneurship under Ivan Grachev and O. Dmitrieva	—	—	—	—	—	1	<1
Democratic Party (Prusak)	—	—	—	—	1	1	1
Liberal Russia	—	—	—	—	0	<1	<1
Other	1	1	1	1	1	0	1
Against all	3	5	5	5	5	5	5

*Note that as of December 2001, Unity and Fatherland merged into a single new party, called United Russia. Percentages reflect only those intending to vote who have decided on a particular party. Columns may not sum to 100% due to rounding.

Source: VTsIOM National Surveys, as posted to **www.wciom.ru/vciom/new/press/press021127**. N = 1,600. Margin of error = 3.8%.

The 1989 and 1990 Elections. The elections of USSR deputies in early 1989 produced the first efforts by like-minded activists to elect candidates sympathetic to their views, as democratically oriented intellectuals organized to elect Andrei Sakharov and other champions of the democratic movement. Then, when the USSR Congress of People's Deputies convened in May 1989, Sakharov and other newly elected deputies formed the first independent legislative caucus in Soviet history: the "Interregional Group of Deputies." In turn, it became the organizational nucleus for the formation of a still broader coalition of democratic candidates running for the Russian Congress of People's Deputies and for seats in lower soviets in the March 1990 elections; this coalition was called "Democratic Russia." After the election, Democratic Russia's deputies in the Russian parliament divided up into several parliamentary factions that sought to coordinate their actions and press for support of economic and political reform. But the creation of the presidency and the growing strength of the anti-Yeltsin opposition in the parliament weakened the democratic forces. Dozens of deputies left parliament to take jobs in the presidential administration.[61]

Both the USSR and Russian parliaments in the transition period had large communist factions that fought bitterly against the dismantling of the state socialist system, but in neither 1989 nor 1990 did the communists form a cohesive electoral bloc that could rally voters to their cause. Likewise the transition parliaments saw organized nationalist and agrarian factions that lacked nationwide electoral organizations. In 1993 these groups competed vigorously with the democrats for electoral support.

The 1993 Elections. Yeltsin's decrees of September and October 1993 dissolving parliament and calling for new elections in December radically changed the incentives facing political parties. Most important was the fact that the electoral law that he enacted by decree introduced a strong proportional representation element into the election of new deputies. Elections in the past had used a single-member district system exclusively. As we know, the new 1993 system divided the seats in the lower house of parliament, the State Duma, into two categories. Each voter would have two votes, one for a candidate running for that electoral district's seat, the other for one of the registered parties putting up candidates on party lists. Half, or 225, of the seats in the Duma would be filled by the winners of single-member district seats. The other 225 seats would go to candidates nominated on party lists, according to the share each party received in the proportional representation ballot, so long as the party won at least 5 percent of the valid party list vote.

The electoral law had been discussed and debated for well over a year before Yeltsin enacted it, and there was a widespread consensus among both pro-Yeltsin and anti-Yeltsin groups that a mixed election system would combine the advantages of a single-member district model (particularly the individual ties between a deputy and a district) with those of a proportional representation system (the stimulus the law gave for the formation of national political parties as a means to stabilize and channel political activity in the country). For party leaders, whether they were opposition, centrist, or reformist, the law provided real benefits. The fact that the party leaders would choose the order in which the candidates running under that party's label were listed on the ballot (the voter could not mark a preference for one candidate on the list over another—the voter simply chose which list he or she preferred) gave the leaders incentives for attracting other politicians to their organization. The electoral law therefore served the political ambitions of party leaders of all ideological camps. Perhaps that is the reason that there was little protest over the details of Yeltsin's electoral law.

The new institutional setting had a strong impact on the outcome of the elections. For one thing, Yeltsin's law set very high requirements on registration of parties.[62] Only twenty-one parties submitted lists to the Central Electoral Commission by the deadline and only thirteen of these were approved.[63] For another, the PR (proportional-representation) portion of the electoral system created one Russia-wide district in which aggregate shares of parties' votes would be tallied, rather than a larger number of multimember districts. This was done to reduce the chances that parties with a strong regional or ethnic appeal might win seats and weaken the state's unity. A third factor was the short time the parties had to organize and mount campaigns. A fourth was the fact that many voters formed their opinions about the parties based on the televised images of their leaders' personalities. The vivid television presence of Vladimir Zhirinovsky, therefore, was converted through the PR system into a large share of seats for his party in parliament. Finally, the law specified that only parties exceeding 5 percent of the party list vote were eligible to receive seats. Again, this was done to filter out potentially destabilizing fringe parties. This feature also had a considerable impact, since five of the thirteen parties competing for the list vote failed to clear the 5 percent hurdle. These features of the electoral law therefore had a very substantial effect: Of dozens, if not hundreds, of organizations that might have attempted to field candidates, only eight succeeded in entering parliament through proportional representation.

Once elected, deputies are free to affiliate with factions and in practice, many deputies leave one faction and join another if they decide that another faction's position is more to their liking. Even deputies elected on one party's list sometimes change factions. Many deputies elected in single-member district races have only loose ties to a party, or run as independents. Once they enter the Duma they choose which faction to join or whether to join one of the factions for independents. For this reason, the results of the party list part of the vote are a poor guide to the actual balance of political forces in parliament.

Table 6.2 indicates the results of the party list voting in the 1993, 1995, and 1999 elections, and Table 6.3 shows how they translated into the shares of seats held by the Duma factions at the beginning of each new convocation. As Table 6.3 indicates, some parliamentary factions have been overwhelmingly composed of deputies elected in the party list portion of the election. A few are evenly balanced between list and single-member district (SMD). And some factions are "start-up" groups made up of independents elected in SMD races who do not wish to affiliate themselves with the party factions.

TABLE 6.2
Party List Vote in Duma Elections, 1993, 1995, 1999

Party	Election year		
	1993	**1995**	**1999**
Democratic parties			
Russia's Choice	15.51	3.9	—
Union of Rightist Forces (SPS)	—	—	8.52
Yabloko	7.86	6.89	5.93
Party of Russian Unity and Concord (PRES)	6.76	—	—
Democratic Party of Russia (DPR)	5.52	—	—
Centrist parties			
Women of Russia	8.13	4.6	2.04
Civic Union[1]	1.93	1.6	—
"Parties of power"			
Our Home Is Russia	—	10.1	1.2
Fatherland-All Russia (OVR)	—	—	13.33
Unity	—	—	23.32
Nationalist parties			
Liberal Democratic Party of Russia (LDPR)[2]	22.92	11.2	5.98
Congress of Russian Communities (KRO)[3]	—	4.3	.62
Leftist parties			
Communist Party of the Russian Federation (CPRF)	12.4	22.3	24.29
Agrarian	7.99	3.8	—
Communists, Laborers of Russia for the Soviet Union	—	4.5	2.22
Against all	4.36	2.8	3.34
Parties failing to meet 5% threshold	8.72	49.28	12.89

[1] In 1995, the same alliance renamed itself the Bloc of Trade Unionists and Industrialists.
[2] In 1999, the LDPR list was named the Zhirinovsky Bloc.
[3] In 1999, this party was called "Congress of Russian Communities and Yuri Boldyrev Movement."

Source: RFE/RL Newsline, various dates; Central Electoral Commission reports.

Thirteen parties won registration to field party lists in the December 1993 election, and eight cleared the 5 percent threshold to parliamentary representation. The election produced a shock—the pro-reform, pro-Yeltsin Russia's Choice did unexpectedly poorly, while Vladimir Zhirinovsky's misleadingly named Liberal Democratic Party of Russia (LDPR) did unexpectedly well. The flamboyant Zhirinovsky, given to extravagant displays of chauvinism and

---
TABLE 6.3

Factional Strength in the State Duma

	1994–1995 Duma[1]			1996–1999 Duma[2]			2000–2003 Duma[3]		
	List deputies	SMD deputies	Total deputies	List deputies	SMD deputies	Total deputies	List deputies	SMD deputies	Total deputies
Russia's Choice	40	33	73	—	—	—	—	—	—
SPS[4]	—	—	—	—	—	—	24	8	32
PRES	18	12	30	—	—	—	—	—	—
Yabloko	20	8	28	31	15	46	16	5	21
Liberal Democratic Union of Dec. 12	0	26	26	—	—	—	—	—	—
DPR[5]	14	1	15	—	—	—	—	—	—
Our Home Is Russia	—	—	—	45	20	65	—	—	—
OVR[6]	—	—	—	—	—	—	30	17	47
Unity	—	—	—	—	—	—	65	17	82
Women of Russia	21	2	23	—	—	—	—	—	—
New Regional Policy	0	66	66	—	—	—	—	—	—
Regions of Russia	—	—	—	0	41	41	6	34	40
Agrarian Party[7]	21	34	55	2	33	35	16	26	42
LDPR[8]	59	5	64	50	1	51	15	1	16
Russia's Way	0	14	14	—	—	—	—	—	—
People's Power	—	—	—	2	35	37	—	—	—
CPRF[9]	32	13	45	95	54	149	50	39	89
Unaffiliated deputies	0	10	10	0	16	16	2	18	20

[1]Figures as of April 1994.
[2]Figures as of February 1996.
[3]Figures as of March 2000.
[4]Union of Rightist Forces.
[5]Democratic Party of Russia.
[6]Fatherland-All Russia.
[7]In the Duma that convened in 2000, the parliamentary faction affiliated with the communist wing of the Agrarian Party renamed itself "the Agro-Industrial Group."
[8]Liberal Democratic Party of Russia.
[9]Communist Party of the Russian Federation.

bravado, liked to boast that he had "won" the elections, although in the end, his poor showing in single-member district races meant that he wound up with only 14 percent of the Duma's seats. The democratic factions received about 38 percent of the seats in the Duma, the left about 20 percent, and centrist factions about 20 percent. No political camp had a majority, but Zhirinovsky's oppositional stance meant the anti-Yeltsin forces had a narrow majority.

The December 1993 elections, Yeltsin decreed, were to elect a transitional Duma. Elections were to be held again two years later, in December 1995, for a new Duma that would have the right to serve out its full, constitutionally man-dated four-year term unless it was dissolved prematurely. The elections were held on schedule on December 17, 1995.

The 1995 Elections. During the 1994–1995 period, some Duma factions lost mem-bers, and new factions formed. The major party factions retained their influence and identity throughout the life of the 1994–95 Duma, however. Each faction in turn then developed a campaign organization and list of candidates to com-pete for seats in the Duma elections of 1995. Altogether 400 (90 percent) of the deputies ran for reelection to the Duma and 158 (40 percent) were successful.

This time an immense array of political groups competed to elect deputies—far more than could possibly be accommodated given that the same 5 percent threshold rule was kept. Some forty-three organizations succeeded in registering and winning a spot on the ballot. But in the end, only four parties crossed the 5 percent threshold: the communists, Zhirinovsky's LDPR, the "Our Home Is Russia" bloc formed around Prime Minister Chernomyrdin, and the Yabloko bloc led by Grigorii Yavlinsky. Of these, the communists were the most successful, with 22.7 percent of the party list votes. Zhirinovsky's party won 11.4 percent; Our Home Is Russia (NDR, in its Russian initials) took 10.3 percent, and Yabloko 7.0 percent. The proliferation of reform-oriented parties associated with prominent personalities split much of the pro-reform vote among them, with the result that 8.2 percent of the votes went to four small democratic par-ties that failed to cross the 5 percent barrier. Another 11.5 percent went to cen-trist groups that also failed to clear the threshold.

Altogether, half of the votes were cast for parties that failed to win any seats on the party list ballot. These votes were redistributed to the parties that did clear the threshold, as is usual in proportional-representation systems. As a result, each of the four winners gained about twice as many seats as they would have been entitled to had there been no wasted votes. Moreover, the communists were quite success-ful in winning district seats, taking more than fifty. Combined with the seats they won through the party list vote, they wound up with one-third of the seats in parlia-ment, the highest share that they or any party had held in the previous Duma.

The 1996 Presidential Election. The 1995 parliamentary election was considered to be a test of strength for Russia's parties and leaders. The big unknown was how Yeltsin would perform. At the beginning of 1996 his popularity ratings were ex-tremely low: In early March, Yeltsin was preferred by only 8 percent of the elec-torate, while 24 percent said they supported Ziuganov.[64] Over the course of the campaign, however, Yeltsin successfully shaped the agenda, emphasizing that vot-ers were choosing between him and communism. The message was that none of the other candidates had a chance of beating Ziuganov, so that if voters wanted to prevent the return of communism, they had no choice but to vote for Yeltsin.

This strategy worked. Yeltsin's displays of vigor during the campaign, his lav-ish promises to voters while out on the campaign trail, and his domination of media publicity, all contributed to a remarkable surge in popularity. In the first round, Yeltsin received 35 percent to 32 percent for Gennadii Ziuganov, his

——————————————— **TABLE 6.4** ———————————————
Presidential Election Results (in percent)

	First round (June 16, 1996)	Second round (July 3, 1996)
Boris Yeltsin	35.28	53.82
Gennadii Ziuganov	32.03	40.31
Aleksandr Lebed'	14.52	—
Grigorii Yavlinskii	7.34	—
Vladimir Zhirinovsky	5.70	—
Svyatoslav Fedorov	0.92	—
Mikhail Gorbachev	0.51	—
Martin Shakkum	0.37	—
Yurii Vlasov	0.20	—
Vladimir Bryntsalov	0.16	—
Aman Tuleev	0.00	—
Against all candidates	1.54	4.83

communist rival.[65] In the second round, Yeltsin received almost 54 percent of the vote to Ziuganov's 40.3 percent.[66] (See Table 6.4.) Russia's great campaigner had won his last election.[67]

The 1999 Elections. The fact that forty-three parties ran for election on the party list portion of the ballot in 1995 was discouraging from the standpoint of hopes for the consolidation of a party system. But politicians drew lessons from 1995 and began to form larger coalitions aimed at clearing the 5 percent threshold. For instance, democratically oriented candidates formed a bloc called the "Union of Rightist Forces," which united several prominent liberal political leaders. In the end, twenty-six parties appeared on the party list ballot. (See Figure 6.1.)

A measure of the weakness of Russian political parties was the fact that they had very little impact on single-member district races. Only the communists had much presence in local races, running candidates in two-thirds of the districts. Party competition tended to be far more focused on the party list vote than on winning single-member district seats.

Six parties cleared the 5 percent threshold in the party list vote. Three had been in the previous two Duma; three were new players (although including some politicians with previous Duma experience). Among them, they won just over 81 percent of the list vote, so that there were far fewer "wasted" votes than there had been in 1995. This suggested that voters, too, were beginning to learn to discriminate between the more viable and less viable parties.

Putin and the 2000 Presidential Race. The presidential election of 2000 was held earlier than scheduled due to President Yeltsin's early resignation. Under the constitution, the prime minister automatically succeeds the president upon the premature departure of the president, but new elections for the presidency must be held within three months. Accordingly, the presidential election was

ИЗБИРАТЕЛЬНЫЙ БЮЛЛЕТЕНЬ

для голосования по федеральному избирательному округу на выборах депутатов Государственной Думы Федерального Собрания Российской Федерации третьего созыва

19 декабря 1999 года

город Москва

РАЗЪЯСНЕНИЯ ПОРЯДКА ЗАПОЛНЕНИЯ ИЗБИРАТЕЛЬНОГО БЮЛЛЕТЕНЯ

Поставьте любой знак в пустом квадрате справа от наименования только одного избирательного объединения, избирательного блока, за федеральный список кандидатов которого Вы голосуете, либо в квадрате, расположенном справа от строки "Против всех федеральных списков кандидатов".

Избирательный бюллетень, в котором любой знак проставлен более чем в одном квадрате либо не проставлен ни в одном из них, считается недействительным.

Избирательный бюллетень, не заверенный подписями членов участковой избирательной комиссии и печатью участковой избирательной комиссии, признается бюллетенем неустановленной формы и при подсчете голосов не учитывается.

1 "КОНСЕРВАТИВНОЕ ДВИЖЕНИЕ РОССИИ"
УБОЖКО Лев Григорьевич, БУРЕНИН Владимир Арсеньевич, ТИШКОВ Андрей Николаевич
региональная группа "Город Москва":
КРАСИЛЬНИКОВ Андрей Николаевич, ДАВЫДЧЕНКОВ Василий Тихонович, КУЗНЕЦОВ Сергей Анатольевич

2 "РОССИЙСКИЙ ОБЩЕНАРОДНЫЙ СОЮЗ"
БАБУРИН Сергей Николаевич, ЛЕОНОВ Николай Сергеевич, ПАВЛОВ Николай Александрович
региональная группа "Город Москва":
НАРОЧНИЦКАЯ Наталия Алексеевна, ЛЕМЕШЕВ Михаил Яковлевич, ДОРОШЕНКО Николай Иванович

3 "ЖЕНЩИНЫ РОССИИ"
ФЕДУЛОВА Алевтина Васильевна, КАРЕЛОВА Галина Николаевна, ВЕСЕЛОВА Нина Григорьевна
региональная группа "Москва":
ДУХАНИНА Любовь Николаевна, ПАРШИКОВА Ольга Васильевна, НАРКЕВИЧ Екатерина Михайловна

4 "ДВИЖЕНИЕ "СПАС"
БАРКАШЕВ Александр Петрович, ДАВИДЕНКО Владимир Иванович, БЕЛИК Дмитрий Васильевич
региональная группа "Особая федеральная":
АМЕЛИН Валерий Анатольевич, ТИМОФЕЕВ Анатолий Петрович, БУРЛАКОВА Людмила Ивановна

5 "СТАЛИНСКИЙ БЛОК - ЗА СССР"
("ООПД "Трудовая Россия", "ОПО "Союз офицеров", "Народно-патриотический союз молодежи", "ООПД "Союз")
АНПИЛОВ Виктор Иванович, ТЕРЕХОВ Станислав Николаевич, ДЖУГАШВИЛИ Евгений Яковлевич
региональная группа "Город Москва":
РЫБАКОВ Александр Владимирович, КУЧЕРОВ Сергей Иванович, ЗИНОВЬЕВ Аркадий Васильевич

6 "ОБЪЕДИНЕНИЕ "ЯБЛОКО"
ЯВЛИНСКИЙ Григорий Алексеевич, СТЕПАШИН Сергей Вадимович, ЛУКИН Владимир Петрович
региональная группа "Город Москва":
ИВАНЕНКО Сергей Викторович, АВЕРЧЕВ Владимир Петрович, БОРЩЕВ Валерий Васильевич

7 "КОММУНИСТЫ, ТРУДЯЩИЕСЯ РОССИИ - ЗА СОВЕТСКИЙ СОЮЗ"
("Коммунисты, трудовая Россия - за Советский Союз", "Советская Родина", "Российская коммунистическая рабочая партия")
ТЮЛЬКИН Виктор Аркадьевич, КРЮЧКОВ Анатолий Викторович, АСЕЕВ Владислав Игнатьевич
региональная группа "Город Москва":
ДАВЫДОВ Михаил Владимирович, ЯЦУНОВ Николай Алексеевич, КОНДРАТЬЕВ Валентин Константинович

8 "МИР. ТРУД. МАЙ"
("Движение "Промышленный союз", "Движение "Родное Отечество")
БУРКОВ Александр Леонидович, ТРУШНИКОВ Валерий Георгиевич, ТАТАРКИН Александр Иванович
региональная группа "Город Москва":
ЛОБАХ Эрик Наэльевич, ТЕМНОВ Алексей Николаевич, БОБРОВСКИЙ Александр Васильевич

9 "БЛОК ГЕНЕРАЛА АНДРЕЯ НИКОЛАЕВА, АКАДЕМИКА СВЯТОСЛАВА ФЕДОРОВА"
("Союз народовластия и труда", "Партия самоуправления трудящихся", "Союз реалистов", "Социалистическая партия трудящихся", "Надежда России", "Инженерный прогресс России")
НИКОЛАЕВ Андрей Иванович, ФЕДОРОВ Святослав Николаевич, МАЛЮТИНА Татьяна Григорьевна
региональная группа "Город Москва":
БАЛАШОВ Евгений Борисович, ЧУРСАЛОВ Владимир Петрович, ТИТОВ Юрий Иванович

10 "ВСЕРОССИЙСКОЕ ОБЩЕСТВЕННО-ПОЛИТИЧЕСКОЕ ДВИЖЕНИЕ "ДУХОВНОЕ НАСЛЕДИЕ"
ПОДБЕРЕЗКИН Алексей Иванович, ПРОСКУРИН Петр Лукич, ВОРОТНИКОВ Валерий Павлович
региональная группа "Московская":
ИСАЙЧЕНКОВ Виктор Николаевич, АРИСТОВ Виталий Васильевич, ЛУНЬКОВ Юрий Гаврилович

11 "КОНГРЕСС РУССКИХ ОБЩИН И ДВИЖЕНИЕ ЮРИЯ БОЛДЫРЕВА"
("Конгресс Русских Общин", "Межнациональный союз")
БОЛДЫРЕВ Юрий Юрьевич, РОГОЗИН Дмитрий Олегович, ГЛУХИХ Виктор Константинович
региональная группа "Город Москва":
САВЕЛЬЕВ Андрей Николаевич, СЕРЕБРЯННИКОВА Ольга Сергеевна, ЯКОВЛЕВА Елена Юрьевна

12 "ПАРТИЯ МИРА И ЕДИНСТВА"
УМАЛАТОВА Сажи Зайндиновна, СТЕПАНОВ Виктор Федорович, АНТОШКИН Николай Тимофеевич
региональная группа "Центральный регион":
ПОЛЕНЯЧЕНКО Игорь Иванович, ГАПОНЕНКО Альфред Григорьевич, МИХАЙЛОВ Сергей Викторович

13 "РОССИЙСКАЯ ПАРТИЯ ЗАЩИТЫ ЖЕНЩИН"
РОЩИНА Татьяна Николаевна, МАХОВА Жанна Мухамедовна, КРЕМЕНЕЦ Ирина Васильевна
региональная группа "Москва":
ФАНЯЕВ Константин Владимирович

14 "МЕЖРЕГИОНАЛЬНОЕ ДВИЖЕНИЕ "ЕДИНСТВО" ("МЕДВЕДЬ")
("РХДП", "Общероссийская общественно-политическая организация - Народно-патриотическая партия", "ОПОД "Рефах"
("Благоденствие")", "Движение "Моя семья", "Общероссийское политическое движение "В поддержку независимых депутатов",
"Всероссийский союз поддержки малого и среднего бизнеса", "Российское движение "Поколение свободы")
ШОЙГУ Сергей Кужугетович, КАРЕЛИН Александр Александрович, ГУРОВ Александр Иванович
региональная группа "Центр":
КЛИНЦЕВИЧ Франц Адамович, КОМИССАРОВ Валерий Яковлевич, КОВАЛЕВ Олег Иванович

Figure 6.1 The 1999 Duma Election Party List Ballot

The party list ballot for the Duma election in December 1999 listed twenty-six parties and organizations (three were disqualified late in the process due to irregularities in their registration documents, so are crossed off the list). Each party or electoral association is indicated by its official name, its logo if it had one, the names of the top three candidates on its central list, and the names of the top three candidates on the list for the region where

15		**"СОЦИАЛ-ДЕМОКРАТЫ"** региональная группа "Город Москва": БЕЛЯЕВ Владимир Никитич, ЦЫБА Татьяна Федоровна, ПОПОВ Василий Гавриилович	☐
16		**"ОБЩЕРОССИЙСКОЕ ПОЛИТИЧЕСКОЕ ДВИЖЕНИЕ "В ПОДДЕРЖКУ АРМИИ"** ИЛЮХИН Виктор Иванович, МАКАШОВ Альберт Михайлович, САВЕЛЬЕВ Юрий Петрович региональная группа "Московская": ПАНКРАТОВ Юрий Иванович, РЯБЦЕВ Юрий Степанович, КАНДЫБОВИЧ Сергей Львович	☐
17		**"БЛОК ЖИРИНОВСКОГО"** ("Партия духовного возрождения России", "Российский союз свободной молодежи") ЖИРИНОВСКИЙ Владимир Вольфович, ФИНЬКО Олег Александрович, СОЛОМАТИН Егор Юрьевич региональная группа "Центральный регион": ЛЕМЕШОВ Геннадий Владимирович, ДЬЯЧКОВСКИЙ Сергей Алексеевич, ОСТРОВСКИЙ Алексей Владимирович	☐
18		**"ЗА ГРАЖДАНСКОЕ ДОСТОИНСТВО"** ПАМФИЛОВА Элла Александровна, ДОНДУКОВ Александр Николаевич, ШКИРКО Анатолий Афанасьевич региональная группа "Российский Центр": ПОПОВ Валерий Валерьевич, ДУПЛЯНСКИЙ Леонид Александрович, ЛЕБЕДЕВА Галина Федоровна	☐
19		**"ОТЕЧЕСТВО - ВСЯ РОССИЯ"** ("Отечество", "Регионы России", "За равноправие и справедливость", "Аграрная партия России", "Союз христианских демократов России") ПРИМАКОВ Евгений Максимович, ЛУЖКОВ Юрий Михайлович, ЯКОВЛЕВ Владимир Анатольевич региональная группа "Московская": БООС Георгий Валентинович, ТЯЖЛОВ Анатолий Степанович, КОНДАКОВА Елена Владимировна	☐
20		**"КОММУНИСТИЧЕСКАЯ ПАРТИЯ РОССИЙСКОЙ ФЕДЕРАЦИИ"** ЗЮГАНОВ Геннадий Андреевич, СЕЛЕЗНЕВ Геннадий Николаевич, СТАРОДУБЦЕВ Василий Александрович региональная группа "Московская": САЙКИН Валерий Тимофеевич, КУВАЕВ Александр Александрович, СУЛЬЯНОВ Юрий Анатольевич	☐
21		**"РУССКОЕ ДЕЛО"** ("Российское общенародное движение (РОД)", "Союз соотечественников "Отчизна", "Союз Христианское Возрождение") ИВАНОВ Олег Анатольевич, ПЕТРОВ Юрий Николаевич, СИДОРОВ Михаил Викторович региональная группа "Московский регион": СОЛОМОНОВ Владимир Иванович, КОНДРАШОВ Александр Никифорович, ЛЕБЕДЕВА Татьяна Васильевна	☐
22		**"ВСЕРОССИЙСКАЯ ПОЛИТИЧЕСКАЯ ПАРТИЯ НАРОДА"** АКСЕНТЬЕВ-КИКАЛИШВИЛИ Анзори Иосифович, БУРЕ Татьяна Львовна, ШАИНСКИЙ Владимир Яковлевич региональная группа "Московская": ГЕРАСИМОВ Александр Иванович, ВЕРЕТЕННИКОВ Алексей Владимирович, КАЛИНИЧЕНКО Владимир Иванович	☐
23		**"СОЮЗ ПРАВЫХ СИЛ"** ("Партия "Демократический выбор России", "Движение "Новая сила", "ОПОД "Россия Молодая", "Юристы за права и достойную жизнь человека") КИРИЕНКО Сергей Владиленович, НЕМЦОВ Борис Ефимович, ХАКАМАДА Ирина Муцуовна региональная группа "Москва": ГАЙДАР Егор Тимурович, НАУМОВ Олег Георгиевич, МУРАШЕВ Аркадий Николаевич	☐
24		**"ЭКОЛОГИЧЕСКАЯ ПАРТИЯ РОССИИ "КЕДР" (ЗЕЛЕНЫЕ)"** ~~ПАНФИЛОВ Анатолий Алексеевич, ПЕТРОВ Владимир Анатольевич, ОХЛОБЫСТИН Иван Иванович~~ региональная группа "Столица": ~~ПАСЬКО Григорий Михайлович, СОСУНОВА Ирина Александровна, ПИМЕНОВ Валерий Иванович~~	☐
25	НДР	**"ВОПД "НАШ ДОМ - РОССИЯ"** ЧЕРНОМЫРДИН Виктор Степанович, РЫЖКОВ Владимир Александрович, АЯЦКОВ Дмитрий Федорович региональная группа "Город Москва": БУНИЧ Павел Григорьевич, ДЕНИСЕНКО Бэла Анатольевна, ОСИПОВ Жудекс Иосипович	☐
26		**"СОЦИАЛИСТИЧЕСКАЯ ПАРТИЯ РОССИИ"** РЫБКИН Иван Петрович, МАЙОРОВ Леонид Сергеевич, БЕЛИШКО Андрей Дмитриевич региональная группа "Город Москва": БИРЮКОВ Дмитрий Дмитриевич, КОНДРАШОВ Вячеслав Юрьевич, ШАРКОВ Валерий Николаевич	☐
27		**"ПАРТИЯ ПЕНСИОНЕРОВ"** РЯБОВ Яков Петрович, КОНТАШОВ Анатолий Павлович, МАРКОВА Римма Васильевна региональная группа "Центральная": УТОЧКИН Валентин Григорьевич, ХИМИЧЕВ Борис Петрович, ВИКТОРЕНКО Александр Степанович	☐
28		**"РУССКАЯ СОЦИАЛИСТИЧЕСКАЯ ПАРТИЯ"** БРЫНЦАЛОВ Владимир Алексеевич, БРЫНЦАЛОВ Игорь Юрьевич, БРЫНЦАЛОВ Юрий Григорьевич региональная группа "Московия": ПОГОДИНА Лилия Николаевна, ФИРСОВ Анатолий Васильевич, КУРЕННОЙ Игорь Иванович	☐
29		**~~"РОССИЙСКАЯ КОНСЕРВАТИВНАЯ ПАРТИЯ ПРЕДПРИНИМАТЕЛЕЙ (РКПП)"~~** ~~ТОПОРКОВ Михаил Николаевич, ГОКИНАЕВ Виктор Александрович, ПАШКОВСКИЙ Владимир Игоревич~~ региональная группа "Город Москва": ~~ЖУКОВ Владимир Николаевич, ГУБАРЬКОВ Сергей Анатольевич, КРАШНИКОВ Юрий Александрович~~	☐

ПРОТИВ ВСЕХ ФЕДЕРАЛЬНЫХ СПИСКОВ КАНДИДАТОВ	☐

Figure 6.2 *(continued)*

the election precinct was located. The order of parties was chosen at random. Yabloko is number 6; the Communist Party of the Russian Federation is number 20. The voter was instructed to place a mark in the box next to the party for which he or she wished to vote. The last box was marked "against all federal lists of candidates" and allowed voters to cast a valid vote against all the parties running. This option was chosen by 3.3 percent of the voters.

scheduled for March 26, 2000. The early election gave the front-runner and in-cumbent, Vladimir Putin, an advantage because he was able to capitalize on his popularity and the country's desire for continuity. Putin ran the Russian equiva-lent of a "rose garden" campaign, preferring to be seen going about the normal daily business of a president rather than going out on the hustings and asking for people's votes. He counted on the support of office holders at all levels, a media campaign that presented a "presidential" image to the voters, and the voters' fear that change would only make life worse. His rivals, moreover, were weak. Several prominent politicians prudently chose not to enter the race against him. Putin's campaign managers' real concern was to convince voters to turn out for the elec-tion, wanting to ensure a broad mandate for their candidate.

In the event, Putin won an outright majority on the first round, with a rea-sonably high turnout of 69 percent. Table 6.5 shows the results.

Party Ideologies

Despite the high turnover in the array of parties and candidates competing for vote support in Russian parliamentary and presidential elections, there is a high degree of continuity in the ideological tendencies represented by them. Moreover, voters appear to be able to make coherent choices among parties and candidates reflecting their own assessments of where the parties stand on the basic issues. As we have seen, the main political families of parties can be classified in four basic types: democratic, communist, nationalist, and nonideological. Many of the presi-dential candidates can also be classified in these categories. Let us examine these ideological tendencies and the parties that represent them more closely.

Democratic Parties. This category comprises parties that promote liberal demo-cratic political values and market-oriented economic values; they want to

---

TABLE 6.5
Presidential Election Results, March 26, 2000 (in percent)

Vladimir Putin	52.94
Gennadii Ziuganov	29.21
Grigorii Yavlinskii	5.8
Aman Tuleev	2.95
Vladimir Zhirinovsky	2.70
Konstantin Titov	1.47
Ella Pamfilova	1.01
Stanislav Gororukhin	0.44
Yuri Skuratov	0.43
Alexei Podberezkin	0.13
Umar Dzhabrailov	0.10
Against all	1.88

dismantle the political and economic framework of state socialism and replace it with an open, pluralistic, free-market system along Western lines. Some emphasize a more laissez-faire approach, others a more social-democratic approach. But they would all agree that Russia must guarantee political and economic freedoms for its citizens, protect property rights, and strengthen the rule of law, and they fight against socialist and collectivist tendencies in the political and economic spheres.

Russia's democrats first mobilized in the glasnost era and formed a movement called Democratic Russia to compete for seats in the Russian parliament in 1990. Soon they split up into different groups, but in 1993 a number of democratic figures allied under the name "Russia's Choice" headed by the prominent architect of economic reform, Egor Gaidar. Russia's Choice counted on a major electoral success in 1993 and was bitterly disappointed when it took only 15.5 percent of the list vote. As time passed, its electoral fortunes sagged further. In 1995 (renamed Russia's Democratic Choice), it took only 3.9 percent—not enough to qualify for seats in the Duma.

As the 1999 elections drew near, a number of politicians from the Russia's Choice and other groups pooled their resources and formed a new electoral alliance called the Union of Right Forces (SPS, for its Russian initials). They put a trio of younger, appealing leaders at the top of their party list, and their campaign emphasized that Prime Minister Putin had endorsed (if rather vaguely) their economic program. This time their strategy paid off, and they entered parliament with 8.5 percent of the list vote. Their success showed that Russia's democrats, hammered and discredited by the results of the economic reforms with which they were associated, still commanded a significant following among Russia's voters.

Yabloko is a party that promotes itself as the "democratic opposition" to Yeltsin, Putin, the liberals, and their economic reform program. It is headed by the prominent political leader Grigorii Yavlinsky. It espouses a general theme of a socially-oriented economy and a pro-Western external policy. Yavlinsky himself ran for the presidency in 1996 and again in 2000, receiving around 7 percent of the vote in 1996 and 5.8 percent in 2000. Yabloko has received a rather constant share of the vote in parliamentary elections: 7.86 percent in 1993, 7.0 percent in 1995, and 5.8 percent in 1999. It has been an active force in parliament, sponsoring much legislation and forging tactical alliances with other parties to get bills passed, but until recently it resisted forming any permanent alliance with other groups. In June 2000, it announced that it was entering into a formal alliance with the Union of Right Forces to coordinate their legislative agenda in parliament. The efforts by SPS and Yabloko to form a coalition for the 2003 parliamentary elections and the 2004 presidential elections have foundered on the ambitions of their leaders and the mutual antipathy on the part of many of their leading figures.

Communist Parties. The communists are in a very different position. They have consistently been in opposition to Russia's president and government throughout the period since the Soviet Union broke up, so they have had to rely on their own resources for support.

The Communist Party of the Russian Federation (CPRF) is the major successor party to the old CPSU. Other splinter groups exist that are more militantly Stalinist; the CPRF has cautiously embraced certain elements of the market and has declared that it no longer believes in violence and revolution as means to achieve its policy goals.[68] But the party vehemently opposes the market reforms and privatization programs of the last decade, and demands immediate restoration of state ownership and planning in heavy industry. Given its history and hostility to Yeltsin's policies, it may seem surprising that the CPRF has chosen to take part in the electoral arena at all. But it has evidently decided to make use of the rules of the parliamentary game to influence national policy, trying to show that, unlike Yeltsin who violated the constitution in dissolving parliament in 1993, it respects the principle of constitutionalism. The CPRF also attacks Western influence in Russia: This writer heard its leader, Gennadii Ziuganov, declare at a press conference in June 1994, having just returned from a tour of the provinces, that the process of "Americanization" of Russia had advanced to the point of "vampirization." As evidence for this, Ziuganov cited his observation that in every town and village one could now see Russian children wearing baseball caps. In addition to anti-Westernism, Ziuganov has also worked hard to align the party with the religious and spiritual traditions of Russian culture, overlooking Marx's and Lenin's militant enmity toward religion. Ziuganov frequently invokes the traditional mutual support between the Russian state and the Russian Orthodox Church. So far, however, the Patriarch has refrained from endorsing the Communist Party.

The CPRF is the most partylike of Russia's parties, by a considerable margin. Unlike any other party, it has a substantial organizational base, a well-defined electoral following, a large membership (estimated at around a half million), a large network of local party newspapers, and, probably most important, the heritage of Communist Party discipline, which it took over from the Communist Party of the Soviet Union. Divisions within the party are muted by the party's ability to speak and act with one voice. But it has clear weaknesses as well. Its voters tend to be older than average, and it appeals to them by its association with the old regime. Moreover, it is ideologically straitjacketed: If it moves too much to the center of the political spectrum, it will lose its distinctiveness as a clear alternative to the government, but if it moves further to the left, it will marginalize itself. The result is that the CPRF has a rather stable share of the electorate, but one that (so far, at least) prevents it from winning a majority in parliament or capturing the presidency. In 1993, it took 12.4 percent of the party list vote; in 1995, 22.7 percent; and in 1999, 24.29 percent. In presidential elections, its leader, Gennadii Ziuganov, is the perennial runner-up: In 1996, Ziuganov won 32 percent of the vote in the first round, and 40.3 percent in the second; in 2000, he took 29.2 percent. It appears that while the ideology, reputation, and organization of the communists give them a certain base level of electoral support, the same factors also set a ceiling on their chances.[69]

Until 1999, the Agrarian Party of Russia (APR) was closely allied with the CPRF on most issues, but its political activity was almost entirely focused on agricultural issues. The APR staunchly and effectively opposed the privatization of land in Russia and persistently and successfully lobbied for credits and subsidies, including price supports, to the country's collective and state farms. The APR was more a lobby for collective and state farm managers than a political party aggregating interests across sectors. For that reason, its interests sometimes diverged from those of the communists. Not only were the APR's interests focused specifically on the agricultural sector, but it also was willing to support the government's position on some issues where the communists were not. The agrarians did poorly in the 1995 election, failing to take any party list seats and winning only 20 district seats. Appealing to other single-mandate district winners, and "borrowing" members from the large communist party faction, they managed to enroll thirty-five members and thus to register as a recognized faction in the Duma in January 1996. In 1999 they finally split. The more moderate wing joined the Unity coalition, while the procommunist members formed a separate deputy group in parliament.

Nationalist Parties. The most visible nationalist party, the Liberal Democratic Party of Russia (LDPR)—Zhirinovsky's party—differs from the communists in certain important respects. Zhirinovsky's party stresses the national theme, even more than the communists, appealing to feelings of injured ethnic and state pride. Zhirinovsky calls for aggressive foreign policies and harsh treatment of non-Russian ethnic minorities. However, his economic policy is much fuzzier. While demanding that the government relieve the distress of Russians who have suffered under market reforms, he also distances himself from the socialist economic system of the past and poses as a "third force," which is tied neither to the old communist regime nor to the new order.[70] Finally, he also sends a clear message that he is seeking the presidency, the powers of which he will use dictatorially to right wrongs and settle accounts with Russia's enemies.

Zhirinovsky cultivates a vivid, theatrical public persona, which works effectively on television. He appeals to many voters who are angry over the current situation but unenthusiastic about returning the communists to power. However, as he has come to be identified with the Moscow political establishment more and more, his party's vote support has fallen. From its unexpectedly strong showing in 1993, when his party won almost 23 percent of the list vote, its vote share has dropped roughly by half in each of the next two elections: to 11.4 percent in 1995, and less than 6 percent in 1999. The fall in Zhirinovsky's popularity is also reflected in the votes he has received in presidential elections: 5.8 percent in 1991, 5.7 percent in 1996, and 2.7 percent in 2000.

Bombastic as Zhirinovsky's rhetoric is, the party's actual voting record has been surprisingly tame and has grown tamer as its electoral popularity has waned. On a number of key votes in parliament, Zhirinovsky has supported the president and government; the most celebrated instance occurred in May 1999, when the Duma was trying to remove Yeltsin through impeachment. Following heavy lobbying by the president's representatives, the LDPR faction declared that they would have nothing to do with the vote and refused to take their ballots. As a result, there were not enough votes in favor of impeachment to clear the two-thirds (300 vote) threshold required for the impeachment motion to succeed. In the Duma that convened in 2000, the LDPR declared itself to be a strong supporter of President Putin. Under President Putin, Zhirinovsky's faction has supported the Kremlin consistently in parliamentary voting.

Zhirinovsky's LDPR has been the most successful of the parties competing for the nationalist vote. A great many other parties have attempted to build successful followings around themes such as the need to restore the Soviet Union, to make Russia a great world power again, to cleanse Russia of the ethnic "outsiders" who contaminate it, or to bring back the tsar. But these parties either have failed in their bid for parliamentary votes and then splintered and faded, or have concentrated their efforts on forming a small but dedicated corps of militant (sometimes armed and militarily organized) followers. Among the nationalist parties attempting to follow the parliamentary route was the Congress of Russian Communities (KRO), which put the prominent, popular army general Alexander Lebed' on the number 2 spot on its party list in the 1995 parliamentary election. However, KRO received only 4.3 percent of the list vote and thus failed to enter parliament. Other, far more extreme groups have also made some effort to run for parliament as well. Two examples are the Russian National Union and the Russian National Unity. The Russian National Union was planning to compete in the 1999 elections when it was charged with the crime of propagating fascist ideas, prompting a split in the organization. The Russian National Unity, which uses a swastika-like symbol for an emblem and imitates Nazi styles in uniform and organization, has been banned in several regions, and an electoral bloc formed by its leader was banned from competing in the 1999 elections on the grounds that it had falsified some of its registration documents. Such groups have been able to attract media attention by staging marches and demonstrations, but they have little popular support.[71]

Parties of the Center, Parties of Power. One of the enduring paradoxes of Russian politics over the past decade is the fact that no viable centrist party—positioned between the communists on the left and the democrats on the right—has arisen despite the fact that survey research regularly shows that voters favor policies and values that could form the basis for such a party. In some European democracies, social democratic parties fill this niche. But in Russia no significant social democratic party has formed. This is not for lack of trying. Many leaders, among them former USSR President Mikhail Gorbachev, have launched parties with an explicitly social democratic platform. None has managed to win more than a negligible share of the vote. Table 6.1 shows that Gorbachev's United Social Democratic Party has the support of only around 1 percent of the population.

Institutional reasons help explain this paradox. For one thing, organized labor, as we saw, is fragmented. Social-democratic parties in Western Europe generally have strong relationships with well-organized labor movements that can supply organizational resources, funding, and blocs of voters. Russia's divided labor unions have not been able to build an electoral base for a social-democratic party. A second, and perhaps even more important institutional barrier to the formation of a serious centrist or social-democratic party is the fact that parties tend to depend heavily on the government for staffing and other organizational help. Once again we see the pervasive tendency for a weak society to call upon the powerful resources of the state for the ability to organize, with the result that social organizations themselves lose both their autonomy and their viability.

In the case of political parties, the state authorities sometimes form their own parties as a way of keeping themselves in power. Typically such parties claim that they are moderate, pragmatic, and centrist. In fact, they are centrist only in the sense that they avoid offering the voters any clear policy commitments at all and thus make it difficult for voters to hold them accountable for their policies. They promise stability, which makes it difficult for them also to offer any coherent solutions to the voters' grievances. The classic example of this type of party was Our Home Is Russia. It originated in the run-up to the 1995 parliamentary elections, when President Yeltsin's political advisers proposed using the Kremlin's political resources to create a progovernment, centrist but moderately reformist, political movement. Yeltsin asked then-Prime Minister Chernomyrdin to head it up. Benefiting from government official support and promoting a reassuring image of stability and pragmatism, Our Home did succeed in crossing the 5 percent threshold in December 1995, with 10.3 percent of the list vote. However, Our Home never succeeded in defining a clear programmatic position for itself, and was mostly a coalition of officeholders, particularly big-city mayors, regional governors, and presidents of ethnic republics. For this reason it soon became known as "the party of power." And once Chernomyrdin was dismissed from the government in 1998, Our Home began to implode. In 1999 it won only 1.2 percent of the list vote. Soon thereafter, it dissolved itself.

The 1999 election was peculiar in that it offered voters at least three "parties of power." Besides Our Home Is Russia, two other blocs also competed that had strong links to the state authorities. The Fatherland-All Russia alliance united several powerful regional leaders and its list was headed by former Prime Minister Evgenii Primakov. But the real phenomenon of 1999 was the third "party of power," Unity. Unity formed only three months before the election, by all accounts with the active assistance of Boris Berezovsky and of President Yeltsin's entourage in the Kremlin. Its trump card was Vladimir Putin. Appointed prime minister on August 9, 1999, Putin actively aided in the formation of the new movement, commenting at one point that "as a citizen," he intended to vote for Unity. Thus state officials who wondered which was the "true" party of power (fearing to back the wrong party!) could safely conclude that Unity was the right choice, particularly as Putin's public popularity soared. As the once-dominant Fatherland-All Russia bloc's ratings fell, Unity's support rose: Unity went from 4 percent on November 2, to 9 percent on November 22, to 18 percent on November 29; and it received 23.3 percent of the vote on election day.[72] The reason for its success was that governors and other officeholders quickly switched their allegiance to it once they saw that it was going to be the *real* party of power.

In parliament, Unity quickly showed itself to be a vehicle through which President Putin could enact his desired legislative program. Voting with remarkable discipline, Unity's members formed alliances with other parliamentary factions and passed nearly every bill proposed by Putin and the government. Unity liked to describe itself as a "ruling party," but in fact it did not control either the government or the presidency: It was largely the parliamentary appendage of a very strong president. Putin spoke in vague terms about the desirability of building a viable party system and even of moving to the point where parties would name the candidates for president. But, like President Yeltsin before him, he himself found it expedient to remain above the battlefield of party politics. True to the logic of Russia's parties, however, Unity soon began organizing for the next election. In December 2001, Fatherland (Moscow Mayor Yuri Luzhkov's political vehicle) merged with Unity to form a new "party of power" called United Russia. (This is why Table 6.1 does not list Unity and Fatherland separately after December 1, 2001.) The new party promised to develop a party program but has found it extremely difficult to define a set of specific issue positions. For example, one of its leaders stated that the party's goal would be to appeal to the "middle class" for support, claiming that Russia's middle class accounted for 75 percent of the society. This was hardly likely to be a viable campaign strategy, since sociological surveys regularly find that fewer than 20 percent of Russians are in fact "middle class" by any reasonable objective standard.[73] Therefore any campaign slogans appealing to middle-class voters are likely to alienate many more voters than they attract. The Kremlin apparently shares observers' skepticism about the prospects for United Russia in the 2003 parliamentary elections, because it has quietly encouraged a second "party of power"—called People's Party—to form, apparently as a reserve option. The core of the People's Party is a group of Duma deputies who were elected in single-member districts, without party affiliations, who have adopted a strongly pro-Kremlin stance. Like Unity and other parties of power, People's Party is top-heavy with Moscow-based politicians eager to stay in office. How much it will be able to appeal to ordinary voters remains to be seen.

The history of Russian parties of power illustrates the point that when parties are the creatures of official government sponsors, they lack the ability to formulate their own independent appeals to voters and to generate distinctive bases of support. Their policy positions are fluid and shifting, and when their sponsors in the state lose power, they vanish. Parties of power are similar to patronage-based parties in some West European countries that exploit their entrenchment in government to provide material benefits to supporters and promises of elective office to ambitious politicians. The difference is that Russian parties of power do not get an opportunity to take responsibility for government, so that voters and politicians do not make any long-term commitments to them.

Party Strategies and the Social Bases of Party Support

The mixed electoral system used in Duma elections allows for different types of representation across the two mandate types, encouraging parties to form and reach out to particular electorates in the party list portion of the ballot, and encouraging both party-nominated and independent candidates to form more direct, personal ties with voters in the single-member district races. Surveys find that while voters tend to be suspicious of parties in general (recall that, as Table 5.2 shows, parties are trusted almost as little as investment funds), they are nevertheless able to pick parties to vote for that they think will represent their interests. Surveys conducted by Arthur Miller and his colleagues at the University of Iowa have found rising levels of party support among Russian voters. Asked "is there one particular party that expresses your views better than any of the other parties?" only 16 percent of Russians in 1992 responded favorably, while in 1995, 52 percent did so, and in 1997, 61 percent did so.[74]

Survey researchers have also found distinct differences in party support among various categories of the population. Both age and education levels are correlated with party preferences; younger voters are more likely to support the democratic camp or Zhirinovsky's party than are older voters, while older voters are disproportionately drawn to the communists. In 1999, well-educated voters were likelier than others to prefer Yabloko and the Union of Right Forces, while less educated voters were likelier than the average voter to support the communists or Zhirinovsky. A strong influence on party preference is household income. Most of the communists' support has come from voters whose household income is below the median, while most of the support for the Union of Right Forces and Yabloko comes from voters in the upper half of the distribution.[75] Table 6.6 indicates how the parties differed in the social bases of their support. Note that the table should be read downward. For example, it tells us that 48 percent of communist supporters were men and 52 percent were women; in contrast, 62 percent of Zhirinovsky's supporters were men and only 38 percent were women.

The table reveals differences in the appeal of the different parties. The communists took over half of their support from citizens aged fifty-five and older; none of the other parties depended so heavily on pensioners. Similarly, the parties have markedly different profiles by income category, with the market-oriented Union of Right Forces (SPS) drawing a substantial amount of its support from better-off citizens, and the communists from among those who are barely scraping by. Finally, education also strongly affects party support. Note that the liberal Yabloko and SPS parties draw 80 percent of their support from people with secondary and higher educational levels, whereas the communists get half of their support from among people with less than a full secondary education.

Russia's parties also differ in the ways they compete for vote support. The communists rely on their inherited organizational networks, their habits of party discipline, a clear-cut ideological profile, and their association with the socialist legacy of the old regime. The various "parties of power," such as Our Home Is Russia, Fatherland-All Russia, and Unity, depend almost completely on the patronage of executive officeholders and almost not at all on an ideological platform or indigenous party organization. LDPR and Yabloko have relatively weak electoral organizations but have well-known, visible political leaders and defined programmatic appeals.

—————————————————— TABLE 6.6 ——————————————————
Social Bases of Party Support, 1999

	CPRF	Unity	Fatherland	Yabloko	Right Forces	Zhirinovsky
Age						
18–24	5	10	10	12	25	18
25–39	17	38	29	40	37	42
40–54	26	24	25	29	23	23
55+	53	28	36	19	15	18
Gender						
Men	48	50	44	47	42	62
Women	52	51	56	54	58	38
Education						
Elementary or less	15	8	8	5	3	10
Incomplete secondary	36	24	26	16	17	26
Secondary	20	27	22	24	26	30
Vocational	18	25	21	28	29	29
Higher+	11	16	23	27	25	5
Economic situation						
Barely make ends meet	45	33	28	24	17	32
Have enough for food	40	41	46	41	44	37
Enough for food and clothes	13	23	21	30	31	28
Can buy durables easily	2	3	5	6	8	3

Note: Table columns read vertically and indicate the share of each party's supporters who belonged to one of the row categories in each set of social groups. Thus, for example, 48 percent of communist supporters were men, 52 percent women; in contrast, 62 percent of Zhirinovsky's supporters were men and only 38 percent were women.

Source: VTsIOM preelection polls, December 1999. Total *N* = 6,400. (From **www.russiavotes.org**, 1 October 2000.)

Party Fragmentation or Consolidation?

Party development in Russia has been hampered by the constitutional arrangements, particularly the heavy propresidential tilt in the balance of power. Since the president is directly elected and does not need a majority in parliament to exercise his substantial policy-making powers, he prefers to win a personal mandate rather than a mandate as standard-bearer of a party. Both Yeltsin and Putin stayed outside party politics, sometimes conferring their blessing on one or another party, but never joining a party or seeking its endorsement. Moreover, the president appoints the government; the government is not formed out of a party majority in parliament. Therefore, even though the government does require majority support in parliament to remain in office, it does not need to frame a specific policy program or to fill cabinet positions in proportion to the strength of parties in parliament. Government is more responsible to the president than to the parliament, and the parliament's levers of control over government are blunt, crude, and ineffective. Parliament can bring down the government, but it cannot instruct the government on a particular direction for national policy.

As a result, the ability of parties to perform the functions of aggregating the interests of citizens and formulating practical policy options is severely compromised. Indeed, parties are likely to find it much more rewarding either to concentrate on extravagant criticism of government, distancing themselves from responsibility for its policies; to make vague emotional appeals that cannot be translated into meaningful policy actions; or to rally support around imagery and leaders' personalities. Under these circumstances, where parties never take responsibility for government, voters have no way to measure their performance as policy makers. Politicians face a parallel situation. Why should politicians form durable commitments to building up parties, if parties will never reward them with political office? Politicians treat parties as disposable objects, good for one-time use, but not intended for repeated or long-term use. In Russia parties have often been formed for a single election; once they have served their purpose, they are discarded. Politicians join up to form shot-gun political weddings, but do not expect to stay married for long. As a result, there has been substantial turnover in the array of parties running in each of the parliamentary elections since 1993. Only four parties have contested all three, the CPRF, LDPR, Yabloko, and Women of Russia. And only the first three managed to clear the threshold each time. As Richard Rose argues, Russia has a "floating party system," in which neither politicians nor voters consider themselves firmly attached to particular parties, parties often lack clear policy programs, and executive authorities avoid affiliating themselves with parties. Such a system inhibits both democratic choice and accountability.[76]

Yet notwithstanding the high turnover and low accountability in Russia's party system, there are reasons to believe that a consolidation of the party system is taking place. The electoral law has a powerful effect on the party system, encouraging parties, on the one hand, to enter the arena through the party list ballot, but also requiring to build broad bases of support to overcome the 5 percent hurdle to winning seats. Another effect comes from the way parliament is organized. Deputies in parliament have an incentive to unite in parliamentary factions, because by doing so they acquire important privileges, such as office space and funding for staff support, as well as a voice on the powerful Council of the Duma, which directs the work of the Duma. If a party wants to use the parliament to showcase a favored bill, investigation, or resolution, to hold a press conference or parliamentary hearings, to force a vote or to prevent a vote, the Council of the Duma allows it to do so. *Parties thus use parliament for their policy and electoral purposes.* It is desirable, therefore, for individual members of parliament who want to further their political careers or to shape policy to affiliate with one or another parliamentary faction. And there is considerable evidence that once in parliament, members want to stay there. In 1995, 90 percent of the deputies in the Duma ran for reelection. Of these, half ran simultaneously in a district and on a party list and almost a hundred more ran only on a list. Therefore legislative officeholders identify themselves with political parties, some for the organizational and financial resources they can gain, some because they have no chance of winning election unless they are on a party list, and some out of ideological conviction. The complementary interests of voters in supporting a particular organized political entity, on the one hand, and of officeholders in affiliating themselves with a particular party organization to win power and influence policy, on the other, are thus influencing the development of Russia's nascent democracy to move, albeit at a snail's pace, in the direction of a competitive party system.

Finally, although there has been high turnover in the specific parties that have run for election in the 1990s, we have seen that they fall into a stable, coherent set of party *families*. And the evidence shows that voters are able to make reasonable choices among them based on their understanding of the parties' positions. Voters for parties in each of the major political tendencies generally held rather similar outlooks on the basic policy choices confronting Russia, and voters' attitudes on such fundamental issues as communism versus a market economy, or whether they approved of the enlargement of NATO in Eastern Europe, generally determined their preferences among those parties. One of the strongest influences on party preferences is whether a person thinks of himself or herself as a "Soviet person." Those who do are much likelier to support the communist or agrarian party.[77] On the other hand, these issues are so fundamental to the identity of the very regime that their prominence indicates that in some ways, party competition is less about government policy than about whether the regime should exist at all.

These results give us clues about what motivates Russians to vote, despite their alienation from political life. Voters are beginning to be able to link their interests with particular political tendencies, labels, and personalities, but the party system, as a whole, lacks a stable foundation in society. Few voters or politicians feel much loyalty to particular parties. This helps explain the fact that, almost a decade after the first open parliamentary elections in Russia, the party system remains fragmented and fluid. Yet Russia's emerging political system does possess certain features that produce incentives for politicians to form up into parties. The politicians themselves have shaped both the electoral law and the governance of parliament in such a way as to further the parties' influence over policy making and elections in Russia. These rules motivate the politicians to try to rally the voters behind party banners: Slowly the politicians are learning to adapt the *supply* of party candidates, programs, and policies to meet the voters' *demands* for a better life. They structure the choices that voters face on election day. Parties have a reason to try to overcome the alienation ordinary Russians feel toward national politics. The next step toward the formation of a stable system of competitive parties, however, will require that parties and elections give voters an opportunity to pass judgment on the policies pursued by government—and they will not be able to do so until government itself has a party identity.

President Putin and his allies in parliament have often declared that they believe that a consolidation of the party system would be desirable for stabilizing Russia's political life, and they have been sponsoring institutional changes to bring this about. However, their proposals appear to be intended to give United Russia, the current party of power, a near-monopoly on power. For instance, in 2001 Putin pushed through a law on political parties that imposed a high membership threshold as a requirement for registration and restricted participation in parliamentary elections to registered parties, while allowing registered parties to receive state financing for their activities. Furthermore, they have succeeded in amending the electoral law to be used in the 2007 parliamentary elections to raise the threshold for seats for party list seats to 7 percent from the current 5 percent—making it all but impossible for more than two or three parties to clear the barrier.[78] Taken together, these changes were intended to give the major current parties, such as United Russia and the communists, something close to a monopoly on parliamentary representation unless their rivals can unite into cohesive coalitions. These changes illustrate the point that institutional reforms are generally enacted to give advantages to those already in dominant positions. Yet often such institutional reforms have turned out to have unexpected consequences.

Summing Up

In this chapter we reviewed the nature of interest articulation and aggregation in contemporary Russian politics. We observed that while political systems require organized channels that link people's needs and desires with the policy processes of government, the availability and effectiveness of such means is not guaranteed. What sorts of interest groups and political parties operate in a particular political system at a particular time depends on the distribution of organizations and the resources needed by organizations. In a time of great political upheaval, the inherited parties and associations may correspond poorly to people's actual needs and wishes. An association may find itself unable to formulate a positive policy agenda even though the constituency it represents is large and important. The old official trade unions have turned out to be weak and uncohesive as representatives of Russian labor's political demands, but continue to exist due to their control over the collection and distribution of state social funds. In Russia's transition, both interests and the organizations articulating them have changed. Old organizations either have adapted to the new environment or have fallen away, and new organizations have formed. Some groups have long-standing interests that could not be effectively represented under the communist regime; others represent new interests that have been created as a result of the economic and political liberalization of the society.

Still, as in most societies, Russia's interest groups tend to be more organized and more effective when they serve constituencies whose members have more resources, whether these are material resources or ties of social trust. Interest articulation in Russia is not clearly statist, as it was in the old regime, and efforts to put it on a corporatist footing have failed. A pluralist political arena is emerging, as much by default as by design.

Political parties also operate in an environment of change: Out of the old ruling Communist Party have come several successor parties, most important the CPRF, but the eruption of new interests and identities that occurred in the glasnost period also left behind it some proto-parties that have adapted themselves to the new rules and institutions of post-Soviet Russia. The party system is defined around four major tendencies: Democrats advocate market reform and liberal democracy, while communists want to reestablish state socialism. Nationalists call either for restoration of a Russian empire or for a purely ethnic Russian national state. The fourth tendency is the recurrent attempt to create broad-based, nominally "centrist" parties by using the state's own administrative levers, resulting in a succession of new "parties of power."

Generally, parties are heavily focused on Moscow and their roots outside the capital are feeble. But the structure of the national representative institutions—especially the large PR component of the Duma—forces politicians to line up with one or another party in order to seek and hold elected office. To a large extent, politicians still treat parties as disposable objects, vehicles to ride to office, and avoid having to be held to account for their actions, and they are greatly assisted in this by the constitutional set-up, which allows the president and government to make policy decisions with little reference to the balance of party forces in parliament. What little interest aggregation there is through political parties owes far more to the "top-down" and "supply-side" strategies of ambitious politicians than to the "bottom-up," "demand-side" processes of social mobilization. Whether Russia will succeed in producing a healthy, competitive party system remains to be seen. There can be little doubt, however, that if democracy is to become consolidated in Russia, a working party system will be essential.

REVIEW QUESTIONS

1. What does "collective action" mean? What factors facilitate collective action in Russia, and what inhibits it?
2. What are "democrats," "reds," and "browns"? Why do "reds" and "browns" sometimes find common cause?
3. What are "statist," "corporatist," and "pluralist" patterns of interest articulation? Why has the post-Soviet Russian system seen much more pluralist interest-group activity than corporatism?
4. Comparing groups such as the RUIE, the FITUR, the Committees of Soldiers' Mothers, and the Orthodox Church, what factors explain why a group is influential or not?
5. What is interest aggregation? How does it differ from interest articulation?
6. What are the main features of Russia's "floating party system"? In what ways is it fluid and unstable, and what gives it stability and continuity?
7. What were the effects of the 1993, 1995, and 1999 elections on the development of the party system?
8. Boris Yeltsin, Gennadii Ziuganov, and Vladimir Zhirinovsky all ran for president more than once in the 1990s. What were the different political appeals each made, and how strong was their support? How does President Putin's public persona compare with theirs, and how would you explain his high popularity among Russian citizens?

9. If you were advising the liberal parties, what would you tell them to do to increase their share of the vote? What would you advise the communists to do to improve their electoral results? Why?
10. What are the main influences on voters as they choose parties to vote for in parliamentary elections?
11. What changes in political culture, interest-group organization, social structure, or political institutions would help contribute to the consolidation of a stable, competitive party system? What factors retard this process?

ENDNOTES

1. In October 2002, a national survey by VTsIOM found that 54 percent of the population consider that their lives had gotten "somewhat" or "significantly" worse in the last fifteen years; only 29 percent said that their lives had improved.
   Yuri Levada, "Ogliadyvaias' no proidennoe i neprodumannoe: 1987–2002," posted on Polit.ru Web site, 27 December 2002, **www.polit.ru/printable/522413.html**.
2. Mancur Olson, *The Logic of Collective Action: Public Goods and the Theory of Groups* (Cambridge, Mass.: Harvard University Press, 1965).
3. According to Gregory J. Kasza, such "administered mass organizations" as Stalin-era trade unions and youth groups have been a characteristic feature of a number of the mobilizing regimes of the twentieth century. Gregory J. Kasza, *The Conscription Society: Administered Mass Organizations* (New Haven, Conn.: Yale University Press, 1995).
4. Frederick C. Barghoorn, "Faction, Sectoral and Subversive Opposition in Soviet Politics," in Robert A. Dahl, ed., *Regimes and Oppositions* (New Haven, Conn.: Yale University Press, 1973), pp. 27–88.
5. Philip G. Roeder, *Red Sunset: The Failure of Soviet Politics* (Princeton, N.J.: Princeton University Press, 1993).
6. Robert Conquest, *The Great Terror: A Reassessment* (New York: Oxford University Press, 1990). The terrible famine of 1932, which struck the Ukraine and certain other regions with particular force, was itself the product of deliberate policy as Stalin and his associates expressly prohibited sending relief to the affected areas, apparently in order to break any resistance to the collectivization campaign. See also Robert Conquest, *The Harvest of Sorrow: Soviet Collectivization and the Terror-Famine* (New York: Oxford University Press, 1986).
7. Jane I. Dawson, *Eco-Nationalism: Anti-Nuclear Activism and National Identity in Russia, Lithuania, and Ukraine* (Durham, N.C.: Duke University Press, 1996).
8. On the emergence of informal social groups in the glasnost period, see Judith B. Sedaitis and Jim Butterfield, eds., *Perestroika from Below: Social Movements in the Soviet Union* (Boulder, Colo.: Westview, 1991); and Michael Urban, *The Rebirth of Politics in Russia* (Cambridge, England: Cambridge University Press, 1997). A valuable overview of the emergence of nationalist movements in the Gorbachev period is Chapter 4, "Nationalism and Nation-States: Gorbachev's Dilemmas," in Ronald Grigor Suny, *The Revenge of the Past: Nationalism, Revolution, and the Collapse of the Soviet Union* (Stanford, Calif.: Stanford University Press, 1993), pp. 127–60.
9. The labels "*red*" and "*brown*" are widely used to refer to these ideological tendencies in Russian discussions. "Red," of course, is the symbolic color of the Bolsheviks, of communism and revolution; it was the dominant color of the Soviet flag. "Brown"

represents extremist nationalism after the "brown shirts" who were early Nazi followers of Adolf Hitler in Germany in the 1920s. Thus they are regarded as quasi-fascist ultranationalists.

10. RFE/RL Newsline, 13 June 2001.

11. EastWest Institute, Russian Regional Report, Vol. 6, no. 42, 28 November 2001.

12. Jack L. Walker, Jr., *Mobilizing Interest Groups in America: Patrons, Professions, and Social Movements* (Ann Arbor: University of Michigan Press, 1991), p. 9.

13. In a system where all prices were set by the state, there was no meaningful measure of profit in any case. Indeed, relative prices were profoundly distorted by the cumulative effect of decades of central planning. The absence of accurate measures of economic costs is one of the major reasons that Russia's economy continues to be so slow to restructure.

14. Information on Civic Union may be found in Stephen White, Graeme Gill, and Darrell Slider, *The Politics of Transition: Shaping a Post-Soviet Future* (Cambridge, England: Cambridge University Press, 1993), pp. 166–69. A more detailed study is Peter Rutland, *Business Elites and Russian Economic Policy* (London: Royal Institute of International Affairs, 1992). See also Michael McFaul, "Russian Centrism and Revolutionary Transitions," *Post-Soviet Affairs* 9:3 (July/September 1993), pp. 196–222. Wendy Slater, "The Diminishing Center of Russian Parliamentary Politics," *RFE/RL Research Report* 3:17 (29 April 1994), discusses the fate of Civic Union through the 1993 elections.

15. Quoted in Andrei Shleifer and Daniel Treisman, *Without a Map: Political Tactics and Economic Reform in Russia* (Cambridge, Mass.: MIT Press, 2000), p. 28.

16. McFaul, "Russian Centrism," p. 206; Michael McFaul, "State Power, Institutional Change, and the Politics of Privatization in Russia," *World Politics* 47 (1995), pp. 229–30; Pekka Sutela, "Insider Privatization in Russia: Speculations in Systemic Change," *Europe-Asia Studies* 46:3 (1994), p. 420. The other variants included one giving a greater share of stock to outside interests and one requiring insiders to bid for the right to restructure the enterprise.

17. *Izvestiia*, 21 June 2001. The 80 percent figure should not be taken too literally, but it conveys some idea of the scope and clout of the group.

18. *Segodnia*, 7 October 2000.

19. RFE/RL Newsline, 13 September 2002.

20. Article 59 of the 1993 Constitution provides that young men of conscription age who are conscientious objectors to war may do alternative service rather than being called up to army service, but legislation specifying how this right is to be exercised only passed in 2002, as a result of strong opposition by the military. Thus would-be conscientious objectors and courts were in a legal limbo for nearly ten years.

21. **www.soldiersmothers.spb.org**. On the Soldiers' Mothers, see Valerie Sperling, *Organizing Women in Contemporary Russia: Engendering Transition* (Cambridge, England: Cambridge University Press, 1999), pp. 206–7; *Christian Science Monitor*, February 24, 2000.

22. Quoted in Annemarie Gielen, "Soldiers' Mothers Challenge Soviet Legacy," on Web site of Initiative for Social Action and Renewal in Eurasia, **www.isar.org/isar/archive/GT/GT8Gielen.html**, 5 July 2002.

23. Mendelson and Glenn, "Democracy Assistance," p. 35.

24. Sperling, *Organizing Women*, pp. 255–56.

25. James Richter, "Evaluating Western Assistance to Russian Women's Organizations," in Sarah E. Mendelson and John K. Glenn, eds., *The Power and Limits of NGOs: A Critical*

Look at Building Democracy in Eastern Europe and Eurasia (New York: Columbia University Press, 2002), p. 80.

26. The FITUR reached a Faustian bargain with the government over the terms of a new Labor Relations Code, which was adopted in 2001. Under the new legislation, employers no longer have to obtain the consent of the unions to lay off workers. But collective bargaining will be between the largest union at each enterprise and the management unless the workers have agreed on which union will represent them. Thus the new labor code favors the FITUR at the expense of the smaller independent unions.

27. Richard Rose, *New Russia Barometer VI: After the Presidential Election* (Glasgow: Centre for the Study of Public Policy, University of Strathclyde, Studies in Public Policy, no. 272), p. 6; Richard Rose, *Getting Things Done with Social Capital: New Russia Barometer VII* (Glasgow: Centre for the Study of Public Policy, University of Strathclyde, Studies in Public Policy, no. 3), p. 15. In 1996, the question was: At any point during the past twelve months, have you received your wages or pension late? In 1996, 78 percent responded yes, 21 percent no. In 1998, the question was: At any point during the past twelve months, have you received your wages late? Seventy-five percent responded yes, 25 percent no.

28. RFE/RL Newsline, 13 January 1997; 17 January 1997; 18 February 1997; 25 November 1998; 14 January 1999; 27 January 1999; 15 September 1999; 26 June 2000.

29. Linda J. Cook, *Labor and Liberalization: Trade Unions in the New Russia* (New York: The Twentieth Century Fund Press, 1997), pp. 76–77.

30. RFE/RL Newsline, 3 October 2000, citing estimates published in *Nezavisimaia gazeta—religii*. Another survey placed the number of Russians considering themselves to be Russian Orthodox at 55 percent; 9 percent were adherents of other religions, while the number calling themselves atheists was 31 percent. See RFE/RL Newsline, 10 May 1999, citing a survey by the Russian firm Public Opinion.

    Religious identity is closely tied to ethnicity. A few ethnic groups of Russia, including the Buryats, are Lamaist Buddhist by tradition. Many groups, among them the Tatars, Bashkirs, and most of the Northern Caucasus nationalities, are historically Muslim. The Jews are considered an ethnic group of their own. A number of other nationalities have preserved and even revived traditional animist rites and practices including shamanism.

31. An accessible and sympathetic introduction to Orthodox history and doctrine is Timothy Ware, *The Orthodox Church* (New York: Penguin Books, 1984).

32. John Dunlop, "The Russian Orthodox Church as an 'Empire-Saving' Institution," in Michael Bourdeaux, ed., *The Politics of Religion in Russia and the New States of Eurasia* (Armonk, N.Y.: M.E. Sharpe, 1995), pp. 15–40; and Dimitry V. Pospielovsky, "The Russian Orthodox Church in the Postcommunist CIS," in ibid, pp. 41–74.

33. On the issues surrounding proselytization in Russia, see the special issue of the *Emory International Law Review* edited by John Witte Jr., titled "Soul Wars: The Problem of Proselytism in Russia," 12:1 (Winter 1998); also see Harold J. Berman, "Religious Freedom and the Rights of Foreign Missionaries under Russian Law," *The Parker School Journal of East European Law* 2:4/5 (1995), pp. 421–46.

34. *Segodnia,* 19 June 1997.

35. RFE/RL Newsline, 22 September 1997.

36. RFE/RL Newsline, 24 November 1999; *Segodnia,* 24 November 1999.

37. This came in a case involving the Jesuits, whose right to registration was upheld by the Constitutional Court in April 2000 although the Society had only existed in Russia since 1992.

38. RFE/RL Newsline, 14 February 2002.
39. John Witte Jr., "Introduction—Soul Wars: The Problem and Promise of Proselytism in Russia," *Emory International Law Review* 12:1 (Winter 1998), p. 38.
40. Similar oligarchs have also arisen in Ukraine and several other postcommunist countries, where the state opened the economy just enough to allow entrepreneurs to profiteer from partial reform but not enough to force them to compete with other entrepreneurs on a level playing field.
41. Steven L. Solnick, *Stealing the State: Control and Collapse in Soviet Institutions* (Cambridge, Mass.: Harvard University Press, 1998).
42. Rose Brady, *Kapitalizm: Russia's Struggle to Free Its Economy* (New Haven, Conn.: Yale University Press, 1999), pp. 206–7.
43. Quoted in Brady, *Kapitalizm*, p. 207.
44. EastWest Institute, Russian Regional Report, Vol. 5, no. 13, 5 April 2000 (online edition); RFE/RL Newsline, Vol. 4, no. 78, Part I, 19 April 2000.
45. Peter Rutland, "Putin and the Oligarchs," in Dale R. Herspring, ed., *Putin's Russia: Past Imperfect, Future Uncertain* (Lanham, Md.: Rowman & Littlefield, 2003), p. 141.
46. Anne Applebaum, "Russian with a Western Way," **www.Washingtonpost.com**, 19 November 2002.
47. RFE/RL Daily Report, 13 September 1994.
48. RFE/RL Daily Report, 1 September 1995.
49. EastWest Institute, Russian Regional Report, 5 May 2000 (Internet edition).
50. RFE/RL Newsline, 22 October 2001.
51. RFE/RL Newsline, 12 March 2002.
52. Polit.ru, 28 November 2002.
53. Nanci Adler, *Victims of Soviet Terror: The Story of the Memorial Movement* (Westport, Conn.: Praeger, 1993).
54. Sophie Lambroschini, "Russia's Growing Network of Private Associations," RFE/RL Newsline, Part I, 2 December 1999.
55. EastWest Institute, Russian Regional Report, Vol. 5, no. 33, 13 September 2000.
56. RFE/RL Newsline, 13 June 2001.
57. Polit.ru, 21 November 2001; RFE/RL Newsline, 26 November 2001.
58. Quoted in Richard Rose, Neil Munro, and Stephen White, *The 1999 Duma Vote: A Floating Party System* (Glasgow: Centre for the Study of Public Policy, University of Strathclyde, 2000), p. 3.
59. M. Stephen Fish, *Democracy from Scratch: Opposition and Regime in the New Russian Revolution* (Princeton, N.J.: Princeton University Press, 1995); Michael Urban, with Vyacheslav Igrunov and Sergei Mitrokhin, *The Rebirth of Politics in Russia* (Cambridge, England: Cambridge University Press, 1997).
60. Good accounts of the political campaigns surrounding the 1989 and 1990 elections include Brendan Kiernan, *The End of Soviet Politics: Elections, Legislatures, and the Demise of the Communist Party* (Boulder, Colo.: Westview, 1993); and Michael McFaul and Sergei Markov, *The Troubled Birth of Russian Democracy: Parties, Personalities, and Programs* (Stanford, Calif.: Hoover Institution Press, 1993). Good accounts of the elections of 1993, 1995, and 1999 can be found in Stephen White, Richard Rose, and Ian McAllister, *How Russia Votes* (Chatham, N.J.: Chatham House, 1997); and Richard Rose and Neil Munro, *Elections without Order: Russia's Challenge to Vladimir Putin* (Cambridge, England: Cambridge University Press, 2002).
61. On the growing confrontation between Yeltsin and the Congress of People's Deputies/Supreme Soviet over the 1990–1993 period, see Thomas F. Remington,

"Ménage à Trois: The End of Soviet Parliamentarism," in Jeffrey W. Hahn, *Democratization in Russia: The Development of Legislative Institutions* (Armonk, N.Y.: M. E. Sharpe, 1996), pp. 106–39.

62. First, parties and electoral associations had to have been registered by the Ministry of Justice to form lists. Second, they had to collect 100,000 signatures nominating petitions, of which no more than 15 percent could be obtained in any one province. And third, they had to gather the signatures and submit them to the Central Electoral Commission by November 6. On the way in which the design of the electoral law affected the campaign, see Michael Urban, "December 1993 as a Replication of Late-Soviet Electoral Practices," *Post-Soviet Affairs* 10:2 (1994), pp. 136–39.

63. The CEC disqualified eight on the grounds that some of the signatures were invalid or too many were collected in one region.

64. White, Rose, and McAllister, *How Russia Votes* (Chatham, N.J.: Chatham House, 1997), p. 254.

65. Based on results published in *Rossiiskaya gazeta* on 22 June 1996, and taken from the OMRI Daily Digest of 25 June 1996. The percentages are calculated based on the number of voters participating in the voting (75,587,139), the method used in the 1995 Duma elections.

66. *Segodnia,* 10 July 1996.

67. White, Rose, and McAllister, *How Russia Votes,* pp. 241–70.

68. Wendy Slater, "The Russian Communist Party Today," *RFE/RL Research Report* 3:31 (12 August 1994), p. 4.

69. On the CPRF, see Richard Sakwa, "Left or Right? The CPRF and the Problem of Democratic Consolidation in Russia," *Journal of Communist Studies and Transition Politics* 14:1 & 2 (March/June 1998), pp. 128–58; and Joan Urban and Valerii D. Solovei, *Russia's Communists at the Crossroads* (Boulder, Colo.: Westview, 1997).

70. Many of Zhirinovsky's writings, including an autobiography, have been collected and published by the party in a volume titled *O sud'bakh Rossii* (n.p., 1993).

71. Michael McFaul, Nikolai Petrov, and Andrei Ryabov, with Elizabeth Reisch, *Primer on Russia's 1999 Duma Elections* (Moscow: Carnegie Endowment for International Peace, 1999), pp. 96–97.

72. Olga Shvetsova, "Resolving the Problem of Pre-Election Coordination: The Parliamentary Election as an Elite Presidential 'Primary,'" in Vicki Hesli and William Reisinger, *Elections, Parties and the Future of Russia: The 1999–2000 Elections* (Cambridge, England: Cambridge University Press, 2002).

73. RFE/RL Newsline, 15 November 2002, and 23 December 2002.

74. Arthur H. Miller, Gwyn Erb, William M. Reisinger, and Vicki L. Hesli, "Emerging Party Systems in Post-Soviet Societies: Fact or Fiction?" *Journal of Politics* 62:2 (May 2000), p. 462.

75. Rose, Munro, and White, *The 1999 Duma Vote,* pp. 20–25.

76. Rose and Munro, *Elections without Order.*

77. Miller, et al., "Emerging Party Systems," pp. 471–76.

78. The chairman of the Central Electoral Commission, Alexander Veshniakov, has proposed a set of reforms along these lines, as have members of the Unity faction in the Duma. See Alexander Kornilov, "Putin Shares Communists' Parliamentary Dream," on the Web site **www.gazeta.ru** for 12 September 2000.

7

The Politics of Partial Reform

THE DUAL TRANSITION

One reason Russia's transition from communism was so wrenching was that the country remade both its *political* and *economic* institutions while simultaneously redefining itself as a new national state following the disintegration of the union. The relations between the political and economic dimensions of the reform raise serious questions about whether market liberalization and political democratization reinforce or undermine one another. Considering the dismal economic performance of communist regimes, few doubt that a market economy leads to both higher economic growth and greater dynamism over the long term than does state socialism. But the transition from a state-controlled economy to a market system generates enormous dangers, such as deepening corruption, economic depression, and the collapse of social-welfare structures. As a result, many observers think that it is preferable to delay democratization until the transition to capitalism is well advanced.

How we evaluate Russia's postcommunist economic performance depends on what our point of reference is. Sometimes Russia's transition is contrasted with the paths of development of Asian countries such as China. Because of China's remarkable record of high economic growth rates in the 1980s and 1990s, many believe that China offers a model that can be emulated elsewhere. Certainly China's thriving economy is all the more impressive when compared to the spectacle of breakdown and decline seen in Russia over the last decade, as Tables 7.1 and 7.2 show.

In Russia, the economy steadily shrank over the 1990s while China recorded high output growth and investment rates, although from a very low base. As Table 7.1 shows, economic growth in China has been rapid, and has brought per capita national income to a level about half that of Russia, while keeping inequality much lower than in Russia and raising life expectancy to a level significantly higher than Russia's. Table 7.2 indicates the growth of two key indicators of economic performance: gross domestic product and price inflation. Altogether, Russia's economy shrank by about half over the decade of the 1990s and only began to recover in 1999. China's reforms have been far more successful in raising economic productivity. Since the Chinese communist leadership retained control over political power while setting the country firmly on the path

--- TABLE 7.1 ---

Russian and Chinese Economic Performance Compared

	GDP growth (average annual % growth, 1990– 2000)	Inflation (average annual %, 1990– 2000)	External debt (% of gross national income, 1999)	% living below poverty line	Gini index (1998)	Life expec- tancy at birth (1999)	Per capita national income (2000) ($US)
Russia	−4.8	162.0	72	27.0[1]	48.7	66	$1,666
China	10.3	7.1	14	4.6[2]	40.3	70	$840

[1]Russian State Statistical Agency figure for November 2002 (refers to percentage of population living below subsistence level).
[2]1998.

Source: World Bank, *Building Institutions for Markets: World Development Report 2002* (Washington, D.C.: World Bank, 2002), pp. 232–7.

--- TABLE 7.2 ---

Russian Annual GDP Growth and Price Inflation Rates, 1991–2002

	1991	1992	1993	1994	1995	1996	1997	1998	1999	2000	2001	2002[1]
GDP	−5.0	−14.5	−8.7	−12.6	−4.3	−6.0	0.4	−11.6	3.2	7.6	5.0	4.0
Inflation	138.0	2,323.0	844.0	202.0	131.0	21.8	11.0	84.4	36.5	20.2	18.6	15.1

Note: GDP is measured in constant market prices. Inflation is measured as the percentage change in the consumer price index from December of one year to December of the next.

[1]*Source:* Press reports of Russian State Statistical Service (**www.gks.ru**). Preliminary estimates.

toward market-oriented growth and prosperity, the Chinese case raises difficult questions about the relationship between economic and political liberalization.

On the other hand, among the postcommunist countries of Eastern Europe and the former Soviet Union, Russia's economic performance is neither particularly poor nor particularly good.[1] As Table 7.3 shows, some of the postcommunist countries suffered huge declines in production in the years following the political transition, with economic growth only barely resuming by the end of the 1990s. In others, economic growth turned positive in the mid-1990s and has continued steadily since then. Figure 7.1 illustrates the wide diversity of economic performances by several postcommunist countries. Russia, where recorded economic output in 2001 stood at about two-thirds of its 1988 level, is in the middle of the range. Its downturn lasted for most of the 1990s, but it has experienced steady economic growth since then.

The worldwide debate over the best package of policies and institutions for promoting economic development is prompted in part by a sharp backlash against the policies promoted by the International Monetary Fund and the

TABLE 7.3

Annual GDP Growth Rates, Selected Postcommunist Countries

	1989	1990	1991	1992	1993	1994	1995	1996	1997	1998	1999	2000	2001	2001 as percentage of 1988 GDP
Poland	0.2	−11.6	−7.0	2.6	3.8	5.2	7.0	6.0	6.8	4.8	4.1	4.0	2.0	129.38
Czech Republic	1.4	−1.2	−11.6	−0.5	0.1	2.2	5.9	4.8	−1.0	−2.2	−0.8	3.1	3.5	102.54
Slovakia	1.4	−2.5	−14.6	−6.5	−3.7	4.9	6.7	6.2	6.2	4.1	1.9	2.2	3.0	107.16
Hungary	0.7	−3.5	−11.9	−3.1	−0.6	2.9	1.5	1.3	4.6	4.9	4.2	5.2	4.5	109.66
Estonia	8.1	−6.5	−13.6	−14.2	−8.8	−2.0	4.6	4.0	10.4	5.0	−0.7	6.9	4.5	93.68
Lithuania	1.5	−5.0	−5.7	−21.3	−16.2	−9.8	3.3	4.7	7.3	5.1	−3.9	3.9	4.0	68.51
Latvia	6.8	2.9	−10.4	−34.9	−14.9	0.6	−0.8	3.3	8.6	3.9	1.1	6.6	6.5	72.83
Ukraine	4.0	−3.4	−8.7	−9.9	−14.2	−22.9	−12.2	−10.0	−3.0	−1.9	−0.2	5.8	7.0	46.44
Georgia	−4.8	−12.4	−20.6	−44.8	−25.4	−11.4	2.4	10.5	10.8	2.9	3.0	1.9	3.0	33.69
Armenia	14.2	−7.4	−11.7	−41.8	−8.8	5.4	6.9	5.9	3.3	7.2	3.3	6.0	6.0	76.01
Azerbaijan	−4.4	−11.7	−0.7	−22.6	−23.1	−19.7	−11.8	1.3	5.8	10.0	7.4	11.1	8.0	53.68
Moldova	8.5	−2.4	−17.5	−29.1	−1.2	−31.2	−1.4	−7.8	1.3	−6.5	−4.4	1.9	5.0	37.08
Kazakstan	−0.4	−0.4	−13.0	−2.9	−9.2	−12.6	−8.2	0.5	1.7	−1.9	2.7	9.6	10.0	75.79
Russia	0.0	−4.0	−5.0	−14.5	−8.7	−12.7	−4.1	−3.5	0.9	−4.9	5.4	8.3	5.0	66.46

Source: European Bank for Reconstruction and Development (EBRD), *Transition Report 2001: Energy in Transition* (London: EBRD, 2001), p. 59.

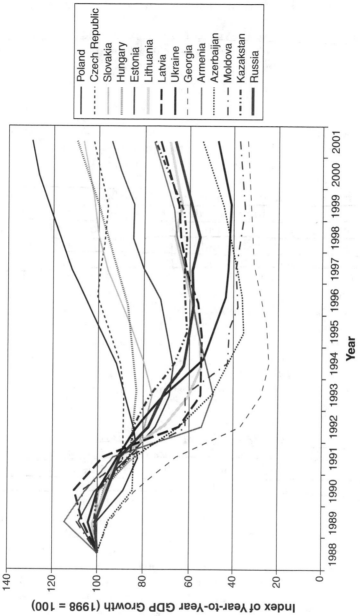

Figure 7.1 Comparative Postcommunist Economic Performance

Legend:
Poland
Czech Republic
Slovakia
Hungary
Estonia
Lithuania
Latvia
Ukraine
Georgia
Armenia
Azerbaijan
Moldova
Kazakstan
Russia

Y-axis: Index of Year-to-Year GDP Growth (1998 = 100)
X-axis: Year — 1988 1989 1990 1991 1992 1993 1994 1995 1996 1997 1998 1999 2000 2001

United States for reforming the postcommunist economies. In this chapter we ask whether and how much the reform policies adopted in Russia were responsible for its poor record of performance in the 1990s.

Stabilization

Russia pursued two major sets of reforms in the 1990s, macroeconomic stabilization and privatization. The stabilization program has often been called "shock therapy" but the official term for stabilization programs such as the one Russia attempted to implement is *structural adjustment*. Stabilization puts an economy on an austerity regime in order to restore a balance between what society spends and what it earns. Stabilization gives the national currency real value, which requires eliminating chronic sources of inflation. This means making drastic cuts in state spending, raising taxes, ending price controls, and opening the economy to free foreign trade so that foreign products can compete with domestic ones. Structural reform of this kind always lowers the standard of living for some or most groups of the population, at least in the short run. Therefore, until living standards begin to rise again for most strata, such reform creates powerful political opponents. These are the groups that had formerly enjoyed the benefits of state-controlled wages and prices, high state spending to subsidize priority sectors of the economy, protection from competition from foreign industries, and welfare entitlement programs. Often these groups are well-organized, voicing their opposition to reform through strong trade unions, associations of directors of state-owned firms, and political parties whose primary constituencies are those most vulnerable to reform.

Those who are made worse off by stabilization are not the only enemies of reform, however. Joel Hellman has argued persuasively that in a number of the postcommunist countries, it is precisely the "early winners" from reform who step in to block subsequent measures to open the economy to free competition. These include officials who have acquired ownership rights to monopoly enterprises and then work to shut out potential competitors from their markets. Or they may be state officials who benefit from collecting "fees" to issue licenses to importers and exporters or permits for doing business. They may be bankers who obtain cheap state-subsidized credits from the central bank and then lend out money to entrepreneurs at exorbitant rates. Some enterprise directors may set up profitable sideline businesses, while using the state enterprise as a cheap source of production equipment, raw materials, and labor; the state enterprise then records losses while the private sideline business makes the director and his friends a tidy profit. And all these newly advantaged groups cultivate ties with policy makers who will act to protect them from either a rollback of the reforms or their advancement to the next stage. Hellman argues that these groups have been a powerful brake on reform in postcommunist countries such as Russia.[2]

The question for the architects of reform therefore is what mixture of policies and institutions is most likely to launch the economy on a path of growth and development and keep it on that path despite political opposition. Reformers may have only a very short window of opportunity in which to act, and they must be politically realistic. If they alienate too many powerful interests, a powerful coalition of groups is likely to form and block reform. But if they give away too much to the "early winners," reform may stall partway.

From Communism to Capitalism

The legacy of communism makes these problems more acute in the postcommunist world than in countries where the basic infrastructure of a market economy is in place. Communist regimes carried out a far more sweeping destruction of autonomous economic and cultural institutions in their societies than did other authoritarian regimes.[3] In the postauthoritarian states of South America and Southern Europe, the economic dimension of transition consists more in liberalizing the foreign trade regime and privatizing state and parastatal enterprises than in creating a capitalist economy from scratch.[4] In the communist world, many fundamental features of a market-oriented economy were absent, including a coherent set of enforceable legal rights to ownership and control of capital assets; a system of prices that approximated equilibrium between demand and supply; a set of financial institutions buying and selling loans at market prices; and regulatory institutions enforcing fair rules of market exchange.

As far as Russia was concerned, the conversion of the world's largest state socialist economy into a market-oriented economy would have been extraordinarily difficult regardless of the policy instruments chosen. In the short and medium term, the process would create winners and losers, depending on how particular enterprises, classes, age groups, ethnic groups, regions, industrial branches, and other actors were positioned. Some would benefit by the opening of competition; others would suffer. Liberalizing prices meant that the elderly and others on fixed incomes would suffer a severe drop in living standards and people would see a lifetime of savings wiped out.

Communist systems differed from other authoritarian regimes in ways that made their economic transitions more difficult. But the Soviet Union possessed certain features that have made its successor states' transition to a capitalist economy even more painful than it has been for many other communist societies. For one, the economic growth model followed by Stalin and his successors tended to seek economies of scale by concentrating large shares of the production of particular goods in particular enterprises. Consequently, many large enterprises entered the new era with near-monopolies in their line of production. In 1988, a small number of giant enterprises with more than 2,000 employees, a group comprising only 9 percent of all enterprises, produced over 60 percent of all output.[5] This meant that once state price and production controls were freed, these enterprises could raise prices with impunity and collect monopolists' rents.[6] Their dominance of the market in their sectors raised the barriers to entry for new enterprises after the system of central planning ended.[7]

The concentration of production in a relatively small number of relatively large enterprises meant that many local governments are entirely dependent on the economic health of a single employer: Almost half of Russian cities have only one industrial enterprise, and three-fourths have no more than four.[8] Since Russian industrial firms were traditionally responsible for a broad range of social-welfare functions—building and maintaining housing for their work forces, and managing health, recreational, educational, and similar facilities—such towns are heavily dependent on these firms for the provision of basic social services and are the mainstay of employment. Therefore economic transition created severe problems for maintaining social welfare since local governments are unable to assume financial responsibility for these tasks.

A second problem facing Russia was the enormous commitment of its economic resources to military production. Since the real level of Soviet GDP (gross domestic product) per capita as of 1985 was something like one-third that of the United States, the actual share of gross economic output devoted to the military sector was around 25 percent, not 14 to 15 percent, as most Western analysts previously believed.[9] In some regions, at least half the work force was employed in defense plants. The end of the Cold War and the cutback in military spending hit such plants very hard, and it was often impossible for them quickly to re-tool equipment, retrain workers, and find new markets.

A third factor is the vast size of Russia. Creating new infrastructure, such as highways and rail lines, high-speed data transmission and microwave communications links, and organizational structures spanning Russia's vast territorial expanse, would be a huge task for any economy, let alone one needing to finance a massive program of retooling and restructuring. For the same reason, aid in the form of credits and grants from Western governments and financial bodies could represent only a tiny fraction of Russia's requirements for new capital. Sometimes Russia's experience is compared with East Germany's. After the collapse of communism there, and the country's merger into West Germany, West German economic investment and social-welfare funds have been poured into the much smaller former East German territory—some $100 billion each year, for a population of 16 million people. Modernization of the telephone system alone had cost $37 billion by the end of 1992.[10] To invest resources in Russia on the same per capita scale would take $1 trillion per year.[11] The huge physical scale of Russia's economy imposes limits on the speed of change.

The final issue has to do with human capital. It is not that the Soviet population was uneducated: Literacy was nearly universal and educational attainment levels were among the highest in the world. Russia's state enterprise managers were highly skilled at coping with the demands on them under the system of planned production targets. Rather, the incentive system built into state and social institutions encouraged skill in coping with a heavily hierarchical, state-centered economy, but discouraged the kinds of risk-and-reward-centered behavior that a market system requires. For example, the directors of Soviet state firms were rewarded for meeting output targets under difficult conditions, such as uncertainty about whether needed inputs would be delivered in time and in the right assortment. As noted, they were also responsible for a broad array of social-welfare functions for their employees, their families, and the population of the towns and regions where they were located. Profitability and efficiency were well down the list of priorities of Soviet managers.[12] Almost no Soviet employees or managers had firsthand experience with decision making in the conditions of a market economy.

Indeed, to the extent that it meant incurring risk and investing effort in a venture for private gain, entrepreneurship was certainly not unknown in the USSR: Rather, it was highly illegal. Indeed, the criminal code prescribed the death penalty for large-scale economic crimes, such as currency speculation. A great deal of private enterprise existed, but as part of the black market. Many citizens, both those who viewed profit-making enterprise with the deepest suspicion and those who risked prosecution and became black marketeers, took it for granted that any profit-making business was illegal and immoral. Many who accepted the risk and went into illicit business viewed the law as an inconvenience to be circumvented. There was no pool of managers and entrepreneurs, therefore, immediately ready to take advantage of new opportunities for legal gainful enterprise when the political regime changed. For this reason, a high proportion of the first generation of new Russian entrepreneurs came from among young scientific and technical employees in state institutes and universities.[13]

These conditions sharpened the contradiction between economic and political reform in Russia by making economic transition more painful than it would have been had conditions been more favorable.

Supporters and Opponents of Reform

Economic and political liberalization can be compatible if the populace of a country understands and accepts the necessity of tough reforms. But moments of consensus that market reform is necessary whatever the cost are historically rare. How much agreement was there among Russians about the desirability of radical market reform? The available evidence suggests that in 1990–1991, about half the adult population expressed support for radical economic reform to bring about a rapid transition to a market economy. Two qualifications must be made. First, Russians had little experience with market principles. Many undoubtedly associated them with the prosperity of Western societies rather than with the problems of transition. Second, public attitudes about the market have proven to be more volatile than have attitudes about democracy. That said, it is important to recognize the degree to which the reforms did have a solid foundation of public support in 1992.[14]

The August 1991 coup further fueled support for radical reform. Both in the Russian Congress of People's Deputies and in public opinion, the response to the coup was a surge of support for Yeltsin and his radical reform program. Addressing the Russian Congress of People's Deputies on October 28, 1991, Yeltsin demanded special powers to enact radical reform by decree, and on November 1, received them by a decisive margin. He named himself prime minister and head of government, and formed a cabinet of young, radically minded intellectuals drawn from academic institutes. Egor Gaidar, then thirty-five years old, became deputy prime minister and overall architect of the reform program. Yeltsin proceeded to issue a set of decrees liberalizing foreign trade and the circulation of hard currency.[15] On January 2, 1992, under Yeltsin's political protection, the new government undertook a major initiative to push Russia toward a market system by abolishing most controls on wholesale and retail prices and cutting government spending sharply.

Almost immediately, opposition began to form to the new program. Within two weeks of the introduction of the program, Ruslan Khasbulatov, now chairman of the Russian Supreme Soviet but previously Yeltsin's deputy as head of the parliament, came out strongly against the program and called on the government to resign. Since Yeltsin formally was head of government, this was a direct attack on Yeltsin. Quickly Vice President Rutskoi sided with Khasbulatov and the conservative opposition in parliament. Economists and politicians took sides. Dispassionate analysis of, and even basic information about, the effects of the stabilization program became virtually impossible to get. The shock therapy program was an easy target for criticism, even though there was no consensus among critics about what should be done. Opponents demanded that the pace of reform be slowed so that Russians would have more time to adjust to the new conditions; they complained that the Gaidar team might be capable theorists but had no idea how to run a government; they demanded creation of a safety net to cushion the blow of the transition for the indigent, the elderly, and the displaced. It became commonplace to say that the program was all shock and no therapy.

The confrontation between President Yeltsin and his parliamentary opposition reached its violent climax in October 1993 (see Chapter 3). Yeltsin's victory and the adoption of the new constitution gave him the ability to use his decree power to put many of the elements of his reform program into effect. But the government's limited control over the state bureaucracy, regional authorities, and the Central Bank meant that many elements of the stabilization program were not implemented as intended. And neither Yeltsin nor his government spent much effort building public support for the reforms.

Consequences of Reform

The first task of macroeconomic stabilization is to stop inflation and to prevent hyperinflation even as price controls are lifted.[16] The idea is that once inflation is under control, the economy can be restored to health. High inflation threatens both democracy and productivity because it undermines faith in the currency and in the future. Defenders of stabilization argue that the pain caused by reform is temporary and that real economic growth can come about only if economic actors have confidence that the value of their earnings will not be wiped out by inflation. By cutting government spending, letting prices rise, and raising taxes to squeeze inflationary pressure out of the economy, stabilization aims at stimulating production by stabilizing money and prices. This creates incentives for producers to increase output and encourages them to look for new niches in the marketplace where they can make and sell products for a profit. Increases in production should in turn bring prices back down. If producers do not respond by raising productivity, society suffers from a sharp, sudden loss in purchasing power. People go hungry; bank savings vanish. This is what happened in Russia: The producers did not respond to the new economic incentives as the theory dictated they should, and the economy fell into a protracted slump.

Enterprise managers, accustomed to assured sources of supply and credit, found it extremely difficult to begin producing for new markets. Directors of top-priority defense plants that produced missiles that could deliver payloads to destinations anywhere in the world found it unthinkable to have to develop new product lines. Factories cut back on production, reduced work forces, and stopped paying their bills and taxes. The economy went into a severe recession. Those directors of state and private enterprises who did want to retool or expand operations, however, faced a severe credit crunch. The state cut back on the supply of cheap loans and credits in an effort to get inflation under control. Organized crime rackets preyed on any firm enjoying even a little success in the market. Firms that were politically connected were able to survive by winning cheap credits and production orders from government, which dampened any incentive they might otherwise have had for improving productivity. This resulted in a situation that the McKinsey Global Institute, in a comprehensive report on Russia's economy in 1999, summed up by pointing out that the most productive sectors of the economy were the least profitable ones, while the least productive sectors were the most profitable.[17]

Small wonder then that one line of criticism directed against the Yeltsin/Gaidar government, its Western advisers, and the international financial organizations that were supplying loans, was that they were seeking to "de-industrialize" Russia—that is, trying to destroy the great industrial plant that had been built up at such cost over many years. Some of the critics went further and said that the West was deliberately trying to sabotage Russia by forcing it to follow the shock therapy prescription. Communists and nationalists got a rise out of audiences by depicting Gaidar and the other radical members of the 1992 government as the traitorous hirelings of a malevolent, imperialist West.[18]

A more moderate and more widespread viewpoint, however, is that the economic assumptions underlying the reform program were flawed. They are sometimes referred to as the "Washington consensus" because they represented the conventional wisdom promoted by the United States and many economists in the 1980s. The Washington consensus emphasized macroeconomic stabilization, privatization, deregulation, and trade liberalization as ways of squeezing out inflationary pressures and injecting painful but necessary doses of competitive pressure into the economy. The idea was to reduce the amount of state intervention into the economy as much as possible and as quickly as possible. You can't jump across an abyss in gradual steps, they pointed out; prolong the pain of reform and the opposition will only grow stronger. Gaidar and his team embraced this philosophy, for both economic and political reasons. Economically, they believed that Russia would never progress if it remained wedded to a Stalin-era industrial system where heavy and defense industry received the lion's share of capital resources and consumer goods and services were perennially starved of investment. Politically, they wanted to act as quickly as possible in order to make movement toward the market economy irreversible: Price liberalization and mass privatization would raise the costs of rolling back reforms to unacceptably high levels.

The deeper questions are twofold: How much effect did the shock therapy program in fact have on the economy, and how much choice did the reformers have in choosing policies?

Both critics and defenders of the program assume that the government's policies actually had the effects they intended. In fact it is by no means clear how much impact the program had. National policies in Russia frequently are accompanied by considerable publicity and attract intense controversy, but rarely are they implemented in the way intended by their sponsors and still more rarely do they achieve their objectives. In the case of the shock therapy program, not all resistance was visible. Many officials simply circumvented the policies. Directors of important industries wheedled credits from the Central Bank (which was not under the government's control) or persuaded ministries to place orders for products simply to keep production going.[19] Rather than respond to the new financial austerity, many directors simply continued to turn out and ship their products without being paid, allowing interenterprise arrears to mount. The Gaidar government lacked full control over the government, so it could not completely shape the structure of incentives to which enterprise managers responded. The credibility of its policies was never secure. Since the effectiveness of a stabilization program depends on producers' calculation of the government's commitment to staying the course, the government's imperfect control over the money supply distorted the effects of the policy. The government did not carry price liberalization out fully in any case, keeping heavy controls on energy and electric power, which may have protected consumers and producers but at the cost of allowing severe price distortions to accumulate throughout the economy.

The Gaidar team had a very limited choice of policy instruments with which to put Russia on a self-reinforcing path toward economic liberalization, and it inherited an economy on the verge of breakdown. Through 1991, as traditional lines of control via the Communist Party and state bureaucracy weakened, regional and local governments began erecting barriers to interregional trade. Some set tariffs; others erected roadblocks preventing the "export" of goods from their territories. Moscow and other big cities introduced identity cards with residents' photographs to prevent out-of-towners from coming in and purchasing goods from the relatively better-stocked stores in cities. The network of internal wholesale and retail trade was breaking down. Tax collections fell precipitously. Administrative measures probably would have failed to restore them, short of martial law. But the drastic price liberalization of January 2, 1992, which allowed producers and retailers to set any price that the market could bear for most goods and services, did immediately eliminate the internal trade wars and restored the circulation of goods, albeit at high and often ruinous prices.

Privatization

Stabilization was followed shortly afterward by another, equally important program—the privatization of state enterprises. In contrast to the shock therapy program, privatization enjoyed considerable public support, at least at first, and offset the unpopularity of stabilization. Privatization is the transfer of ownership of state firms to private owners. Market theory holds that under the right conditions, private ownership of productive assets is more efficient for society as a whole than is monopoly or state ownership, because in a competitive environment owners are motivated by an incentive to maximize their property's ability to produce a return. Whereas a monopolist does not care if the firm he or she owns is inefficient, the owner of the firm in a market system wants to increase the productivity and therefore the market value of the firm. For this reason, most economists consider it essential to transfer ownership of state assets from the state to private owners as part of the transition from socialism to a market economy in order to stimulate growth and productivity in the economy as a whole. In short, a system of private property not only benefits the individual owners, but also benefits the whole society.

The theory is generally valid. But, as is often true of good theories, many circumstances can interfere with its application to the real world.

We must distinguish the privatization of state-owned firms in Russia from the creation of new, private start-up businesses. Although private entrepreneurs and foreign interests have created a large number of new, independent businesses, these are usually small in scale. The fate of Russia's state enterprises has profound political importance because the overwhelming majority of the population is tied to them for their livelihoods as well as the wide range of social benefits which, as we have noted, are supplied through jobs at state enterprises. The form privatization should take also has major political repercussions. One method is simply to give away state assets to the public as a democratic gesture that quickly turns the entire population into property holders and gives them a stake in the reform process. An alternative is to require auctions in which groups and individuals submit competitive bids to purchase assets, thereby creating real value that can be used as investment capital, but allowing rich or corrupt elements of the population to capture control of state enterprises. Russia combined these two methods, first distributing free vouchers to all citizens, who were then able to use the vouchers to bid for shares of privatized firms at special auctions, and then holding auctions of shares for cash.

The legal right to start a private company is much less politically controversial than was the design of the privatization program. As early as 1986, Soviet law was changed so as to permit individuals and family members to start their own businesses, as well as to allow groups of people to start private commercial businesses organized as cooperatives.[20] As of 1996, Russia had around 900,000 small private businesses. Of these, just over 100,000 were small state establishments that had been privatized, and about 800,000 were start-up businesses.[21] Most of these small firms work in the service sphere. Altogether they account for only about 9 percent of total employment. Of greater political significance, there-fore, is the question of privatization of larger state firms. Privatization programs are usually politically sensitive, since someone must decide how to set value on state enterprises in the absence of capital markets; whether to privatize enter-prises for cash or for government-provided coupons; how much to favor the workers and managers of the enterprise in gaining control over their own work-place; whether to allow foreigners to buy privatized enterprises; and which levels of government can privatize which assets. Disputes over these issues have often stalled privatization programs in postcommunist countries.

Voucher Privatization. The Russian parliament gave Yeltsin and his government the authority to enact privatization by decree but disagreements within the gov-ernment produced fits and starts in the policy. Some in the government wanted to use auctions as much as possible to sell off state enterprises, especially retail and service establishments where it was reasonable to think that purchasers might have sufficient resources to buy them. Others believed it was more just to distribute some sort of coupon or bank account to every citizen that they could use to bid on and buy enterprises. Although the government generally agreed that for the sake of both fairness and social stability, workers should be given pri-ority in acquiring title to the enterprises in which they worked, there were two objections to taking this idea too far. One was that not every citizen worked in an enterprise that could be privatized. Retired people, military servicemen, bal-lerinas, scientists, teachers, and many government employees, for instance, might still be unable to share in the privatization program. Another was that if workers were able to gain control over their enterprises, the managers would be able to use their power within the enterprise to gain both ownership and con-trol over the workplace.

The Russian Supreme Soviet approved legislation on the privatization of state enterprises in July 1991. In December, Yeltsin issued a decree stepping up the pace of privatization and changing the procedures envisioned in the July laws.[22] Privatization of thousands of small- and medium-size enterprises, and a smaller number of large firms, proceeded under the methods that the laws and decrees laid out. One method was for workers and managers who had leased their firms simply to buy them. Another was to hold an auction or to invite bids from investors proposing alternative reorganization plans. A third was to reorga-nize the firm into a joint-stock company and issue shares, in which case the work-ers and managers could acquire a fixed proportion of the shares at a discount.

In the forms of privatization used in 1991 and the first half of 1992, buyers used cash rather than state-issued vouchers. Auctions and the sale of shares were supposed to serve the goal of efficiency by creating a material interest on the part of an investor in the value of the newly acquired assets. It was hoped that in-vestors, be they the workers of the firm themselves or outside buyers, would be interested in maximizing the return on their investment by seeing that the firms were run profitably and efficiently. But when efficiency became the principal ob-jective of cash privatization schemes, fairness was jeopardized. Cash privatization had the effect of making the rich richer and giving ownership of enterprises to the officials who had run them before. Ordinary citizens often were excluded from benefiting from the most profitable opportunities as insiders acquired the stock of the most promising firms. And the poor, of course, had no chance at all to buy shares. In the interests of dispersing ownership rights as widely as possible, parliament's law envisioned that all citizens would be given special bank accounts to buy shares of privatized enterprises.

Yeltsin's December 1991 decree promised that eventually everyone would be issued a voucher to buy shares, while deciding that this would not take effect for a year. Meantime the process of transforming state firms into stock companies and issuing shares would be stepped up, and the cash buyouts of leased and transformed enterprises would continue. In April 1992, however, as opposition to the stabilization program was gaining force, Yeltsin changed course again and decreed that a program of vouchers would begin in the fourth quarter of 1992. Under the program, every citizen of Russia would be issued a voucher with a face value of 10,000 rubles. People would be free to buy and sell vouchers, but they could be used only to acquire shares of stock in privatized enterprises through auctions where voucher owners could bid vouchers for shares of enterprises. People were also allowed to use their vouchers to acquire shares of mutual funds investing in privatized enterprises, or they could sell them to other people. The program was intended to ensure that everyone became a property owner instantly. Politically the aim was to build support for the economic reforms by making citizens into stock owners and thus giving them a stake in the outcome of the market transition. The designers of the program hoped that even though the voucher privatization program did not itself represent new investment capital, it would eventually spur increases in productivity by creating meaningful property rights.[23]

Beginning in October 1992, 148 million privatization vouchers were distributed to citizens. A citizen could sell the voucher to someone else or invest it directly in enterprise stock or in an investment fund. The program established three ways in which vouchers could be exchanged for stock shares. These differed according to how much stock could be acquired by employees of privatized enterprises and on what terms. Each method balanced the demands of managers and workers of state enterprises for control over their own enterprises against the demand of outsiders for the right to bid freely for shares, and each combined the objective of letting citizens acquire stock for free with that of creating a real capital market where stock had tradable value. The State Privatization Committee and its regional and local offices oversaw the entire privatization process, organizing auctions and approving privatization plans drafted by enterprises. This powerful agency, and its chairman, Anatolii Chubais, became targets for vehement criticism from all sides—from those accusing the committee of selling off assets too cheaply and not protecting enterprises to those distressed at the way in which state managers usually wound up with the controlling share of stock. With Yeltsin's protection, however, Chubais carried out the program over the objections of all critics.

Chubais's team was unwilling simply to give away Russia's vast capital stock to the powerful state enterprise directors. Instead it wanted to diffuse ownership rights as broadly as possible. The political realities, however, dictated that the government allow enterprise directors certain advantages. In the short run, at least, the consent of the directors to the program was essential to maintaining economic and social stability in the country. The managers could ensure that labor did not erupt in a massive wave of strikes. As we have seen, they also represented one of the most powerful collective interests in the country. The government, therefore, allowed a good deal of "insider privatization," in which senior enterprise officials acquired the largest proportion of shares in privatized firms. Of the three options, the second, under which employees could acquire majority stakes in the enterprises, proved to be the most widely used. Three-quarters of privatized enterprises opted for this method, most often using vouchers. On average, only 22.5 percent of shares of enterprises were sold at voucher auctions, where the public could bid for them. Real control wound up in the hands of the managers.[24]

Around 18,000 medium- and large-scale firms were privatized by 1996. Privatization for most of them did not immediately bring about major changes in the way they were run. One reason is that privatization did not bring an infusion of new investment capital to modernize their plant and equipment. And one reason for this is that managers strenuously resisted allowing their firms to be taken over by outside investors. Asked in one major survey of enterprise directors whether they would be willing to sell a majority of the shares of their enterprise to an outside investor who would bring the capital needed to invest in modernizing the firm, two-thirds said they would not be willing. In other words, they preferred to remain majority owners of an unprofitable enterprise than the minority owners of a much more profitable one.[25] Very few firms experienced much management turnover and even fewer engaged in extensive restructuring of their operations to make them more productive or efficient.

All vouchers were to have been used by December 31, 1993. President Yeltsin extended the expiration date until June 30, 1994. By that time 140 million vouchers had been exchanged for stock out of 148 million originally distributed, according to Anatolii Chubais.[26] Some 40 million citizens had become property owners. About 70 percent of large- and medium-size firms and 80 percent of all small businesses had been privatized. The voucher privatization phase had ended. The next phase was to bring about the privatization of most of the remaining state enterprises, but by means of auctions of shares for cash. This also included the infamous "loans-for-shares" scheme that we discussed in the last chapter. By 1996, about 90 percent of industrial output was being produced by privatized firms and about two-thirds of all large- and medium-size enterprises had been privatized.[27] As of 2000, around 70 percent of Russian GDP was produced in the private sector.[28]

Consequences of Privatization. How much did privatization transform Russia's economy? It is fair to say that privatization did not make Russia's economy more productive in the short run, and it did deepen corruption. A famous theorem in economics holds that if the costs of economic transactions are sufficiently low, then regardless of how property rights over some set of economic assets are initially allocated, bargaining among owners will eventually achieve an optimally efficient distribution of ownership and control rights over those assets.[29] But note the *if*. The theorem stipulates that the distribution of property rights reaches optimum efficiency *if* the costs of reaching agreements are low. In fact, in any real society, the costs of transactions—the difficulties of bargaining, incomplete information about the qualities of what is being sold, the problem of enforcing an agreement after it has been reached—can be formidable.[30] In Russia, the uncertainty surrounding the change in economic and political conditions made markets extremely hazardous and inefficient. Owners of many firms preferred to capitalize on their political leverage and take advantage of inefficiency rather than to restructure. Many firms have not changed in the way they are managed and continue to be closely tied to state life-support systems such as cheap loans and subsidies.[31]

Not surprisingly, the actual process of privatization was shaped by the inherited structure of power and wealth in society. The dominant pattern was acquisition of title through insider privatization, rather than through open competitive bidding. Moreover, the program allowed many unscrupulous wheeler-dealers to prey on the public through various financial schemes. Some investment funds promised truly incredible rates of return; most Western investors would have dismissed these claims as outrageous and fraudulent. But in a country lacking experience with capitalism, hope often triumphs over good sense. Many people lost a great deal of money by investing in funds that went bankrupt or turned out to be simple pyramid schemes, where the dividends for the early investors were supplied by the contributions of later investors. The Russian government lacked the capacity to protect the investors. Many people were disenchanted with the entire program as a result.

Moreover, the privatization program contributed little to the urgent task of modernization and retooling of the economy. Vouchers, the dramatic instrument used in the first phase for mass privatization, were not inflationary because they could not be used as legal tender for other transactions.[32] But neither were they forms of productive capital, as stocks and bonds are in countries with established financial markets. So the vouchers did not expand the pool of resources enterprises could use to increase productivity. They were intended to give an impetus to the consolidation of a market economy. The policy makers believed that mass privatization would establish an interest on the part of new property owners in increasing the value of their assets, which they would achieve by investing in the modernization and retooling of the firms. In turn, the need for capital would induce a healthy capital market into being. However, the lack of an institutional infrastructure for market exchange and a lack of confidence in the future deterred entrepreneurs from investing capital. The result has been massive capital flight out of Russia: One estimate is that some $300 billion has fled Russia since 1990, an amount greater than Russia's annual national income.[33]

Weak Capital Markets and the August 1998 Crash. Privatization was carried out in the absence of strong, impartial institutions regulating capital markets, and the newly minted big business owners have not been eager to see such institutions created. The channels by which market economies convert private savings into investment in companies, such as financial institutions, pension and insurance funds, and stock and bond markets, are extremely weak in Russia. For so large a country, with so great an industrial potential, stock and bond markets are tiny. In turn, the weakness of financial institutions resulted in a vicious cycle of illiquidity that helped trigger a financial crash in 1998: Enterprises, starved for working capital, failed to pay their wages and taxes on time, and traded with one another using barter. By 1998, at least half of enterprise output was being "sold" through barter trade.[34] Barter creates a world of unreal values, a "virtual economy," as economists Clifford Gaddy and Barry Ickes termed it, where it is impossible to calculate the cost of goods and where investors cannot make intelligent judgments about where capital investment will have the greatest return. A virtual economy is profoundly inefficient.[35]

By the mid-1990s, the government's own long- and short-term goals were in conflict. In the long run the government hoped privatization would create property rights and capital markets. But in the immediate term, the government needed to raise cash to compensate for shortfalls in its tax revenues. Privatization of enterprises for cash allowed the government to generate one-time infusions of revenue into the budget by auctioning off state-owned shares of stock in industrial firms. Unfortunately, the government found that demand for shares was often weak, and sold off the assets at embarrassingly, even scandalously, low prices, as in the case of loans for shares. Moreover, at the same time the government was trying to auction off shares in enterprises, it was also trying to raise revenues by issuing bonds (GKOs) at extremely high rates of return.[36] The market for the lucrative GKOs crowded out the capital market for investment in industry. One government policy goal—that of financing budget expenditures by issuing bonds—was directly in competition with another—that of accelerating private ownership of state-owned enterprises.

The government fell into an unsustainable debt trap. To pay off the interest on the loans it had taken, it needed to raise still more cash, which it did through foreign borrowing, issuing high interest–bearing domestic bonds, and privatization. As lenders became increasingly certain that the government could not make good on its obligations, they demanded ever higher interest rates, deepening the trap. Ultimately the bubble burst: In August 1998, the state could not honor its obligations. It declared a moratorium on its debts, and let the ruble's value collapse against the dollar. Overnight, the ruble lost two-thirds of its value and credit dried up.[37] The government bonds held by investors were almost worthless. Importers went out of business. The effects of the crash rippled through the economy. The sharp devaluation of the ruble made exports more competitive and gave an impetus to domestic producers, but also significantly lowered people's living standards.

Privatization of land has been much slower to develop. Until 2001–2002, the communist-agrarian-nationalist forces in parliament blocked private ownership of land. Over 90 percent of agricultural land continues to be owned by the old collective and state farms.[38] Almost all of these have been legally transformed into joint-stock companies, but continue to be run as in the past. There was a small and largely off-book market for land parcels, but large-scale privatization was blocked by the impasse between Yeltsin and his left-wing opposition. In 2001–2002, however, with the active support of President Putin, parliament passed legislation making the private purchase and sale of land—including farmland—legal. Together with new legislation allowing land to be used as security for bank loans, these laws should give an impetus to the development of a market for land.

Financial-Industrial Groups. As we have seen, despite the goal of encouraging widespread property ownership through the mass privatization program, capital became highly concentrated as financial capital merged with industrial capital, in a manner reminiscent of Marxist caricatures of "monopoly capitalism." A small number of powerful *financial-industrial groups* (FIGs) gained concentrated ownership of Russian industry. Financial-industrial groups are holding companies in which a leading bank owns controlling shares in a number of enterprises in a particular branch. In a few cases, a former ministry dissolved itself in such a way that its financial department formed a bank to service the enterprises that once were administered hierarchically by the ministry; thus the ministry re-created itself as a holding company with its own financial base. In other cases the government created a holding company to replace a ministry, and set up a bank to finance the company's operations. Most common, however, are conglomerates created by new, nominally private banks.[39]

For different reasons, both parliament and the president encouraged the formation of such powerful conglomerates in the 1990s. Conservative elements in the state bureaucracy and parliament viewed FIGs as a means of keeping the old state-owned industrial sector afloat and staving off competition from the foreign or domestic market. Industrial managers in these groups welcome an assured source of financing. The new entrepreneurial class gains greater opportunities to collect rents and finance profitable lines of activity, while forcing the Central Bank or Finance Ministry to cover their losses from the less profitable areas. In some cases, control over governance through a financial-industrial group allows a bank to force firms to become more efficient and productive in the domestic and international markets. However, this form of ownership also restricts open competition for financing in the capital and debt markets, a goal directly contrary to the liberal precepts of Russia's government and president. Nonetheless, the de facto strength of a coalition of bureaucratic industrialists and newly ascendant business interests has allowed them to flourish.

Overall, then, privatization through vouchers and cash has created property rights and a class of property owners. This class is still narrow, however, as ownership of many assets is concentrated in the hands of the few rather than the many. Capital markets have been extremely slow to get off the ground, and the August 1998 crash set back the development of both stock and debt markets. Yet 1999 brought signs of recovery, and if President Putin carries through on his commitment of creating an equal playing field for all market players, privatization may well come to be regarded as a painful but necessary passage to the birth of a market economy in Russia.

ECONOMY AND SOCIETY

How badly did the economy suffer from the reforms? Output fell for most of the 1990s. There was a slight recovery in 1997, but it was wiped out by the financial collapse of 1998. The crash resulted in an inflationary shock, as the price of the dollar and of goods purchased for hard currency rose three to four times in relation to the ruble. Therefore inflation rose sharply in 1998 while output fell (see Table 7.2).

It is true that official figures overstate the depth of the decline. Consumption declined less than production. Observers skeptical of official output statistics point out that in the past, industrial managers had every reason to *overstate* their actual levels of output, since they were under pressure to fulfill the production plan, whereas now they are more likely to *understate* their actual output in order to avoid taxes. Moreover, the very structure of national income has shifted. Much more of Russia's economic activity is occurring in the sphere of services, which is poorly captured in output statistics. The share of services in the economy has dropped much less than that of industry or agriculture. Since services are much easier to conceal from the authorities, the service sector might even have grown overall in the 1990s if unrecorded transactions are included. There is certainly a great deal of off-book economic activity taking place, some of it legal but outside the scrutiny of the tax police, and some of it illegal. A conservative estimate of the scale of total output of unregistered goods and services is 20 percent of GDP, but some place the figure as high as 40 percent.[40]

Still, the fact remains that Russia's economy sank into deep depression by the mid-1990s, was hit further by the financial crash of 1998, and then began to recover in 1999. Russia's economic decline was far more severe and more protracted than was the Great Depression experienced by the United States or Western Europe following 1929. It was about half as severe as the catastrophic drop caused by the effects of World War I, the Bolshevik Revolution, and the Civil War.[41] The shock therapy and privatization policies pursued by the Russian government, coupled with the restrictive conditions imposed by international financial institutions in return for loans and credits, are only part of the reason for this outcome. Other postcommunist countries experienced much shallower declines and quicker recoveries, as we saw in Table 7.3 and Figure 7.1. The table shows that *all* of the countries that underwent a transition from communist rule experienced an initial decline, as their economies absorbed the shock of the breakup of the socialist trading bloc and the end of central planning. In all of them, economic output fell at least three years in succession. In countries such as Poland, Hungary, the Czech Republic, and Slovakia, however, the economies recovered and began to grow again by the mid-1990s.

For Russia, it would be more accurate to say that real economic reform was never tried since it was quickly subverted by actors outside the government's control, such as the Central Bank, ministries, regional governments, and industrial managers. In some cases, their resistance to reform was not based on an ideological opposition to a market economy as much as it was part of an effort to capture benefits, such as economic rents, from ownership and control over valuable assets and privileges. This reflects the "early winners" syndrome in which initial beneficiaries of the first steps toward privatization and commerce act to shut the doors to other would-be market participants.

The depression was also the aggregate outcome of many local survival strategies. Starved of cash, some enterprises formed alliances with regional governors to pay lower taxes to the regions, while pressuring the regional branches of the federal tax collectors to let them defer their tax obligations to the central government.[42] Recognizing that major oil, gas, and electric power firms were suffering from huge unpaid bills from their customers, the federal government effectively allowed them to avoid paying much of their federal taxes in return for keeping key customers, such as military bases and major industrial enterprises, supplied with energy and power. Each link in the chain coped with the shortage of cash and credit in the economy, but the net outcome was a deep structural crisis. The government was perennially short of money with which to meet its obligations, including pensions and pay for teachers and other state employees. People coped by working outside the official economy, earning unrecorded incomes and hoarding money. No one knows exactly how much cash is sitting under people's mattresses, both in rubles and in dollars, but the state statistical agency estimated in 2000 that people had some $17 billion stashed away at home.[43] This sum, and another $12 billion or so held in ruble and dollar savings accounts in banks, could be an enormously important source of investment capital, if only banks and other institutions were working more effectively to translate savings into financial assets.

A number of indicators suggest both that the economy has begun to recover from its decade-long posttransition depression and that investors have greater confidence in the economy's future. Capital flight is slowing, and some offshore money is starting to move back to Russia. Some of Russia's largest companies have been undertaking structural reforms, hoping to attract international investment and to be listed on overseas stock exchanges. The result is that investment has been increasing. Over the 1999–2001 period, investment, in real terms, increased 32 percent, with the largest share going into the oil and gas industry.[44] Russia's production of oil has been increasing rapidly, and Russia now rivals Saudi Arabia as the largest producer of oil in the world.[45] Although Russia's recovery has been led by the oil and gas industry, it has spilled out into many other sectors as well. Between 1999 and 2001, GDP rose nearly 20 percent in real terms, and manufacturing grew 30 percent.[46] Real incomes rose, as wages and pensions were increased (and were usually being paid on time). In turn, the greater liquidity in the economy and improved bureaucratic performance have improved tax collections sharply. Higher tax collections and rises in the international price of oil allowed the government to realize a significant budget surplus in 2001 and 2002, which it has used to accelerate the repayment of foreign debt and to create a reserve fund. However, if oil prices drop, budget revenues will also fall since exports of oil and gas contribute about 22 percent of GDP.[47] It is estimated that for every dollar by which the price of oil declines, the budget will lose about 130 billion rubles (or about $4 billion) in revenues.[48] Thus the recovery since 1999 is in part a result of better policies and better governance, but it is also in large measure the consequence of a favorable conjunction of circumstances. To make economic development self-sustaining, Russia still needs to undertake major policy and structural reform.

Social Conditions

The economic changes in the country have had an enormous impact on living standards. A small minority have become wealthy, and some households have improved their lot modestly. A majority of the population, however, has suffered a net decline in living standards as a result of unemployment, lagging income, and nonpayment of wages and pensions. Richard Rose's 1998 survey of Russians asked how people rated their family's economic situation. Seventy-two percent rated it as unsatisfactory or very unsatisfactory. Many people rely on their own sources of food. About 71 percent of the households surveyed reported that they had a plot of land where they grew food for their family.[49]

A much larger share of the populace lives in poverty than was the case in the Soviet era. As of 2002, 27 percent of the population was estimated to live in poverty (this is a considerable decline since 2000, when the poverty rate stood at over 40 percent).[50] Several factors account for the high poverty rate. Unemployment is one major factor, and the persistent lag of wages behind prices is another. As of June 2002, unemployment stood at about 8.1 percent of the work force (5.9 million unemployed out of about 72.5 million working-age citizens).[51] Large-scale unemployment has been particularly painful for a country whose citizens were used to nearly full employment in the communist era and where the state-funded social safety net works poorly. As elsewhere in the former communist countries, unemployment has affected women more severely than men. Women are less likely than men to find offsetting employment, as are residents of small towns and people with lower educational levels.[52] Since the vast majority of single-parent households are headed by women, rising unemployment has pushed more women and children into poverty.[53] One estimate is that 55 percent of households headed by a single mother with small children live in poverty.[54] Another is that whereas 28 percent of men between the ages of 31 and 59 live in poverty, 43.6 percent of children below the age of 17 live in poverty.[55] Also vulnerable to the economic trends of the past few years have been groups whose incomes are paid directly out of the state budget, such as those living on pensions and disability payments, as well as teachers, scientists, and health care workers. Although they have received periodic increases in their earnings levels, these often have been insufficient to keep up with increases in prices.

Wages in state industry have also lagged behind price increases, particularly in the early stages of the liberalization program, when prices rose rapidly. In 1992, when the price index for consumer goods rose twenty-six times over the course of the year, average real per capita incomes fell three times. Incomes rose gradually thereafter more quickly than prices. However, real incomes in money terms still have not caught up with their prereform level; according to official figures, average real incomes in mid-2002 had nearly recovered to their 1998 levels but were still below their 1991 levels.[56]

However, two other changes somewhat offset the decline in living standards. First, in-kind and unreported forms of income (such as enterprises paying workers in the goods they produced, or people's consumption of products they grow themselves on garden plots) have risen. So have unreported earnings from off-book employment, often second and third jobs. Second, whereas in the prereform period, goods were scarce at the official state prices, people spent long hours standing in line at stores, and prices on the black market were high, after the reforms, consumer goods became available in all major cities and lines disappeared. Since the cheap prices on basic subsistence goods set by the Soviet authorities had often been purely hypothetical—what use is a cheap price if the good is unavailable?—many people's living standards have improved. One estimate is that by early 2002, living standards had recovered to their 1993 levels if the quality and availability of goods are taken into account.[57]

Along with poverty, inequality has grown sharply since the end of the Soviet era. While most people were suffering falling living standards, a few were becoming wealthy. One commonly used measure of inequality is the Gini Index, which is an aggregate measure of the total deviation from perfect equality in the distribution of wealth or income in a country. In a highly egalitarian country such as Finland, Sweden, or Norway, the Gini Index for income distribution stands at about 25. Countries with moderately high levels of income inequality, such as Great Britain, France, and Italy, fall in the range between 27 and 37. High-inequality countries such as the United States have a Gini index of around 40. In Russia, in 1993, the equivalent index reached 48, double the level of 1988, and higher than any other postcommunist country except Kyrgyzstan.[58] As Table 7.1 shows, it has continued to be high throughout the 1990s (48.7 in 1998). So high a gap between the incomes of the rich and poor—inequality in Russia is comparable with the level of countries such as Mexico and Venezuela—represents an enormous shock to a society brought up on the socialist doctrine of class equality.

Tied to the deteriorating economic performance has been the erosion of public health. Mortality rates have risen, especially among males. Life expectancy for males in Russia is at a level comparable with poor and developing countries. The State Statistics Committee estimated in 1999 that life expectancy at birth for males was fifty-eight and for females seventy-one, a remarkable discrepancy, generally attributed to the higher rates of abuse of alcohol and tobacco among men. Demographers warned that although life expectancy was beginning to rise again, at the present rate of mortality, 40 percent of Russia's sixteen-year-old boys would not reach their sixtieth birthday.[59] Other demographic indicators are equally grim. Every year Russia's population declines by over half a million people or more due to the excess of deaths over births. The rate of deaths per year is 70 percent higher than the rate of births.[60] Rates of incidence of HIV and other infectious disease, murders, suicides, drug addiction, and alcoholism are rising. Policy makers consider the demographic crisis to be one of the gravest threats to the country's national security.

Against the background of high unemployment, poverty, and inequality, the stabilization of price levels and of the ruble's exchange value is a mixed blessing. As we saw, a major objective of stabilization is to give the national currency stable value so that it becomes the currency of choice for producers and consumers. Although confidence in the ruble is growing, Russia's economy remains heavily reliant on U.S. dollars, which are still a more trusted medium of exchange and store of value than rubles.[61] Table 7.4 indicates that rubles have finally stabilized against the dollar. The ruble lost two-thirds of its value from 1991 to 1992, and again from 1992 to 1993, and again from 1993 to 1994 before stabi-

---
TABLE 7.4
Ruble Exchange Rate Against the U.S. Dollar, as of December 31 of Given Year ($1.00 =)[1]

1990:	25 rubles
1991:	170
1992:	415
1993:	1,240
1994:	3,500
1995:	4,650
1996:	5,600
1997:	6,000
1998:	20
1999:	27
2000:	28
2001:	30
2002:	31.8

[1]Calculated by the author. Figures represent approximate value in rubles of one U.S. dollar at legal exchange points in Moscow.
Note: On January 1, 1998, the government introduced a currency reform. 1,000 old rubles were set equal to 1 new ruble. Therefore prices in real terms were unchanged, and consumers simply dropped three zeros to convert from the price in old rubles to the new price.

lizing somewhat. Then the August crash brought about another sharp devaluation, as the ruble lost two-thirds of its value again. The low ruble certainly favors exporters and has helped to bring about Russia's recovery under Putin through a healthy foreign-trade surplus. But many sectors of the economy are suffering because imported goods and supplies are extremely expensive.

Putin's Agenda

Vladimir Putin has repeatedly stated that he intends to set the economy firmly on the path of growth again by creating an economic climate conductive to investment and entrepreneurship. Some of the reformers who were part of the Gaidar government of the early 1990s—including Gaidar himself—are actively involved in drafting legislation on tax reform, administrative reform, privatization, and other crucial policy issues. In his messages to parliament each year, Putin has emphasized the importance of lowering marginal tax rates, protecting property rights, reducing burdensome government regulation of business, liberalizing the labor market, shifting the pension system more toward pension insurance and private savings, eliminating the tariff and bureaucratic obstacles that prevent Russia's entry into the World Trade Organization (WTO), and creating a market for buying and selling land.

Moreover, he has backed up his rhetoric with a well-coordinated effort to draft new legislation on these and many other subjects. His almost total control of both chambers of parliament has let him pass nearly everything he proposes.[62] Step by step, Putin's policy team has hammered out the legislative foundation for a market-oriented economic system. However, some of the most controversial reforms still lie ahead, including reform of natural monopolies such as the state-owned electric power monopoly (RAO EES) and Gazprom, which controls the extraction, processing, and distribution of most natural gas. There was also stiff resistance to the government's plan to put housing and communal services on a commercial footing. Still, the pace of policy reform under Putin has been remarkable. The real test is whether these policies will be implemented as intended, or whether officials in the central and regional state bureaucracy will manage to sidetrack them.

Putin's program and the steps he has taken to improve the effectiveness of governance have begun to bear fruit. As we have seen, growth, real incomes, and investment have risen, while poverty and unemployment have declined (inequality remains extremely high, however). These favorable trends are due both to business confidence in Putin and his policies, and to a strong international market for Russian oil and gas. Most observers believe that to achieve high and self-sustaining economic growth, Russia must still undertake more reforms (particularly of its financial system) and drastically improve the quality of governance. President Putin has made his policy objectives clear: He wants an orderly, efficient, business-friendly economy that will attract domestic and foreign investment and yield high, self-sustaining economic growth. But the institutional tools he has chosen to accomplish his goals are a throwback to the familiar impulse of Russian rulers to centralize state power rather than to democratize it. Therefore, like Russian rulers before him, he is finding it far easier to enact policy decisions than to ensure that they are carried out.

Summing Up

The economic reform policies of the early 1990s had a number of unexpected and undesirable consequences. The economy's performance plummeted for most of the 1990s before recovering again at the end of the decade. At the beginning of the decade, the government of the newly sovereign Russia lacked real control over many of the administrative and financial agencies of the state. In order to carry out its stabilization and privatization program, it had to make major concessions to powerful stakeholders in the economy, such as enterprise directors and regional leaders, which in turn distorted the entire reform process. The legacy of the communist system also helps explain firms' unwillingness to restructure by seeking out new markets and new lines of production. And the extremely unfavorable conditions with which Russia had begun its difficult transition to a market economy further complicated the economy's response to the central government's reform policies.

The situation resembled that of developing economies where economic growth is crippled by a perverse structure of incentives for investment, where wealthy capitalists flaunt their riches in conspicuous consumption and send their profits to safe havens abroad, where social inequality widens, and where political pressures for government intervention to preserve living standards through price controls and secure employment in state-controlled firms become irresistible. Such economies fall prey to the dilemma posed by the cycles of stagnation and inflation until economic incentives are restructured in such a way as to encourage growth-inducing behavior by society. In Russia, groups that gained power and wealth in the late Soviet period were able to take advantage of the opening to a market system by gaining control over lucrative assets, and in turn using their political connections to manipulate the system to their advantage further. As a result, while the reforms were not rolled back, neither was the economy opened up to full and fair competition under strong and impartial government regulation. Clearly, an efficient, competitive market economy would benefit most groups in Russia's society, but, as is the case with efficient and honest government as well, the groups who profit from the status quo are strong and well organized, giving them an advantage in the political arena over the large but unorganized interests that would be made better off from a successful economic reform. The task of leading the way out of the trap of partial reform now falls to President Putin.

REVIEW QUESTIONS

1. Define the terms "stabilization" and "privatization." How are they related to one another? What are the aims of these policies? How fully did Russia implement them?
2. Describe Russia's program of voucher privatization. What were its political and economic objectives? What were its main consequences?

3. What are "oligarchs" and how did they become oligarchs? How similar are they to America's "robber barons" of the late nineteenth century?
4. What was the "loans-for-shares" scheme? Why did the Russian government agree to it?
5. What explains the sharp rise in both poverty and inequality in the 1990s?
6. What are President Putin's main goals in economic policy? How effective have his policies been in bringing about an improvement in economic performance?

ENDNOTES

1. For a valuable overview of the economic and political transformation of postcommunist countries, see Valerie Bunce, "The Political Economy of Postsocialism," *Slavic Review* 58(4) (Winter 1999), pp. 756–93.
2. Joel S. Hellman, "Winners Take All: The Politics of Partial Reform in Postcommunist Transitions," *World Politics* 50:1 (1998), pp. 203–34. Also see Anders Åslund, *Building Capitalism: The Transformation of the Former Soviet Bloc* (Cambridge, England: Cambridge University Press, 2002).
3. Juan J. Linz and Alfred Stepan, *Problems of Democratic Transition and Consolidation: Southern Europe, South America, and Post-Communist Europe* (Baltimore, Md.: Johns Hopkins Press, 1996).
4. On the economic policy dilemmas facing new democratic regimes in Latin America, see John Sheahan, "Economic Policies and the Prospects for Successful Transition from Authoritarian Rule in Latin America," in Guillermo O'Donnell, Philippe C. Schmitter, and Laurence Whitehead, eds., *Transitions from Authoritarian Rule: Comparative Perspectives* (Baltimore, Md.: Johns Hopkins University Press, 1986), pp. 154–64.
5. Roman Frydman, Andrzej Rapaczynski, and John S. Earle, et al., *The Privatization Process in Russia, Ukraine and the Baltic States* (Budapest, London, New York: Central European University Press, 1993), p. 7.
6. An economic rent is defined as the price of a good that is fixed in supply. The price is therefore determined entirely by demand. Rent seeking is the attempt to keep supply fixed in order to be able to collect rents. A monopolist who successfully lobbies government for the right to maintain the monopoly will be able to collect monopoly rents. The concept of rent seeking is useful in understanding much of the political activity of Russia's "early winners."
7. There is a school of thought holding that the problem of monopolization in the Russian economy is not severe: that in comparative perspective, the Russian industrial economy is less dominated by monopolies and oligopolies than many Western economies, but that there are also many fewer small-scale firms than in the West. This argument misses an important point, however. In the absence of a working capital market—including a free flow of capital in and out of the country—Russian industrial firms tend to be price setters more than they are price takers. That is, they are rather free to set prices because they face such limited competition. See the discussion of this point in Anders Åslund, *How Russia Became a Market Economy* (Washington, D.C.: Brookings Institution, 1995), pp. 152–56.
8. Åslund, *How Russia Became a Market Economy,* p. 154.
9. Anders Åslund, "How Small Is Soviet National Income?" in Henry S. Rowen and Charles Wolf Jr., eds., *The Impoverished Superpower: Perestroika and the Soviet Military Burden* (San Francisco: Institute for Contemporary Studies, 1990), p. 49.

10. Robert W. Campbell, "Economic Reform in the USSR and Its Successor States," in Shafiqul Islam and Michael Mandelbaum, eds., *Making Markets: Economic Transformation in Eastern Europe and the Post-Soviet States* (New York: Council on Foreign Relations), pp. 131–32.

11. Jeffrey Sachs, "Western Financial Assistance and Russia's Reforms," in ibid., pp. 145–46. Sachs is an American economist who was the principal Western architect of the strategy of macroeconomic stabilization that was applied in Poland in 1991 and partly in Russia in 1992, and he developed a similar strategy for Latin American economies in the 1980s. His prescription for rapid, anti-inflationary measures that achieve fiscal stabilization as a precondition of other reforms has been the target of tremendous controversy.

12. Two useful studies of Soviet managers are Paul Lawrence and Charalambos A. Vlachoutsicos, eds., *Behind the Factory Walls: Decision Making in Soviet and US Enterprises* (Cambridge, Mass.: Harvard Business School Press, 1990); and Sheila M. Puffer, ed., *The Russian Management Revolution: Preparing Managers for the Market Economy* (Armonk, N.Y.: M. E. Sharpe, 1992).

13. An interesting portrait of forty such individuals based on interviews is provided in the book edited by Igor Bunin, *Biznesmeny Rossii: Sorok istorii uspekha* (Moscow: OKO, 1994).

14. Gennady M. Denisovsky, Polina M. Kozyreva, and Mikhail S. Matskovsky, "Twelve Percent of Hope: Economic Consciousness and a Market Economy," in Arthur H. Miller, William M. Reisinger, and Vicki L. Hesli, eds., *Public Opinion and Regime Change: The New Politics of Post-Soviet Societies* (Boulder, Colo.: Westview, 1993), pp. 225–27.

15. Hard currency is the term used for the U.S. dollar, German mark, Japanese yen, and other national currencies that are freely traded on world markets. Soft currencies are those where governments set a value and then protect that value against foreign currency markets.

16. Economists generally say that once prices start rising by 50 percent a month and more, the economy is in a state of hyperinflation.

17. McKinsey Global Institute, *Unlocking Economic Growth in Russia* (Moscow: 1999).

18. Some Western observers are also highly critical of the "shock therapy" program although for different reasons. Stephen F. Cohen argues that the United States attempted to impose an entirely inappropriate economic model on Russia out of willful blindness to Russian realities; Peter Reddaway and Dmitri Glinski argue that Russian reformers failed to build a political consensus for a more moderate reform program and used crash methods instead with disastrous results; and Jerry Hough claims that the failure of the program was in fact intended all along by Yeltsin's team, who were using it to exploit the industrial and natural-resource producers for the sake of subsidizing consumers in the big cities. Stephen F. Cohen, *Failed Crusade: America and the Tragedy of Post-Communist Russia* (New York: W. W. Norton, 2001); Peter Reddaway and Dmitri Glinski, *Tragedy of Russia's Reforms: Market Bolshevism against Democracy* (Washington, D.C.: U.S. Institute of Peace, 2001); Jerry F. Hough, *The Logic of Economic Reform in Russia* (Washington, D.C.: Brookings Institution Press, 2001).

19. Joseph R. Blasi, Maya Kroumova, and Douglas Kruse, *Kremlin Capitalism: Privatizing the Russian Economy* (Ithaca, N.Y.: Cornell University Press, 1997), p. 171; Andrei Shleifer and Daniel Treisman, *Without a Map: Political Tactics and Economic Reform in Russia* (Cambridge, Mass.: MIT Press, 2000), p. 42. A good account of the Central Bank's high-handedness in this period is Juliet Johnson, *A Fistful of Rubles: The Rise and Fall of the Russian Banking System* (Ithaca, N.Y.: Cornell University Press, 2000), Ch. 3, "The Central Bank of Russia" (pp. 64–97).

20. In a cooperative, all the employees are co-owners of the business and share in its profits.

21. Blasi, et al., *Kremlin Capitalism*, p. 189.

22. Lynn D. Nelson and Irina Y. Kuzes, *Property to the People: The Struggle for Radical Economic Reform in Russia* (Armonk, N.Y.: M. E. Sharpe, 1994), pp. 28, 44.

23. The goals of the privatization program are laid out in a volume of essays by its chief Russian designers and their Western advisers. See, in particular, Anatoly B. Chubais and Maria Vishnevskaya, "Main Issues of Privatisation in Russia," and Maxim Boycko and Andrei Shleifer, "The Voucher Programme for Russia," both in Anders Åslund and Richard Layard, eds., *Changing the Economic System in Russia* (New York: St. Martin's Press, 1993), pp. 89–99, 100–111.

24. Pekka Sutela, "Insider Privatization in Russia: Speculations on Systemic Changes," *Europe-Asia Studies* 46:3 (1994), pp. 420–21.

25. Blasi, et al., *Kremlin Capitalism*, pp. 179–80. The authors have conducted a major national annual survey of the managers of privatized enterprises in Russia.

26. Radio Free Europe/Radio Liberty Daily Report, 1 July 1994.

27. Blasi, et al., *Kremlin Capitalism*, p. 50.

28. European Bank for Reconstruction and Development (EBRD), *Transition Report 2001: Energy in Transition* (London: EBRD, 2001), p. 12.

29. This is known as the Coase Theorem, after the economist Ronald H. Coase. It is very often misrepresented: Coase was calling attention to the sensitivity of markets to the costliness of transactions. Where contracts and property rights are not consistently enforced and information is scarce, the theorem predicts that the initial distribution of property rights will be an obstacle to efficiency-improving economic exchange.

30. This perspective underlies the field of institutional economics. Cf. Douglass C. North, *Institutions, Institutional Change and Economic Performance* (Cambridge, England: Cambridge University Press, 1990).

31. Blasi, et al., *Kremlin Capitalism;* Michael McFaul, "State Power, Institutional Change, and the Politics of Privatization in Russia," *World Politics* 47 (1995), pp. 210–43.

32. They were backed by the federal government's share of the proceeds of the sale of stock from state enterprises. Each enterprise had to offer at least 35 percent of its stock for vouchers. This corresponded to the share of ownership that the federal government claimed for itself. The federal government's share in the sale of privatizing enterprises was thus distributed to the citizens in the form of vouchers.

33. The $300 billion figure comes from RFE/RL Business Watch, Vol. 2, no. 26, 2 July 2002. The World Bank estimates that Russian GDP was about $251 billion in 2000. World Bank, *Building Institutions for Markets: World Development Report 2002* (Washington, D.C.: World Bank, 2002), p. 27.

34. At least half of the output of Russian industry is "sold" through barter. EBRD Transition Report 1998, p. 186.

35. On the virtual economy, see Clifford G. Gaddy and Barry W. Ickes, "Russia's Virtual Economy," *Foreign Affairs* 77 (September–October 1998), pp. 53–67; and David Woodruff, *Money Unmade: Barter and the Fate of Russian Capitalism* (Ithaca, N.Y., and London: Cornell University Press, 1999); Stephen S. Moody, "Decapitalizing Russian Capitalism," *Orbis* 40:1 (Winter 1996), pp. 123–43.

36. In spring 1996, when the presidential election campaign was at its height, Russian state treasury obligations were selling at ruinously high interest rates—over 200 percent effective annual yields on six-month bonds. Little wonder that investors were

uninterested in the stock market. Because of the instability of the political climate and the fear of default, the great bulk of this paper was short term.

37. Thane Gustafson, *Capitalism Russian-Style* (Cambridge, England: Cambridge University Press, 1999), pp. 2–3, 94–95.

38. European Bank for Reconstruction and Development, *Transition Report 1995: Investment and Enterprise Development* (London: 1995), p. 55. There is a large market in small parcels of land for country cottages and gardens, however.

39. Ol'ga Kryshtanovskaia, "Finansovaia oligarkhiia v Rossii," *Izvestiia*, 10 January 1996, p. 5. The author is a respected sociologist who heads the sector for the study of the elite of the Institute of Sociology of the Russian Academy of Sciences. Also see Blasi, et al., *Kremlin Capitalism*, pp. 155–57.

40. OMRI Daily Digests for April 20 and May 30, 1995; Gustafson, *Capitalism*, p. 25.

41. The Russian Civil War (1918–1921) was fought between the Bolshevik ("Red") forces and the anticommunists ("Whites") following the communist revolution. The Whites comprised a diverse set of enemies of the new regime—among them both monarchists and socialists—whose inability to unite against the Bolsheviks ensured their ultimate defeat at the hands of the Red Army.

42. Shleifer and Treisman, *Without a Map*, pp. 113–36.

43. RFE/RL Newsline, 30 March 2000.

44. Standard & Poor's, "Rossiiskaia Federatsiia," 5 March 2002, from Web site **www. standardandpoors.ru**, 10 July 2002.

45. Saudi Arabia has vastly greater reserves of oil, however, than Russia.

46. Ibid.

47. Standard & Poor's.

48. Ibid.

49. Richard Rose, *Getting Things Done with Social Capital: New Russia Barometer VII*, paper no. 303, Studies in Public Policy (Glasgow: Centre for the Study of Public Policy, University of Strathclyde, 1998), pp. 25, 1.

50. RFE/RL Russian Political Weekly, 13 November 2002.
    Poverty is defined by the State Statistics Committee as monthly income below the subsistence minimum. In 2000, the minimum monthly income considered necessary for subsistence was (on average for all groups of the population in all regions) 1,210 rubles, or about $43 U.S. At that time the average money income per capita was about $78 per month. Goskomstat Rossii, *Rossiiskii Statisticheskii Ezhegodnik 2001: Statisticheskii Ezhegodnik* (Moscow: Gosudarstvennyi komitet Rossiiskoi Federatsii po statistike, 2001), p. 189.

51. Figures of the Russian State Statistics Committee, cited in RFE/RL Newsline, 23 July 2002.

52. Ekaterina Khibovskaia, "Rossiiane stali bol'she opasat'sia poteriat' rabotu," *Segodnia*, 26 July 1995.

53. Gail Kligman, "The Social Legacy of Communism: Women, Children, and the Feminization of Poverty," in James R. Millar and Sharon L. Wolchik, eds., *The Social Legacy of Communism* (Washington, D.C.: Woodrow Wilson Center Press and Cambridge University Press, 1994), p. 261; Mary Buckley, "The Politics of Social Issues," in Stephen White, Alex Pravda, and Zvi Gitelman, eds., *Developments in Russian and Post-Soviet Politics*, 3rd ed. (London: Macmillan, 1994), pp. 192–94.

54. G. Pirogov and S. Pronin, "The Russian Case: Social Policy Concerns," in Yogesh Atal, ed., *Poverty in Transition and Transition in Poverty: Recent Developments in Hungary, Bulgaria, Romania, Georgia, Russia, Mongolia* (New York: Berghahn Books/Paris: UNESCO Publishing, 1999), p. 189.

55. RFE/RL Russian Political Weekly, 13 November 2002.
56. RFE/RL Business Watch, 7 May 2002.
57. Vesa Korhonen, "Looking at the Russian Economy in 2001–02," Bank of Finland, Institute for Economies in Transition, "Russian Economy: The Month in Review," 11 February 2002, on Web site **www.bof.fi/bofit**.
58. Branko Milanovic, *Income, Inequality, and Poverty During the Transition from Planned to Market Economy* (Washington, D.C.: The World Bank, 1998), p. 41; see the World Bank figures for most countries in the world in its annual World Development Report. World Bank, *Building Institutions for Markets: World Development Report 2002* (Washington, D.C.: World Bank, 2002), pp. 234–35.
59. RFE/RL Newsline, 8 March 1999.
60. RFE/RL Newsline, 23 March 2000; 20 March 2002.
61. Russian lore is rich in illustrations of this point. Rubles are colloquially called "wooden money" while dollars are called "live money" or *baksy* (bucks). A popular anecdote, illustrating both the reputation for ignorance of the wealthy "new Russians" and the fact that dollars are widely used in the business world, has a "new Russian" visiting America for the first time. When he comes home, he tells his friends: "Can you believe it? I was in America, and they use our *baksy* there too!"
62. In 2001, Putin signed into law measures permitting the purchase and sale of land, including agricultural land; a new Labor Code allowing employers to dismiss workers without the explicit consent of the labor unions; comprehensive tax reform; judicial reform; restrictions on government regulation and licensing of businesses; measures to fight money laundering; and several measures reforming banking and the stock market.

8 Toward the Rule of Law

DEMOCRATIZATION AND THE RULE OF LAW

In Russia, the law has often been a tool of those in power. Consequently, one of the most important goals of democratic reformers in Russia since the end of the communist regime has been to make the legal system fairer by making it independent of those who hold political power. In fact, the drive to make the judicial branch more independent goes back well before the collapse of the Soviet system. From the 1950s onward, reformers worked to make the justice system a stronger barrier to the exercise of arbitrary power by the state. Since 1991, however, there have been significant changes to the organization of the judicial branch and to the codes of law and procedure which have moved Russia closer to the rule of law.

The constitutional scholar Stephen Holmes has distinguished between the "rule of law" and "rule by law." In rule-by-law, a powerful elite concentrating political power uses law to protect its prerogatives. In the rule of law, power is sufficiently dispersed among groups and organizations in society to prevent any one group from monopolizing access to the law. Many citizens and groups can turn to the law to defend their rights and interests, and their diversity and competition help to preserve the law's independence.[1] This means, therefore, that reforming legal codes and structures alone is not sufficient to make the legal system impartial: As Holmes argues, "Russia's legal reforms will succeed only to the extent that the country as a whole develops in a liberal, pluralistic, and democratic direction."[2]

Efforts to reduce the state's arbitrary use of legal institutions to protect the rulers' interests date to the post-Stalin period, but they were stepped up substantially under Mikhail Gorbachev. When Mikhail Gorbachev declared the "law-governed state" *(pravovoe gosudarstvo)* to be one of the cardinal objectives of his reform program, it was a significant step.[3] By a "law-governed state," Gorbachev meant that both rulers and ruled would obey the law. Its opposite would be a condition where the rulers exercised power arbitrarily; the rulers could freely violate the state's own constitutional and statutory rules, as had often happened under the Soviet regime when Communist Party, KGB, and other officials often ignored constitutional and legal norms in exercising their power, but they expected their subjects to obey the law. Since 1991, the ideal of the law-governed state has continued to attract lip service from Russian leaders even when they took actions violating the constitution. President Vladimir Putin, for instance, declared that Russia must be governed by a "dictatorship of law," which certainly has ambiguous implications (does it mean that the law must be supreme over the state, or a dictatorship by means of law?). Since the end of the communist regime, reforms of the constitutional and judicial systems have strengthened legal institutions by making them less subject to political abuse. The judicial system has grown somewhat more independent and effective. The legal principles essential to a democratic and pluralistic society have begun to be established. One of the most significant changes is the creation of a Constitutional Court empowered to adjudicate disputes arising between the branches of government and between the federal level of government and the constituent territories. An important statutory change is the adoption of a body of law recognizing private property rights.

Still, movement toward a genuinely independent judicial branch has been stymied by several problems. At the federal level, the enormous power of the president limits the courts' ability to apply the law impartially. For instance, the Constitutional Court has been very cautious about crossing the president on matters concerning presidential prerogatives. Many court rulings go unenforced because of the ability of powerful interests to flout judicial decisions, while other decisions clearly reflect high-level political intervention. At the regional and local levels, courts remain vulnerable to the power of local political authorities, and as a result often defer to them in their decisions. A huge problem is the corruption of the courts: Russian surveys have found that the courts and police are considered among the most highly corrupted of Russian institutions.[4] To some extent, this stems from the rapidity of the change in the political and economic system. The meltdown of the Soviet system created vast opportunities for criminals to amass wealth and use it to corrupt law enforcement officials. Legitimate business owners often find themselves forced to turn to illegal protection rackets because the police and courts fail to protect their basic interests. Many citizens report that they cannot afford to turn to the law for the redress of their grievances, because they cannot afford to pay the bribes that they believe are expected. Trust in the courts and Procuracy is low, as Tables 5.2 and 5.3 illustrated.[5]

Yet despite the low trust, people turn to the courts in rising numbers. The Chairman of the Russian Supreme Court, Viacheslav Lebedev, estimated in 2000 that the number of cases heard in Russian courts had tripled since 1994.[6] Judges are overwhelmed by the caseload, are often paid far less than the attorneys who appear in court, and face primitive or substandard working conditions (for example, only 40 percent of judges have computers).[7] There are only a quarter as many bailiffs as are needed to enforce judicial rulings.

Legal reformers emphasize two basic principles: Individual rights should take precedence over the power of the state, and judicial power should be separated from legislative and executive power. Observance of these two principles would represent a large step toward greater respect for law and away from the many abuses of law that the Soviet state committed in the past. For instance, the Bolsheviks held that since "revolutionary justice" was higher than any written law, the rights and obligations of rulers and citizens must be subordinate to the political interests of the regime. But this instrumental view of the law was not held by the Bolsheviks only. Many in and outside of President Yeltsin's administration expressed a similar view that the goal of eliminating the foundations of communist rule took precedence over observance of the letter of the law: The populace must obey the law—but the authorities (*vlast'*) could choose when to observe it and when not to, according to their judgments of expediency.

The decades-long subordination of the legal system to the political interests of the communist regime was not the only impediment to judicial reform. Law enforcement in Russia has traditionally weighted the scales of justice in favor of the *Procuracy*—the agency charged with supervising the justice system, investigating crimes, preparing and prosecuting cases, and ensuring that the rights of *both* state *and* individuals were upheld—and at the expense of both the courts and the defense attorneys. Judicial reformers long have urged that judges be given greater authority with which to supervise pretrial investigations and court proceedings, and that individuals accused of criminal acts have more effective means to defend themselves. But the Procuracy has proven itself to be a powerful bureaucratic interest group, and has blocked many of the reforms that might improve the justice system.

The movement to reform legal institutions began well before Gorbachev.[8] After Stalin, Soviet political leaders and members of the legal profession attempted with mixed results to effect both institutional and statutory changes designed to make the rights of citizens somewhat more secure. One of the most important institutional changes made in the late 1950s was to place the secret police under stricter legal control. Extrajudicial trials, judgments, and sentences, which were a common practice in the time of Stalin's terror, were prohibited, and criminal defendants were granted important rights. New codes of criminal law and criminal procedure were adopted in the union republics, and official policy promoted a concept of "socialist legality." Like many slogans of the post-Stalin period, this was a formula meant to paper over contradictory policy goals. The idea was that the legal system should be less subject to political caprice than under Stalin, but still uphold socialist principles and practices. In fact, under the post-Stalin regime, the party and police could still use legal procedures as a way of legitimating actions taken in the interests of the regime's power and security. The criminal codes themselves contained articles providing legal penalties for "anti-Soviet agitation and propaganda" and for "circulation of fabrications known to be false which defame the Soviet state or social system." In the post-Stalin period these were frequently used against individuals whom the regime considered to be political dissidents.[9] Alternatively the authorities sometimes resorted to the practice of declaring a dissident mentally incompetent and forcibly incarcerating him in a mental hospital, where he could be further punished by being administered mind-altering drugs.[10] The continuation of these practices for political repression until the late 1980s attests to the inability of the law to protect the rights of individuals whom the party and KGB for any reason decided to suppress.

The struggle for legal reform continued even in the Brezhnev era, although results were meager, and accelerated in the Gorbachev and post-Soviet eras. As early as 1977, the new Brezhnev constitution included a principle that individuals had the right to sue state officials if the latter had violated their legal rights through an official action. As is common in Soviet and Russian constitutional practice, however, the constitutional text provided that the procedure for exercising this right would be prescribed by a statute to be enacted in the future.[11] In April 1993, however, after the USSR collapsed, the Russian parliament passed a new statute providing that individuals whose rights had been violated by state officials could sue for remedy regardless of whether the action had been taken by individual officials or organizational entities. In principle, at least, this represents a highly significant normative change.[12] As with other innovations in statutory law, however, its effectiveness depends upon the willingness of judges and procurators to enforce it. The new federal criminal code that came into force in January 1997 makes it a criminal offense for state officials to withhold information from citizens concerning their rights; President Yeltsin singled this provision out in particular in his message to parliament in March 1997, calling on law enforcement bodies to uphold it.[13]

Judicial Reform

Full establishment of the rule of law would mean that no arm of the state would be able to bend or violate the law for political ends. In turn, this would require that the judiciary be independent of political influence. Through much of the Soviet period, however, judges were readily influenced by political pressures, some direct, some indirect. One of the most notorious forms of political influence was called "telephone justice." This referred to the practice whereby a party official or some other powerful individual would privately communicate instructions to a judge on a particular case.[14] Telephone justice was symptomatic of a prevalent pattern in which the law was held in relatively low repute and legal institutions possessed little autonomy of the policy-implementing organs of government. The party might direct judges to be especially harsh in passing sentences on a particular class of criminals if it was attempting to conduct a propaganda campaign against a social problem, such as alcoholism, hooliganism, or economic crimes. A party official might direct prosecutors to crack down on some previously tolerated activity, or to gather incriminating evidence on someone it wished to punish. In the past, pressures such as these often pushed adjudication over the line from full and vigorous enforcement of the law into abandonment of the law in pursuit of political ends.[15] By the same token, an unwritten but firmly observed norm made it impossible to prosecute a high-ranking member of the political elite without the party's consent. Even where improper political influence was not involved, many judges routinely accepted the prosecutor's case for a defendant's guilt, a reflection of the advantage of the Procuracy over the defense in criminal proceedings.

The judicial reforms under Gorbachev set in motion significant policy changes but did not bring them to completion. Still, the record of judicial reforms undertaken during the Gorbachev period raises an important point. A fair and impartial judicial system is an ideal that both right and left can agree upon because it serves ultimately to protect all citizens, regardless of their political persuasions, from the arbitrary exercise of political power. The obstacles to achieving it have less to do with the struggle between reformers and conservatives than with the struggle between change itself and the self-interest and inertia of existing state agencies. Often a consensus between legal experts of very different ideological camps emerges on the principles of judicial reform, but is opposed by the interest groups whose power would be threatened by reform, such as the Procuracy and regional executives.

Under Gorbachev, several important reform measures were enacted, but generally the legislation took the form of "framework" laws that allowed particular republics to decide how to apply them locally. In the Russian Republic, the Supreme Soviet made several changes that went further than those envisioned by the union. For example, with respect to a defendant's right to counsel, the Russian Republic legislature removed the limitations that had been set by the USSR legislature. Now accused persons could hire defense counsel immediately upon arrest and discuss their case with their attorney in confidence at any point during the investigation. The Russian parliament also adopted a law in July 1993—shortly before Yeltsin dissolved the parliament—providing that a defendant in a criminal case could request a jury trial. Below we will discuss the introduction of jury trials in more detail.

Another example of a reform enacted in a partial and tentative way in the 1989–1991 period at the union level but more fully by the Russian Republic is the creation of a constitutional court. While the USSR legislature established a compromise creature called the "Committee on Constitutional Supervision"— an entity somewhat stronger than an advisory council but not quite an actual court—the RSFSR legislature in 1991 adopted a law creating a regular Constitutional Court. The court was given the power to adjudicate the constitutionality of acts of the legislative and executive branches of state power, as well as of actions of the governments of the constituent regions, and of decisions of other courts. Yeltsin suspended the activity of the Russian Constitutional Court as one of his actions in September–October 1993 when he dissolved parliament, but he did not dissolve the court—it continued to exist but its activity was frozen until the 1993 constitution was ratified and the Duma passed a law defining its structure and powers. In 1995 the newly organized Court resumed its functioning. Below we will review the record of its decision making.

Since 1989, reforms of Russia's legal system have gradually expanded the effectiveness and independence of judicial institutions and strengthened individual legal rights vis-à-vis the state. These institutional and statutory changes have not always pitted democrats against communists, but have often met the resistance of powerful agencies of the state such as the Procuracy that are threatened by losing power to judges, defense attorneys, and juries. In the 1990s parliament passed and the president signed a number of significant institutional changes, including a reorganization of the court system and statutory changes affecting the criminal code, code of criminal procedure, and criminal corrections code. At the same time, progress in the other factors that would enable Russia to move toward the rule of law has been slower. Those in power still sometimes intervene in judicial decision making, and the poor working conditions under which the police and courts operate invite corruption.

Let us now consider in more detail the nature of recent changes in five domains of the legal system: the Procuracy; the judiciary; the *advokatura;* the Constitutional Court; and the reform of legal and procedural codes.

The Procuracy

Russia's legal system traditionally vested a great deal of power in the Procuracy: The Procuracy was considered to be the most prestigious branch of the law. A procurator is an official corresponding to a prosecutor in U.S. practice, but has wider powers and duties. Procurators are given sweeping responsibilities for fighting crime, corruption, and abuses of power in the bureaucracy, and for both instigating investigations of criminal wrong-doing by private citizens and responding to complaints about official malfeasance. The Procuracy, more than the judiciary, has traditionally been seen as the principal check on illegal activity by officials and abuses of power. One of the Procuracy's assigned tasks is to supervise all state officials and public organizations to ensure that they observe the law. In addition, the Procuracy is responsible for overseeing the entire system of justice, including the penal system. Finally, the Procuracy has the primary responsibility for bringing criminal cases to court. It supervises the investigation of a case, prepares the case for prosecution, and argues the case in court.

One of the most important tasks of the Procuracy is to enforce federal law throughout Russia. As regional political establishments have grown powerful and independent, the center's ability to compel compliance with federal law in the regions declined, placing more pressure on the Procuracy to enforce federal law. Formally, the regional branches of the Procuracy are subordinate to the procurator-general in Moscow, but in practice some local procurators have formed alliances with strong governors. President Putin has demanded that the Procuracy once again be centralized so that it can enforce common legal standards throughout the country. When Putin created the seven new federal "super-districts" in May 2000, the Procuracy announced that it was creating new structures of the Procuracy in each new super-region. These were charged with riding herd on the branches of the Procuracy in each of the eighty-nine subjects of the federation, and thus helping to recentralize control within the Procuracy.

Not surprisingly, the Procuracy has a difficult time coping with the comprehensive tasks that the law assigns to it, because of the difficulty of effectively supervising the vast economic bureaucracy and overcoming the entrenched political machines of central and regional governments. The procurator-general complained in a newspaper interview in 1997 that the Procuracy has only 7,090 investigators (of a total staff of 28,677) but that in 1996 they issued more than 400,000 arrest warrants and took more than a million cases to court, while also looking into another million complaints from citizens about violations of their rights. Meantime procurators were investigating cases of fraud in privatization and corruption among state officials.[16]

The Procuracy does have substantial political influence, which it exercises to protect its institutional prerogatives. Complaining that its resources leave it grossly underequipped to meet even the most elementary demands placed upon it, such as investigating the most serious violent crimes and bringing the offenders to justice, the Procuracy's representatives plead for more resources rather than fewer responsibilities. The Procuracy has even lobbied vigorously in defense of its institutional prerogatives when it believed that a proposed reform would weaken its power. For example, it has staunchly opposed giving arrested persons the right to consult with an attorney at any time during the pretrial investigation; it stubbornly opposed the adoption of the jury trial system; it fought reforms giving the courts the right to review procurators' decisions on the pretrial detention of criminal suspects; and it has battled successfully to retain the responsibility to supervise criminal investigations. The Procuracy has won some of its fights, and in others it has succeeded in watering down reforms intended to strengthen other legal institutions. Both Russian statist tradition (including the experience of legal institutions in the Soviet and prerevolutionary eras) and Russia's use of a continental, or inquisitorial, system of legal procedure,[17] reinforce the Procuracy's central role in the judicial system. However, the reformed Criminal Procedure Code that came into effect on July 1, 2002, significantly reduced the legal powers of the Procuracy by providing that warrants for arrests, wiretaps, searches, seizures, and a number of other pretrial procedures could no longer be issued by the Procuracy, but only by the courts.[18]

Because of the centrality of the Procuracy in the Russian legal system, the position of procurator-general, who directs the Procuracy throughout the country, is of enormous political sensitivity. Under the 1993 constitution, the president nominates a candidate for procurator-general to the Federation Council, which has the power to approve or reject the nomination. Likewise, the president must obtain Federation Council approval to remove the procurator-general. Only rarely in postcommunist Russia has the procurator-general taken a position directly opposing the president, but in one important precedent-setting instance at least, the Procuracy did demonstrate its political independence. In February 1994, the State Duma approved an amnesty for several categories of persons, including those who were in jail awaiting trial for their participation in the attempted coups d'état of August 1991 and October 1993. The Duma was exercising the power of amnesty that the newly adopted Constitution had granted (although no law had yet been adopted specifying how this power was to be exercised). However, President Yeltsin expressed outrage at the decision and his advisers presented a variety of legal opinions purporting to demonstrate that the Duma's action was unlawful. Nonetheless, the procurator-general at the time, although believing that the Duma had exceeded its constitutional powers, complied with the Duma's decision and ordered the release of the prisoners.

When President Yeltsin pressured him to halt the release, the procurator-general refused to comply and resigned instead. The release was duly carried out. Then, for several months afterward, the Federation Council refused to confirm Yeltsin's nominee for a new procurator-general.[19]

More recently, the Procuracy became involved in a major political scandal when Procurator-General Yuri Skuratov initiated an investigation of corruption among some of President Yeltsin's closest associates and family members. To force him out, Skuratov's enemies then arranged to have a videotape discrediting Skuratov aired on Russian television in early 1999. The videotape showed Skuratov (or someone resembling him) cavorting in a bathhouse with two women. Skuratov tendered his resignation but the Federation Council refused to allow him to resign. Yeltsin then issued a decree suspending Skuratov from his duties pending the outcome of a criminal investigation opened against him. The Federation Council appealed to the Constitutional Court for a ruling on whether Yeltsin had to right to remove Skuratov without the approval of the Federation Council; its reasoning was that since its approval was needed for a new procurator-general to be appointed, the president could not dismiss a procurator-general without its approval as well. In December 1999, the Court ruled that Yeltsin did have the right to remove a procurator-general from office pending the outcome of a criminal investigation on the grounds that the president may act by decree where preexisting legislation does not exist. Finally, in April 2000, after Putin's election, the Council of the Federation voted to accept Skuratov's dismissal. The episode revealed that the legal system continues to be threatened by the ability of power holders to abuse it when their vital interests are at stake. Yet unlike the Soviet system, however, today's political system contains several institutional obstacles to the manipulation of law for political purposes.

The Judiciary

In contrast to the clout that the Procuracy has traditionally wielded in Russia, the bench has been relatively weak and passive. Traditionally judges have been the least-experienced and lowest-paid members of the legal profession, and the most vulnerable to external political and administrative pressure.[20] There are around 16,000 judges in courts of general jurisdiction, and most are holdovers from the Soviet era. If judges are to supervise the legality of arrests, ensure fair trials, and render just decisions in the face of intense external pressure, they will need greater legal training, experience, and social esteem. As Eugene Huskey observes, "independent courts are more difficult to create and nurture than representative institutions."[21] Judges are being called upon to raise their standards of professionalism, moreover, at a time of rapid change in law, legal procedure, and social conditions. In a few instances, judges have been murdered when they attempted to take on organized crime. Many judges have left their positions to take higher paying jobs in other branches of the legal profession. As the volume of court cases that come before the courts increases, judges find themselves hard-pressed to keep up.[22] Moreover, despite the introduction of a new institution of "bailiff-enforcers" in 1997 to assist in enforcing parties to legal judgments to comply with court decisions, courts still often find it difficult to implement their decisions in the face of determined resistance.[23]

Policy makers recognize the importance of an independent judiciary but disagree on the conditions needed to achieve it. In the past, judges were formally elected by the local soviet of the jurisdiction in which they served; in actuality they were part of the Communist Party–controlled *nomenklatura* system and thus were appointed to their positions by the party staff. Reforms beginning in the late 1980s attempted to increase judges' independence by lengthening their term of office and placing their election into the hands of the soviet at the next-higher level to that of the jurisdiction in which they served. But this still allowed powerful regional executives to sway judicial decision making. Therefore reformers pushed a law through the Federal Assembly that put the power of appointment of all federal judges into the president's hands, although the president was to choose from among candidates screened and proposed by the Russian Supreme Court and Supreme Commercial Court.[24] The president was also obliged to take into account the suggestions of the legislatures of the regions where federal judges would serve. Judges' terms of office are not limited, but under new legislation passed in 2001, they must retire at age sixty-five (age seventy for the highest courts).[25]

The judicial reform law passed at the end of 1996 took a significant step in the direction of establishing a single legal order throughout the Russian Federation.[26] Over the objection of some of the heads of the national republics and other regions, both chambers of parliament and the president agreed that all courts of general jurisdiction would be federal courts and would be guided by federal law, the federal constitution, and the instructions of the federal Supreme Court. The law establishes an institution of local justices of the peace (*mirovye sud'i*), which had existed in Russia in the prerevolutionary era, but they may only consider the most minor cases. Thus in contrast to the United States's multitiered system of justice, Russia's law establishes a single federal judiciary throughout the country.

Until very recently, all judicial decisions in Russian courts in criminal cases were rendered by a judge and two lay assessors. *Lay assessors* are ordinary citizens who are given paid leave from their place of work for a period of time in order to serve as co-judges in presiding over criminal trials; their participation is a form of community service for citizens designed to bring the justice system closer to the values and interests of the public. The judge and lay assessors have equal votes in deciding on the verdict and sentence, but, in practice, lay assessors tend to defer to the superior legal knowledge and experience of judges. More recently, a serious practical problem has arisen with the system of lay assessors. Fewer and fewer citizens are willing to leave their jobs to serve as lay assessors, and many trials must be conducted without them.

A number of legal reformers have pushed to replace the old system of judges and lay assessors with a jury trial system in criminal justice. Those supporting the jury trial believe that it will help make citizens feel themselves to be part of the legal system, and, by extension, the political system, rather than passive and helpless objects of its will. Jury service would allow people to experience directly the responsibilities associated with civic self-government. Reformers assert that jury trials will also make the legal system more honest and effective, since it will be more difficult for police, investigators, prosecutors, and judges to get away with abuses and misconduct. Finally, they argue that the jury trial will redress the bias of criminal procedure by countering the strong advantages presently possessed by the Procuracy and establishing a more level playing field between accuser and accused. As the distinguished Russian legal scholar, Alexander M. Yakovlev, wrote:

> The introduction of jury trials into the Russian system of justice marked an important step from the inquisitorial principle to the accusatorial one. The jury represented the real third party, the umpire before whom the defendant and the prosecutor became equal. This meant a great deal in a country where the prosecutor personified the omnipotence of the state and the defendant was considered just a despised transgressor of the laws prescribed by the state, where the presumption was not of innocence but of guilt, and where to be accused meant mostly to be sentenced and punished.[27]

Trial by jury certainly is not a *necessary* condition for democracy: Other judicial fact-finding procedures are also perfectly consistent with democratic principles. But in Russia, where there are long traditions of local self-government and strong if latent norms of egalitarianism and communalism, the jury trial may indeed have indirect effects that reinforce democratic values. Moreover, it is an institution with substantial roots in Russian society. It was introduced and widely used in Russia as part of the great reforms of the 1860s, and juries became an important instrument of civic participation.[28] Following the October 1917 revolution, however, the Bolsheviks eliminated the jury trial.

The reformers succeeded in passing a law in 1993 that authorized the introduction of the jury trial in Russia. With help and advice from distinguished legal specialists in Moscow as well as the American Bar Association and other outside organizations, an experiment was launched in a number of regions in Russia to employ the jury trial in criminal cases when the defendant requested it. The details were based on the prerevolutionary Russian model more than on the Anglo-American system. For example, a Russian defendant can request a jury trial even if he or she admits guilt, hoping that the jury will recommend a lenient sentence. (Note that Russian judicial practice lacks a procedure for plea bargaining, where a defendant is allowed to plead guilty to a lesser charge in return for a lighter sentence and no trial.) In the first years in which the jury system was used on an experimental basis, juries were somewhat more sympathetic to defendants than judges would be, a tendency noted also in Britain and America; acquittal rates were significantly higher than in regular courts.[29] The institution was introduced in nine regions on an experimental basis, but under the new Code of Criminal Procedure, it is now to be adopted in the entire country over the next five years.

Generally, after many initial misgivings, legal experts in Russia and abroad have come to regard trial by jury favorably. Judging from the experience of the nine regions where it was introduced on a trial basis, the new system seems to be having a positive impact on the quality of the judicial system. Prosecutors are being forced to prepare their cases more carefully and defense attorneys are more equal in status in judicial proceedings with the prosecution. In turn, the system is making the judges into neutral arbiters rather than participants in the prosecution.[30] To be sure, there are problems with the jury trial system. They are more costly than traditional trials (courtrooms need to be refitted for jury boxes, and jurors need to be compensated).[31] Many citizens do not appear when summoned to serve and courts find it hard to enforce their summons.[32] In any case, juries are only used in more serious criminal cases (overall, only about 1 percent of all cases are heard by juries). But they are very important, both legally and politically. A 1999 Constitutional Court decision held that a person could be sentenced to death only if a jury had convicted the defendant (Russia has suspended the death penalty in any case as a condition for membership in the Council of Europe).[33] And politically, juries help to democratize the legal system by broadening participation in the administration of justice.

Regional and republican courts serve to hear appeals from lower-level courts, as well as hear certain cases as courts of the first instance. At the pinnacle of the system of general courts is the Russian Supreme Court, which hears cases referred from lower courts and also issues instructions to lower courts on judicial matters. Its reasoning in rendering decisions is published and may be taken as guidance by lower courts in reaching decisions (bringing the Russian system closer to the recognition of legal precedents as binding). The Supreme Court does not have the power to challenge the constitutionality of laws and other normative acts adopted by legislative and executive bodies. That power is assigned by the constitution to the Constitutional Court. Under the constitution, judges of the Supreme Court are nominated by the president and confirmed by the Council of the Federation. Likewise, the chairman of the Supreme Court is appointed by the president and confirmed by the upper house.

There is another pyramid of courts designed to adjudicate cases arising from civil disputes between firms or between firms and the government. These are called *arbitration,* or *commercial,* courts *(arbitrazhnye sudy)*.[34] There is one arbitration court in nearly every subject of the federation, and there are another ten regional courts to hear appeals. At the head of this system stands the Supreme Arbitration Court. Like the Supreme Court, the Supreme Arbitration Court is both the highest appellate court for its system of courts, as well as the source of instruction and direction to lower commercial courts. Also, as with the Supreme Court, the chairman of the Supreme Arbitration Court is nominated by the president and confirmed by the Council of the Federation. As the volume of commercial transactions in Russia has grown, so has the workload of the arbitration courts; currently they handle over 600,000 cases a year and the caseload is growing.[35] These courts not only hear suits between private firms or between private firms and the government, but also handle an increasing number of cases arising from tax disputes (including a rapidly growing number of cases, often successful, when private firms take the government's tax authorities to court). The new arbitration courts have issued a number of crucial rulings that have helped establish the legal foundation for a market economy. The courts have often had a hard time enforcing their rulings, but a new institution of judicial bailiffs has helped somewhat. Moreover, enterprises sometimes find it useful to obtain a ruling in a dispute against another enterprise, even if they are unsure whether it will be enforced, in order to have a precedent that they can use in future litigation.[36] The chairman of the Supreme Arbitration Court, Veniamin Yakovlev, commented that even though the arbitration courts are a part of the state and paid by it, the judges consider themselves an independent branch of state power, and have been reasonably successful at defending their independence even in litigation where the state has been a party.[37]

In 2001 the Putin administration drafted a comprehensive set of legislative proposals to strengthen the judicial system. One of the aims of the reforms was to increase the accountability of judges for their actions, but increasing accountability and independence at the same time proved thorny. After extensive deliberation by legal experts, judges, presidential staff people, and parliamentarians, the reforms were enacted. They consisted of a substantial increase in judges' salaries and improvement in their working conditions; organizational changes in the way judges were appointed and removed; and the changes to the criminal procedure code that were noted earlier that expanded the rights of judges to supervise pretrial criminal procedures.[38] On paper, at any rate, the Putin reforms went a long way to increase the status and political independence of the judiciary and to expand the judicial protection of civil liberties. How the reforms will work in practice is an open question.

The Constitutional Court

Because the Soviet regime had no legal institution to ensure that legislative and administrative acts of the state conformed with the Soviet constitution, legal reformers in the Gorbachev period called for creating a constitutional court, equivalent to such bodies as the Constitutional Council in the French Fifth Republic or the Constitutional Court in Germany, that would rule on the constitutionality of laws and would adjudicate disputes between the union and the republics. As a cautious initial experiment with such a body, a constitutional amendment creating a "committee on constitutional supervision" (*komitet konstitutsionnogo nadzora*) was passed in December 1988. This body came into being on January 1, 1990. One of its early decisions was that there would be no Communist Party organization within it—a small symbolic indication that the committee's members considered the law superior to the dictates of the party. The committee's first official decision, in September 1990, found that Gorbachev had acted unconstitutionally when he had decreed earlier in the year that as president he had the power to forbid or allow demonstrations within Moscow. Gorbachev did not challenge the committee's ruling. But the committee found itself powerless to overcome the paralyzing effects of the "war of laws" between union, republican, and local government authorities. Moreover, since it was not a court, the committee could not adjudicate cases. Nevertheless, the committee's creation, and the care it exercised to avoid making decisions that would be flagrantly ignored, indicated that an important precedent had been established.

The committee dissolved along with the rest of the union government in December 1991. Russia, however, had established a constitutional court by a constitutional amendment in July 1991. The fifteen members of the Constitutional Court were elected by the Congress of People's Deputies for life terms. The Congress elected a relatively young legal scholar, Valerii Zor'kin, as chairman.

The Russian Constitutional Court made several significant decisions in its first year of existence. Among them was a finding in December 1991 that an action of President Yeltsin merging two state ministries into a single body was unconstitutional; the president complied with the decision, establishing the precedent of effective judicial review. Another very important decision concerned Yeltsin's decrees in the fall of 1991 outlawing the Communist Party and nationalizing its property. Reviewing the constitutionality of his actions, the court held in November 1992 that Yeltsin acted within his rights when he banned the Communist Party's executive organs but that he had no right to prohibit members of the party from forming primary organizations (PPOs or cells). Moreover, the court said that the state had the right to confiscate the party's property, but that in cases where the title of an asset was unclear or disputed, only the Supreme Arbitration Court could rule on the state's rights. This decision was widely regarded as juridically sound and politically shrewd, in that it allowed both the communists and the president's side to claim victory. The court also, perhaps wisely, avoided taking sides on the president's assertion that the CPSU was itself unconstitutional. The court thus positioned itself as a politically neutral institution. This was no mean achievement in the tense, polarized environment of the time.

A final success for the court in the 1991–1993 period was the intervention by its chairman into the severe confrontation that arose between President Yeltsin and the Congress of People's Deputies in December 1992 over the rightful powers of the president and the legislature. Chairman Zor'kin proposed a resolution of the crisis that both sides accepted: that a national referendum be held to decide on the basic constitutional principles to govern Russia. Here the chairman of the court came close to entering the political fray directly, but, unfortunately for the court, he did not stop there. Zor'kin soon came to agree with the chairman of the Supreme Soviet, Ruslan Khasbulatov, that the referendum should not be held after all, and supported the Congress's decision in early March 1993 to cancel it. When Yeltsin immediately thereafter appeared on television to declare his intention to suspend the Congress and impose special presidential rule, Chairman Zor'kin quickly issued a condemnation of Yeltsin's statement: But he did so without having reviewed the text of Yeltsin's proposed decree and on his own authority, rather than as a decision of the full membership of the court. When Yeltsin's decree was finally published a few days later, it had dropped the legally offensive provisions about declaring a special form of presidential rule and suspending the activity of the Congress. Perhaps Zor'kin's condemnation had helped to deter Yeltsin from taking such authoritarian steps.

But it was clear that Zor'kin had acted precipitously, revealing a zeal more political than judicial.

Soon Zor'kin began supporting Khasbulatov's political positions routinely and thus forfeiting the court's claim to be politically neutral. In October 1993, following Yeltsin's decrees dissolving parliament and calling for new elections and a constitutional referendum, Yeltsin also suspended the operation of the Constitutional Court until the new constitution was ratified, new judges were elected to fill vacancies, and a new law governing its activity was enacted by parliament. Under the new law on the Constitutional Court passed by parliament in summer 1994, there were to be nineteen members and the members themselves would elect their own chairman. Their terms were limited to twelve years. Thirteen of the original members of the court remained members (including Zor'kin, whom Yeltsin removed as chairman of the court but who continued to be a full member of it and who was elected chairman of the court again in 2003). The president then nominated six new justices to fill the vacancies on the court and presented them to the Council of the Federation for confirmation. The Council refused to confirm three and the stage was set for a new round of political bargaining between the president and parliament in order to find mutually acceptable candidates. Over the next eight months, the president proposed fourteen different candidates altogether, and the Federation Council rejected eight, until finally the full complement of nineteen judges was confirmed. Thus for a year and a half, from October 1993 to March 1995, Russia lacked a functioning Constitutional Court. The accumulation of unresolved disputes between the executive and legislative branches and between the federal government and lower governments ensured that once the court did begin to operate again, it would face a heavy workload.

When the newly configured Court resumed work in March 1995 it quickly established its right to interpret the constitution in a variety of areas. It ruled on several ambiguous questions relating to parliamentary procedure (it found, for instance, that the constitution's provision that passage of a law required a majority "of the total number of deputies" in fact meant a majority of the total number of seats envisioned for that chamber, regardless of whether or not all the seats in the chamber were currently filled). It overturned some laws passed by ethnic republics within Russia, and struck down a provision of the Russian Criminal Code that limited individual rights. Generally, in cases involving disputes between individuals and state authorities, the court has found in favor of individuals, thus widening and reaffirming the sphere of individual legal rights. For example, the court issued an important ruling in March 2002 demanding that the new legislative rule that the arrest of a person for more than forty-eight hours required a court order must take effect as of July 1, 2002.[39]

Of all the spheres in which the Constitutional Court has made politically significant rulings, its decisions in the area of *federalism* are perhaps the most significant. Repeatedly the court has been called upon to delimit the powers of territorial subjects of the federation in relation to the federal constitution. Generally it has defended the legal unity of the federation in the face of the demands of the regions for autonomy. However, it has also tried to be careful not to issue rulings that will be ignored and thus will undermine the court's legitimacy. A particularly contentious example of the type of dispute it has dealt with is the Udmurtia case. The legislature of the Udmurt Republic (an industrial territory located in the western part of the Urals area) passed a law in 1996 that dissolved the elected governments of the cities and districts throughout the republic, and required that the executive branch instead be headed by officials appointed by the republic government. The mayor of the capital city, joined by President Yeltsin and the Russian State Duma, took the matter to court and sought a ruling from the Constitutional Court. In January 1997 the Court ruled that while the Udmurt legislature was within its constitutional rights to pass a law on local government for the republic, it did not have the right to nullify the authority of previously elected government officials without taking into account the will of its citizens. An interesting outcome of the decision was that both sides claimed that they had won. For several weeks the regional legislature ignored the court's requirement that it reinstate the officials it had removed from office. Twice President Yeltsin went so far as to issue an edict demanding the region's compliance with the court's decision. After temporizing briefly, the region finally backed down.[40] Observers hailed this as an important precedent in establishing the court's legitimacy in adjudicating disputes arising from ambiguities in the rules of Russian federalism.

Throughout the 1990s, the court rendered a series of decisions upholding federal law against the efforts by regional executives and legislatures to assert their autonomy. However, the court was always mindful of the political climate and therefore recognized that the federal government had only limited capacity to enforce its decisions in the regions. The election of President Putin changed the political balance sharply. Putin made it clear that he intended to reclaim for the federal government some of the power and prerogatives that had been claimed, de facto, by regional governments. Two crucially important rulings by the Constitutional Court in the spring of 2000 reinforced Putin's position. First was a ruling in April 2000, which declared that a procurator (in fact, *any* citizen) could contest whether a law or regulation passed by a regional or local authority was consistent with federal law. An ordinary court (court of general jurisdiction) was entitled to suspend such a law or regulation if it found that it did indeed violate federal law. Only the Constitutional Court had the power to strike down such a law as completely invalid. But a local court, guided by previous decisions of the Constitutional Court and its own reading of the federal law, could declare that the law or regulation was "not in force."[41] The effect of this ruling was to allow procurators and courts throughout the country to enforce the primacy of federal law over arbitrary acts by local authorities.

The other major decision by the court came in response to an appeal by the president of the ethnic republic of Gorno-Altai, who sought clarification about the constitutionality of several provisions of its constitution. Among other things, he asked the court to rule whether its constitution had the right to declare the republic "sovereign" and to declare the natural resources located on the territory of the republic the "property" of the republic. The court ruled that not only did the provisions on sovereignty and the ownership of natural resources violate the federal constitution (on the grounds that only the Russian Federation is sovereign), but declared explicitly that the analogous provisions in all the other republic constitutions that contained such points were also unconstitutional. To drive the point home, the court met with the heads of the constitutional courts of all six republics whose constitutions possessed such provisions. It explained that these provisions were all automatically rendered invalid and should be removed. Clearly the court was taking advantage of Putin's vigorous drive to centralize power to assert its own legal doctrine of the primacy of federal law and constitution over regional claims to sovereignty.

Because the court has been politically prudent, reluctant to issue a decision that will be flagrantly ignored, it has tiptoed cautiously around the huge domain of presidential authority. Even here, however, the court has managed to limit the president's power. One was its ruling in the "trophy art" case, when it decided that President Yeltsin was required to sign a law after both chambers of parliament overrode his veto.[42] Another was its decision that the use of the proportional-representation system in the electoral law to elect half of the deputies of the Duma was entirely compatible with the constitution (observers generally thought that the case, which was brought by one of the regional legislatures, had the tacit support or even sponsorship of the Kremlin). And the court ruled that President Yeltsin was not entitled to run for a third term.[43]

In other and more significant cases, however, the court has tended to side with the president. One of the court's first and most important decisions concerned a challenge brought by a group of communist parliamentarians to the president's edicts launching the war in Chechnia. The court ruled that the president had the authority to wage the war through the use of his constitutional power to issue edicts with the force of law. More recently, as we saw, the court upheld the president's right to dismiss the procurator-general if a criminal case had been opened against him. The court has had to steer an extremely delicate course between being regarded as a tool of the president, and crossing the president on a significant issue only to have its ruling flagrantly ignored.

The Constitutional Court proceeds by deciding whether to accept a case or inquiry. Usually if it does so, it has determined that a challenge to an existing law, decree, or official action has legal merit. It then holds hearings where parties and experts representing both sides of the issue make statements to the court. Each side listens to the arguments presented by its opponents and seeks to counter them with superior arguments. The court then takes the information presented under advisement and renders its judgment. Dissenting opinions are published separately, but in recent years there have been very few of these; the court far prefers to speak with a single voice.

The court tends to act slowly. Most cases require two to four weeks to decide, with most of that time being spent on the painstaking task of drafting their decision. The court issues, however, a great many findings (determinations, or *opredeleniia*), as many as ten in a single day, which fall short of being full rulings on a case but which decide a case by finding that the issues it raises were decided in a previous case. It therefore has begun to introduce a form of law by precedent. This form of decision making eases the strain on the court's growing workload.

Turnover of members will bring about a change in the court's political complexion in response to changes in public opinion and the political tendencies of future presidents and parliaments. With time, the court's stature is likely to increase to the extent that it can steer the difficult narrow course between the Scylla of excessive zeal in upholding constitutional law that brings it into unwinnable confrontations with powerful state officials, and the Charybdis of excessive caution that may render it a passive instrument of the rulers.[44]

The Advocates

Change of another sort has been occurring among members of that branch of the legal profession who represent individual citizens and organizations in both criminal and civil matters: "advocates" *(advokaty)*. Comparable to defense attorneys in the United States, Soviet advocates often oppose procurators and other state bodies in judicial proceedings, in both criminal and civil cases. As the volume of commercial transactions has grown, so has their activity in this area, as have their opportunities for material gain.

The advocates have long enjoyed a certain corporate autonomy through their self-governing associations, called *collegia,* through which they elect officers and govern admission of new practitioners. In the Soviet era, when they were supervised by the Ministry of Justice and the Communist Party, their ability to make effective use of the rights given them was limited. But in recent years, their independence and prestige have risen markedly, partly as a result of the new emphasis on legality under Gorbachev and the rapid growth of the private economic sector in the early 1990s. They have begun organizing their own professional association and codifying corporate ethical standards, often struggling with the Ministry of Justice to free themselves of interference from the state. Today there are around 42,000 advocates, and 145 judicial collegia.[45]

One of the most telling indicators of a change in the status of advocates was the revision of the previous rules limiting their earnings. As of September 1988, an advocate was theoretically free to take on as many cases as he or she wished and to charge any fee agreed upon with the client. With the new freedom to form cooperatives, some lawyers have begun forming legal cooperatives and competing with the collegia of advocates in dispensing legal assistance to citizens; the collegia of advocates have begun to organize their own for-profit legal cooperatives in response. Advocates have become popular guests on national television programs and have contributed a number of articles on legal subjects to mass periodicals, suggesting widespread popular interest in learning about the law.[46] Many advocates work in commercial firms licensed by local governments and some have become celebrities. The legal profession has become highly attractive to many young people for its opportunities to gain status and high incomes.

Statutory Reforms

In addition to these changes in judicial institutions, reformers have made far-reaching modifications to the codes of criminal, civil, and administrative law and procedure. The objectives here are broadly consistent with those we have outlined and with the general goal of a "law-governed state" in Russia, in that they extend protections for individual legal and civil rights. More generally they create legal conditions for the existence of civil society through laws recognizing the rights of social and public organizations such as religious communities, political parties, charitable associations, labor unions, and business firms. To a surprising degree, this statutory foundation for the rule of law has been achieved by the laborious process of bargaining and consensus building among interested groups, including judges, legal experts, and politicians of the left and right, rather than by decree or dictate. The area of consensus is larger than might be imagined, given the deep division between those who want to advance Russia toward a democratic, market-based society, and those who want to preserve the state-dominant, socialist character of Russia. As has been emphasized, both reformers and conservatives can support the principles of judicial independence, impartiality, and fairness.

To be sure, much of the change is confined to paper: At the center and in many regions, the actual behavior of judicial institutions is still often subject to the sway of wealth and power. Nevertheless, the passage of a body of important federal laws governing the judicial process has had a substantial impact. The legal system has become another check on the exercise of arbitrary political power, although not a consistent or reliable one. The fact that some defendants have won significant legal victories in the courts against powerful political actors has encouraged more people to turn to the courts to protect their rights. Between 1993 and 1997 alone, the number of civil cases heard in the courts more than doubled.[47]

One of the milestones of statutory reform of legal procedures is the new Civil Code, which regulates civil relations among individuals, organizations, and the state, and provides legal guarantees for property rights. Another important achievement was the new Criminal Code, finally signed into law by President Yeltsin in June 1996 following a year and a half of negotiations and deliberations among specialists, concerned state bodies, the presidential administration, and members of parliament. The new code brought the criminal law into closer conformity with the demands of the post-Soviet environment. It reduced the number of crimes subject to capital punishment, differentiated closely among crimes according to their seriousness, emphasized the need to protect individual legal rights as opposed to the state's interests, decriminalized some activities that had been illegal in the Soviet era, and at the same time introduced definitions of new types of crimes that had been previously unheard of, such as money laundering and unfair competition. "On the whole," Peter Solomon remarked, "the new code represented a moderate consensus document that promised to de-Sovietize and modernize Russian criminal law."[48] The set of laws reforming the judiciary adopted in December 2001 was a significant step toward improving the working conditions of courts and expanding the legal powers possessed by courts. These included the new Code of Criminal Procedure and a law on the status of judges, as well as a substantial increase in state spending on the judicial branch.[49] For these statutory changes to bring about major progress toward real judicial independence, however, the necessary political conditions will have to come about: The president and other state officials will need to demonstrate respect for the law by their own behavior, and political pluralism will need to increase.

OBSTACLES TO THE RULE OF LAW

How close has post-Soviet Russia come to realizing the ideal of a "law-governed state"? While substantial change in legal institutions has occurred, the reforms have not yet succeeded in fully checking the arbitrary use of state power by executive authorities. Moreover, the severity of the problems of corruption and organized crime indicates how weak law enforcement is in the face of power and determined criminal interests. Rampant crime and corruption in turn discourage the spread of respect for the law and legal institutions.

The problem of crime and corruption is so serious that it requires separate attention. First let us note three other weaknesses in the capacity of the law and legal institutions to restrain the arbitrary exercise of power by the state. These are the extralegal powers of the successor bodies of the KGB; the ability of bureaucratic agencies to circumvent national policy through administrative rules and regulations; and the propensity of chief executives—the president of the country and the governors and presidents of the subjects of the federation—to ignore constitutional limits on their power.

The Continuing Power of the State Security Agencies. Under Soviet rule, the Committee for State Security (KGB) exercised very wide powers, including responsibility for both domestic and foreign intelligence. It also conducted extensive surveillance over society to prevent political dissent or opposition, and in its exercise of power, it often operated outside the law. In October 1991, following the August 1991 coup (when the KGB chairman was one of the principal organizers of the seizure of power), Yeltsin dissolved the Russian republican branch of the KGB and divided it into several new agencies: the Ministry of Security, which was to guard the state's security in domestic matters; the Foreign Intelligence Service, which took over the KGB's overseas espionage and intelligence functions; the Federal Agency for Governmental Communications and Information (FAPSI), which maintained security in the country's telecommunications system; the Federal Border Guard Service (FSP); and the Federal Tax Police (FSNP). The reorganization altered the structure and mission of the successor bodies, but they were never subjected to a thorough-going purge of personnel. Like Gorbachev, Yeltsin and Putin have preferred to cultivate a close political relationship with the security agencies rather than to antagonize them. Although many of the archives containing documents on the past activities of the secret police[50] have been opened to inspection, thus exposing many aspects of the Soviet regime's use of terror, no member or collaborator of the security service has ever been prosecuted legally for these actions. None of the KGB's informers have been exposed to public judgment. Indeed, the security police claim that they were themselves a victim of arbitrary rule and terror under Stalin, and therefore that today they strongly uphold the rule of law. Whether this position is credible is another matter.

Through the 1990s the successor bodies were further reorganized. In 1993 the Ministry of Security was reorganized as the Federal Counter-Intelligence Service, and in 1995 President Yeltsin reorganized it yet again into the Federal Security Service (FSB), assigning it comprehensive duties and powers. Some idea of how wide-ranging its powers are is suggested by the description of the new body's mandate given by a senior Russian government official to the press. The new FSB, he stated, would "be able to infiltrate foreign organizations and criminal groups, institute inquiries, carry out preliminary investigations, maintain its own prisons, demand information from private companies, and set up special units and front enterprises." Its duties would include foreign intelligence activities to boost Russia's "economic, scientific, technical, and defense potential" and "to ensure the security of all government bodies."[51]

The KGB's successor agencies have been skillful at adapting to the new post-Soviet political environment, and have found new security tasks that enable them to retain power and resources. An example is the Federal Agency for Governmental Communications and Information (FAPSI), which is responsible for ensuring the security of state telecommunications. FAPSI is believed to provide telecommunications services to a number of governmental, financial, and commercial organizations, giving it unusually privileged intelligence-gathering opportunities. FAPSI's role in monitoring all forms of mass-communications and telecommunications systems has been greatly enhanced by the approval of a sweeping new doctrine on "information security," which the Security Council drafted and which President Putin signed on September 12, 2000. Defining virtually all areas of information processing, communication, and use as vital to Russia's national security, the doctrine enumerates a series of threats to Russia's information security. Among them are Russia's inability to compete effectively in world markets for news and information, the leakage of state secrets, the ability of unauthorized persons to gain illegal access to Russian databases and electronic servers, vulnerability to "information weapons" directed against Russia, and efforts by "Western countries" to "further destroy the scientific-technological integrity" of the former Soviet Union by trying to bring it under Western influence. The document establishes doctrinal grounds for a considerable expansion of the powers (and budget allocations) of FAPSI and other security agencies in order to control the flow of information in and out of Russia.[52]

Besides these agencies, there are two services responsible for providing security for state buildings and state officials. One of these, the presidential guard service, was headed by a close friend of President Yeltsin, Alexander Korzhakov, until Yeltsin fired him from that position in June 1996. Korzhakov had shown an alarming eagerness to offer advice, commentary, and demands on a number of policy matters—urging Prime Minister Chernomyrdin to slow down economic reform, for instance, and floating an opinion that presidential elections were a needless source of tension and expense and should be canceled. Leaning heavily on his close relationship with the president, Korzhakov engaged in various Kremlin plots and intrigues to advance the interests of a coalition of antireformers. After firing Korzhakov, Yeltsin then merged the two state protection services into a single agency.

Although they have been eager to aggrandize power, the security agencies that formed from the KGB have generally maintained a reputation for competence and incorruptibility. Many former security officers have gone to work for private organizations because they are considered to be honest and professional. And a number of leading politicians have backgrounds in the security organs, including, most famously, President Putin. Putin has drawn upon the security agencies for many of his senior personnel appointments, although whether this is because he finds these individuals professional and reliable, or because he shares their preference for solving Russia's political problems by means of police methods, remains unclear. It is characteristic of the contradictions of the Putin presidency that on the day following Putin's approval of the broad new "information security doctrine" that—potentially, at least—gives the state sweeping rights to control all information flows in the country, the Presidium of the Supreme Court issued a ruling that the security police bitterly opposed. The case concerned retired Navy captain Alexander Nikitin, who in 1995 supplied an international environmental organization with documents revealing the extent of the danger that aging Russian nuclear submarines posed to the environment as their reactors deteriorated. Acting at the behest of the Federal Security Service, the Procuracy pressed charges against Nikitin, claiming that he had committed treason by illegally revealing state secrets to foreign powers. When Nikitin was acquitted by a St. Petersburg city court, the procurator appealed to the Supreme Court. The Supreme Court upheld the city court's decision. The procurator than appealed to the Presidium of the Supreme Court, the highest appellate instance in criminal cases in the country. On September 13, 2000, the Presidium of the Supreme Court confirmed the decisions of the lower courts, and freed Nikitin. Commenting on the verdict, one representative of the Security Council remarked that the law on the media needed to be amended so as to make actions such as Nikitin's punishable by law.

Since the end of the Soviet era, despite taking on new tasks such as fighting international narcotics trafficking and terrorism, Russia's security police have continued to demonstrate a Soviet-style preoccupation with controlling the flow of information about the country. In 2002, embarrassed by the defections to the West of two senior officers, they obtained convictions in absentia of both defectors on charges of treason. Under Putin the authorities have arrested several Russian journalists and scientists for espionage, and in 2001 the security police sent a directive to the Academy of Sciences demanding that scholars report all contacts with foreigners. A deputy director of the FSB denied that his agency was fanning a "spy-mania" but claimed that the activities of foreign intelligence services in Russia had become "more aggressive, conspiratorial, and sophisticated."[53] The fact that the police were reviving Soviet-era practices under a president who made his career in the KGB has raised serious concerns about Putin's commitment to the rule of law. Some Russian political figures have expressed serious concern that under Putin, the security police have become more powerful and assertive and have cast a long shadow over society. The deputy chairman of the Duma's Security Committee recently commented that he had the impression that Russia had "returned again to the period at the end of the 1970s and early 1980s. Now in Russia a like-mindedness is observable absolutely everywhere— . . . a constant fear and the strengthening of the position of the first committee for state security. For any society the KGB-ization of the government is an abnormal occurrence."[54]

A further indication of the strengthening of the state security police under President Putin was the president's decision in March 2003, enacted in a series of decrees, to dissolve FAPSI and the Federal Border Guard Service (FSP) and merge them into the Federal Security Service. Since both of these services had operated as divisions of the KGB in the Soviet era, observers commented that the FSB was returning to the model of a "super-agency," much as the KGB had been. One Russian political analyst, Nikolai Petrov, observed that the main problem was not so much the reorganization itself as the absence of any meaningful oversight of the security agencies by civil society and parliament. As he noted, "Over the last ten years, the KGB was broken up into numerous agencies, but society did not much increase in its oversight over the special services."[55]

Bureaucratic Rule Making. The second impediment to the primacy of law reflects the immense inertia of a heavily bureaucratized state. In Russia today, as in Russia in ages past, the power of the central policy makers is frequently thwarted by the tendency of administrative agencies to issue normative acts—decrees, regulations, instructions, orders, directives, circular letters, and many other kinds of official and binding rules—applying not only to subordinates in the same agency but, often, to other governmental agencies and to Russian citizens generally. In the Soviet period, where the legislative branch was purely a ceremonial adjunct of the party and executive bureaucracy, the practice of bureaucratic rule making through what are called "sub-legal normative acts" was extremely widespread. Some indication of the magnitude of this practice is suggested by the fact that over the first seventy years of Soviet power, the USSR legislature adopted fewer than 800 laws and decrees, whereas over the same period, the union-level government issued hundreds of thousands of decrees and other normative acts. In 1985, according to one estimate, there were 27,000 legal norms enacted by the USSR Council of Ministers that were still valid.[56] Tens of thousands more binding rules issued by particular government ministries and state committees also remained on the books. The profusion of rules and regulations, complementing, interpreting, and often contradicting one another, creates ample opportunities for evasion, as well as generates pressures for intervention by powerful individuals to cut through the jungle of red tape.

Much of the rule making by bureaucratic agencies, moreover, is secret, and rulings issued by lower levels of the bureaucracy often take precedence over the law. As political scientist Eugene Huskey observes, the bureaucratic hierarchy "may also be conceived of as an iceberg. A small portion is visible but obscured from view is that vast body of departmental instructions that gives direction to Soviet life. As one goes further down the pyramid, glasnost lessens. There is, to put it in an American context, no *Federal Register.*"[57] Most regulations are issued in numbered copies to a small list of authorized personnel, with most of these being classified "for internal use only." Even the Procuracy, which is given official responsibility for ensuring the legality and consistency of governmental regulations, lacks full access to all legal acts of the bureaucracy.[58] Often, laws passed by the parliament remain dead letters until they are "interpreted" and given concrete, binding content by bureaucrats in state agencies. Although the rules and regulations that the departments issue are supposed to be consistent with both the language and spirit of the law, in practice they frequently gut it, so that reforms adopted by the legislature may be eviscerated and weightless by the time they reach the level where they are supposed to be acted upon.

The 1993 constitution does not give parliament an explicit right to oversee *(kontrolirovat')* the executive branch, a power considered essential to the checks and balances between the American legislative and executive branches. However, as parliament has gained experience in using the powers it does have—particularly the budget process, investigations, hearings, and the Auditing Chamber[59]—it has gradually acquired greater de facto power to oversee the bureaucracy's compliance with legislative requirements. On the other hand, it is frequently difficult to know what the legislature's will is. A persistent problem with legislation passed by the Federal Assembly and signed into law is that as laws pass through the legislative mill, their more controversial points are removed or replaced with bland statements that give bureaucrats wide latitude to issue rules "interpreting" the law. In such cases, parliament sometimes has to go back and amend the law when it is displeased with how the law has been implemented.

The bureaucracy's ability to derail the implementation of policy decisions made at the center not only contradicts the primacy of law, but also hampers the ability of a reform-minded central leader to ensure the implementation of his wishes. The bureaucracy's ability to issue regulations on how laws are to be implemented can distort and water down a leader's policies. For this reason, President Putin has repeatedly denounced the bureaucracy's propensity to sidetrack laws with rules and regulations that displace the goals of the policy. He has been particularly critical of administrative overregulation of business for stifling economic initiative. For example, in his April 2001 message to parliament he called on the bureaucracy to eliminate excessive rules and regulations and on parliament to pass better quality laws:[60]

> Bureaucratic rule making *[vedomstvennoe normotvorchestvo]* is one of the chief brakes on the development of entrepreneurship. A bureaucrat is used to acting according to an instruction which, after one or another law has come into force, often is inconsistent with the law itself, but yet for years is never rescinded. . . . The government, ministries and departments should, finally, take radical mea-

sures with respect to bureaucratic regulation—even going so far as to eliminate the whole body of departmental regulations in cases where there are already federal laws of direct force in place.

More generally, Putin has begun the arduous process of reforming the entire system of state service in order to raise the quality and professionalism of civil servants. In 2002 he issued two decrees laying out general principles to guide the state bureaucracy, but these are extremely broad. A state employee, Putin decreed in August, must show "tolerance and respect toward the customs and traditions of the peoples of Russia, facilitate inter-ethnic and inter-confessional concord, observe political neutrality, and respectfully relate to the activity of representatives of the mass media." "Observing and defending human rights and freedoms," the decree stated, "constitute the meaning and content of the activity of organs of state power." Although such vague declarations are unlikely to have any effect on the power of the bureaucracy, Putin has also charged his advisors with the task of preparing a comprehensive set of laws reforming the structure and operation of the state bureaucracy. As all observers agree, any serious reform of the Russian bureaucracy will meet extremely stiff resistance.[61]

Executive Discretion. A third threat to the rule of law is the ability of the president and of regional chief executives to ignore constitutional or statutory limitations in the pursuit of political ends. Russia's president has a broad range of informal levers of power to reward and punish state officials and private businesses. The presidential administration, for example, can intervene in government ministries on personnel or policy issues and wield carrots and sticks to persuade members of parliament to vote as the Kremlin wishes. Similarly, although the president's decree power is exceptionally wide by comparative standards, both Yeltsin and Putin have sometimes used it in ways that exceeded even the broad limits allowed under the constitution.[62] The clearest example, of course, is President Yeltsin's set of decrees in September and October 1993 that dissolved parliament. They were unconstitutional, even though they called for a national referendum to determine the constitutional principles that Russia was to adopt for the future. Yeltsin further authorized the army to use crushing military power to suppress the resistance to these decrees, and for many citizens, the artillery shelling of the parliament building in October 1993 was more than the outcome of a national tragedy—it was the final sign that President Yeltsin was willing to use dictatorial means to defend his power. His actions had the result of resolving a constitutional crisis and allowing a new set of constitutional institutions to begin operating, their legal legitimacy buttressed by the outcomes of popular elections. But his defiance of the law set a dangerous precedent for a future president, and for lower executive officials who judge the limits of their own permissible behavior by observing the behavior of the president.

President Yeltsin and, at least initially, President Putin, used their decree power extensively in matters such as privatization, banking reform, reorganization of the executive branch, and criminal procedure. For instance, President

Putin used his decree power to establish the seven new federal "super-districts" where appointed presidential representatives would be stationed to monitor the observance of federal law in the regions. Some critics objected that since these new bodies lacked any legislative foundation, they represented an authoritarian step on the president's part, while other critics noted that since no other existing laws envisioned structures at this level, the appointed representatives would find themselves legally powerless. There was also criticism from some (especially the communists) when Putin used his decree power on December 31, 1999, to grant outgoing President Yeltsin and members of Yeltsin's family full legal immunity for the rest of their lives. Moreover, the fact that at least two of President Putin's major decrees (the decree setting up a special administration for Chechnia and the decree establishing the seven federal "super-districts") were prepared by the staff of the Security Council raised concerns among many observers that the real decision making in the Putin administration was going on behind the scenes under the influence of the security forces.[63]

When Yeltsin used his decree power, he often invited the legislature to follow up the decree with permanent legislation. Sometimes he did so knowing that once he had altered the status quo with a decree, it would be much harder for the legislature to undo the results of his decree. As a result, Yeltsin's enemies often accused Yeltsin of exceeding decree-making power. Certainly the decree power gives a president a considerable advantage in setting policy: He can issue a decree before parliament has acted on an issue and then use the threat of a veto to block legislation if parliament tries to change his policy. Moreover, his right to initiate legislation, his ability to threaten to dissolve the Duma (for instance, the president could nominate a grossly unacceptable candidate for prime minister, and then dissolve the Duma when it fails to confirm his choice), and his ability to block a bill in the Council of the Federation by using carrots and sticks, mean that he has leverage over the legislative process at a number of pressure points.

Some indication of the scale of the president's use of his decree power may be seen in the fact that during the 1994 and 1995 period, parliament passed 461 laws, 282 of them being signed by the president. Around 100 of the latter were major regulatory or distributive policy acts in areas such as budget appropriations, social welfare, and reform of state political institutions, law enforcement, and the judicial system.[64] Over the same period, the president issued approximately 4,000 decrees, most of them of minor significance, such as appointing individuals to state positions or awarding honors for merit. A few, however, were highly important because they shaped major national policy. These included the terms of the privatization of shares of the state television and radio company, the delineation of powers of regional government, and the determination of which enterprises were subject to privatization for cash. Often the parliamentary opposition vehemently objected to the president's use of his decree power to bypass the regular lawmaking process, but had no legal means to counter it.[65] By 1998 and 1999, however, President Yeltsin's decrees had become much less significant as policy decisions. The great majority concerned minor issues such as state symbols, or nullified earlier decrees that had been superseded by federal legislation.[66]

President Yeltsin was equally creative in using his constitutional role as "guarantor of the constitution" when it came to dealing with regional leaders. Between 1994 and 1998, as we saw in Chapter 3, he concluded forty-six bilateral "treaties" with the heads of federal territories.[67] These treaties often gave particular regions special rights and privileges not enjoyed by other regions. The entire process of negotiating and signing the treaties was not regulated by any law and the treaties themselves were never ratified by parliament. While they may have been justified under the circumstances as short-term expedients that preserved some semblance of stability to federal relations, they vividly illustrate the point that Yeltsin considered himself entitled to wield his presidential powers as he saw fit.

The ability of the president to circumvent the law and constitution when it suits him using decree power or more informal means is echoed in the behavior of many regional governors and local executives. Some governors rule as autocrats in their territories. They control all bodies of state power in their regions including the regional branches of federal structures, bully the mass media, intimidate (or worse) their political opponents, and build up powerful patronage machines through control of local business firms.[68] Neither Yeltsin nor Putin has exhibited much appetite for fighting such governors, and they usually have preferred to reach an accommodation with them. In one famous case early in 2001, President Putin finally managed to force out the firmly entrenched governor of Primorsk territory in the Far East, Evgenii Nazdratenko. But, although Putin persuaded Nazdratenko to resign as governor, he gave him a consolation prize by putting him in charge of the state committee for the fishing industry— a position that carries with it the extremely lucrative right to distribute licenses for fishing quotas in coastal waters.

As serious a threat to the rule of law as the discretion of chief executives is— both their constitutionally mandated and informal powers—an even greater danger may be the *weakness* of executive authority. As political scientists who have studied strongly presidential systems point out, a high degree of centralization of power in the presidency challenges the ability of *any* president, even the most energetic and capable, to manage it.[69] Russia's huge presidential apparatus is filled with officials who are adept at manipulating the president's power. The problem is exacerbated at times when the president is weakened by illness or exhaustion, as was Yeltsin for much of his second term as president. The drift and decay of executive control that occurs when the president is incapacitated in a hyper-presidential system can be as serious a problem as the overconcentration of power in one person's hands.

Organized Crime and Corruption

Organized Crime. Both criminality and official corruption have been stimulated by a substantial rise in the power of organized crime. But although organized crime has been discussed extensively in the Western and Russian press, reliable indicators of its scale are elusive.[70] By all accounts, however, organized crime is deeply entrenched and broad in scope. A 1994 article in the newspaper *Izvestiia* observed:

> 'Godfathers' of the mafia exist in many countries, but there for the most part they control illegal business, such as narcotics, gambling, thieves' hang-outs. Here they have established total control over ordinary commerce. As a result we pay for our daily bread, for our basket of consumer goods, around 20–30 percent more. In the farmers' markets exotic fruits cost less than tomatoes and cucumbers—because of the tribute to the mafia that is paid. Thus the population is supporting two states with its money—the legitimate government and the criminal one—that exist in parallel. Or rather, the legal state more and more depends on the power of the criminal one.[71]

Certainly the police often appear to be incapable of solving major crimes committed by organized crime groups. Hundreds of people—politicians, businesspeople, bankers, journalists, and others—have been assassinated in contract murders, but few cases have resulted in an arrest, let alone a conviction. Nine members of the Duma have been killed in contract murders since 1994. One of the most shocking such incidents occurred in November 1998, when the well-known political figure Galina Starovoitova was murdered in her apartment. The crime has yet to be solved. In April 2003, the prominent liberal democrat Sergei Yushenkov was killed as he returned to his apartment from the Duma. Observers assumed that the motive was political, because Yushenkov (like Starovoitova) was not involved in any business dealings. In all, the Ministry of Internal Affairs estimates that there are between 500 and 600 contract killings per year.[72]

A disturbing report on the severity of organized crime was given by Interior Minister Anatolii Kulikov at a press conference in June 1997. Kulikov declared that there were some 9,000 criminal groups in Russia with around 100,000 members. He asserted that the number of registered crimes by organized groups had increased by almost 95 percent during the previous five years. He claimed that law enforcement bodies were making headway in solving crimes but acknowledged that some 3,700 murders committed in the first half of 1997 alone remained unsolved.[73] At a press conference in June 2000, a first deputy minister of internal affairs presented a slightly different set of figures: He claimed that Russia now had eleven major criminal groups, with about 50,000 members, and that as many as 5,000 firms were controlled by as few as one-third of these groups.[74] Whatever the exact scale of organized crime, analysts agree that two conditions help it to flourish: First, the state bureaucracy is highly susceptible to corruption and has allowed organized crime to penetrate it deeply, and second, regular businesses frequently find it impossible to operate except by turning to organized crime for "security services," which include paying protection rackets, forcing partners to make good on agreements, and obtaining scarce supplies.

To understand why organized crime is so powerful we must recognize the vicious circle formed by the interlocking relationship among three sets of actors: government, legitimate business, and criminal organizations. Many businesses, both small-scale entrepreneurs and the owners of large companies, purchase protection from protection rackets (of course, racketeers often commit acts of violence against businesses to force them to purchase their protection services). Government, particularly the police, is weak, and weakened further by corruption. Organized crime groups penetrate both business and government, providing business with services such as protection as well as short-term loans and the enforcement of business contracts, and paying off law enforcement officials to let them operate with impunity.[75]

Each side in this triangle depends on the others. Businesses frequently find that they must pay bribes to corrupt government officials simply to be able to operate or to be allowed to get around the law. Moreover, unable to count on the courts to protect their property rights and enforce their business agreements, they often turn to organized crime rackets for protection. Taking advantage of the state's inability to enforce the law (and, through penetration of the state, keeping it weak), organized crime preys on business and corrupts government. And government officials often find it easier, safer, and more lucrative to accept bribes than to fight crime and corruption or to provide legitimate public goods such as fair enforcement of the laws. The fact that Russia is a federal state probably exacerbates the problem, since the existence of governments at different levels multiplies the number of officials who demand bribes as condition for doing business.[76]

Corruption. Corruption is fed both by the interests of businesses in evading laws and regulations and by organized crime rackets that want to keep government weak and subservient. Although corruption is notoriously difficult to measure with any precision, all observers agree that it has increased substantially since the end of the Soviet period and that it is not decreasing. It is widespread both in everyday life and in dealings with the state. A recent large-scale survey by a Moscow research firm gives some indication of the nature and scale of corruption. At least half the population of Russia is involved in corruption in daily life.[77] For instance, the survey found that the probability that an individual would pay a bribe to get an automobile inspection permits was about 60 percent. The likelihood of paying a bribe to get one's child into a good school or college, or to get good grades, was about 50 percent. There was about a one-third probability that one would bribe a repairman to fix a problem in one's apartment. There was a 26 percent chance of paying a bribe to get a favorable ruling in a court case. Altogether, the study estimated that the country spends the equivalent of about $2.8 billion every year in bribes for everyday services of this type. The areas where the largest sums are spent are health care, education, courts, and automobile inspections; these alone make up over 60 percent of the market for corruption in everyday life.[78]

Bribery in the dealings between business and the state is of a far larger magnitude. The survey's authors estimate that 82 percent of business firms engage in giving bribes to government officials and that the total annual volume of such corruption is $33.5 billion, a sum equal to about 50 percent of the federal budget.[79] By far the largest share of such payments goes to local officials. Nearly 99 percent of such bribes are paid to executive branch officials rather than to legislative or judicial branch, and nearly all of this money goes to officials in charge of licensing, taxation, and regulation of business.[80] Moreover, about a third of the firms surveyed acknowledged trying to affect policy decisions by state officials, for example, to obtain a favorable law or regulation or an exemption from one.

Corruption is hardly unique to Russia or to the former communist world, but it is especially widespread in Russia and the other former Soviet states. The World Bank conducted a survey of business firms in sixty-nine countries in all parts of the world in 1996 and found that the region with the highest levels of corruption was the former Soviet Union.[81] The organization Transparency International, which publishes an annual ranking of countries according to the perceived level of honesty of government, ranks Russia as one of the most corrupt countries in the world—in seventy-ninth place out of ninety-one countries on the scale in 2001.[82] Corruption on this scale represents a severe drag on economic development, both because it diverts large quantities of resources away from public needs and because it undermines people's willingness to invest in productive activity. World Bank experts estimate that in an economy where firms pay bribes on a large scale to capture private benefits from state officials, economic growth over a three-year period is 10 percent lower on average than in economies where such activity is at a low level.[83] Moreover, much corruption is associated with organized crime, which bribes government officials for protection and which drives legal businesses under. For example, in a number of cases, criminal organizations have forced legitimate businesspeople to sell out at the risk of being murdered, and the payment of protection money by businesses to organized crime groups is very widespread. The corruption of the police and courts helps to ensure that such crimes go unpunished and forces legal businesses to compete in the corruption market with illegal ones. When citizens themselves come to believe that public institutions such as courts, police, universities, hospitals, and tax collectors are corrupt, they perpetuate the corruption by offering bribes. Indeed, the study cited above found that the vast majority of bribes are initiated by the bribe givers, not by the bribe takers. And, most significantly, it found that businesses that refused to engage in corruption were no less successful than those that did.[84] This suggests that corruption is partly a matter of mutual expectations. If the public and the government both believe that corruption is not necessary or expected, then the individual is less likely to offer a bribe and the official is less likely to demand one.

Corruption in Russia has deep roots and many Russians assume that it is an ineradicable feature of Russian society. Comparative studies of corruption demonstrate, however, that the culture of corruption can be changed by changing the expectations of the public and the government. For example, some countries have created powerful independent agencies to fight corruption. When their commitment to their mission is credible, people begin resisting corruption and refusing to engage in it, and government officials begin providing services without expecting to receive bribes.[85] The key is for the political leadership to make a serious commitment to fighting corruption, and to back this commitment up with institutional reform and sustained attention to the problem. In Russia, corruption is so pervasive that it is a significant drag on the economy and a threat to the integrity of the state. Both the political leadership and big business recognize the seriousness of the problem. Former Prime Minister Evgenii Primakov, for instance, declared in 1999 that criminal organizations "control up to 40% of the economy, and half the banking resources of the country." Corruption, he said, had reached the point where it threatened national security and was undermining Russia's very statehood.[86] The question, therefore, is not whether the leadership recognizes the problem, but whether they have the political will to address it.

Conclusion

Despite some steps toward realization of the ideal of the rule of law since the end of the communist regime, Russia remains closer to a system of "rule by law" than to the rule of law. The precedence of law over political and administrative power in the state would reduce the ability of officials in the bureaucracy, the security police, and the president to exercise power arbitrarily. Respect for the law on the part of officials and citizens would help establish habits of civic initiative and responsibility, which are essential to democracy. These are among the reasons that legal reformers have actively propagated the ideal of the "law-governed state" and have taken several steps that begin to put the ideal into practice. As with many other institutional reforms, however, success in the realm of law will ultimately require large-scale changes in political culture and behavior.

The radical implications of a shift to a law-governed state have generated opposition from a number of entrenched interests both inside and outside the state. In some cases the opposition is due to bureaucratic unwillingness to relinquish administrative power; in other cases it stems from the lucrative opportunities that lax and corrupt fiscal practices create for self-enrichment by officials. The continuing hold among many who wield power and among many in the population of the traditionally skeptical attitude toward the law—the view of the law as no more than an instrument of the policy goals of those in power—may also impede movement in this direction. However, there is ample evidence that a substantial base of support exists for the concept of law as a set of impartial rules to which both state officials and ordinary citizens would be subordinate. Despite serious limitations and setbacks, a slow and long-term movement in the direction of the rule of institutions rather than individuals can be discerned since the fall of the Soviet order.[87] As we have seen in this chapter, both reformers and their opponents can agree on a core set of legal principles that are essential to the primacy of law. They have enacted a number of reforms that have strengthened law and legal institutions. The constitution now corresponds much more closely to the actual political system than it did in the Soviet era, and some of the changes in legal institutions and codes strengthen civil rights. The Constitutional Court has become an important instrument for upholding the principle of constitutionalism.

But there are still many obstacles to the realization of the rule of law. The weakness of law enforcement, the deep penetration of the state by organized crime, and the old habit for Russian rulers and Russian citizens generally of treating the law instrumentally continue to impede progress toward the primacy of law. President Putin has taken a number of steps that, if fully implemented would strengthen the independence of the judiciary from both political pressure and corruption. At the same time, both his own willingness to use the courts as weapons against his political opponents, and the powerful corrosive effect of corruption, continue to subvert the integrity of the legal system.

REVIEW QUESTIONS

1. What is the difference between "rule of law" and "rule by law"?
2. What have the main goals of legal reformers in the Soviet and post-Soviet periods? What institutional changes have they called for to improve the fairness and efficiency of justice?
3. What is the Procuracy? How does it differ from the institution of public prosecutors in the United States?
4. What effect would you expect the introduction of the jury trial system throughout the country to have on the administration of justice in Russia? Why?
5. How does the Constitutional Court exercise the power of judicial review? What political factors limit its autonomy?
6. What are the main obstacles to the realization of the rule of law? What changes in the political system would be required to overcome them?
7. What are the main reasons for the flourishing of corruption? What measures would be effective in combating it?

ENDNOTES

1. Stephen Holmes, "Introduction," *East European Constitutional Review* 11:1/2 (Winter/Spring 2002), p. 91.
2. Holmes, "Introduction," p. 92.
3. On the legal reforms of the Gorbachev period, see Donald D. Barry, ed., *Toward the "Rule of Law" in Russia? Political and Legal Reform in the Transition Period* (Armonk, N.Y.: M. E. Sharpe, 1992); and Alexandre Yakovlev with Dale Gibson, *The Bear That Wouldn't Dance: Failed Attempts to Reform the Constitution of the Former Soviet Union* (Winnipeg, Manitoba, Canada: University of Manitoba, Legal Research Institute, 1992).
4. See the discussion of corruption, below.
5. See pp. 136 and 137.
6. Robert Orttung, "A Long Way to Go in Establishing Effective Courts," Russian Regional Report, EastWest Institute, 5:46 (13 December 2000).
7. Orttung, "A Long Way to Go."
8. A seminal study of the influences on the development of law in the Soviet Union is Harold J. Berman, *Justice in the U.S.S.R.*, rev. ed. (Cambridge, Mass.: Harvard University Press, 1963).
9. Full texts of these articles of the RSFSR Criminal Code together with commentary can be found in Harold J. Berman, ed., *Soviet Criminal Law and Procedure: The RSFSR Codes,* 2nd ed. (Cambridge, Mass.: Harvard University Press, 1972). Analogous articles were contained in the criminal codes of other republics as well.
. Sidney Bloch and Peter Reddaway, *Psychiatric Terror: How Soviet Psychiatry Is Used to Suppress Dissent* (New York: Basic Books, 1977).

11. Alexandre M. Yakovlev, *Striving for Law in a Lawless Land: Memoirs of a Russian Reformer* (Armonk, N.Y.: M. E. Sharpe, 1996), p. 201.

12. Ibid., p. 202.

13. *Poslanie Prezidenta Rossiiskoi Federatsii Federal'nomu Sobraniiu* (Moscow: n.p., 1997), p. 23.

14. One of the early products of glasnost was the exposure of "telephone justice" as a prevalent practice. See, for example, Arkadii Vaksberg, "Pravde v glaza," *Literaturnaia gazeta,* 17 December 1986, p. 13.

15. Robert Sharlet, "The Communist Party and the Administration of Justice in the USSR," in Donald D. Barry, et al., eds., *Soviet Law After Stalin, Part III: Soviet Institutions and the Administration of Law* (Alpen aan den Rijn, The Netherlands and Germantown, Md.: Sijthofff and Noordhoff, 1979), pp. 321–92. In another article, Sharlet details several ways in which the regime acted to repress individuals for political acts, including administrative penalties such as job dismissal, officially sponsored acts of hooliganism, psychiatric internment, forced emigration, and criminal trials. See Robert Sharlet, "Party and Public Ideals in Conflict: Constitutionalism and Civil Rights in the USSR," *Cornell International Law Journal* 23:2 (1990), pp. 341–62.

16. RFE/RL Newsline, 14 March 1997.

17. Inquisitorial procedure is contrasted with the adversarial model used in Anglo-American judicial proceedings. In the inquisitorial system, the presiding officer (judge, magistrate) actively seeks to determine the full truth of the case at hand rather than serving as an impartial referee in a contest between an accuser and a defendant. In Soviet and Russian tradition, the powerful procurator is the central figure in the proceeding; the judge may actively participate in questioning witnesses and ruling on matters of law, but the procurator is expected to serve the higher cause of justice and not simply to present the state's best case against the accused. From the standpoint of the Anglo-American tradition, this puts the procurator in a potentially contradictory position: While the procurator is required to ensure the legality of the entire proceeding (including, as appropriate, the obligation to defend the accused's rights), he or she must also seek to prosecute and win the case. Since the procurator has already overseen the pretrial investigation and concluded that there is sufficient evidence to proceed with the trial, it is extremely rare for a procurator to decide that the case lacks merit and should be dropped. From the standpoint of the Anglo-American criminal process, it is as though the procurator were wearing the hats of prosecutor, defender, judge, and jury all at the same time. In any case, in Soviet times, judges tended to be highly deferential to the procurators. As a result of the Procuracy's power and prestige, very few criminal cases in the Soviet period resulted in acquittal, although in some cases, a higher court set aside a questionable conviction or remanded it for further investigation, effectively reversing a lower court's verdict.

    For a discussion of the Soviet Procuracy that places it in the context of both Western continental models and earlier, Russian historical precedents, see Berman, *Justice in the USSR,* pp. 238–47.

18. Peter H. Solomon Jr., "Putin's Judicial Reform: Making Judges Accountable as Well as Independent," *East European Constitutional Review* 11:1/2 (Winter/Spring 2002), p. 121.

19. Donald D. Barry, "Amnesty under the Russian Constitution: Evolution of the Provision and Its Use in February 1994," *Parker School Journal of East European Law* 1:4 (1994), pp. 437–61.

20. Eugene Huskey, "The Administration of Justice: Courts, Procuracy, and Ministry of Justice," in Eugene Huskey, ed., *Executive Power and Soviet Politics: The Rise and Decline of the Soviet State* (Armonk, N.Y.: M. E. Sharpe, 1992), pp. 224–31.

21. Ibid., p. 224.

22. A report in *Izvestiia* in 2001 commented that there are 8 million cases per year in Russian courts, and that on average, any given court hears 500 cases per year. Courts are growing increasingly backlogged as a result. See RFE/RL Newsline, 27 March 2001.

23. On the new system of bailiffs, see Peter H. Solomon Jr., and Todd S. Foglesong, *Courts and Transition in Russia* (Boulder, Colo.: Westview, 2000), pp. 165–71; also Peter L. Kahn, "The Russian Bailiffs Service and the Enforcement of Civil Judgments," *Post-Soviet Affairs* 18(2) (April–June 2002), pp. 148–81.

    Press reports indicate that the introduction of the new system of "bailiff-enforcers" has helped reduce noncompliance somewhat, but there are still numerous cases where court decisions are ignored. For example, in one incident, a group of eighteen bailiffs appeared at a factory on the outskirts of Moscow at 6:30 one morning. They were enforcing a court order upholding the decision of a shareholders' meeting of the company to replace the old director with a new one. The bailiffs were there to ensure that the new director gained access to the director's office, and to prevent the old director from entering the premises. A group of workers and guards attacked the bailiffs with rocks and stones, water from a fire hose, and tear gas. Four bailiffs were wounded and all eighteen suffered injuries from the tear gas. As the news report put it, "further attempts to enter the firm have been called off for the time being." See Polit.ru, 10 April 2002.

24. Peter H. Solomon, "The Limits of Legal Order in Post-Soviet Russia," *Post-Soviet Affairs* 11:2 (April–June 1995), pp. 96–97.

25. The new legislation on the status of judges also reformed the makeup and powers of the "judicial qualifications commissions," which are composed of judges and legal experts and which screen appointments, promotions, and removals of judges. See Solomon, "Putin's Judicial Reform," pp. 120–21.

26. Eugene Huskey, "Russian Judicial Reform after Communism," in Peter Solomon, ed., *Reforming Justice in Russia, 1864–1994* (Armonk, N.Y.: M. E. Sharpe, 1997).

27. Yakovlev, *Striving*, p. 208.

28. In one of the most famous trial verdicts in Russian history, Vera Zasulich, a young Russian revolutionary who had attempted to assassinate the chief of police of St. Petersburg in 1878, was acquitted by a jury following a fiery speech by her lawyer that scathingly denounced the injustices of the Russian government.

29. A majority of seven votes out of the twelve jurors suffices to decide on a conviction, but only six votes are needed to acquit. Solomon, "Limits," p. 103.

30. Stephen C. Thaman, "The Resurrection of Trial by Jury in Russia," *Stanford Journal of International Law* 31 (1995), p. 130. This is a comprehensive survey of the early experience of the use of the jury system in several regions.

31. Irina Dline and Olga Schwartz, "The Jury Is Still Out on the Future of Jury Trials in Russia," *East European Constitutional Review* 11:1/2 (Winter/Spring 2002), pp. 104–10.

32. "Sud prisiazhnykh griadet," *Izvestiia*, 22 January 2003, **www.izvestia.ru/day/article29136**.

33. Pamela Jordan, "Russian Courts: Enforcing the Rule of Law?" in Valerie Sperling, ed., *Building the Russian State: Institutional Crisis and the Quest for Democratic Governance* (Boulder, Colo.: Westview, 2000), p. 202.

34. It is misleading to call these *arbitration* courts, since they use judicial procedure, not arbitration, to adjudicate disputes. They were created out of the "arbitration boards" used in Soviet times to resolve disputes among economic entities such as enterprises and ministries, but now form a separate branch of the federal judiciary.

35. *Segodnia,* 20 February 2001.
36. See Kathryn Hendley, Barry W. Ickes, Peter Murrell, and Randi Ryterman, "Observations on the Use of Law by Russian Enterprises," *Post-Soviet Affairs* 13:1 (January–March 1997), pp. 19–41.
37. *Segodnia,* 30 November 1999.
38. Solomon, "Putin's Judicial Reform," pp. 117–23.
39. The new Criminal Procedure Code that was passed by parliament in December 2001 and came into force on July 1, 2002, included this provision, which had been opposed by the Procuracy. The Duma agreed to delay its implementation, however, on the grounds that the courts needed time to prepare for it (judicial administrators claimed that they would need another 3,000 judges and 700 million rubles to handle the increased caseload that would result from implementation of the reform). The Constitutional Court ruled that the provision must be implemented immediately on July 1, along with the rest of the new Code.
40. *Segodnia,* 30 January 1997; OMRI Daily Digest, 10 March and 11 March 1997.
41. *Segodnia,* 12 April 2000.
42. This case arose when President Yeltsin refused to sign a law that parliament had passed that he considered unconstitutional. The law nationalized cultural artifacts and artworks that the Soviet Army had seized in Nazi-occupied Europe during World War II. Parliament overrode his veto but Yeltsin still refused to sign. Parliament sent a protest to the Constitutional Court, which found that Yeltsin had no right to withhold his signature when parliament overrode a veto; it did find some provisions of the law unconstitutional but warned that a president had no right to declare a duly passed law unconstitutional—only the Court had that power.
43. *Segodnia,* 21 February 2000.
44. A thorough examination of the recent history and legal status of the court is the article by Herbert Hausmaninger, "Towards a 'New' Russian Constitutional Court," *Cornell International Law Journal* 28 (1995), pp. 349–86. Also see Robert Sharlet, "Transitional Constitutionalism: Politics and Law in the Second Russian Republic," *Wisconsin International Law Journal* 14:3 (1996), pp. 495–521. Other information on the court is drawn from interviews with judges on the court.
45. RFE/RL Newsline, 1 November 2001.
46. An informative article about the advocates, based on interviews in the winter of 1988–1989, is Michael Burrage, "*Advokatura:* In Search of Professionalism and Pluralism in Moscow and Leningrad," *Law and Social Inquiry* 15:3 (Summer 1990), pp. 433–78. An article analyzing the statute of the Russian Republic that governs the activity of the advocates is Harold J. Berman and Yuri I. Luryi, "The Soviet *Advokatura:* The 1980 RSFSR Statute with Annotations," *Soviet Union/Union Sovietique* 14:3 (1987), pp. 253–99.
47. Solomon and Foglesong, *Courts and Transition in Russia,* p. 115.
48. Solomon, "Limits," pp. 93–94.
49. For a review of these laws, see Solomon, "Putin's Judicial Reform," pp. 117–23.
50. The KGB was the institutional successor to the powerful instruments of coercion that the Soviet regime used since the revolution to eliminate its political enemies, including the Cheka (created within six weeks of the October Revolution), the GPU, and the NKVD. In the post-Stalin era, according to its press representatives, the KGB had nothing in common with these predecessor organizations and was dedicated to upholding the law while carrying out its mission of defending the security of the state and its citizens. Often KGB press representatives discussed the modern efforts of the organization in combating drug trafficking and terrorism. Evidently keen to be portrayed in a positive light in the media, the KGB promoted itself in the 1980s as a

heroic organization, a body performing its difficult duties with scrupulous respect for the law as well as ingenuity and courage.

51. OMRI Daily Digest, 7 April 1995.

52. The doctrine was posted to the Internet on several sites, among them **www.regions.ru**.

53. RFE/RL Newsline, 7 May 2002.

54. RFE/RL Newsline, 18 December 2002, quoting Yabloko deputy Yuri Shchekochikhin.

55. Quoted in Polit.ru, 11 March 2003.

56. Eugene Huskey, "Government Rulemaking as a Brake on Perestroika," *Law and Social Inquiry*, 15:3 (Summer 1990), pp. 421–22.

57. Ibid., p. 424.

58. Ibid., pp. 424–25.

59. The Auditing Chamber *(Schetnaia palata)* is an auditing agency created by the parliament, comparable to the General Accounting Office (GAO) in the United States. Like the GAO, it serves the legislative branch by conducting audits of the books of executive agencies and presenting reports of its findings.

60. Following are my translations from the published versions of the president's message, as posted to the presidential Web site, **http://president.kremlin.ru/events**.

61. Polit.ru, 13 August, 14 August and 21 November 2002.

62. For comparisons of Russia's president's decree authority with the decree powers of presidents in other countries, see John M. Carey and Matthew Soberg Shugart, eds., *Executive Decree Authority* (Cambridge, England: Cambridge University Press, 1998); and Timothy Frye, "A Politics of Institutional Choice: Post-Communist Presidencies," *Comparative Political Studies* 30:5 (1997), pp. 523–52.

63. Ilia Bulavinov and Elena Tregubova, "Druz'ia, prekrasen nash Sovbez!" *Kommersant Vlast'*, 13 June 2000, pp. 14–17.

64. *Segodnia*, 23 December 1995.

65. In spring 1996, after President Yeltsin issued an edict reaffirming earlier edicts on the right of members of collective and state farms to acquire parcels of land from the farm as private property, the communist–agrarian coalition in the Duma hurried through the legislature a law "clarifying" the procedures under which farmers could exercise these rights. The "clarification" had the effect of annulling farmers' right to own land as property.

66. Thomas F. Remington, "The Evolution of Executive-Legislative Relations in Russia since 1993," *Slavic Review* 59:3 (November 2000), pp. 499–520.

67. On the bilateral bargaining between Yeltsin and the regional governors, see Steven L. Solnick, "Federalism and State-Building: Post-Communist and Post-Colonial Perspectives," in Andrew Reynolds, ed., *The Architecture of Democracy: Constitutional Design, Conflict Management, and Democracy* (New York: Oxford University Press, 2002), esp. pp. 189–92.

68. On the ability of regional governors to control federal agencies located on their territories, see Kathryn Stoner-Weiss, "Central Weakness and Provincial Autonomy: Observations on the Devolution Process in Russia," *Post-Soviet Affairs* 15:1 (January–March 1999), pp. 87–106.

69. Juan Linz, "Presidential or Parliamentary Democracy: Does It Make a Difference?" in Juan J. Linz and Arturo Valenzuela, ed., *The Failure of Presidential Democracy: Comparative Perspectives* (Baltimore, Md., and London: Johns Hopkins University Press, 1994) pp. 3–90; Stephen White, "Russia: Presidential Leadership under Yeltsin," in Ray Taras, ed., *Postcommunist Presidents* (Cambridge, England: Cambridge University Press, 1997), pp. 38–66.

70. A useful but somewhat lurid account of the subject is the book by Stephen Handelman, *Comrade Criminal: Russia's New Mafiya* (New Haven, Conn.: Yale University Press, 1995); a study emphasizing the operation of protection rackets in one Russian city is Federico Varese, *The Russian Mafia: Private Protection in a New Market Economy* (New York: Oxford University Press, 2001). Also see Vadim Volkov, "Who Is Strong When the State Is Weak? Violent Entrepreneurship in Russia's Emerging Markets," in Mark R. Beissinger and Crawford Young, *Beyond State Crisis? Postcolonial Africa and Post-Soviet Eurasia in Comparative Perspective* (Washington, D.C.: Woodrow Wilson Center, 2002), pp. 81–104.

71. "Neizvestnaia voina . . . s korruptsiiei," *Izvestiia,* 22 October 1994.

72. RFE/RL Newsline, 28 July 2000.

73. RFE/RL Newsline, Vol. 1, No. 53, Part I, 16 June 1997.

74. Polit.ru (Internet news site), 8 June 2000.

75. Varese, *The Russian Mafia;* and Volkov, "Who Is Strong?"

76. Political scientist Daniel Treisman has conducted a comparative analysis of corruption in Russia and other countries. He found that most of the explanation for corruption in countries lay in four factors: relatively low per capita income, low experience with democracy, low level of foreign trade, and its federal structure. Once these factors were accounted for, Russia was not particularly more corrupt than other countries. See Daniel Treisman, "The Causes of Corruption: A Cross-National Study," *Journal of Public Economics* 76(3) (2000), pp. 399–457.

77. G. A. Satarov, *Diagnostika rossiiskoi korruptsii: Sotsiologicheskii analiz* (Moscow: Fond INDEM, 2002).

78. Satarov, *Diagnostika,* pp. 16–17.

79. Ibid, p. 21.

80. Ibid, p. 22.

81. World Bank, *World Development Report 1997: The State in a Changing World* (New York: Oxford University Press, 1997), pp. 34–36. The average number of firms across all world regions reporting having to pay bribes to officials to get things done as a matter of course was 40 percent. In advanced industrial societies, the figure was 15 percent, in Asia 30 percent, and in the CIS—that is, the former Soviet states excluding the Baltic states—the figure was over 60 percent.

82. The Corruption Perceptions Index compares the results of numerous surveys of businesspeople and experts about their perception of the level of corruption in ninety-one countries. Transparency International then produces an aggregate ranking of each country on the scale, which it publishes on its Web site. In 2001, Russia was tied with Ecuador and Pakistan for seventy-ninth place. See **www.transparency.org/cpi/2001/cpi2001.html**.

83. Joel S. Hellman, Geraint Jones, and Daniel Kaufmann, "'Seize the State, Seize the Day': State Capture, Corruption, and Influence in Transition," Policy Research Working Paper, no. 2444 (Washington, D.C.: World Bank Institute, September 2000).

84. Satarov, *Diagnostika,* p. 25.

85. Susan Rose-Ackerman, *Corruption and Government: Causes, Consequences, and Reform* (Cambridge, England: Cambridge University Press, 1999), pp. 159–62.

86. *Segodnia,* 15 October 1999. Primakov was speaking at a special session of the Council for Foreign and Defense Policy, a prestigious group of policy makers and experts.

87. Robert Sharlet, "Reinventing the Russian State: Problems of Constitutional Implementation," *The John Marshall Law Review* 28:4 (Summer 1995), p. 786.

9 Russia and the International Community

Russia's thousand-year history of expansion, war, and state domination of society has left behind a legacy of autocratic rule and a preoccupation with defending national borders. In the twentieth century alone, Russian society has undergone several deep traumas. Twice the regime collapsed—in 1917 and again in 1991—and twice world wars have taken tens of millions of lives. During the Soviet era, civil war and Stalin's terror killed tens of millions more. In the light of such terrible trials, it is understandable that Russians should regard the preservation of statehood and order as the foremost priority for their country. Likewise this history of catastrophe, much of it self-induced, helps explain why President Putin calls for continuity with the past rather than another rupture, and why Russians remain so averse to any more social transformations.

Indeed, Russians continue to harbor a high sense of insecurity. A national survey conducted early in 2000 found that almost a quarter of Russians believed that it was probable ("likely" or "very likely") that another country would initiate a military attack on Russia in the coming five years. Seventy percent believed that the threat had grown significantly over the past two or three years. Assessments of who Russia's enemies were varied widely: around a quarter named China and about the same number identified Iraq as countries that posed a "big threat" or "some threat" to Russia. Forty-three percent cited non-Russians living in Russia as a significant security problem. Nearly half of the Russian respondents believed the United States was a significant threat for Russia.[1] More Russians believed that the greatest challenges to Russia's security came from terrorism and Islamic militants than believed that NATO or China were the sources of serious threats.[2]

The anxiety Russians express about their place in the world has at least as much to do with the fear that outside powers will take advantage of their weakness at a time of deep political and social change as it does with the actual shifts in the balance of international power.[3] Russians historically have learned to associate periods of domestic turmoil with attempts by foreign powers to take advantage of Russia's weakness. Interludes of regime collapse and civil disorder, such as the Time of Troubles in the early seventeenth century or the fall of the Romanov dynasty in 1917 during World War I, which led to the February and October Revolutions, tempted external powers to intervene in Russia and seize

Russian-ruled territories. Many Russians today regard the period of the late 1980s and early 1990s in a similar light, believing that Gorbachev's concessions to the West, his willingness to allow the union to dissolve, and his abandonment of Communist Party rule left Russia weakened and humiliated and subject to the dictates of the West. Little wonder that there is such strong support for rebuilding some sort of union out of the former Soviet republics. In early 2000, nearly half the Russian public believed that they would be better off living in a larger political union, and two-thirds supported a closer union with Ukraine and Belarus. Seventy percent agreed (either "completely" or "somewhat") with the statement that "it is a great misfortune that the Soviet Union no longer exists."[4]

The collapse of the Soviet regime has required Russia to rebuild its political institutions, economic system, national identity, and relations with the outside world. During the Soviet period, the state's propaganda emphasized the theme of an enduring international struggle between capitalism and socialism as a way of keeping society regimented, secretive, and semiclosed, and of justifying the regime's enormous devotion of resources to military production. Without the ideological contest between the Soviet bloc and the West as an instrument for legitimating communist political control, post-Soviet Russian leaders have to forge an entirely new relationship to the international community. This has required choosing between a strategy of *balancing against* the West and one of *joining* it but on Western terms. Gorbachev, Yeltsin, and Putin have all decisively opted for a strategy of integration with the democratic and capitalist world. Yet, as they have worked to define a new national identity for Russia in relation to the liberal capitalist countries of the West and in relation to the countries in the regions on which it borders, including East Asia, Central Asia, the Transcaucasus, and the Near East, they have sought to build bridges in all directions rather than choosing between an exclusively "European," "Asian," or "Eurasian" orientation. Their leverage is constrained by the fact that Russia's power resources are severely limited: Russia cannot project its political or diplomatic power to the degree it did when its military power was at its apogee. The substantial decline in the size and capability of its military forces and the severe shrinkage of its economy have meant that its capacity to exert influence has fallen sharply.

The country's leaders accept that the only way of rebuilding Russia's power and prosperity lies through closer economic and political integration into the global capitalist economy. This theme has been a consistent element of President Putin's public statements. Putin has clearly and repeatedly insisted that there is only one way forward for Russia—by adopting democratic and market-based political and economic institutions. As he wrote in an article posted to the Russian government's Web site in December 1999,

> The way to the market and democracy was difficult for all states that entered it in the 1990s. They all had roughly the same problems, although in varying degrees. Russia is completing the first, transition stage of economic and political reforms. Despite problems and mistakes, it has entered the highway by which

the whole of humanity is travelling. Only this way offers the possibility of dynamic economic growth and higher living standards, as the world experience convincingly shows. There is no alternative to it.[5]

Achieving this goal is made difficult, however, by the economy's technological backwardness relative to the developed countries, the ingrained suspicion and hostility toward the outside world that many elites and citizens continue to feel, the tendency to think of the former Soviet states as still forming part of the country, and the vast size of Russia's territory. Following the breakup of the Soviet Union, Russia bordered on sixteen countries, including eight that had been republics in the Soviet Union.[6] Many of these were influenced by long histories of hostile relations with Russia.

Gorbachev, Yeltsin, and Putin have all regarded closer integration of Russia with the developed democracies as being strategically important for Russia. Gorbachev was willing to allow communist regimes to fall throughout Eastern Europe for the sake of improved relations with the West. Yeltsin accepted the expansion of NATO into Eastern Europe as a necessary condition for close relations with the United States and Europe.[7] Putin repeatedly emphasized that he regarded Russia's admission to the World Trade Organization (WTO) as being critical for Russia's long-term economic success. Following the September 11, 2001, terrorist attacks on the United States, Putin immediately telephoned President Bush to offer his support. Putin clearly saw an advantage for Russia in aligning itself with the United States against Islamic terrorism, which he has often identified as an immediate threat to Russia's (and the world's) own security. Putin repeatedly cited Russia's own war in Chechnia as part of the global struggle against Islamic terrorists.[8] When the United States commenced military operations against the Taliban regime in Afghanistan, Putin proceeded to supply the United States with military intelligence based on the Soviet Union's own disastrous involvement in Afghanistan during the 1980s. Putin also offered to open Russian airspace to American overflights, pledged humanitarian assistance in Afghanistan, and increased Russia's military aid to the Northern Alliance in Afghanistan (the main military opposition to the Taliban). Putin justified his unqualified support for the United States's campaign against the Taliban in his message to parliament in April 2002:

> For our state, which has long been confronted with terrorism, there was no difficulty in deciding whether to support efforts to destroy its lair or not—especially as these measures did indeed help to strengthen security on the southern borders of our country and, to a considerable extent, helped to improve the situation.[9]

In turn, the Bush administration warmly welcomed Russian assistance and immediately dropped its criticism of Russian military tactics in Chechnia.[10]

To be sure, Putin has not complied with all the United States's demands. Russia continues to sell to Iran both military supplies and nuclear-power technology that the United States believes can be used to produce fuel for nuclear weapons. In the case of Iraq, Russia opposed the Bush administration's demands to find Iraq in material breach of its obligations under a series of UN Security Council resolutions and thus subject to international military sanctions. The sharp division over Iraq between the United States, on the one side, and France and Germany, on the other, allowed Putin to try an old Soviet tactic: aligning Russia with continental Europe against a seemingly, unreliable, and aggressive America. Putin was strongly critical of the American-led military operation against the Saddam Hussein regime in Iraq, calling it a blow to the principles of international law. Yet at the same time, he warned against overreacting or succumbing to anti-Americanism, and he offered the prospect of cooperation with the United States in other areas, such as dealing with North Korea's nuclear weapons program. However, the speed with which the Saddam Hussein regime collapsed embarrassed Putin and led him to chastise Russian intelligence for providing him with faulty estimates of Iraq's military capability.

Because they all pursued the same fundamental strategy of integrating Russia into international trade, diplomatic, and security networks, Gorbachev, Yeltsin, and Putin were all criticized sharply by many elements of the political establishment for making too many unreciprocated concessions. Neither trade nor investment has blossomed as Russia had hoped, and Russia has continued to depend on its raw-materials exports to maintain a positive trade balance. Except over Iraq, President Putin has generally taken a very pragmatic line toward the United States, choosing not to oppose the United States strenuously when confrontation would be both futile and counterproductive. For instance, Putin downplayed the importance of the abandonment of the 1972 ABM Treaty, which Russian leaders had previously regarded as a fundamental element of international security, when in December 2001 President Bush announced that the United States would unilaterally abrogate it and proceed with its own missile defense program. Many Russian critics objected that Putin was standing by and letting the United States dictate the terms of the relationship. Nor did Putin allow Russia's objections to the expansion of NATO to interfere with Russian–American relations as the United States pushed for the admission of new members in Eastern Europe. (Russia was given a symbolic compensation in the form of a new "NATO-Russia Council" where Russia could discuss matters of mutual concern with the nineteen members of NATO but in which Russia had no direct influence over NATO policy.[11]) Russia mildly criticized NATO's November 2002 decision to admit seven more members, including the three Baltic states, remonstrating only that it demonstrated NATO's "inability to respond to new challenges," but chose not to make the issue into a serious source of contention. Some in the Russian political establishment also criticized Putin for unilaterally abandoning the large intelligence-gathering facilities that Russia inherited from the Soviet Union in Lourdes, Cuba, and Cam Ranh Bay, Vietnam, and for allowing the United States to establish military bases in Central Asia to support the war in Afghanistan. Even on Iraq, Putin commented that the U.S.–Russian relationship had matured to the point where the two countries could hold a "frank dialogue."

In other areas Russia has rejected international pressure. In the wars in the former Yugoslavia, President Yeltsin supported the dictator Slobodan Milosevic in the face of overwhelming evidence of Milosevic's responsibility for mass murder against Bosnians and Kosovars. In its military campaign in Chechnia, Russia has used massive bombardment against civilian settlements, costing tens of thousands of lives and forcing hundreds of thousands of refugees from their homes. The capital city, Grozny, has been almost completely razed. Russia has conducted brutal "sweep" operations in refugee camps to round up suspected guerrillas, who are often killed or detained. Insisting that the war is a matter of domestic sovereignty and that it is fighting bandits supported by international terrorism, it has refused to allow international human rights organizations to monitor its operations, and, under Putin, it has forced the mass media to report a sanitized, distorted picture of the situation.

Putin has pledged that Russia will meet the conditions set by the World Trade Organization for membership, but the process of Russia's admission will be slow. Membership in the WTO will require Russia to lift many of the tariff and other legal barriers to international trade that currently protect its inefficient domestic producers. Many firms in branches such as automobile and aircraft manufacturing, chemicals, banking, and insurance are extremely nervous about the consequences of membership, fearing, with some justification, that they may not be able to compete with Western products and services once protectionist tariffs and subsidies are eliminated.[12] Some sectors, however, are eager for Russia to join the WTO, confident that they can compete successfully in overseas markets. The beer-brewing industry is an example. An industry that does not receive state subsidies, it has become a thriving sector in the 1990s, successful in the Russian domestic market, and ambitious to compete in foreign markets.[13]

Russia's oil industry is another sector that has responded dynamically to the opportunities of an open economy after several years of decline in the early 1990s after it was subjected to privatization. A significant signal of international business confidence in Russian oil was the announcement that British Petroleum (BP) would invest $6.75 in a new business venture in Russia in which it would own 50 percent of the shares and a consortium of Russian oil firms would own the other 50 percent. BP's chief executive officer indicated that the decision reflected Russia's "greatly improved economic stability, improved legal system, and increasing commitment to the international rules of trade and business," a testimonial that suggested that Putin's policies were taking hold.[14] But the fact that the size of this one deal was equal to about a quarter of *all* foreign direct investment in Russia since 1992, suggesting how little overseas investment in Russia there has been (by comparison, in 2002, China attracted more than $50 billion in foreign direct investment compared with Russia's $4 billion), showed how far Russia still needs to go to gain the confidence of international business. Capital flight out of Russia still exceeds foreign investment into Russia, although there are some signs that some of Russia's flight capital is slowly making its way back into investments in Russia from its safe havens in Cyprus, Malta, and Switzerland.[15]

Meantime Russia has continued to deepen integration among former Soviet states. Putin has ended the showy ceremonies announcing the "union" of Russia and Belarus that Presidents Yeltsin and Lukashenko used to hold, at which they regularly announced the creation of a new union state with a common currency and customs system—and which remained a dead letter. Instead, Putin has demanded that Belarus accept the Russian constitution as the basis for any union and accept Russia's right to make the main decisions on fiscal and monetary policy. In a similar way, the Commonwealth of Independent States (CIS) remains largely a formality. It provides a framework for periodic consultations for the heads of state, heads of government, or ministers of the member states, and periodically ambitious agreements are reached creating a new "Eurasian Economic Union," "CIS Antiterrorism Center," or "Interstate Eurasian Coal and Metals Association," which is forgotten the day after the documents are signed. Most observers agree that as a working international institution, the CIS does not in fact integrate the economies of the member states; certainly it has done little to harmonize trade, tax, monetary, or security policy. For its first ten years, the CIS's role has been almost exclusively ceremonial. This is hardly surprising in view of the fact that other members would need to cede a substantial share of sovereignty to Russia for the CIS to have any actual power. Yet there are signs that Putin is moving to forge more meaningful institutions involving smaller subsets of members. One of these is the "Shanghai Cooperation Organization," a grouping of five former Soviet republics (Russia, Kazakstan, Kyrgyzstan, Uzbekistan, and Tajikistan) together with China, the focus of which is security in the Central Asian region. Periodic discussions among the members of this group center on problems of terrorism, radical Islamic movements, and drug trafficking in the Central Asian region. Another organization is a new customs union involving Russia, Ukraine, Kazakstan, and Belarus, which is to coordinate trade policy among the four countries.[16] President Putin's involvement in the negotiations leading to the agreement may signal that Russia intends to take this institution more seriously than it has similar agreements in the past.

President Putin has played a very active personal role in Russian diplomacy and promoted good relations with countries that had been allies of the Soviet Union—such as Cuba, India, and North Korea—as well as with countries where relations with the USSR and Russia had been more difficult, such as Japan and Pakistan. For instance, Pakistan's President Pervez Musharaf paid a visit to Moscow in February 2003, the first time in almost twenty years that a Pakistani leader had visited Moscow. Putin visited Japan in September 2000, meeting with Japan's emperor and others, and he received Japan's prime minister in January 2003. Despite the absence of a formal peace treaty ending World War II, Russia and Japan have nonetheless expanded economic ties and agreed to continue to seek a resolution of the conflict over the Kurile Islands.[17] Putin meantime has continued to improve relations with China and South Korea while improving relations with North Korea (North Korea's reclusive leader, Kim Jong Il, traveled to Russia twice, and Putin visited North Korea in 2000). Putin's strategy has been to cultivate good relations with all countries in the regions affecting its security, and to maintain relations with former Soviet allies such as Cuba and Vietnam, while simultaneously building a strong security relationship with the United States. It has been an energetic, pragmatic, and successful policy.

Russia today is far more open than it was under Soviet rule and its leaders recognize that it cannot retreat into isolation and autarky. President Putin clearly recognizes that Russia's economic interests require closer trade and investment ties with the outside world and that its security requires the avoidance of provoking confrontations with any powerful potential enemies. The post–Cold War environment has been more favorable to Russia's strategic interests than most observers expected, however. Russia has grudgingly accepted the United States' preeminent military power and the limits this imposes on Russia's own security strategy (for instance, requiring it to accept NATO's expansion and the end of the ABM treaty regime). But at the same time, Russia has found new opportunities to develop its own international role by playing on the world's concerns about international terrorism and by balancing with Europeans against the United States over issues such as Iraq. The new vulnerabilities and divisions created in the post–Cold War world have given Russia an opening to develop influence not dependent solely on its legacy as the heir to the Soviet Union's nuclear arsenal. This opening encourages Russia to seek a place in the international community commensurate with both its means and its long-term interests.

Russia's postcommunist transition has been difficult and incomplete. Within Russia, many are disenchanted with the promise of democracy. The rule of law remains fragile, vulnerable both to the power of state authorities and to the corrupting influences of wealth, inequality, and social mistrust. At the same time, the end of communism has stimulated groups to organize for the protection of their interests and given them new rights to advance their goals. New institutions for articulating and aggregating these interests remain tenuous. But the spread of political and property rights has resulted in the emergence of a more pluralistic environment.

Russia's vast size, weak government capacity, and cultural legacy of state domination make it likely that democratic consolidation in the postcommunist era will be slow and uneven. The end of the communist regime and the dissolution of the Soviet Union brought about a severe weakening of the state's capacity to enforce the laws, protect its citizens, and provide basic social services. Russian history has seen periods when the breakdown of an old regime and the rise of a new one led to internal weakness and external vulnerability. Is the present period simply a new "Time of Troubles," an interlude between the breakdown of one autocratic regime and the consolidation of a new one? Probably not. International factors such as the dense network of international communications linking societies, the rapid expansion of cross-border trade and investment, and the global spread of norms and expectations centered on democracy, human rights, and the rule of law, together with the effects of domestic social changes such as rising educational levels, make a return to dictatorship unlikely. Russia's rulers want to reconcile the imperative of strengthening a weakened state with the principles of an open economy and a democratic political system. Effective governance, this book has argued, requires effective institutions for collective action by society and the aggregation of people's needs and interests. While President Putin may give priority to constructing a coherent administrative structure for implementing state policy over the observance of democratic principles, the viability of Russia's postcommunist state will ultimately depend on how responsive and adaptive its institutions are to the demands of Russia's citizens in a globalized and interdependent world.

REVIEW QUESTIONS

1. We have seen evidence that there is a high level of anxiety and insecurity in Russian public opinion about Russia's place in the world. What factors in Russian history help explain this fact? What developments in the 1990s explain the rise in the sense of threat from the United States?
2. What are the main points of continuity in the foreign policies of Gorbachev, Yeltsin, and Putin? What are the main differences among them?
3. How might the reintegration of some of the former Soviet republics into a new federal union affect Russia's relations with the outside world?

ENDNOTES

1. Stephen White, Ian McAllister, Margot Light, et al., "A European or a Slavic Choice? Foreign Policy and Public Attitudes in Post-Soviet Europe," *Europe-Asia Studies* 54:2 (2002), p. 185. In a comprehensive survey of the attitudes of the Russian public and Russian elites about foreign policy, William Zimmerman finds that the view of the United States as a threat to Russian security has risen significantly in the 1990s. Indeed, for elites, the perception that the United States threatens Russia's security is closely associated with views on a range of other security issues as well. See William Zimmerman, *The Russian People and Foreign Policy: Russian Elite and Mass Perspectives, 1993–2000* (Princeton, N.J.: Princeton University Press, 2002), pp. 91, 103.
2. Ibid., p. 186.
3. A valuable overview of the deep continuities in the evolution of Russia's relations with the outside world through the twentieth century is Robert Legvold, "The Three Russias: Decline, Revolution, and Reconstruction," in Robert A. Pastor, ed., *A Century's Journey: How the Great Powers Shape the World* (New York: Basic Books, 1999), pp. 139–90.
4. White et al., "European or Slavic Choice?" pp. 191–92.
5. Vladimir Putin, "Russia at the Turn of the Millenium," on Web site **www.gov.ru**, 31 December 1999.
6. Russia has a small exclave located on the Baltic Sea, called Kaliningrad, which borders on Lithuania and Poland. Now that Lithuania is independent, Russia no longer has direct physical access to Kaliningrad. This is creating growing problems between Russia and its European neighbors.
7. An excellent account of U.S.–Russian relations during the Clinton administration is provided by Strobe Talbott, *The Russia Hand: A Memoir of Presidential Diplomacy* (New York: Random House, 2002).

8. In November 1999, Putin published an op-ed article in the *New York Times* that sought to justify Russia's scorched-earth tactics to eliminate the Chechen rebels on the grounds that Russia was responding to unprovoked terrorist attacks. He asked Americans to imagine how they would feel if they were suddenly attacked without warning by terrorists in their own country—and to imagine how they would respond. "Imagine ordinary New Yorkers or Washingtonians asleep in their homes. Then, in a flash, hundreds perish at the Watergate or at an apartment on Manhattan's West Side. Thousands are injured, some horribly disfigured. Panic engulfs a neighborhood, then a nation." *New York Times,* 14 November 1999.

9. Matthew Evangelista, *The Chechen Wars: Will Russia Go the Way of the Soviet Union?* (Washington, D.C.: Brookings Institution, 2002), p. 182.

10. James Goldgeier and Michael McFaul, "George W. Bush and Russia," *Current History* 101:657 (October 2002), pp. 317–19.

11. NATO admitted Poland, Hungary, and the Czech Republic in 1999. In July 2002 NATO ratified the creation of the new NATO–Russia Council. In November 2002, NATO invited Slovakia, Slovenia, Romania, Bulgaria, Estonia, Latvia, and Lithuania to begin the process of applying for membership, a process that is expected to be completed in 2004. See RFE/RL Newsline, 6 December 2002.

12. RFE/RL Newsline, 6 February 2002.

13. Polit.ru, 2 August 2002.

14. *New York Times,* 11 February 2003.

15. RFE/RL Business Watch, 25 February 2003.

16. RFE/RL Newsline, 24 February 2003.

17. Following World War II, Russia occupied a string of islands separating Russia's Sakhalin Island from Japan; Russia calls them the Kurile Islands, while Japan refers to them as the Northern Territories. These islands have been the subject of a dispute since the nineteenth century, but following Japan's defeat in World War II, Russia claimed them. A 1956 agreement promised that Russia would transfer two of them to Japan following the conclusion of a peace treaty, but the treaty has never been signed and the terms of the transfer have not been settled. Japan regards the issue as an obstacle to the conclusion of a peace treaty and the improvement of relations.

Index